May this book stand as a testament to the atrocities visited on the Dakota of Minnesota, not for posterity, but as an opportunity for us to finally tell our story. May this book be recognized as part of the healing process that restorative justice champions and as bringing some understanding to the atrocities still inflicted on Dakota people, for only with understanding can healing come. May this book give rise to the dominating society taking responsibility for setting things right with Dakota descendents, for, just as our people and communities live with the legacy of historical trauma, so, too, do Whites live with the legacy of the atrocities that their ancestors committed. May this book be recognized as articulating a pattern visited upon all Indigenous Peoples of this continent and throughout the world—the pattern of colonization and oppression. May this book be part of undoing these negative patterns, which unfortunately still thrive today.

Harley Eagle, enrolled member in the Wapaha Ska Dakota First Nations Reserve
(Saskatchewan, Canada)

IN THE FOOTSTEPS OF OUR ANCESTORS

—◄○►—

In the Footsteps of Our Ancestors

◄O►

The Dakota Commemorative Marches
of the 21st Century

Edited by

WAZIYATAWIN ANGELA WILSON

Living Justice Press

St. Paul, Minnesota

2006

Living Justice Press
St. Paul, Minnesota 55105

First edition

For information about permission to reproduce selections from this book, please contact:
Permissions, Living Justice Press, 2093 Juliet Avenue, St. Paul, MN 55105 Tel. (651) 695-1008

Cataloging-in-Publication
(Provided by Quality Books, Inc.)

In the footsteps of our ancestors : the Dakota commemorative marches of the 21st century / edited by Waziyatawin Angela Wilson. —1st ed.
    p.   cm.
    Includes bibliographical references and index.
    LCCN 2006923882
    ISBN 0-9721886-2-2
1. Dakota Indians—Minnesota—Relocation.
2. Indians of North America—Government relations—1789–1869. 3. Indians of North America—Minnesota. 4. Dakota Indians—Ethnic identity—21st century. 5. Dakota Indians—Politics and government—21st century. I. Wilson, Angela Cavender.
E99.D1I25 2006
978.004'975243   QBI06-600094

11 10 09 08 07 06   5 4 3 2 1

‑‹o›‑

Production and promotion coordinated
   by Loretta Draths
Marketing research by Mary Joy Breton
Copyediting by Cathy Broberg
Cover design by David Spohn

Interior design by Wendy Holdman
Composition at Prism Publishing Center,
   Minneapolis, Minnesota
Printed by Sheridan Books, Inc.,
   Ann Arbor, Michigan

Expressing Our Gratitude for Support

—◄○►—

We at Living Justice Press are deeply grateful to those who have made this book financially possible. For several years now, the Sisters of Charity of the Blessed Virgin Mary (Dubuque, Iowa) and Yvonne Sexton of the Sexton Foundation (Saint Cloud, Minnesota) have given Living Justice Press most generous grants that have enabled us to proceed with our publishing work, especially concerning Native Peoples. We continue to be grateful to Betsy Fairbanks and Don Lane at the Fund for Nonviolence for their faith in us during our first years. And we are very grateful to the Archie D. and Bertha H. Walker Foundation for their grant to support this book and its distribution.

We have received generous support from individuals as well, including Jeannine and Mike Baden, Ernest J. Breton, Mary Joy Breton, Clark Erickson, Sid Farrar, Deb Feeny, Barbara Gerten, Ava-Dale and Charles Johnson, Christopher Largent, Ruth Newman, Kay Pranis, and Pat Thalhuber. One individual donor who gave most generously wishes to remain anonymous. Diane Wilson, one of the Dakota Commemorative March organizers, donated a computer to Living Justice Press. And two young people, Robyn Skrebes and Paul Cole, who came to the door soliciting donations for clean water in Minnesota, returned the next day to donate money to support this book after having heard the story of the 1862 history and the present-day marches.

Realizing that this would be an expensive book to produce, we sent a fundraising letter explaining the history here in Minnesota, the Dakota Commemorative March, and our work on this book to two hundred churches located on Mini Sota Makoce (now called Minnesota). One church group, the Minnesota Conference of the United Church of Christ, sent a donation for the book. The First United Church of Christ in Northfield, Minnesota, and the Justice and Witness Ministries of the United Church of Christ in Cleveland, Ohio, donated to the march. This is significant, because various accounts of the chronology of the death march indicate that the Dakota may very well have passed through New Ulm about church time that Sunday morning.

Contents

—◄o►—

2004 Commemorative March Commentaries

Manipi Hena Owas'in Wicunkiksuyapi

(We Remember All Those Who Walked)

WAZIYATAWIN ANGELA WILSON

◄◦►

Although the past and its implications are self-evident, we are complicit in their denial because it is too painful or arduous or costly to imagine an existence unbound from the lies. Emotionally and psychologically, we are attached to this mythology of colonialism because it explains the Euroamerican conquest and normalizes it in our lives. The perpetrators know that it is wrong to steal a country and deny it is a crime; the victims know that it is shameful to accept defeat lying down. Yet, complacency rules over both because the thought of what might come out of transcending the lies is too . . . fearsome.[1]

◄ Taiaiake Alfred ►

We've never really come out of that grief and mourning. We are yet afflicted with that. We seem to be a mourning people at times.[2]

◄ Ed Red Owl ►

The Dakota populations of the United States and Canada continue to suffer deeply from decades of historical trauma and the effects of an ongoing colonization. Even in the age of casinos, cigarette and gas sales, declarations of sovereignty, and a seemingly expanding political influence, our people are burdened with a sense of pain and grief that continues to affect our daily lives. This grief combines with the pain caused by the near daily assaults on our humanity that we still experience at the dawn of the twenty-first century. The weight of these burdens contributes to the many social ills destroying the lives of our People, yet we struggle with how to liberate ourselves from this encumbrance. The Dakota Commemorative Marches of 2002 and 2004 have been an attempt to unburden ourselves of this suffering by examining in a profound and meaningful way one historical antecedent that contributes to our current pain and by challenging the colonialist representation of that event.

On November 7, 2002, a couple dozen marchers set out from the Lower Sioux Reservation on a 150-mile journey to a concentration camp site at Fort Snelling in St. Paul, Minnesota. Eventually several hundred others joined the walk. This journey was conceived as a commemorative event to honor the Dakota people—primarily women and children—who were forcibly marched roughly the same route November 7–13, 1862, at the close of the U.S.-Dakota War of 1862. We were also there to remember the equally horrific journey of our Dakota men who were sentenced to death for war crimes and were awaiting their execution. On November 8, 1862, these men were shackled, placed on wagons, and transported to the concentration camp in Mankato, where those who were not hanged would spend a difficult winter.

These forced journeys marked the first phase of Dakota expulsion from our homeland; they were the first phase of forced removal. The following spring, all were ousted from Minnesota as part of a successful policy of ethnic cleansing. While the primary intent of our march was to remember and honor our ancestors who suffered on these journeys, it was also about giving testimony to the truth about a shameful past that had been largely hidden over the previous 140 years. We walked again in 2004 and will continue to walk every other year until the 150th commemoration of the original forced march.

The idea of a commemorative march was first conceived in the summer of 2001 during a discussion among a small group of us who were attending a conference in New Ulm, Minnesota. My *deksi* (uncle) Leo Omani suggested the idea to me, Yvonne Wynde, and Gabrielle Tateyuskanskan.[3] We realized that while our Dakota People have sponsored commemorative events over the years to honor the thirty-eight who were hanged in Mankato, little had been done to remember

the suffering endured by the others involved, especially the women and children. The four of us agreed that it was important to remember and honor these ancestors. As we contemplated the purpose and meaning of such a commemorative march, we realized that this event must be an honest commemoration, that is, a rendering of the event in the context of the oppression and colonization in which it occurred.

◄○►

Though the first essay of this volume offers a more detailed historical overview, some additional context may help readers gain a more thorough understanding of what happened. The forced march and removal of the Dakota People from our homeland has been justified as a reasonable course of action by generations of scholars and writers who positioned it as an inevitable consequence of the "Sioux Uprising of 1862." The master narrative surrounding this event reasoned that if "Sioux" men were savage enough to spontaneously rise up and viciously attack innocent White settlers, the removal of the Dakota was not only warranted but also necessary for the safety of the settler families who were simply trying to live peacefully while making proper use of the land. Thus, while the particular brutality shown to Dakota women and children might be deemed unfortunate, it was still considered an acceptable and understandable response to the savageness of the hostile Indians. The forced march was given little attention and was often mentioned only briefly in entire books on the U.S.-Dakota War of 1862, apparently considered to be largely unremarkable. The story of the condemned men was treated similarly. Rather than being depicted as the defenders of Dakota land and way of life that they were, the men were cast as bloodthirsty savages worthy only of contempt and hatred. Those controlling how the history was written made little comment on this first phase of forced removal. The perpetrators kept only limited records of the events, and few oral accounts among the victims have been documented.

The broader context for this first phase of forced removal is the cycle of invasion, conquest, removal, and colonization that occurred repeatedly in the settlement of America. Specifically, the U.S.-Dakota War of 1862 sheds considerable light on this first phase of ethnic cleansing, because it helps to explain the mind-set of White settlers and their ability to carry out unjust acts in their relentless desire for Dakota lands. The 1862 war offered the rationale Whites needed to seize all Dakota lands. It thus remains a major turning point in Dakota history, because it marks the loss of our homeland and the subsequent diaspora of our People.

Historians of the last several decades have written about the circumstances leading up to the U.S.-Dakota War of 1862—circumstances that left the Dakota with little choice but to go to war or die.[4] The injustices perpetrated upon the Dakota are well documented, and they set a clear pattern of invasion, oppression, conquest, and colonization. While the Dakota had trading relations with Europeans by the 1660s, the Dakota were able to maintain control of their resources until the beginning of the nineteenth century.

The Treaty of 1805 marked the first land cession for the Dakota, but it was so fraudulently negotiated by Zebulon Pike that its ratification by the Senate was shameful. Only two Dakota signatures graced the treaty (for which they immediately received alcohol and presents), and they were considered by the U.S. government to be representative of the entire "Sioux Nation," a population estimated by Pike to be 21,675.[5] Pike's mission was to establish United States sovereignty in the area, in competition with the British who sought to maintain their own influence. From this perspective, the Dakota were merely pawns in the imperial enterprises of more powerful nations. Unfortunately, because Fort Snelling was erected on lands from that original cession, its establishment opened the way for soldiers, missionaries, Indian agents, and settlers to invade Dakota lands further.

Because an immediate war with the Dakota over lands and resources would be both dangerous and costly, more peacefully negotiated land cessions became the method of choice for further dispossession. More land cessions followed in 1830, 1837, 1851, and 1858. In all instances, the U.S. government used foul means to obtain signatures, and they often ensured the wealth of agents and traders in Dakota lands. For example, in 1837 the Dakota believed they were being summoned to negotiate a peace treaty with the Sacs and Foxes, but instead they were pressured into signing away lands east of the Mississippi. In the 1851 treaties, the Dakota were illegally threatened and bullied into ceding remaining lands that would then confine them to a 20-mile wide, 140-mile long strip of reservation land.

Furthermore, the government consistently violated the treaties it negotiated, which should have meant the return of lands ceded. For example, though the Doty Treaties of 1841 were never ratified, the letter from James Duane Doty to the Secretary of War accompanying the treaty signed by the Bdewakantunwan Dakota acknowledges the repeated treaty violations by the U.S. government:

> In consequence of the failure of government to pay to Indians their annuities at the time appointed by the treaties with them, and at the seasons of the year when these necessities require, the supplies which they can only obtain on a *credit* from their traders, or with their annuities, the system of *credits* has been continued, and indeed been absolutely necessary in many instances to save the Indian from suffering. Nothing but punctuality on the part of Govt. can establish the relations which ought to exist between the Indians and the Govt.—that is, the Indians should feel dependent on the *Government*, and not on the *Trader*. Unless this dependence is established, it is in vain for the Govt. to attempt to exercise any influence over them, except that of force.[6]

By the 1840s, the Dakota were facing incremental land dispossession through treaties, which were nonetheless repeatedly violated. However, as this excerpt highlights, the Dakota were additionally subjected to a policy of forced dependency that was already well established.

—◦—

The first phase of forced removals was a devastating experience for our Dakota ancestors. It was also a major and necessary course in the opening of prime agricultural Dakota lands to White settlement by White standards. Yet until 2002, there was no public recognition of these removals either to memorialize the suffering of the Dakota or to recognize the treacherous means by which White hegemony was achieved. If memorials are commissioned and built among a community with shared and admired values that are expected to continue into the future, the glaring absence of memorials to Dakota suffering makes it eminently clear that Minnesota's citizens and planners assumed a future without a Dakota presence.[7] It is equally clear that Minnesotans have not wanted reminders of the costs paid by us for their occupation of our homeland. It is precisely because the ethnic cleansing was so complete that no public memorials dedicated to the forced removals exist.

Publicly and collectively invoking Dakota historical memories of these forced marches becomes a site of political contestation, because it sends shock waves to the foundation that has upheld the master narrative. When that narrative is disrupted, the social order is called into question and challenged. Throughout the first century of historical scholarship on the 1862 war, the Dakota are depicted as militant, hostile, savage "Sioux" Indians who spontaneously rose up and viciously slaughtered innocent White settlers. This sentiment was graphically recorded in the earliest accounts from the era and continued to be echoed, albeit more subtly, in subsequent decades. Even the name that was eventually applied to the war, "The Sioux Uprising of 1862," is a phrase that both captures and embeds this interpretation.

Just as the Little Big Horn has been sanctified as having been, to use history and memory scholar Edward Linenthal's words, "hallowed by the blood of America's warriors," so too have many sites in Minnesota been sanctified. Linenthal comments, "These kinds of sacred places and martial rituals have communicated a parochial ideology and awakened a certain kind of patriotic enthusiasm, a mood that affirmed the rightness of American arms and aims in its wars."[8] While the attention given to the U.S.-Dakota War of 1862 has not captured the American imagination on the same scale as Little Big Horn, the messages carved in stone are the same.

The numerous obelisk monuments that dot the landscape of southern Minnesota have literally fixed in stone this historical narrative. They may be seen in places like Acton Township, where they mark the site of the first White casualties, or at battle sites such as Wood Lake, Fort Ridgely, and New Ulm, where citizens and soldiery valiantly defended themselves against Dakota aggression. A monument in New Ulm was dedicated to the "Guardians of the Frontier." According to the master narrative, the title of guardians was wrested [i.e., stolen] from the Indigenous occupants and bestowed upon the new settlers now guarding Indigenous lands against Indigenous attack. This is the colonial perversion of reality referred to by African intellectual Ngugi wa Thiong'o.[9] Dedicated to preserving the settler's memory of the 1862 war, they make frequent reference to the heroics demonstrated by the White settlers in the face of "Sioux violence and brutality," and the settlers who lost their lives in the war have been cast as martyrs.

Few memorials to Dakota people exist, and those that do reflect a colonialist agenda. Six Dakota men are honored through commemoration in stone in a smaller background monument at Birch Coulee for saving the lives of White settlers. These men would be considered traitors by Dakota standards, but they are given celebrity status within the colonizing class because of their assistance in furthering the colonialist agenda.

In Hutchinson, Minnesota, a statue of Chief Little Crow was erected by their celebrated hometown artist Les Koubas. Situated there, the statue carries a particularly ironic message. Though this is the place where a White father and son, Nathan and Chauncey Lamson, killed Little Crow to collect a bounty payment, the accompanying text makes no mention of this Minnesota policy of ethnic cleansing. Instead, the text marker reads: "The red of the sunset upon these waters reminds us that all blood is red—even that of the red-skin who fought us for possession of this stream, and in the mist which rises from the river we see the smoke of the pipe of peace between all peoples curling upward forever from the valley of the crow."[10] Yet, Hutchinson is at peace only because the Dakota presence was eradicated.

In another example, the Milford State Monument just west of New Ulm commemorates fifty-two White settlers killed during the war. The figure was created to symbolize Memory (with a capital M), but their notion of memory was restricted to that which would support colonialist claims to the land.[11] In southern Minnesota, the Dakota memory of resistance became nonexistent, metaphorically exterminated and removed, just as our ancestors bodily suffered the same fate.

> « IT IS ABOUT TIME THAT WE QUESTION THESE MONUMENTS AND THE IDEOLOGIES THEY REPRESENT. »

In view of the larger context in 1862, the elderly people, men, women, and children who suffered these assaults are Dakota martyrs. Yet in Minnesota, we do not see monuments to them, either individually or collectively. We do not see buildings, counties, roads, schools, or parks named in their honor. Indeed, these honors are reserved for those who believed in their superior right to our land, who believed the Dakota did not even have a right to go to war over wrongs committed, and who believed Dakota people should be either exterminated or removed from our homeland. Our homeland is littered with monuments erected to glorify the bravery and martyrdom of those who invaded our lands and fought our People, some of whom lost their lives. Southern Minnesota markers also celebrate those who helped in our annihilation and expulsion. It is about time that we question these monuments and the ideologies they represent. Some have suggested that we need to dedicate additional monuments to the Dakota People (such as the more recent markers at Mankato and Fort Snelling), but this is not nearly enough. While these kinds of memorials are a step in the right direction of re-educating the public about the events of 1862, they do not erase the continuing assaults on our spirits from the ongoing celebration of the colonizers.

—◦—

In the last several decades, scholarship on the 1862 war has perceptibly challenged this narrative, and the crimes perpetrated against the Dakota have been increasingly acknowledged. However, even in the mid-1960s, the rightness of American invasion was still defended, as this telling passage from one historian on the expulsion of the Dakota from Minnesota shows: "While the state mourned the loss of her citizens, the removal of the Indians was a source of untold benefit, for the whites occupied the land in peace, and this extensive domain is the pride of the state, and increasing years will add to its value and its greatness."[12]

In this narrative, what happens to the Indigenous population is assumed to be inconsequential as long as peace and prosperity have since reigned in the state for the White population. While more recent scholarship (and I am referring specifically to the work of scholars such as Gary Anderson, Roy Meyer, and Kenneth Carley) has largely transcended this Manifest Destiny dogma, it has nonetheless configured the war as a closed chapter in American history. These scholars write from the perspective that, though unfortunate, the damage has been done, as if there were only one window in time for justice to occur. Though much useful information may be gleaned from their analyses, such scholarship remains ultimately disempowering to the Dakota population because it rules out present and future justice.

This work, then, stands as a narrative that reclaims our right to tell our stories in our own way and for our own purposes. This is not a collection that supports the power base and status of the people, institutions, and structures that have subjugated our nation. Rather, it is designed with Dakota empowerment in mind, as a valuation of Dakota voices, perspectives, worldview, and historical and contemporary experiences. Oral histories take a prominent position in this collection, as does the need for a multitude of Indigenous voices. The connection between past and present is clearly illuminated. The imagery, perspectives, and stories of the past impact the present in profound ways, and this message is conveyed in every contribution to this volume. This historical consciousness is very different from the histories written by non-Dakota. We cannot separate what was from what is. On a broad scale, then, this project is part of a growing Indigenous movement toward reclaiming our past through more appropriate and accurate renderings of Indigenous history. On a local level, this work is about taking back our Dakota history.

In addition, as we voice repeated objections to our illegal and immoral dispossession that occurred in 1862–63, we also raise questions about our long-term struggle as Dakota People indigenous to Minnesota. By bringing these previously suppressed perspectives to the forefront, we shed light on some truths of Minnesota history that necessarily challenge the state and its people to rethink their treatment of its Indigenous inhabitants. In this confrontation, Minnesotans must either reaffirm the White supremacist values and greed that caused our historical dispossession in the first place, or they must reject these values and join us in our ultimate quest for justice. Perhaps others will fall somewhere in between, but we are pushing them to do so consciously by honestly assessing their motivations and positions.

—◄o►—

The first step in realizing the humanity of our ancestors who suffered in 1862 is to remember them by name. At the beginning of this collection, we have included the names of those who were victims of this first phase of forced removal in 1862—

both the group of primarily women and children who were force marched to Fort Snelling, and the group of condemned men who were shackled and forced to make the trip in wagons to Mankato where they awaited their execution orders.

« WE NEED TO BEGIN TO CREATE A RECORD OF THOSE WHO WE KNOW WERE ON THE MARCH AND WHO WERE IMPRISONED AT FORT SNELLING, SO THAT WE CAN REMEMBER THESE ANCESTORS BY NAME AS WE CONTINUE TO WALK IN THE FUTURE. »

The first list includes the Dakota names that were recorded as heads of families by the U.S. Army after their arrival at the Fort Snelling concentration camp site. This was the list of names that we used to make the stakes we planted along the 150-mile route, marking each mile we walked. In the U.S. Army record, beside each name is a number representing the number of people under that head of household. To date, all those represented as numbers remain largely nameless. We need to create a record of those who we know were on the march and who were imprisoned at Fort Snelling, so that we can remember these ancestors by name as we continue to walk in the future. The second list includes the names of the men who were sentenced to death or imprisonment as a consequence of their participation in the war. While these lists are imperfect, they provide a starting place for Dakota people to identify their ancestors who were forcibly removed to concentration camps in 1862.

The circle of wooden stakes with the names of the three hundred heads of families listed on the rolls at Fort Snelling in 1862. In November of 2003 these were placed in a circle at the Fort Snelling site so that descendents can find their family names and leave prayer offerings. Photo by Molly Schoenhoff

The forced removals are significant because they mark the first phase of Dakota expulsion from our homeland of *Minisota Makoce* (Land Where the Waters Reflect the Skies). In addition, the forced march of elders, women, and children to Fort Snelling was perpetrated upon the noncombatants: the women, the children, and the elders. This treatment of Indigenous Peoples by the colonizing forces in U.S. history was not unusual; in fact, it was quite routine, as several essays in this collection document.

After the list of names of our ancestors who experienced this first phase of ethnic cleansing in 1862, the contemporary writings begin with a poem entitled "Shadows of Voices" by Gabrielle Tateyuskanskan. Gaby is a poet, mother, and educator dedicated to the perpetuation of Dakota cultural traditions and the restoration of well-being to our People. She also served as co-coordinator for the 2002 event. As many of us were inspired to reflect on our experience during the Commemorative March, Gaby chose a form of expression in which she is particularly gifted. This poem offered at the beginning reflects not only the strong connection to homeland for our People but also the damage wrought by genocide and oppression in "a road made of bones." Our collection also ends with one of Gaby's poems, "Wounded Hearts." Here she speaks of the pain associated with the 1862 march but also highlights the reality of regenerated strength as we walk with moral courage in our search for "Humanity, Justice, and Peace."

◄◊►

The first essay of the 2002 Commemorative March Commentaries, "Decolonizing the 1862 Death Marches," provides a historical overview of the first phase of the Dakota removal from our homeland of Minisota Makoce. In two groups, Dakota people were forced into concentration camp sites in either Mankato or Fort Snelling in November 1862. Laced with a critical and stinging commentary, for the first time in a written history, my article argues that, because "Violence is never initiated by the oppressed," and a state of oppression certainly existed for the Dakota in 1862, there were no innocent White settlers in Minnesota in 1862.[13]

This is likely to be another controversial aspect of this collection, namely, the way in which it challenges the master narrative. This approach is not, however, simply about casting blame for the purpose of seeking punitive justice; rather, it is intended to wake people up to the extent to which the colonization and oppression of Dakota People are ongoing, even in our ancient homeland. The "righteous anger" evident in this work, though discomforting and unpleasant, is a necessary step in unburdening Dakota grief and suffering from this difficult period in our past.[14] It is also an equally necessary indictment of contemporary Minnesota residents for the way colonization continues.

In his contribution to this volume, my *ate* (father), Chris Mato Nunpa, places the forced removal of the Dakota from Minnesota in 1862–63 in the broader context of U.S. Indian policy. Drawing appropriate parallels to the Tsalagi Trail of Tears and the Long Walk of the Diné, he argues that, in trying to make sense of these horrendous atrocities, "The genocidal and imperialistic mind-set present in the Euro-American population provides a context for understanding these 'ethnic cleansings' of the Indigenous Peoples by the United States and its citizens." Not only does he discuss the event within a national arena, but he also broadens the discussion by making a connection between the treatment of the Jews under the Nazis and the treatment of the Dakota by the Americans. As he points out, the treatment of the Dakota fulfills the criteria for genocide under the UN Genocide Convention.

Because many Minnesotans have never examined the events of 1862 from this larger perspective, his arguments have met with considerable resistance in some circles. He decided to use this resistance as an educational opportunity and so shares with us recent exchanges with non-Dakota regarding these issues. He closes his essay by describing his most memorable experiences on the Commemorative March.

In her essay, Mary Beth Faimon explains the Commemorative March by referring to "social work micro and macro practice principles," which lead her to examine the event as having caused considerable historical trauma. She explains, "Indescribable terror consumed the Dakota, and the legacy of that terror remains 140 years later, as evidenced in repression, dissociation, denial, alcoholism, depression, doubt and devaluation of self and culture, and the helplessness suffered by many Dakota descendants." As a non-Dakota, Mary Beth is uniquely positioned to offer insight into the responsibility of White Minnesotans in supporting Dakota efforts to seek justice. To counteract the effects of trauma, Mary Beth suggests that the public acknowledgment of the genocidal policies perpetrated against Dakota Peoples is a step in the right direction. She points out that the Commemorative March made strides toward this end: "The march itself brought into public consciousness a reminder of the events of 1862 in the towns and surrounding communities where the event occurred." She closes her essay with a discussion of the meaning of the march from a personal and professional perspective.

Not everyone who wanted to walk with us in 2002 or 2004 was able to join us. A few months before the first Commemorative March, I received a letter with a return address from the South Dakota State Penitentiary. It was from George Blue Bird, a Lakota man writing to let me know that he and other members of the Lakota/Dakota/Nakota Spiritual Group in Jameson Prison were praying for us. While they could not be there in body, they would walk with us in spirit. We were all deeply appreciative of their support. With George's eloquent encouragement of our

efforts and his obvious knowledge of tribal history, I asked him if he would be willing to offer some comments to include in this collection. In this piece, he reminds us of our profound need for healing and makes connections between the experiences of all Lakota, Dakota, and Nakota people, those who comprise the *Oceti Sakowin* (Seven Council Fires) of the Dakota *Oyate* (Nation). He calls on the support of all of our People in the prison systems, stating, "The reason the prisoners are asked to help is because they symbolize the spirits of our relatives who were kept in Fort Snelling and other stockades or concentration camps." In so doing, he makes an incontrovertible and powerful statement linking past and present institutions of oppression.

His essay is followed by my personal narrative, "A Journey of Healing and Awakening," in which I share some of my experiences on the 2002 Commemorative March. Rather than presenting a detached, scholarly description of the walk, I intend this to be a reflective thought piece that I hope captures the mood and spirit of the event from someone who served as co-coordinator and who walked every day from beginning to end. Much of what I wrote came from my own need and desire to process this transformative, powerful experience in a creative and productive way. Ultimately, I conclude that this commemorative walk was about empowerment: "Despite the physical and emotional hardship—or maybe even because of it—we were taking hold of our past and controlling our history in a powerful, public effort. We were beginning a process of reclamation, steeped for seven generations in the memory and strength of our ancestors."

It was Leo Omani's vision that inspired this

walk. He and his nephew Gerald Standing were on the march in 2002 from beginning to end, and many of us relied heavily on their strength and compassion. Deksi Leo came back again in 2004, and his little red car led the way for us for the second time. In this contribution, he discusses his reasons for suggesting the march and his reasons for participating. Highlighting the disconnection experienced among our People as we have been separated from one another, he explains the immediate and important need for our people to reconnect. Leo views the rebinding of relatives as an essential component in the rebuilding of our nation, and he believes the Dakota Commemorative Marches will bless the future generations of the Dakota People.

Unlike Leo Omani, Molly Schoenhoff's participation in the commemoration of these events has been not as an attached descendent of the original marchers but rather as a compassionate outside observer committed to addressing issues of social injustice. Her commitment demonstrates the far-reaching ramifications of an event like this and the possibility of affecting change on a broad scale. Molly is one of my colleagues at Arizona State University, though her area of expertise and skill is far different from mine as a historian. Molly is in the School of Design and has brought her skills as an artist to the project. When she invited me to speak in her class about my work with the oral tradition in October of 2002, I shared with them my grandmother's story about the forced march and discussed the Commemorative March on which we were about to embark. When I returned, Molly and I began working on a text-art project involving my grandmother's story. As we worked on the proj-

ect, Molly's interest in the subject continued to grow, so much so that she joined us in November of 2003 when we met at Fort Snelling to further commemorate the forced removal and internment at the Fort Snelling concentration camp.

Since then, Molly has agreed to help begin the ambitious project of creating a living memorial for this phase of the 1862 forced removals, which she has envisioned as Native red plantings along the 150-mile stretch of road to signify not only the blood that was shed along the way but also the lifeblood of contemporary Dakota people. As Molly describes it,

> The change in the earth's surface would acknowledge the cultural and physical genocide that accompanied the establishment of the United States. Moreover, it would be a gesture of reclamation for Dakota People—a means of expressing their heritage and deep connection to the place they know as Minisota Makoce (the Land Where the Waters Reflect the Skies).

Her idea was discussed at the 2003 public commemorative event and has been enthusiastically supported by Dakota people. Since Molly articulated this idea in print, new possibilities have emerged that may help propel this project into being. The Center for Changing Landscapes at the University of Minnesota has expressed an interest in pursuing either this project further or something similar that would help mark the trail of the Dakota Death March.

The following chapter, "Voices of the Marchers," weaves reflections and comments by march participants about their experiences. While many

The Minnesota River near Henderson, Minnesota. November 11, 2002. The march roughly followed the flow of the Minnesota River from Lower Sioux to Fort Snelling.

of those who came to walk with us did not necessarily want to put their sentiments in writing, their powerful words provide important insights into the original march and the commemorative experience. One of the consequences of the diaspora of our People and the silencing of our history has been that, while we have largely shared a common historical memory—that is, through our oral traditions, most of our People today have had at least a minimal understanding of the forced removals that occurred as a consequence of the 1862 war—we have not had a shared memory of that experience. Avishai Margalit, a philosophy professor at the Hebrew University of Jerusalem, explains that, "A *shared* memory . . . is not a simple aggregate of individual memories. A shared memory integrates and calibrates the different perspectives of those who remember the episode. . . ."[15] Since 1862, the Dakota People have had few opportunities to participate in integrating and calibrating this historical event.

This essay, and indeed this collection, is about beginning the process of creating a shared memory—an effort that is extraordinarily difficult as long as we remain in a state of colonization. While my voice is present to provide context and to discuss the experiences thematically, I hope that the individual voices presented here will begin to comprise a chorus of shared memories. Creating shared memory by recovering Indigenous knowledge is, indeed, part of our larger decolonization agenda.

The last chapter from the section on the 2002 Commemorative March is a creative piece written by Diane Wilson. She begins by offering an eloquent and engaging narrative of her experience on the Commemorative March. Midway through, though, her narrative shifts, "As we continued to walk, the pavement beneath the women's feet began to fade and disappear, the rigid layer of tar and gravel slowly giving way to the prairie beneath." Diane then slips into a moving rendition of the original walk from the perspective of a woman who experienced it in 1862. In this way, we learn how Diane has internalized the experience, combining aspects of the historical record with the understanding she gained from placing her footsteps over those of her ancestors. She then brings us back to the 2002 commemoration and closes with a poem she composed while on the march. The words to this poem were written for music that her brother, Dave Wilson, created, and their composition is now available on CD. Diane's chapter ends the section on the Dakota Commemorative March of 2002.

◄o►

On November 8, 2003, we gathered once again at Fort Snelling. This event was to honor our ancestors from 1862 and to say prayers on their behalf. It was also an opportunity for us to thank the people who supported us in 2002 with a small giveaway and feast. It was very cold that day, but we stood in silence around the circle of wooden lathes Gaby Tateyuskanskan brought from Sisseton and planted on the concentration camp site. They were the same kind of stakes that were made for the walk in 2002. Phyllis Redday said a prayer, and *Kunsi* (Grandmother) Carrie Schommer quietly read the names of all the heads of household who arrived at Fort Snelling in No-

vember of 1862. That circle of stakes stood for nearly a year at Fort Snelling, affording a way for people to seek out their family names and leave offerings.

◄o►

In November 2004, we again met at Lower Sioux and began the second Dakota Commemorative March. This, too, was an inspiring and uplifting experience that deeply marked all of its participants. We had increased participation and heard new stories about Dakota experiences from 1862 that were passed on through the oral tradition by generations of Dakota families. Our relatives came home, and we all grieved and laughed together.

From a logistical perspective, everything went smoother, though new issues arose with law enforcement. While Scott McConkey, a state trooper who has been an incredible ally and supporter of the march, helped us make it safely to Henderson in both 2002 and 2004, other state law enforcers were not so kind. They raised issues that we will have to address in future marches, but nothing so serious as to prevent us from walking again in future years. Despite a few difficulties, we arrived at Fort Snelling on November 13 and successfully completed another 150-mile commemorative journey.

◄o►

Because the 2004 Commemorative March involved so many new marchers, we wanted to give those people an opportunity to share their reflections about their experiences in this volume. Their contributions come next.

We have two visual art contributions in this section. The first comes from Craig Marsden, who stumbled across information on the first Commemorative March and decided he wanted to learn firsthand what we were commemorating and why. He was raised in Pipestone, Minnesota, and when he arrived, he was in the process of creating a documentary film about his hometown entitled *The Song of Hiawatha*. Unafraid to call attention to the ongoing racism and colonialism in Minnesota as well as their peculiar ironies, Craig sought out stories that would expand his understanding of the history of the area. The story of the ethnic cleansing of the Dakota People was one such story, and he began filming and photographing the Commemorative March in 2002. In 2004, Craig met up with us in New Ulm, and we were delighted to see him again. He remained with us until we all said our good-byes at the American Indian Center in Minneapolis on the last day of the march, and he plans on walking with us again in 2006. He created a series of photo collages from his collection of Commemorative March photographs. They comprise the first contribution to the 2004 section of this volume.

The second visual arts contribution comes from one of my former students at Arizona State University. David Miller was taking an American Indian history class with me in fall 2004 when I discussed the Commemorative March and handed out brochures to interested students. Three students of mine from ASU paid their own airfare and expenses and traveled to Minnesota to walk with us. While David could spend only a few days with us, he used his talents as a photographer to capture some wonderful images. In his photographs, he was able to render both the happiness and sorrow existent among the marchers.

Gabrielle Tateyuskanskan similarly captures the wide-ranging emotions felt by the marchers in her essay "The Terrible Truth of a Beautiful Landscape." I have had the opportunity to hear her present portions of this essay before an audience on a couple of occasions, and both times she moved the audience to tears. Gabrielle has skill with words because she speaks from her heart, and as a consequence her words seem to resonate with others. In this chapter, she situates her own Dakota family history amidst the beautiful landscape of the Minnesota River Valley and the horrors of the 1862 war. She comments on the inhumanity all around us and asks difficult questions about those who become complicit in human injustices: "It is troubling when high ideals such as equality and justice are not applied to all human beings in America. Where are those individuals who believe in moral accountability? Are their numbers so small or are their voices silent?" We hope that our Commemorative March will help to push for those answers.

In the next essay, Myla Vicenti Carpio draws attention to her own tribal history and the forced removal of her nation, the Jicarilla Apaches, pointing out that many Indigenous Peoples throughout the United States have suffered similar fates as a consequence of American colonialism. She describes the lessons she learned through the Dakota Commemorative March, especially the importance of reconnecting to land and history. She explains that, though we can read about historical events in a written history text, reliving the experiences ourselves creates a whole new dimension of understanding. She uses the Commemorative March as an example of a decolonizing activity because, she says, "Decolonization is not just about reconnecting with historical events; it is reconnecting the past and the present. That reconnection reminds us of our relationships and our obligations to our Peoples, our cultures, our religions, and our lands."

Edward Valandra's essay, "Oyate Kin Unkanikupi Pelo (The People, We Are Coming Home Bringing You All)," also broadens the discussion of the Dakota Commemorative March by placing the march in the context of other commemorative events, such as the Big Foot Memorial Ride and the Fort Snelling–Mankato Spiritual Run. He has participated in some capacity in all three, and he speaks about all of them as part of the resurgence and healing of the Oceti Sakowin. Walking in solidarity with his eastern relatives, Edward also offered some important insights about male involvement in the march, "I walked for those Dakota men who, because of the circumstances of that extremely difficult time, were absent during this horrendous 150-mile journey." He was fulfilling a vital role on our Commemorative March as a supporter and protector of the women and children, a role that most Dakota men were denied in 1862.

In her essay, "Pazahiyayewin and the Importance of Remembering Dakota Women," Ramona Stately describes what the march has meant to her in terms of reconnecting with her great-great-grandmother. She describes how our culture has been impacted by American patriarchy and how, as a consequence, even we have not always remembered to honor our women the way we have honored our male ancestors. Participation in the Commemorative March has reawakened her sense of admiration for and connection to her grandmother who was on the forced march in 1862. She describes how she walked in mindfulness of her ancestor, "As I walked, I thought of Pazahiyayewin and I felt her there. This was my way of walking in her path, acknowledging her suffering, reclaiming my identity, and teaching this to my children who walked by my side." She provides a moving testament to the power and unity developing among Dakota women that also draws on the strength and resiliency of our grandmothers and the power of stories.

The stories from our oral tradition are central to this Commemorative March, in part because the documentary evidence has failed to tell this story of genocide in any satisfactory detail. Written evidence for the forced removals in 1862 is scarce, but in her essay, Lisa Elbert sheds further light on these events by examining archival evidence produced by *Wasicu* (White) sources, primarily maps, newspaper accounts, and soldiers' diaries. In this chapter, she attempts to retrace the route that the women, children, and elders were forced to walk from Lower Sioux to Fort Snelling, as well as the route the condemned and shackled Dakota men followed to Mankato in their wagon-trains. The evidence raises more questions than it answers, since much of it conflicts with other archival sources, secondary literature, and the Dakota oral tradition. Yet in presenting all of the data that she uncovered, Lisa allows readers to make their own determinations about the veracity of the evidence.

By presenting the Wasicu perspective of the forced march, Lisa's article also reveals the mentality of the Whites most directly involved. Some Whites who have read her article in the context of the other articles leading up to it have found it to be the most damning article about Whites in this book in terms of exposing their Nazi-like detachment to the horrific suffering they were inflicting upon the most vulnerable among our People. By contrast, some of the Whites who have read Lisa's article out of the context of this book regarded it as a normal account—entirely what they expected from Whites in those situations and not anything out of the ordinary. Both reactions speak truths about the Wasicu that Dakota people have observed before 1862 and since.

Many of us have known Lisa Elbert since her first years as a Dakota language student at the University of Minnesota. We were thrilled when she first pulled up to join the 2002 Commemorative March, and we saw the banner on the back of her truck that read *Manipi Hena Owas'in Wicunkiksuyapi*. This is the Dakota name for the Commemorative March, which in English translates to "We Remember All Those Who Walked." We were happy that she had come to join us, but were surprised to see her walking with a cane and still bearing the signs of surgery on her face. We learned then that Lisa had been struggling with cancer and numerous surgeries the previous year and in the process had lost her ability to walk. Lisa had been on her own incredible journey of recovery and had just relearned how to walk, yet she was there on the march, wanting to walk with us in honor of our Dakota ancestors. We celebrated with her on the first day when she walked two miles with us. This was a miracle for her. In the special issue of the *American Indian Quarterly* on the 2002 Commemorative March, she wrote about her road of personal suffering and healing and its connection to our walk. In this current collection, she contributes to the body of historical research on the forced removals from a Wasicu perspective.

As an ally in the Dakota struggle for justice, Denise Breton provocatively and skillfully addresses the role of Wasicus in healing the wounds from 1862. She compels Wasicu readers to consider their personal historic and contemporary participation in Dakota oppression within a restorative justice framework. She argues persuasively that if restorative justice is to have a future, it must extend beyond person-to-person harms and address on a much larger scale People-to-People harms. To do this, it must provide a process through which the White colonizers can hold themselves accountable for the harms perpetrated against Indigenous Peoples. In holding herself accountable, Denise models an extraordinary self-reflective behavior for other Wasicu people: "Whether I personally committed these crimes or not, I benefit from them. They were planned and executed precisely so that I could live here now in one of the Whitest states in the country, Minnesota. And I perpetuate these crimes by continuing in the colonizer habits . . . that have been my way of life since birth."

When the colonizers are busy colonizing, one of the myths they perpetuate is that the social ills of the colonized are the responsibility of the colonized. The colonizers' assumption is that individual members of the colonized society, or the colonized society itself, have somehow failed or are somehow inferior to that of the colonizing society—that they are the source of all the problems. Thus, when we drink too much or commit violent crimes, it is because of our personal failing: we are not smart enough or we do not have enough willpower. Or it is our parents' failing because they did not raise us with good moral values. Or it is our community's failing for not providing enough guidance and support. This myth reinforces the sense of superiority among the colonizing class and the sense of inferiority among the colonized.

We know, however, that colonized Peoples all over the world experience the same set of social ills. That being so, either we can draw the conclusion that all are inferior human beings, or we can see that there is something consistent about a colonized status that sends whole nations tailspinning into cycles of poverty, depression, and violence. If the latter is the case, then the actions of the colonizers are the true source of the problems. In the struggle for decolonization, part of our goal is to examine the social problems as an effect of colonialism and to work toward overturning the institutions and systems that have perpetuated our subjugation.

Restorative justice, then, can either realize its full potential and help us address the roots of our suffering, or it can help perpetuate the myth that the harms perpetrated within our communities are based on individual actions and deny the effects of colonialism among our Peoples. When the victims of horrendous crimes against humanity are blamed for their state of crisis, the colonizer's interests are served. Denise is working within the area of restorative justice to help ensure that the forest is also seen, not just the trees. Furthermore, she understands the monumental struggle for justice that is in all of our futures, "Together as Peoples, we can acknowledge the massive harms done, name racism as it operates to hurt Native Peoples, arrange substantive land return, honor the inherent sovereignty and self-determination of Native Peoples, make restitution and reparations, return the billions of dollars in missing trust funds that have been accumulating from the White use of Native resources, respectfully cease behaviors that denigrate Native Peoples (such as using them as sports mascots), and teach everyone the full history of this land." She views the Commemorative March as a means to begin the truth-telling phase and to create awareness about the crimes perpetrated against us—an important stage in preparation for all the others.

Many of us who began walking in 2002 knew we had just begun something significant, but we still are learning what that means. Clifford Canku referred to our first march as "planting the seeds," and I think we are now beginning to realize the magnitude of our undertaking. We have clearly seen on this march, however, how issues of justice are deeply intertwined with our truth-telling and, as a consequence, new paths have been opened for our People.

Ho-Chunk scholar Amy Lonetree also understands the importance of Indigenous Peoples reclaiming control over the production of historical knowledge. In her essay, "Transforming Lives by Reclaiming Memory," she addresses the meaning of the march from a variety of perspectives, including her family and tribal connections to the Dakota forced removals from Minnesota, her scholarly interests in history and memory, and the importance of honoring and remembering Indigenous women. Based on her scholarly research on public monuments and historical representation, she engages a critical discussion about the impossibility of finding closure for catastrophic and life-changing events, such as the Dakota forced removal. She says, "The Native American Holocaust encompasses many 'searing events' in our history and no amount of time can ever diminish the pain we feel." These are issues that we will continue to address on the Commemorative March, but our experience does seem to indicate that the pain of our genocide may never lessen.

In her account of the 2004 March, Diane Wilson relates the moments of hope and despair along the way, highlighting the lessons learned. After coming face-to-face with threats from law enforcement, she realized that "The internalized values of White culture are so pervasive that the most difficult first step is to see the effects of colonization." She describes how most people become comfortable remaining ignorant about the horrors of Minnesota history because to explore that area is painful and difficult. She tells us, however, that "It was an unwillingness to live this way that brought many of us to the march, to see and feel the limitations of old ways of thinking that have been determined by colonization and internalized racism, and to begin the healing process."

Indeed, all the marchers have initiated a healing that comes from an awareness of how we have been affected by historical harms, and a more critical assessment of the injustices perpetrated against us has subsequently emerged. Many of us view this as an extremely positive step, because it moves us out of a position of complacency. What has followed is a reconnecting among individuals and a collective strengthening of our nation. Diane and her brother David have been an important part of that.

The last chapter in this volume before Gabrielle's closing poem is "Voices of the Marchers from 2004." As the similar chapter written about 2002, this piece brings forth the voices and perspectives of the 2004 participants as well as the various conversations we had with one another and with Wasicu townspeople. This piece represents only a smattering of comments from people who were present primarily during our evening discussions in the various towns along the way. I hope that in future years we will hear the thoughts and reflections of many more participants, especially as the descendants of the original marchers decide to walk to honor their ancestors. It is important to remember that this entire series of marches is an event in process, and we are creating our own documentary record of it as we go along. Additional chapters have yet to be written by future participants of the Dakota Commemorative Marches of the Twenty-first Century.

◄○►

I would like to thank all those who helped with the Commemorative Marches of 2002 and 2004. The Dakota Commemorative Marches were successfully completed with the help of numerous individuals, groups, and tribal communities. Those who supported these events with their energy, monetary, or material donations include Lower Sioux, Upper Sioux, Shakopee, and Prairie Island Dakota communities, Sisseton-Wahpeton Sioux Tribe, Santee Dakota Nation of Nebraska, Mendota Dakota Community, Eci Nompa Woonspe, Southwest State University, Lutheran Campus Ministries at Mankato State, Children of Tiospa Zina Tribal School, St. Mary's Catholic School, Coca-Cola, Shetek Lutheran Ministries, Gustavus Adolphus College, Hy-Vee, Gideon Pond Heritage Society, Joseph Brown Heritage Society, Minnesota New Country School, Department of Natural Resources, Fort Snelling State Park, Dakota Meadows School, Southwest State

University Social Work Club, Minnesota Department of Transportation, University of Minnesota Indian Education, Turner Hall, Tim Blue, Winifred Feezor, Leo Omani, Angela and Scott Wilson, Chris Mato Nunpa, Yvonne Wynde, Gaby Tateyuskanskan, Mary Beth Faimon, Tina Hyde, Jon Hoyme, Arlo and Duella Hasse, Wyatt Thomas, Audrey and Randy Fuller, Jeff Williamson, Autumn Wilson, Phyllis Redday and Sisseton Women, Lisa Bellanger, Jim Anderson, Bob Brown, Neil McKay, Juanita Espinoza, Sandra Turpin, Beth Pierce, Bill Means and his family, Art Owen, Mike Forcia and his family, Tara Chadwick, Mary Peters, Loretta Leith, Ron Leith, Arlene Busse, Dee Thomas, Jim Whortman, Judy Thomson, Dan Breva, Richard Runcke, Darla Gebhard, Fred Fritz, Nadarajin Sethuraju, Karen Larson, Brian Kamnikar, Matt Kopperud, Dave Holm, Steve Rasmussen, Don Robertson, Lisa Elbert, Michelle Rhubee, Scott Windschitz, Naomi Stewart, Connie Kerten, Esther Mark-Babel, Peg Lundell, Cheryl Mathieries, Mary and Chris Loetscher, Helen Schneyer, Julie Soehren, Faye Schuetzle, Jean Jore, Joan Wieneke, Colleen Steinman, Nancy Besse, Eileen Campbell, Diane Wilson, Dave Wilson, and the Gordon Bird family.

During the 2004 March many of these same individuals, organizations, and institutions supported us, so we extend a heartfelt "Pidamayaye" to everyone, but we also want to thank specifically those individuals and families who provided our meals, including the Lorna Anywaush family, Audrey and Randy Fuller, Samantha Odegard and the Task Force, Terri Yellowhammer, John Provost and his family (especially Estelle LaPointe and Phoebe Provost), Francis Yellow,

Robert Blaeser, Lenore Scheffler, Penny Scheffler, the Kitto family, Gwen Griffin and her family, Jennifer Brewer and her family, the folks at New Ulm (especially Richard Runcke at Turner Hall), the Henderson townspeople, and Beth Brown and the Dakota/Lakota Language Society at the University of Minnesota.

Many of our Dakota communities came through with funds and resources to support the 2004 march: Prairie Island paid for the sanitation unit; Upper Sioux paid for the liability insurance and the T-shirts; Lower Sioux provided meals and sleeping quarters; Shakopee provided meals, sleeping quarters, and a monetary donation; and Sisseton provided a monetary donation. Also, Tim Blue and his students at Eci Nompa Woonspe made the prayer stakes we planted each mile along the route. Thanks also must be extended to Susanna Short at the Minnesota Historical Society for providing parking passes at Fort Snelling, Dakota Meadows School for providing lodging, Lake Shetek Lutheran Camp for providing the mattresses, and Don Robertson for the trailer and mileage. I express sincere apologies to anyone I have omitted, as it was by no means intentional. We would also like to thank all the people who supported the walk with their physical efforts and the hundreds, even thousands, of people who sent prayers on our behalf, especially the Lakota/Dakota/Nakota Spiritual Group and the Native American Council of Tribes in the South Dakota State Penitentiary.

◄○►

I would encourage any non-Dakota who is interested in demonstrating solidarity with us and our ongoing struggles to walk with us and to help us in our struggle for justice. Jean-Paul Sartre in his introduction to Frantz Fanon's book *Wretched of the Earth* makes a powerful statement regarding the role of the colonizer in the decolonization process. He says, "[W]e in Europe too are being decolonized: that is to say that the settler which is in every one of us is being savagely rooted out. Let us look at ourselves, if we can bear to, and see what is becoming of us." For non-Dakota people, you can begin to help us when you come to terms with your own role as oppressor. Although you cannot gift us our freedom from oppression, as only we can do that for ourselves, you can help to educate those around you and assist us in overturning colonial systems and institutions.

For the next Commemorative March in 2006, you can think creatively about developing ways in which the non-Dakota people of Minnesota can begin their own decolonization process in regards to the U.S.-Dakota War of 1862. We need help from our non-Dakota allies. We need people who are willing to stand with us and commit themselves to fighting injustice. In addition, our non-Dakota allies can help us uncover the truth about Minnesota's history. As Kevin Annett has asked in his quest to uncover the truth about government- and church-perpetrated abuses against the Indigenous Peoples of Canada, "What happens . . . when you try to house the truth alongside the industry of official lies that runs so much of our lives and thoughts? Can both survive in close proximity for long?"[16] Indeed, they cannot. Help us make sure the truth survives.

◂◦▸

As Dakota people, we need to develop our minds critically. We need to train our children to recognize the injustice around us and to foster in them a desire to work toward a just society. Our critical consciousness has been a form of intellect largely suppressed in our lengthy period of colonization. The challenge now is not simply to observe the passing of the years since these forced removals took place but rather to think critically about how we as Dakota People want to commemorate this event, to question the history forced upon us, and to retrieve the voices silenced by the colonizers' brutality. As Chris Mato Nunpa commented at our gathering on November 12, 2005, at Lower Sioux, "Some of our own people now are beginning to write for us, tell our story, instead of having some White person tell it for us, instead of having some White Ph.D. historian or anthropologist or sociologist tell our story. We are telling it from our perspective and that's really important. . . . I am now sixty-five winters, and I am tired of hearing what Wasicus have to say about us." This collection is an attempt to put those voices forward so that we can critically interrogate how our past has been represented and reshape it to reflect our true experiences as Dakota People.

We owe it to our ancestors to commemorate their suffering and their sacrifice by having the courage to stand up and speak the truth, to examine honestly the events of 1862, unencumbered by the shackles that have bound our historical consciousness. This telling of the truth is the first step to our own true healing. After seven generations, it is about time. Please join us as we walk in the footsteps of our ancestors . . .

NOTES

1. Taiaiake Alfred, "Warrior Scholarship: Seeing the University as a Ground of Contention," in *Indigenizing the Academy: Transforming Scholarship and Empowering Communities*, ed. Devon Mihesuah and Angela Wilson (Lincoln: University of Nebraska Press, 2004), 90–91.

2. Ed Red Owl, Minnesota Public Radio, September 26, 2002, "The Remnants of War" by Mark Steil and Tim Post, first section of MPR series *Minnesota's Uncivil War* (available online at the Minnesota Public Radio Web site, http://Minnesota.publicradio.org).

3. Leo Omani is a former chief of the Wahpeton Dakota Reserve just outside of Prince Albert, Saskatchewan. Yvonne Wynde and her daughter Gabrielle (Gaby) Tateyuskanskan are strong cultural leaders from the Lake Traverse Reservation in South Dakota. We had all gathered at a Summer Institute on "Reconciliation—A Bridge to Diabetes and Dakota Language/Culture Education" held in New Ulm, Minnesota, in the summer of 2001. Gaby and I became co-coordinators for the Commemorative March held in 2002.

4. See, for example, Kenneth Carley, *The Sioux Uprising of 1862* (St. Paul: Minnesota Historical Society Press, 1976); Roy Meyer, *History of the Santee Sioux: United States Indian Policy on Trial* (Lincoln: University of Nebraska Press, 1967); Gary Clayton Anderson, *Little Crow: Spokesman for the Sioux* (St. Paul: Minnesota Historical Society Press, 1986); and Duane Schultz, *Over the Earth I Come: The Great Sioux Uprising of 1862* (New York: St. Martin's Press, 1992).

5. Meyer, *History of the Santee Sioux*, 26.

6. Meyer, *History of the Santee Sioux*, appendix on the Doty Treaties of 1841, 421.

7. Harriet Senie, *Contemporary Public Sculpture: Tradition, Transformation, and Controversy* (New York: Oxford, 1992), 1.

8. Edward Linenthal, "Ritual Drama at the Little Big Horn: The Persistence and Transformation of National Symbol," *Journal of the American Academy of Religion* 51, no. 2 (June 1983): 268.

9. See Ngugi wa Thiong'o, *Moving the Centre: The Struggle for Cultural Freedoms* (Oxford: James Curry, 1993), 84

10. I thank Trent Redfield, a former student of mine at Southwest Minnesota State University, for bringing this historical monument to my attention.

11. Carley, *The Sioux Uprising of 1862*, 22.

12. Daniel Buck, *Indian Outbreaks* (Minneapolis: Ross & Haines, 1965), 31.

13. An assertion made by Brazilian liberatory educator Paulo Freire in *Pedagogy of the Oppressed* (New York: Continuum, 2001), 55.

14. "Righteous anger" is defined by Haunani-Kay Trask as "The emotional/psychological response of victims of racism/discrimination to the system of power that dominates/exploits/oppresses them. Righteous anger is *not* racism; rather, it is a defensible response to racism." See Haunani-Kay Trask, *From a Native Daughter: Colonialism and Sovereignty in Hawai'i*, rev. ed. (Honolulu: University of Hawai'i Press, Revised Edition, 1999), 252.

15. Avishai Margalit, *The Ethics of Memory* (Cambridge, MA: Harvard University Press, 2002), 51.

16. Kevin Annett, *Love and Death in the Valley* (Bloomington, IN: Authorhouse, 2002), 15.

Fort Snelling Concentration Camp Dakota Prisoners 1862–63

Heads of families and number of family members
as compiled by the U.S. Army on December 2, 1862

—◄○►—

Wapahasa's Band

Wapahasa	8
Canhpiyuha	5
Wakanhdiota	5
Okisemaye	5
Winuna Tanka	6
Icazuntewin	3
Tiniyukpanin	8
Dowanhdinape	6
Hupahdinazinwin	7
Dowanhdinapewin	4
Hapan	7
Hupahu	4
Iyowin	5
Tukannapinwin	8
Wicinyan	3
Cegabutiwin	4
Akiwiwina	7
Mahpiyadutawin	4
Hdonicawin	6
Winuna Dutawin	4
Tokahewin	4
Tateyuhewin	9
Magasinawin	2
Hapan	5
Tawicin	6

Wospi	6
Tahaya	9
Hotawinna	3
Kapopawin	5
Mahpiyahdegawin	5
Winuna	2

Passing Hail's Band

Wasuhiyayada	7
Tatehota	8
Hapan	6
Tiozanzanwin	7
Saiciyeda	12
Taputadutawin	3
Waste	3
Tahanpaaye	5
Hapstinna	4
Canhdeska	5
Hoganyudwin	5
Hapanau	2
Siiyatukawin	2
Heyake	12
Pezihuta	7
Ninahnihdiwin	13
Zitkadayuzawin	2
Tukanokiyewin	7

Hazawin	3
Hapan	5
Mahpiya	8
Hapstin	6
Wapiyawicsta	3
Winuna	4
Wanbdisanwastewin	7
Tatekinyaniyayewin	5
Tasinatowin	7
Wakankoyakewin	3
Hapan	5
Ogu	6
Hoksida	6
Mazayuhayankewin	8
Maniwakanhdiwin	5
Mazanumpawin	2

Red Leg's Band

Husasa	5
Pepe	4
Hepi	5
Iyotankewin	7
Wakanna	7
Hepan	6
Iyeyawin	6
Haza	5

Pazahiyayewin	5
Mazaiyotankewin	3
Winuna	3
Ptesanwin	7
Canhdeskamaza	5
Hazadutawin	4
Napeya	7
Su-un	3
Hapan	4
Anpetuhiyawin	7
Wakanmaniwin	2
Mazaahdiyahdu	4
Wakanhdiotawin	6
Wageininmapewin	2
Intekiyawin	2
Zitkada	2
Mahpiyunawin	3
Tukananapewin	4
Wakinyanokiyab	8
Wospi	2
Tokanyahpewin	5

Wakute's Band

Wakute	9
Tunwanota	7
Wakanwapiwin	4

Winyanau	6	Cehdupasamsun	2	Aupo	1	Hakewote	11
Hapan	3	Kahdawin	10	Iciyaupiwin	2	Wiyotanhanau	5
Owahca	6	Iyaheyahewin	4	Cajeyatawin	5	Nunpaicaga	7
Nagi	3	Touake	7			Wastemnawin	5
Tatecinwin	4	Hapaupaye	2	**Good Road's Band**		Paza	5
Susu	2	Haza	11			Wahacankamaza	8
Waci	5	Canwiyawa	7	Wamanus'a	7	Tateahpeyab	5
Mahpiyaduzahan	7	Canhdeyayewin	2	Tateayatomni	9	Betsey	4
Upanhdayawin	4	Tawospin	3	Mahtiadizinin	3	Wakinyatawa	8
Kaiyowazewin	5	Tasinainayawin	2	Tatewastewin	3	Hunkamaza	5
Tasinatowin	8	Anpetuwastewin	8	Ahdatewin	7	Inkpawayakapi	4
Wanhdaka	7	Paksiksan	6	Ptandutawin	8	Wanhinkpe	7
Oiceyawin	6	Tamaza	7	Makatokecawin	6	Aupeicage	4
Waktaahdewin	9	Wakanhditaninwin	2	Hinhewin	4	Sunkatoiciye	6
Winyannau	7	Oyewastewin	3	Capaahdewin	4	Caske	7
Wipe-un	13	Wicahpikoyakewin	4	Hohepetakicawin	5	Mahpiyainyanke	7
Zitkadasakoyake	9	Tatehonunwin	4	Kanpeska	5	Tacetansan	5
Mahpiyatankawin	9	Tapeta	1	Hotada	4	Dutawin	5
Aupehdiwin	10	Wiyuhamani	10	Miniskatewin	7	Canohnahiyayeda	9
Tiakunwin	11			Winode	2	Winyan	2
Canku	9	**Black Dog's Band**		Itesan	3	Kandisapa	9
Wakankihna	7			Mahpiyatowin	4	Mahpiyawakanzi	4
Winuna	5	Napesni	5	Hopecutankawin	6	Nagitopawin	6
Cusnawin	7	Mazaiojanjanwin	2	Oyenakisnawin	3	Hotohdinape	7
Tanagidutawin	4	Anpetuiyotankewin	2	Nazan	3	Maza	2
Kanpeskapewin	7	Ptanhiyewin	1	William Adams	2	Sunkemaza	11
Kampeskada	10	Tokahiwin	3	Yucauniwin	3	Wakinyantopa	2
Wakanhdiiyo-		Hoto	5			Nankadutawin	3
tankewin	7	Winuna	3	**Taopi's Band**		Pesaduta	7
Takanheca	6	Kabdecabwin	1			
Itewakanhdiwin	5	Mahpiyuzawin	2	Taopi	5	**Yellow Medicine's Band**	
		Sagyeopahdawin	4	Istazani	7		
Eagle Head's Band		Hapan	4	Wicinyan	4		
		Tasinawakan	3	Wakanhdisapa	9	Anawangmani	8
Huicape	7	Wicanhpidutawin	4	Tukanwicasta	6	Wakanboide	4
Mahpiyahdakin-		Ihawayakapi	4	Wasteiado	7	Tasina	3
yamun	7	Owankatowin	5	Makayewin	6	Wihake	4

Iyegeda	3	Wicacaka	2	Wakamnapiwin	4	Louise Frenier	2
Cetangeda	7	Inihan	5	Wicanhpiwegacin	4	Narcisse Frenier	3
Winyantoiciye	1	Kuwaau	5	Mahpiyakoyakewin	4	Alexis E. LaFram-	
Apahtawin	3	Wakanmani	3	Anpetusa	12	boise	3
Tukaw	1	Upan	6	Hapan	5	Thomas Robinson	2
Mahpiyaayewin	4	Wakankada	4	Sokehcawin	1	Louison Frenier	8
Kandisotawin	5	Mahpiyawinna	10	Mazaonahonwin	3	Jack Frasier	1
Wasusnawin	11	Sakeda	6	Sucanwasocaoun	6	Joseph Lablac	8
Kuteu	3	Peta	7	Hapstin	2	David Fairebault	1
Iya	1	Wakanhdikoyake-				Joseph Monterey	2
Sihapakiye	7	win	8			Mary Tussotts	1
Wanske	2	Mainapewin	4	**Mixed Blood**		A. D. Campbell	8
Anawagkutemani	5	Mizowin	7	**Families**		Scott Campbell	5
Okihipisni	9	Oyatenazinwin	4			Antoine Renville	7
Tunkan	5	Makainapewin	2	John Moore	5	Michael Renville	6
Wakanoiseda	3	Supehiyu	7	Angus M. Robert-		Gabriel Renville	8
Kaskawin	4	Tahazu	5	son	1	Charles Crawford	1
Tukanhdiyotanke-		Mahpiyataninin	6	Gustavus A. Robert-		Frances Roy	8
win	4	Wihniunkawaste	5	son	1	Vetal Boye	3
Dowanmani	6	Wacage	5	Thomas A. Robert-		Daniel Renville	4
Niteopi	7	Tunwanwantiton	6	son	2	Joseph Renville	2
Hapan	4	Dotedutawin	8	Jane Moore	1	Rosalie Renville	2
Mazaska	5	Wiyuha	12	Joseph E. LaFram-		Maline Mumford	4
Wicanhpi Numpa	4	Ecetukiya	4	boise	4	Alek Graham	6
				Louise Moore	3		

Names of the Condemned Dakota Men

◄○►

The first names listed here are those of the thirty-nine who were sentenced by President Abraham Lincoln to be hanged at Mankato (one was reprieved at the last moment). The spellings come from President Lincoln's Executive Order (December 6, 1862), and the suggested translations were provided by Chris Mato Nunpa during the 1987 Year of Reconciliation. The translations, however, were based on the spellings from Daniel Buck's *Indian Outbreaks* (Minneapolis: Ross and Haines, 1965) and vary slightly from the original execution order. The names of the other condemned men immediately follow and are written as they are spelled in the "Addenda" in M. P. Satterlee's *Minnesota Indian Outbreak* (Minneapolis: Satterlee Printing, 1923). These translations of the names are those offered in Satterlee's work, though these should be viewed not necessarily as accurate translations but as helpful guides for descendants to identify their relatives. I have sometimes rearranged the order of information offered in Satterlee's work for the sake of consistency. I also left off the names of those men who were acquitted, as most of them would be represented in the group sent to Fort Snelling.

Te he hdo ne cha—One Who Jealously Guards His Home. Hanged at Mankato.

Ptan doo ta—Scarlet Otter. Hanged at Mankato.

Wy a tah ta wah—His people. Hanged at Mankato.

Hin han shoon ko yag—One Who Walks Clothed in Owl Feathers. Hanged at Mankato.

Muz za boom a du—Iron Blower. Hanged at Mankato.

Wah pay du ta—Red leaf. Hanged at Mankato.

Wa he hna—I Came (?). Hanged at Mankato.

Sna ma ni—Tinkling Walker. Hanged at Mankato.

Ta te mi na—Round Wind. In Lincoln's executive order but reprieved at the last minute.

Rda in yan kna—Rattling Runner. Hanged at Mankato.

Do wan sa—One Who Sings a Lot or the Singer. Hanged at Mankato.

Ha pan—Second-born Child and Male in a Dakota family. Hanged at Mankato.

Shoon ka ska—White Dog. Hanged at Mankato

Toon kan e chah tay mane—One Who Walks by His Grandfather. Hanged at Mankato.

E tay hoo tay—Scarlet Face. Hanged at Mankato.

Am da cha—Broken to Pieces. Hanged at Mankato.

Hay pee don—Third-born Child and Male in a Dakota Family with the Diminutive "Little." Hanged at Mankato.

Mahpe o ke na ji—One Who Stands on a Cloud. Hanged at Mankato.

Henry Milord—Hanged at Mankato.

Chaskay don—First-born Child and Male in a Dakota Family with the Diminutive "Little." Hanged at Mankato.

Baptiste Campbell—Hanged at Mankato.

Tah ta kay gay—Wind Maker. Hanged at Mankato.

Ha pink pa—The Top of the Horn. Hanged at Mankato.

Hypolite Ange—Hanged at Mankato.

Na pay shne—Fearless. Hanged at Mankato.

Wa kan tan ka—Great Mystery. Hanged at Mankato.

Toon kan ka yag e na jin—One Who Stands Clothed with His Grandfather or One Who Stands Cloaked in Stone. Hanged at Mankato.

Ma kat e na jin—One Who Stands on the Earth. Hanged at Mankato

Pa zee koo tay ma ne—One Who Shoots While Walking. Hanged at Mankato.

Ta tay hde don—Wind Comes Home. Hanged at Mankato.

Wa she choon—Whiteman. Hanged at Mankato.

A e cha ga—To Grow Upon. Hanged at Mankato.

Ha tan in koo—Returning Clear Voice. Hanged at Mankato.

Chay ton hoon ka—Elder Hawk. Hanged at Mankato.

Chan ka hda—Near the Woods. Hanged at Mankato.

Hda hin hday—Sudden Rattle. Hanged at Mankato.

O ya tay a koo—He Brings the People. Hanged at Mankato.

May hoo way wa—He Comes for Me. Hanged at Mankato.

Wa kin yan na—Little Thunder. Hanged at Mankato.

Tunkan e cha—To hang.

Tah-e yo kan—To hang.

Wan num dee kean heyaye ina—To hang.

Pejihuta ska—White Medicine. To hang. Pardoned at Rock Island 1866.

Tunkan e hdo mani—Walks by His Grandfather. Said to be "Old Columbus." To hang.

Huntka—Cormorant. To hang. Pardoned 1866.

Wazi duta—Red Pine. To hang. Pardoned 1866.

Wakan inape dan—Appears Mysteriously. To hang.

Oceti duta—Place of Red Fire. To hang. Pardoned 1866.

Akicita wakan—Sacred Soldier. To hang. Pardoned 1866.

Maka a mani waxicum—White Man Walks the Earth. To hang. Pardoned 1863.

W__yan a kita—To hang.

Iyotan ona—Shoots More Than Others. To hang. Pardoned 1866.

Tatanke kute—Buffalo Shooter. To hang.

Maza yuha mani—Carries Iron Walking. To hang. Pardoned 1866.

Ta wa chin hay—To hang.

Wakinyan hiyaye—Forked Lightning. To hang.

Xake hanske—Long Claws. To hang. Pardoned 1866.

Anpao hdi najin—Returns and Stands at Daybreak. To hang. Pardoned 1866.

Waxicum maza—Iron White Man. To hang.

Hoxidan nonpa—Twin Baby Boy. To hang.

Ta peta—His Fire. To hang.

Ta tay wah kun na ki ya—To hang.

Shin ta—To hang.

We cha hin cha maza—To hang.

Wakinyan maza—Iron Thunder. To hang.

Peji rota—Gray Grass (Wild Sage). To hang. Pardoned 1866.

Maza Wakinyan na—Little Iron Thunder. To hang. Pardoned 1866.

Rupahu—Wing. To hang.

Ite hota—Gray Face. To hang.

Tate tokeca—Different Kinds of Wind. To hang. Pardoned 1866.

Too man na—To hang.

Kayo—Carries for Another. To hang. Pardoned 1866.

Wazi duta—Red Pine. To hang. Pardoned 1866.

Hepan na—Little Hepan. Year imprisonment.

Maza iyapa—Striking Irons Together. To hang. Pardoned 1866.

Wicanrpi ota—Many Stars. To hang. Pardoned 1866.

Oyay e cha sna—To hang.

Wasu wakanhdi—Lightning Hail. To hang. Pardoned 1866.

Marpiya tanka—Big Cloud. To hang. Pardoned 1866.

(Error in book) Rewanke—Frost. Pardoned 1866.

Hotanin xica—Bad Voice. To hang.

Tate yuha mani—Carries the Wind as He Walks. To hang. Pardoned 1866.

Xota dan—Cloudy (or Bleary). To hang.

Ta tay wan yag kan—Five years imprisonment.

Tukan aputeg mani—Presses the Sacred Stone with His Hands While Walking. To hang. Pardoned 1866.

Kam pay ska—To hang.

Maza i heyedan—Strikes on Iron. To hang. Pardoned 1866.

Tukan xa iceye—Sacred Stone Paints Itself Red. Later an Indian minister called Solomon. Pardoned 1866.

Tawa hinkpe duta—His Scarlet Arrow. To hang. Pardoned 1866.

Hepan duta—Scarlet Second Born If Son. To hang. Pardoned 1866.

Ta peta tanka—His Big Fire. To hang. Probably pardoned before others.

Wa na pay ya—To hang.

Xunkardo—Dog Growls. To hang. Pardoned 1866.

Ea ska mane—To hang.

Waxte inape—Appears Good. Five years imprisonment, changed to hanging.

We zoo ha—Acquitted, case reopened and ordered to hang.

Toon kan wa kan—To hang.

Bo ga ga—To hang.

Maka—Earth. To hang.

Nagi dan—Little Ghost. To hang.

Toon kan ke yo mane—To hang.

Sitomni—Everywhere (All Around). To hang. Pardoned 1866.

Waxtexte—Several Times Good. To hang. Pardoned 1866.

Karboka—Sailing (or Floating). To hang. Pardoned 1866.

We cha wa ge dan—Year imprisonment.

Sam e che ya—Five years imprisonment.Etay ho mini—To hang.

Kadutedan—Fanning. To hang. Pardoned 1866.

Mash tay—Waxte—Good. To hang.

Anpetu o janjan na—Bright (or Sunny) Day. To hang. Pardoned 1866.

Ta marpiya rota—His Gray Cloud. To hang. Minister called David. Pardoned 1866.

Itay ho pay—To hang.

Wakinyan wicakte—Lightning Kills. To hang.

Iyopte mani—Swift Walker. To hang.

Tate ohomni inyanke—Runs Around the Wind. To hang. Pardoned 1866.

Wa he tay maza—To hang.

Louis Freniere—To hang.

Joe Provencalle—To hang.

E wan kan e nagin—To hang.

Hmun yan ku—Returns with a Buzz. To hang. Pardoned 1866.

Tukan ji dan—Little Rusty (or Brownish) Sacred Stone. Pardoned 1866.

E ta ge ne ya—To hang.

Tukan ji—Yellow Stone. Five years imprisonment. Pardoned 1866.

Thomas Freniere—To hang.

Oyate yanku—People Coming Back. To hang.

John Freniere—Five years imprisonment.

Joseph Freniere—Five years imprisonment.

Tee maze pay waka—To hang.

Wakanhdi to—Blue Lightning. Five years imprisonment.

Ite wakanhdi ota—Many Lightnings in Face. To hang. Pardoned 1866.

Ta ma hpe wa stay—Five years imprisonment.

Ta chan cha wa kan—To hang.

Wamde oo pe dan—To hang.

Xonka waxte—Good Dog. To hang.

Ta sha ka dan to—To hang.

Na pa sni ma za—To hang.

Toonkan to e cha ga to—To hang.

Wakanhdi ota—Many Lightnings. To hang. Pardoned, no date found.

Hocoka—Middle (or center). To hang. Pardoned 1866.

O e cha ga—Three years imprisonment.

Napixtan—Bother. To hang. Pardoned 1866.

Wahorpi—Nest. To hang. Pardoned 1866.

Okaze—Skates (or Slides). To hang. Pardoned 1866.

Tee o wink mane. To hang.

Cetan rota—Gray Hawk. To hang. Pardoned.

Waka etape mane—Three years imprisonment.

Ta canrpi maza—His Iron Tomahawk. To hang.

Kohdamni najin—Headed Off Standing. Pardoned 1866.

Ta tay e cha gay—To hang.

Wakan hdo mane—To hang.

Taninyan na—Little Breath. To hang. Pardoned 1866.

Pa tan in ne ya—To hang.

Hmoon yan ke ya dan—To hang.

Ta najin—To hang.

Waze kute—Pine Shooter.

Ta wotahe duta—His Scarlet Medicine Bag. To hang. Pardoned 1866.

We cha sha che gay—To hang.

Toon wan wan jidan—To hang.

Hepan—Second Born If Son. To hang.

Tunkan koyag i mani—Walks by His Grandfather. To hang.

Ay ha kay dan—To hang.

Wasu hota—Gray Hail. To hang.

Wakan dowan—Sings Sacredly. To hang. Pardoned 1866.

Nina iyopte—Goes Ahead Very Swiftly. Pardoned 1866.

Wakinyan kute—Lightning Shooter.

Peta wanyag mani—Kindles Fire as He Walks. Three years imprisonment.

Anpao hdi najin—Returns and Stands at Daybreak. Pardoned 1866.

O ta hay dan—To hang.

Hay pin kpa—To hang.

Tate hdi najin—Wind Returns Standing. To hang. Pardoned 1866.

Wan wakan kida—Believes His Arrow Sacred. To hang. Pardoned 1866.

Tate peta—Fire Winds (That Burn). To hang. Pardoned 1866.

Ta wipe—His Weapon. To hang.

Hin han e yay yay. To hang.

Maka a inyanke—Runs on Earth. To hang. Pardoned 1866.

Lot ite janjan—Light Face. To hang. Pardoned 1866.

Ta hanpe wakan—His Sacred Moccasin. To hang.

Etay e cha sna mani—To hang.

Cetan—Hawk. To hang.

Anpetu iyokihi—Next to Day. To hang. Pardoned 1866

Ojanjan na—Bright. To hang. Pardoned 1866.

Ta o ha gay—To hang.

Ta wa pa ha ja ta—To hang.

Tawa hinkpe—His Arrow. To hang. Pardoned 1866.

Dowanwan ku—Sings Coming Back. To hang.

Ta canrpi ojanjan—His Tomahawk Is Bright. To hang. Pardoned 1866.

Maza a inyanke—Makes Iron to Run (Melt). To hang. Pardoned 1866.

Waxicum sapa—Black Whiteman (Negro). To hang. Pardoned 1866.

Chin pee ta na—To hang.

Marpiya duta—Red Cloud. To hang. Pardoned 1866.

Maza e day yay dan—To hang.

Han yan to ka ke—To hang.

Marpiya waxicum—Cloud Whiteman. To hang. Pardoned 1866.

Marpiya o he yay—To hang.

Ay cha yan kay—To hang.

Ampaytu ta ka—To hang.

E kpi sapa—To hang.

Wakanhdi hota—Gray Lightning. Three years imprisonment.

Wicaxte maza—Iron Man. Acquitted but on the pardon list of 1866.

Otin iyapa—Echo Maker. Acquitted but on the pardon list of 1866.

We cha hpe nonpa—To hang.

Ta wicaxte—The Whiteman. To hang.

Marpiya hepiya—Lowering Clouds. To hang. Pardoned 1866.

Marpiya ota—Many Clouds. To hang. Pardoned 1866.

Maza de de—To hang.

Marpiya a e hdo—To hang.

O ya tay tanka—To hang.

Chan o man ne—To hang.

Ti yokiti—Occupies His Own Tipi. To hang. Pardoned 1866.

O yay ko ke pa—To hang.

Han yay too wa kan na ne—To hang.

Ho waxte—Good Voice. To hang.

Kam pay ska—To hang.

Rmu ya koo—To hang.

Enape koyag mani—Appears Clothed Walking. To hang.

Wakan ho min koo dan—To hang.

Marpiya akicita—Cloud Soldier. To hang. Pardoned 1866.

Ta xunke wakan—His Sacred Horse. To hang.

Wamdi ji—Yellow Eagle. To hang.

Toonkan e yay we cha yay. To hang.

Marpiya wicakte—Cloud Kills. To hang.

Cetan rota—Gray Hawk. To hang. Pardoned 1866.

Maza kin yan hi ya ya—To hang.

Wakinyan to (iceye)—Lightning Paints Itself
Blue. To hang. Pardoned 1866.

Ta ho coka duta—His Red Middle Voice. To hang.

Choon hdo ka doo ta—To hang.

Kieos mani—Beckons as He Walks. To hang.
Pardoned 1866.

Kawinge—Circles About. To hang.

Wan wakan kida—Believes His Arrows Sacred.
To hang. Pardoned 1866.

Chan hday shka ma za. To hang.

Xake hota—Gray Claws. To hang.

We ya ka—To hang.

Maza wicakte—Iron That Kills. To hang.

E ya na pay—To hang.

Nom ahdi—Brings Back Two. To hang. Pardoned 1866.

Toon kan chan kday shka—To hang.

Xa iceye—Paints Himself Red. To hang. Pardoned 1866.

Tawa hinkpe maza—His Iron Arrows. To hang.

Kin yan hde don. To hang.

Wakanhdi rota—Gray Lightning. To hang. Pardoned 1866.

Marpiya Wakanhdi—Cloud Lightning. To hang.

Tukau ji iceye—Sacred Stone Paints Itself Yellow.
To hang.

Paze najin—Stands Ready. To hang.

E pah tay—To hang.

Marpiya wakan—Sacred Cloud. To hang.

Wicanrpi duta—Red Star. To hang.

Ti nazipe—His Bow. To hang. Pardoned 1866.

Ma za e shkan man ne—To hang. Pardoned
1866.

Ta niyan hdi najin—He Stands Fast. To hang.
Pardoned 1866.

Marpiya cokaya mani—Walks in Center of
Clouds. To hang.

Pa inyanke duta—Rolling a Red Hoop (the hoop
game). To hang. Pardoned 1866.

Tukan waxtexte—Good Sacred Stones. To
hang.

Marpiya ota—Many Clouds. To hang, changed
to five years imprisonment.

Akicita—Soldier. To hang.

Ma ka na sho ta—One year imprisonment.

Tee o ho mni pe. To hang.

Toon wee chock tay. To hang.

E to hna kay. To hang.

Ma ne ke ya. To hang.

Historic Photographs and Images from 1862 to 1863

<o>

The concentration camp at Fort Snelling. *(Photo by Benjamin F. Upton, Minnesota Historical Society.)*

Dakota woman at Fort Snelling concentration camp. *(Minnesota Historical Society.)*

Wa-pa-sto-ka, One Who Is Gentle. *(Photo by Benjamin F. Upton, Minnesota Historical Society.)*

Han-ye-tu Was-te, Beautiful Night, at the Fort Snelling concentration camp. *(Photo by Whitney's Gallery, Minnesota Historical Society.)*

Dakota women at the Fort Snelling concentration camp. *(Photo by R. W. Ranson, Minnesota Historical Society.)*

Apistoka. *(Photo by Benjamin F. Upton, Minnesota Historical Society.)*

Dakota women at the Fort Snelling concentration camp. *(Photo by Joel E. Whitney, Minnesota Historical Society.)*

Dakota boy at the Fort Snelling concentration camp. *(Photo by Whitney's Gallery, Minnesota Historical Society.)*

Dakota people with the tipis provided at the concentration camp at Fort Snelling. *(Photo by Whitney's Gallery, Minnesota Historical Society.)*

Wo-wi-na-pe, the son of Little Crow, and others at the Fort Snelling concentration camp. *(Photo by Whitney's Gallery, Minnesota Historical Society.)*

Illustration showing the attack by the settlers of New Ulm—mostly White women—on the Dakota women, children, and elders being transported to the concentration camp at Fort Snelling. *(Harper's Weekly Magazine, June, 1863.)*

1919 photos of New Ulm settlers and their children seated according to the year of their arrival.

Forced conversion of Dakota people by a Christian missionary. *(Photo by Benjamin F. Upton, Minnesota Historical Society.)*

Pregnant Dakota woman at Fort Snelling concentration camp.
(Photo by Benjamin F. Upton, Minnesota Historical Society.)

Shadows of Voices

GABRIELLE WYNDE TATEYUSKANSKAN

—◄○►—

In awe of the prairie wind and its beauty,
I listen for shadows of voices.
An ancestral memory of
Forgotten rituals,
Forgotten oral narratives,
Forgotten humanity.

The conqueror in its insolence cannot hear the ancient heartbeat of the prairie.
The plowed and plundered grassland
has been sacrificed to a leader's arrogance.
Damaged spirit is the prize for the powerful victor,
given to the vulnerable,
who are unable to save themselves.

There is a language on the ancient landscape.
Symbols that relate ideas traveling from time immemorial to humanity.
Shadows of voices sustain memory in the continuous prairie wind.
Okiya from sacred and wise relatives.
This same prairie wind that caused pioneer women to go mad.

The heart knows ceremony and its healing virtues.
Medicine that can only be felt.
Ancestral narratives tell of Eya's genocide and oppression.
Imperialism has left its reminder,
a road made of bones.

2002 Commemorative March Commentaries

—◄◦►—

Decolonizing the 1862 Death Marches

WAZIYATAWIN ANGELA WILSON

◄○►

In November of 1862, approximately 2,100 Dakota men, women, and children were forcibly moved in two groups from the Lower Sioux Agency to concentration camps at either Fort Snelling or Mankato, Minnesota—events that marked the first phase of expelling our Dakota people from our homeland of Minisota Makoce.[1] These two groups were paying the severest of penalties for the retributive actions of Dakota people who dared to fight the Wasicu invaders. These Dakota dared to fight because they could not take any more offenses; indeed, they dared to fight because they were pushed to desperation and because there appeared to be no other options. In this chapter, I examine existing accounts of these removals from a critical perspective within the broader framework of colonialism. Furthermore, I discuss how necessary remembering and truth-telling are in our commemoration of these removals in order to achieve healing and to restore well-being among Dakota People.

If we apply a framework of colonization, the U.S.-Dakota War of 1862 emerges as just one point on a continuum that carries through to the present day, yet the framework also suggests the possibility for change in the future. At the most basic level, the colonization framework challenges the narrative that seeks to justify policies of invasion, forced removal, and genocide. The narrative of White innocence and Dakota guilt is immediately displaced by one of White oppression and Dakota subjugation. On the topic of violence and oppression, Brazilian liberationist educator Paulo Freire wrote:

> With the establishment of a relationship of oppression, violence has already begun. Never in history has violence been initiated by the oppressed. How could they be the initiators, if they themselves are the result of violence? How could they be the sponsors of something whose objective inauguration called forth their existence as oppressed? There would be no oppressed had there been no prior situation of violence to establish their subjugation.[2]

The term *violence* here encompasses not only the physical assaults but also all injurious abuses perpetrated upon a People, their way of life, and their land. If we examine 1862 in the context of the subjugation and oppression of the Dakota People by the colonizing Wasicu settlers and the United

States government, then it becomes clear that the process of violence had been initiated long before.

When people are faced with oppression, several psychological responses follow: flight, fight, or capitulate. The Dakota had already capitulated to a tremendous degree. Our ancestors had continually sought peaceful resolutions through treaty negotiations over land issues; they had tolerated missionaries, traders, agents, and settlers, even when these Wasicus were illegally occupying Dakota lands and destroying Dakota resources. Some of our ancestors had already fled further west to escape the oppressive forces at work in Minnesota. Other of our Dakota People, however, wished to stay in our ancient homeland. As these Dakota were pushed to desperation with their very survival at stake, fighting increasingly became the most likely option. The violence finally echoed by Dakota warriors was simply a defensive response to the subjugation and oppression they had been enduring for decades.

This is not to excuse the acts of violence perpetrated by Dakota people. This violence did not advance the Dakota cause (though it is unlikely anything would have done so in the face of White greed for Dakota land), and it is a reality that White families were killed during the war. However, to consider another case of subjugation and oppression, Archbishop Desmond Tutu points out that, though the human rights abuses perpetrated by African National Congress (ANC) members against the upholders of apartheid South Africa were legally equivalent with the abuses perpetrated by White South Africans, they were not

> « WITH THE ESTABLISHMENT OF A RELATIONSHIP OF OPPRESSION, VIOLENCE HAS ALREADY BEGUN. »

morally equivalent. In all cases where acts of violence have already been perpetrated, we can make important distinctions between, for example, justifiable homicide and culpable homicide.[3] It may be that all suffer no matter who the perpetrator is, but the culpability of White Minnesota settlers is a story that has not been documented. Instead, the story has been suppressed because of what it suggests about the colonizers.

◄○►

The year 1862 marked perhaps the greatest turning point in the long history of our Dakota People. By the early 1860s, we had already faced for at least several decades tremendous assaults at the hands of the colonizers on our land, our spirituality, our educational system, our communal lifestyle, our subsistence patterns, and our physical being. In August of 1862, our Dakota People were facing starvation because the U.S. government had again violated its treaty obligations and was late in producing the gold necessary to fend off starvation.[4] A few Dakota finally had enough and struck out by killing a family of White settlers in Acton, Minnesota, after a quarrel when some warriors took some eggs. The next day, the Dakota officially declared war upon the United States government and its citizens. The war, however, was short-lived. Within six weeks, the Dakota were defeated by the troops organized against them.

After the 1862 defeat of our People at Wood Lake, it was reported that the leader of Dakota resistance, Bdewakantunwan Chief Little Crow, was despondent and heartbroken. After stepping out of his lodge, he told the people that he was ashamed to call himself Dakota:

> Seven hundred picked warriors whipped by the cowardly whites. . . . Better run away and scatter out over the plains like buffalo and wolves. . . . To be sure . . . the whites had big guns and better arms than the Indians and outnumbered us four or five to one, but that is no reason we should not have whipped them, for we are brave men, while they are cowardly women. I can not account for the disgraceful defeat. It must be the work of traitors in our midst.[5]

Little Crow certainly was betrayed by traitors among his people—by those such as Wabasha and Taopi who negotiated secretly with Sibley and worked toward Little Crow's defeat. Yet for the purposes of this essay and the task of decolonizing the historical record, we can see in his recognition of this reality that Little Crow was also acknowledging the old divide-and-conquer tactics typically used by colonial forces to subjugate a People. He was experiencing this consequence of colonialism through the betrayal by his fellow Dakota.

Colonization was sufficiently extensive by 1862 to prevent the Dakota from taking united action. Far from being accidental, this divide-and-conquer tactic was purposeful on the part of missionaries, agents, traders, and White settlers, who rewarded those who adopted the traditions of the Wasicu.[6] Dakota men who agreed to take up the full-time occupation of farming, for example, were rewarded with food or material goods, while others were punished for refusing to abandon their traditions. Missionaries gained control of treaty-provisioned educational funds and used them to carry out their work of "civilizing" the Dakota, creating a gap between the supposedly "educated" and "uneducated" Dakota and injuring traditional educational systems. To undermine Dakota leadership, government agents were urged by the missionaries to dole out annuities to heads of families instead of chiefs. They encouraged nuclear family settlement with individual plots of land, rewarding housing to those who complied in order to foster individual greed and to break up the communal villages.

More than simply disrupting traditional systems, all of these efforts brought tremendous harm to the fabric of Dakota social, political, and economic life. Previously, the Dakota had constructed an egalitarian society in which generosity was highly valued and the welfare of the group took precedence over individual desires. A comprehensive educational system existed in which individuals were well trained and mentored in skills necessary not only for their own survival but also to produce contributing members to the society. In addition,

« THESE SOCIETAL STRUCTURES WERE . . . TARGETED FOR ATTACK TO SUBJUGATE THE DAKOTA, INSURING U.S. DOMINION NOT ONLY OVER THE PEOPLE BUT ALSO OVER THE LAND AND ITS RESOURCES. »

rather than using their positions of power to amass wealth for themselves, the chiefs gained respect through their ability to give generously to the people by distributing goods and gold. These societal structures were purposely targeted for attack to subjugate the Dakota, ensuring U.S. dominion not only over the people but also over the land and its resources.

Relentlessly pursued, these attacks on Dakota social structures were designed to eventually create a population so weakened and dependent that the way would be totally cleared for Whites to settle and appropriate Dakota land and resources. This pattern was repeated continuously across the continental United States. Thus, by the time the colonizers set their sights on Dakota lands, imperial expansion demanded the eradication of the original inhabitants.

Within this framework, Dakota dispossession was a foregone conclusion. Internal breakdown—and the simultaneous lack of unity necessary for any meaningful resistance—wreaked devastating consequences for the Dakota but served the interests of the colonizers well. Those Dakota who converted to Christianity, dressed in Wasicu clothing, cut their hair to resemble the Wasicu men, and learned to speak English became known as the "friendlies" and reaped the rewards of preferential treatment. Big Eagle, for example, stated, "The 'farmers' were favored by the government in every way. They had houses built for them, some of them even had brick houses, and they were not allowed to suffer. The other Indians did not like this. They were envious of them and jealous, and disliked them because they were favored."[7]

Indeed, the government did not hesitate to pit Dakota people against each other for its own purposes. This occurred, for example, when annuities were illegally withheld from the Dakota until they had attempted to kill or capture Inkpaduta for his attacks on White settlements.[8] Though Inkpaduta may be remembered as one of our fiercest resisters to Wasicu invasion, his fellow Dakota were metaphorically held hostage by the Whites until they agreed to take up arms against him. By 1862, the use of these colonizing divide-and-conquer tactics against the Dakota People and way of life had been so successful that our people were deeply factionalized. Even after the war, those Dakota who served as scouts for the U.S. Army were ordered to kill any Indian trying to return to Minnesota or face military execution themselves. Sisseton elder Ed Red Owl recalls,

> One of the chief scouts here tells . . . of encountering his own nephew. When he saw his nephew coming, he said, "I had tears in my eyes, but yet I had the orders of the United States Army to fulfill. And so before my own eyes, I shot him until he died."[9]

This painful fractionation that began in the nineteenth century became intergenerational and continues today.

◄○►

The punishment of the Dakota after the war officially ended was swift and brutal, resulting in Dakota casualties and losses that have yet to be enumerated. Governor Alexander Ramsey stated unambiguously in September of 1862 that, "The Sioux Indians of Minnesota must be exterminated or driven forever beyond the borders of the State."[10] Henry Sibley was commissioned to carry out these goals, which he did with marked success.[11] At the final Battle of Wood Lake, Dakota people began to surrender, believing that they would be treated as prisoners of war, while others fled north into Canada or west into the Dakotas. Twelve hundred Dakota initially surrendered to Colonel Sibley, and that number quickly grew to two thousand.

It was soon clear that the price for Dakota military resistance to the invasion would be exceedingly high. Upon surrendering, the men were immediately separated from the women and children, shackled, and tried for war crimes before a five-man military tribunal. By November 5, 392 trials had been completed, some having lasted as little as five minutes; 307 Dakota men were sentenced to death, and 16 were given prison terms. An executive order was still required, however, and the trial records were sent to Washington for President Lincoln's review.

> « EARLY SCHOLARSHIP ON THE TOPIC OF 1862 REVEALS A HATRED FOR DAKOTA PEOPLE AND A CLEAR SENSE OF WHITE SUPERIORITY. »

On November 8, the condemned men were forcibly removed to the concentration camp at Mankato, where they continued to await execution orders. On December 26, 1862, at the order of President Abraham Lincoln, thirty-eight of those Dakota men were hanged in what remains the largest mass execution in United States history. In the spring of 1863, those with commuted death sentences were transported to Davenport, Iowa, and imprisoned there for three years. By the time they were finally released in 1866, only 247 were still alive; 120 had died in prison.

Meanwhile, on November 7, 1862, the group of some 1,600 women and children were forcibly marched to Fort Snelling, where they, too, were imprisoned through the winter. In May of 1863, the 1,300 women and children who had survived the death camp were sent to a new reservation beyond Minnesota's borders in Crow Creek, South Dakota.

Once the Dakota were forcibly removed from Minnesota, bounties were placed on the scalps of any and all Dakota people who remained. These bounties began at $25 and eventually were raised to $200. Moreover, the treaty money, which had arrived too late the previous summer to prevent the war, was sent back to Washington and then redistributed to White settlers, totaling $1,370,374 in 1863–64, as recompense for depredations incurred during the war. The Dakota treaties were abrogated, the people were exiled from our homeland, and our lands were opened to White settlement. The legacy of these policies is evident in the extant diaspora of our exiled people and our only minimal presence in our ancient homeland.

Early scholarship on the topic of 1862 reveals a hatred for Dakota people and a clear sense of White superiority. Rampant throughout these narratives is terminology that reflects this perspective. Typical of colonial interlopers on Indigenous lands, writers from the era regularly used words such as "massacre," "slaughter," or "atrocity" to describe Dakota actions upon "innocent," "pure," "brave" White settlers. The Dakota, on the other hand, were depicted as "savages," "red devils," "blood-thirsty demons," "wretches," "beasts," "fiendish perpetrators," and even "government-pampered" Indians, as Minnesota's first schoolteacher, Harriet Bishop McConkey, described us.[12] McConkey's work is representative of many early Wasicu accounts of the war as well as the views held by many of those early Euro-American settlers. In the introduction to her book about the war, she stated:

It is a dreadful tale—one from which the heart recoils and the pen shrinks; but I have girded me for the effort, and what though every hair of the head is erect, and every nerve a vibrating medium, making me, for the time being, as a living, actual witness of all I rehearse; the reading word shall hear, if they cannot see, what young Minnesota has experienced, how her adopted sons and daughters have suffered from the savage bullet and bloody tomahawk, while yet is undulating the clear prairie air, in brutal fierceness, never to die from the ear of the sufferers, the terrible Dakota war-whoop.[13]

Similarly, in their book *A History of the Great Massacre by the Sioux Indians,* Charles Bryant and Abel Murch begin:

The massacre in Minnesota, by the Annuity Sioux Indians, in August, 1862, marks an epoch in the history of savage races. In their westward march across the continent, in the van of a higher civilization, the native red men have, at different times, given sad and fearful evidences of their enmity to the dominant white race; but, from the landing of the Pilgrim Fathers on the rock-bound coast of New England, in the winter of 1620, until their descendents had passed the center of the continent, and reached the lovely plains of Minnesota, no exhibition of Indian character so afflicted and appalled the soul of humanity, as the fearful and deliberate massacre perpetrated by them in August 1862.[14]

These writings lack context. They cite merely the symptoms of the problem rather than its root in the processes of conquest and colonization. In writings from the period, many Wasicu expressed almost a complete astonishment that any act of war would be declared upon them; they seemed to view themselves as entirely innocent. From their perspective, the "Indian problem" was being dealt with appropriately. Settlers arrived on the "Indian frontier"; they pressured the government to negotiate treaties so that legal land title could be claimed, after which Dakota homeland was declared first Minnesota Territory and then in 1858 the State of Minnesota. Their plans were progressing nicely. Such a conquest agenda can be rationalized only by a deeply ingrained myth of self-apotheosis coupled with a simultaneous dehumanization of the Dakota.

◄◦►

Our ancestors, on the other hand, were forced to confront the reality that something had gone horribly wrong. Why were our People being outnumbered and overpowered in our own homeland? What were we to do when this powerful government consistently failed to fulfill its treaty obligations? How were we to subsist while we were being confined to smaller and smaller tracts of land and facing diminishing supplies of food? Were these Wasicu so favored even by our Creator that they could take what was ours and leave us with nothing?

While Dakota people attempted to rationalize these tremendous violations of justice, the Wasicu proclaimed a definitive explanation: The Dakota were not favored by God. Instead, they believed it was the White race that possessed a divine right and responsibility to invade the land, conquer its people, and develop its resources according to their own interests, and we were mere obstacles to the fulfillment of that destiny—that *Manifest Destiny*. The colonization of entire Peoples is always rationalized in such ways. The colonization might have ended in that generation, but every subsequent generation has elected to maintain the status quo instead of challenge it.

Unquestionably, the oppression and colonization of our People was well under way by the mid-nineteenth century. For example, in 1852 when Alexander Ramsey was pressuring the Dakota to sign papers agreeing to the fraudulent traders' claims, the Sisitunwan Dakota Chief Mazasa (Red Iron) stated in their meeting:

We want our pay, and we will sign no paper except a receipt for the money. The snow covers the ground, and we are still waiting for our money. We are very poor; you have plenty. Your fires burn well; your tents are well-closed against the cold. We have nothing to eat. We wait a long time for our money. Many of our people are sick from hunger. We will have to die, because you do not pay us. We may die, and if so we will leave our bones unburied, so that our Great Father may see how his Dakota children died.[15]

For making these comments and refusing to sign the papers, Red Iron was taken prisoner. A head-soldier from Red Iron's band, Lean Bear, then advocated warfare, stating, "I will lead you against the long knives (bayonets and swords) of the white men who have come to swindle us, to rob us of our land, and to imprison us, because we do not assist them to rob our wives and children."[16]

Lean Bear was persuaded against warfare at the time. However, by August 1862, the Dakota were in a life-and-death struggle that required a reaction, and some chose war. In the subsequent period, our People faced complete defeat militarily, outright land theft in the abrogation of our already despicable treaties, genocide in the policies of extermination, and expulsion from our homeland. After these atrocities effectively cleared the way for White settlement, military force was no longer needed, and a quieter period of colonization ensued.

—◦—

To expand the empire, colonization requires the expulsion of the original residents from as much land as possible, and the Wasicu began to expel Dakota people from our Minisota homeland in two successive waves and two distinct groupings. I say two successive waves because, although White sources do not connect the two, my own family's oral accounts make little distinction between the forced marches to the concentration camps and the later banishment from Minnesota. Thus my grandmother learned from her grandmother that "they passed through a lot of towns going to South Dakota."[17]

The first wave of removal occurred when the uncondemned Dakota were sent to Fort Snelling and the condemned men to Mankato. On November 7, 1862, 1,658 of our people were force-marched under heavily armed guard from the Lower Sioux Agency to Fort Snelling under the command of Colonel William R. Marshall, who would later become governor of Minnesota.[18] This armed guard consisted of the Seventh Regiment Minnesota Volunteers and three companies of soldiers. In a four-mile procession, our ancestors were paraded through towns and subjected to additional violence by Wasicu settlers.

Just one day later, the 392 condemned men who were awaiting news of their execution or prison sentencing—forty-eight of them having been acquitted of formal charges but still kept in confinement—made their way to Mankato under the supervision of Colonel Henry Sibley. Also accompanying them were seventeen Dakota women who served as laundresses and cooks, four of their babies, and four of those whom the Whites called "friendly Indians" to assist in caring for the prisoners.[19]

The second wave of removal occurred in late spring of 1863 when our people were physically forced out of our homeland. On April 21, the condemned men—thirty-eight fewer in number after the hanging in Mankato—were sent to a dilapidated prison in Davenport, Iowa, where they remained for three years. While there, they suffered cold, disease, and intensive pressure for religious conversion, as well as White educational training. When they were finally released, roughly one-third, or 120, had not survived the imprisonment. On May 4 and 5, groups of prisoners from Fort Snelling—1,318 in all—boarded boats that brought them down the Mississippi River and then up the Missouri River to the Crow Creek Reservation in South Dakota. One group traveled by boat to St. Louis and then up the Missouri River to St. Joseph, while the second group of 547 prisoners stopped in Hannibal, Missouri, and traveled by train across Missouri to St. Joseph. Once in St. Joseph, both groups boarded a single boat for the rest of the difficult journey. The missionary John Williamson described the trip as "nearly as bad as the Middle Passage for slaves."[20]

This essay and book are concerned with the first phase of removal, when our Dakota people made the journey to concentration camps. I first learned of this forced relocation from my grandmother, Elsie Cavender, who carried a narrative account passed down from her grandmother, Maza Okiye Win (Woman Who Talks to Iron). Maza Okiye Win was ten years old at the time of the war, and thus the accounts she relayed to her children and grandchildren were born of her own traumatic hardships. Kunsi (Grandmother) Elsie entitled this story of her grandmother's "Death March," consciously drawing a parallel between this forced march and that of the Bataan Death March during World War II, during which 70,000 U.S. and Filipino soldiers were forced to walk sixty-three miles to a prison camp while facing starvation and poor treatment. Learning of this event from a relative who had experienced it, she saw similarities with the march her grandmother was forced to endure. The following account, which I recorded in 1990 with my grandmother, remains the most descriptive and lengthy one yet documented. It is relayed here in my grandmother's words:

Right after the 1862 Conflict, most of the Sioux people were driven out of Minnesota. A lot of our people left to other states. This must have been heartbreaking for them, as this valley had always been their home.

My grandmother, Isabel Roberts (Maza Okiye Win is her Indian name), and her family were taken as captives down to Fort Snelling. On the way most of them [the people] walked, but some of the older ones and the children rode in a cart. In Indian the cart was called *canpahmihma kawitkotkoka.* That means "crazy cart" in Indian. The reason they called the cart that is because it had one big wheel that didn't have any spokes. It was just one big round board. When they went, they didn't grease it just right, so it squeaked. You could just hear that noise about a mile away. The poor men, women, old people, and children who had to listen to it got sick from it. They would get headaches real bad. It carried the old people and the children so they wouldn't have to walk. Most of the people just walked. Some of them if they were lucky rode horses.

They passed through a lot of towns, and they went through some where the people were real hostile to them. They would throw rocks, cans, sticks, and everything they could think of—potatoes, even rotten tomatoes and eggs. They were throwing these things at them, but the Indians still had to walk through the main streets. So they had to take all that. Then when they would pass through the town they would be all right. A lot of those towns I don't know the names of in English. They used to say them in Indian. The two towns that were the worst they had to get through were Henderson and New Ulm, Minnesota. I didn't know the name in English, so I said, "Grandfather, do you know how they call them in English?"

"No, I just know their Indian names," he said.

So then I had to go to Mr. Fred Pearsall. In Indian his name was Wanbdi Ska (White Eagle). He was a white man, but he knew a lot of things about the conflict. He talked Indian just like we do. He knew all those things that happened, and he knew just what words to use to describe the times. So I was able to get the names of those towns. They were the worst ones they had to go through.

When they came through New Ulm, they threw cans, potatoes, and sticks. They went on through the town anyway. The old people were in the cart. They were coming to the end of the town, and they thought they were out of trouble. Then there was a big building at the end of the street. The windows were open. Someone threw hot, scalding water on them. The children were all burned and the old people too. As soon as they started to rub their arms the skin just peeled off. Their faces were like that, too. The children were all crying, even the old ladies started to cry, too. It was so hard it really hurt them, but they went on.

They would camp some place at night. They would feed them, giving them meat, potatoes, or bread. But they brought the bread in on big lumber wagons with no wrapping on them. They would just throw it on the ground. They would have them sleep in either cabins or tents. When they saw the wagons coming, they would come out of there. They had to eat food like that. So, they would just brush off the dust and eat it that way. The meat was the same way. They had to wash it and eat it. A lot of them got sick. They would get dysentery and diarrhea and some had cases of whooping cough and small pox. This went on for several days. A lot of them were complaining that they drank the water and got sick. It was just like a nightmare going on this trip.

It was on this trip that my maternal grandmother's grandmother was killed by White soldiers. My grandmother, Maza Okiye Win, was ten years old at the time and she remembers everything that happened on this journey. The killing took place when they came to a bridge that had no guard rails. The horses or stock were getting restless and were very thirsty. So, when they saw water, they wanted to get down to the water right

away, and they couldn't hold them still. So the women and children all got out, including my grandmother, her mother, and her grandmother.

When all this commotion started, the soldiers came running to the scene and demanded to know what was wrong. But most of them [the Dakota] couldn't speak English and so couldn't talk. This irritated them and right away they wanted to get rough and tried to push my grand-mother's mother and her grandmother off the bridge, but they only succeeded in pushing the older one off and she fell in the water. Her daughter ran down and got her out and she was all wet, so she took her shawl off and put it around her. After this they both got back up on the bridge with the help of the others who were waiting there, including the small daughter, Maza Okiye Win.

She was going to put her mother in the wagon, but it was gone. They stood there not knowing what to do. She wanted to put her mother someplace where she could be warm, but before they could get away, the soldier came again and stabbed her mother with a saber. She screamed and hollered in pain, so she [her daugh-ter] stooped down to help her. But her mother said, "Please daughter, go. Don't mind me. Take your daughter and go before they do the same thing to you. I'm done for anyway. If they kill you, the children will have no one." Though she was in pain and dying, she was still con-cerned about her daughter and little granddaughter who was standing there and witnessed all this. The daughter left her mother there at the mercy of the soldiers, as she knew she had a responsibility as a mother to take care of her small daughter.

"Up to today, we don't even know where my grandmother's body is. If only they had given the body back to us, we could have given her a decent funeral," Grandma said. So, at night, Grandma's mother had gone back to the bridge where her mother had fallen. She went there, but there was no body. There was blood all over the bridge, but the body was gone. She went down to the bank. She walked up and down the bank. She even waded across to see if she could see anything on the other side, but no body, nothing. So she came back up. She went on from there not knowing what happened to her or what they did with the body. So she really felt bad about it. When we were small, Grandma used to talk about it. She used to cry. We used to cry with her.

Things happened like this, but they always say the Indians are ruthless killers and that they massacred White people. The White people are just as bad, even worse. You never hear about the things that happened to our people, because it was never written in the history books. They say it is always the Indians who were at fault.[21]

In telling these stories and commenting as she did, my grandmother was clearly aware that she

« IN TELLING THESE STORIES . . . MY GRANDMOTHER WAS CLEARLY AWARE THAT SHE WAS SUBVERTING THE USUAL HISTORICAL NARRATIVES ABOUT THE 1862 WAR. »

was subverting the usual historical narratives about the 1862 war. She was also well aware that the perpetrators of atrocities against the Dakota had gone unpunished. Indeed, whereas the Japanese commander in charge of the Bataan Death March was tried, convicted, and executed by U.S. military commission for his actions, the leaders behind these marches—notably Henry Hastings Sibley and Alexander Ramsey—not only were hailed for their conduct but also remain celebrated heroes in Minnesota history.

Governor Ramsey's call for either the extermination or the forced removal of our ancestors in September 1862 was clearly a policy of ethnic cleansing, yet this has not diminished his appeal to White Minnesotans. Between Ramsey's implementation of his policies and their support by state and federal authorities, it became impossible for the Dakota to live in Minnesota. As one writer commented, "Congress exiled remaining Sioux from Minnesota March 3, 1863, and stopped all further annuities, and thereafter troops stationed in the state felt no compunction in shooting those found within its boundaries."[22]

It is only because the same colonizing class retains power that this obvious genocidal policy can still be rationalized. Genocide and its perpetrators can be celebrated only as long as the colonizers are still colonizing. There was no ambivalence about the call for extermination and forced removal in 1862, nor is there today. None-theless, not only did our Dakota people have to go through the horror of having Ramsey's plan implemented with the full support of White set-tlers in the state, but every Dakota person since then has been assaulted on a near daily basis with a celebration of the very leaders responsible for the "ethnic cleansing" of our People from Min-nesota. Yet, such realities continue to escape the critical eye of the general public. This would be comparable to expecting Jewish people to live in a state where counties, streets, numerous statues, paintings, schools, and parks were created in honor of Hit-ler or Eichmann and bore their names.

Even Colonel William Mar-shall, who was in charge of the soldier who killed my ancestor, went on to become governor of Minnesota. In fact, Samuel Brown, the mixed-blood son of a Sisitunwan Dakota woman named Susan and Major Joseph Brown, celebrates Mar-shall as "one of the bravest and noblest of men." Thoroughly indoctrinated with the racist ideol-ogy that condemned the "savage Indian," Samuel Brown betrayed his Dakota People. He served as a scout and accompanied Colonel Marshall's de-tachment with the uncondemned men, women, and children to Fort Snelling, while his father, the elder Brown, accompanied the condemned men to Mankato. In Brown's eyes, Colonel Mar-shall warranted this characterization because,

> While the train was passing through
> the town one of the citizens, with blood
> in his eyes and half-crazed with drink,

rushed up with a gun leveled at Charles Crawford, one of the friendlies, and was about to fire, when "the bold charger of the plains," Lieutenant-Colonel Marshall, who happened along on horseback, rushed between them and struck down the gun with his sabre and got Crawford out of the way, thus saving a life at the risk of his own.[23]

I would like to know where Colonel Marshall was when my elderly grandmother was stabbed, but perhaps she was not friendly enough to the White cause. Or, why the adjutant general re-ported that Lieutenant-Colonel Marshall's detachment guard-ing the Dakota to Fort Snelling stated, "This detachment re-ceived no molestation from the settlers upon the route, and arrives safely at their destination on the 13th."[24]

This statement is extraordinary given the oral record of what happened to our ancestors on that journey. Brown was one of those who offered a more detailed description of the hardships facing Dakota people on their walk through Henderson in his well-known quote:

> At Henderson, which we reached on the
> 11th, we found the streets crowded with
> an angry and excited populace, cursing,
> shouting, and crying. Men, women, and
> children, armed with guns, knives, clubs,
> and stones, rushed upon the Indians as
> the train was passing by and, before the
> soldiers could interfere and stop them,

« ONLY WHEN THE COLONIZERS ARE STILL COLONIZING CAN PERPETRATORS OF GENOCIDE STILL BE CELEBRATED. »

succeeded in pulling many of the old men and women, and even children, from the wagons by the hair of the head and beating them, and otherwise inflicting injury upon the helpless and miserable creatures.

I saw an enraged white woman rush up to one of the wagons and snatch a nursing babe from its mother's breast and dash it violently upon the ground. The soldiers instantly seized her and led, or rather dragged, the woman away and restored the papoose to its mother, limp and almost dead. Although the child was not killed outright it died a few hours after. The body was quietly laid away in the crotch of a tree a few miles below Henderson and not far from Faxon.

I witnessed the ceremony, which was, perhaps, the last of the kind within the limits of Minnesota; that is, the last Sioux Indian "buried" according to one of the oldest and most cherished customs of the tribe.[25]

Of course the White woman responsible for killing a Dakota baby went unpunished because, though extreme, her act of crime was viewed as an act of retribution against Dakota violence.

Another oral account, this one given by Bain Wilson, recalls the brutality and indignity suffered by women and children along the way. An elderly Dakota woman told him:

My great-great-grandma was on that route when they were taking them to Crow Creek. On the way down she wanted to go to the bathroom. They told her not to go to the bathroom, "If you have to go, go in your pants." But that old lady got out of the wagon and she started to walk toward some trees and some soldiers saw her and they shot her. And that old lady hollered back to the people, she said "They shot me! Makutepi ye!" she said. And so they went back to try to pick up the body and that body was missing, it was already gone.

The elderly woman in this narrative was shot by White soldiers, not because she posed any kind of threat to them or the White settlers, but because she tried to maintain some semblance of her dignity and modesty amidst a seething pool of inhumanity. It was not enough that our Dakota People should be dispossessed of our ancient homelands; it was also necessary that our dignity be smothered in the process. The pain in Wilson's voice was apparent when he continued, "And I couldn't help hear that old lady crying. She said, 'To this day we don't know whatever happened to my great-great-grandma.'" He then wisely and passionately pointed out, "These kinds of stories should bring our Dakota People back together."[26]

⟨○⟩

Few written accounts expressing the Dakota perspective of this march have been documented or translated.[27] Yet other Dakota families still strong in the oral tradition most likely carry accounts about this event. Until these accounts are uncovered, additional insight may be gleaned from the plethora of Wasicu first-person accounts of the war. For example, an account given by Sarah Purnell Montgomery more clearly illuminates my grandmother's story. Montgomery described the Wasicu women's roles in helping to arm the town of New Ulm while Dakota warriors attacked. Montgomery wrote:

> The men not on picket duty, occupied the lower floor, while the floor above was filled with women and children, the latter sleeping on the floor in a small room. For the rest of us, there was no sleep. We filled every available vessel with water from a nearby well, and laboriously carried up an outside stair way. Fires were kept burning to keep the water boiling, and had the Indians attacked us that night, as was their intention, they would have received showers of boiling water upon their heads.[28]

Montgomery was not one of those who threw boiling water on our Dakota elderly and children during their forced march, since she was in the town of South Bend by then, but she likely learned this tactic from her association with the women who did. Nonetheless, in November of 1862, the women of New Ulm apparently kept the fires burning to keep the water boiling in anticipation of the four-mile procession of women, children, and elderly. And they waited to pour the water on the most feeble of the group—the elderly women and the youngest children who rode in the wagon.

◄o►

The group of uncondemned Dakota people arrived at Fort Snelling on November 13 to spend a winter under horrendous conditions. Duane Schultz comments:

The Indians were confined in a fenced camp of tepees on the north side of the river. It was a gloomy, inhospitable site, on bottomland that turned to mud and offered no protection from the icy winter winds. Settlers ran off the Indians' few horse and oxen and taunted them until eventually they grew bored. The army allotted the Indians only meager rations, typically bread for the adults and crackers for the children.[29]

Imprisonment at the Fort Snelling concentration camp meant continued suffering and hardship through the winter of 1862–63, during which time hundreds more died from starvation, disease, and exposure.

◄o►

The day after Marshall's procession left for Fort Snelling, the condemned men—those who had been tried, convicted, and sentenced to execution under the command of commissioned colonel Henry Hastings Sibley—were shackled in groups of two and then placed in wagons holding ten prisoners each. Isaac V. D. Heard described that morning:

> At six o'clock our drums were beating for forward march. The general was one of the earliest of risers. He had all the camp aroused and at breakfast before four. It was a disagreeable morning; "the owl through all his feathers was a-cold," and so were bold "sojer" boys. We soon cantered away, and left the aforesaid quondam kitchen, but henceforth im-

mortalized court-house, in which three of us had slumbered cozily for many a pleasant night, . . . probably forever.[30]

Although these men were relieved from walking the roughly seventy miles from the Lower Sioux Agency to Mankato, their journey was not without pain and hardship. In reference to the trip through New Ulm, Sibley described the attack on their convoy, stating that it was "set upon by a crowd of men, women, and children, who showered brickbats, and other missiles, upon the shackled wretches, seriously injuring some fifteen of the latter, and some of the guards." He went on to say, "The assailants were finally driven back by a bayonet charge. . . . I did not dare to fire, for fear of killing women and children. The Dutch she devils! They were as fierce as tigresses."[31] White settlers were demonstrating an uncontrolled rage and desire for revenge on the Indigenous inhabitants who dared to challenge their right of invasion and conquest.

Heard similarly describes the scene in New Ulm:

Hearing that we were passing by, they all rushed forth—men, women and children, armed with clubs, pitchforks, brickbats, knives and guns, and attacked the prisoners. The women were perfectly furious. They danced around with their aprons full of stones, and cried for an opportunity to get at the prisoners, upon whom they poured the most violent abuse. Many rushed forward and discharged a shower of stones. One woman, who had a long knife in her hand, was especially violent

in her demonstration, and another pounded an Indian in the face until she broke his jaw, and he fell backward out of the wagon.[32]

In his book *Indian Outbreak,* Daniel Buck rationalizes the mob violence against the Dakota by saying, "The principal actors in the attack were mostly women and young people, many of whom had relatives and friends who had suffered from the depredations of these Indians, and who feared that the latter would escape from due punishment of their crimes through the leniency of the United States government."[33]

Sarah Purnell Montgomery also documented her recollections of the procession of condemned Dakota men as they were paraded through their town:

It was on a beautiful Indian summer afternoon a few weeks after we had returned to South Bend, that General Sibley and his staff, in full uniform, and mounted, headed a strange procession that passed through our village. Behind them marched a regiment of infantry. Then came forty wagons drawn by horses containing four hundred of the murderers. They were chained together, and seated on the floor, five on a side, facing one another. Many wore bright shawls that they had taken from the homes of the settlers. Nearly all covered their heads.

Another regiment of infantry was followed by ambulances carrying the wounded settlers, who had been found nearly dead from hunger and exhaustion. The squaws retained to cook and care for the prisoners, rode in army wagons drawn by mules. The camp equipment and supplies was followed by the artillery which comprised the rear guard.

They came to a halt at the Blue Earth river, midway between South Bend and Mankato.[34]

This excerpt illustrates the twisted perceptions of White settlers. Though she failed to comment on the millions of acres stolen from the Dakota in our own homeland, Montgomery felt compelled to discuss the shawls Dakota men took from the homes of the White settlers.

The documents from this era clearly dismantle one of America's favorite images, namely, that of the innocent, pure, and benevolent White pioneer woman. Numerous accounts of the role of White women (and their children) in the civilian attacks on the Indigenous prisoners challenge the notion that their participation in Dakota genocide and dispossession was benign or exculpatory.

While the fierceness of the women in New Ulm is routinely commented upon, only from a soldier's journal do we understand why it was the women who committed most of the violence. In his entry for November 8, 1862, when his company was camped eight miles outside of New Ulm, this soldier noted that a boy had warned them that the citizens of New Ulm were intending to kill the prisoners as they passed through. On November 9, as they made their way into town, he states, "They had planked up their store fronts and had pierced them for rifles, through which they intended to shoot the Indians when

we came through." He went on to say, "About a mile from town, we came to a halt and a guard of infantry was placed between us and the wagons containing the Indian prisoners. We again moved forward and orders were given to allow no man to come within the lines." Thus, if the prisoners were to be murdered, the women of the town would have to be the perpetrators. They did not disappoint:

Women led this drive. They were armed with every conceivable weapon. In a moment all was in an uproar. Stones began to come like hail, smashing the heads and breaking the jaws of the Indians and knocking some out of the wagons. The drivers took shelter behind their horses, which were nearly unmanageable. An Indian was knocked out of the wagon nearest to me and was dragged a long distance by a chain made fast to his leg and to another's held in the wagon. Some women broke through, our men making but little opposition. The infantry made a show of resistance, but nothing in earnest. Our orders were to let *no man* [emphasis in original] through and we didn't.[35]

The half-hearted attempts by the soldiers to keep the women and children at bay resulted in the deaths of Dakota prisoners. The same soldier commented, "Eight out of ten Indians in the wagon that I was guarding were hurt . . . some of the Indians died that night from wounds received during the day."[36]

Perhaps the most graphic description of the condemned men's removal was given by George

Crooks, one of the Dakota men who experienced the events firsthand. This source stated that Crooks was six years old at the time of the war but was with the Indian women who followed their Dakota warriors to battle and traveled with them as they awaited their execution or imprisonment. His account appeared in the February 10, 1909, issue of the *New Ulm Review* while he was living at Lower Sioux. He stated:

After the surrender the Indians were loaded into old Red River carts and started for the Lower Agency and Mankato. The carts were small, drawn by oxen, and it was difficult for any more than four persons to occupy the box. In the cart I was forced to occupy were two Indian men and my sixteen-year-old brother. We were bound securely and on our journey resembled a load of animals on their way to market. We traveled slow, meeting now and then a white person who never failed to give us a look of revenge as we jolted along in our cramped condition.

As we came near New Ulm my brother told me the driver was afraid to go through the town. My heart leaped into my mouth and I crouched down beside my brother completely overcome with fear. In a short time we reached the outskirts of the city and the long looked-for verdict, death, seemed at hand. Women running about and men waving their arms and shouting at the top of their voices convinced the driver that the citizens of the place were wild

in their thirst for blood. Accordingly he turned the vehicle in an effort to escape the angry mob. But it was too late. In an instant the crowd was upon us and pounded us almost to a jelly, my arms feet and head resembling more than anything else raw beefsteak.

How I escaped alive has always been a mystery to me. My brother was killed and when I realized that he was dead I felt that the only person in the world who would look after me was gone and I wished at the time that I might have been killed too.[37]

Some Dakota people report today that George lived because his older brother protected him with his own body, sparing him the worst beatings by bearing the brunt of them himself. However, the sufferings of the condemned men have generally not been depicted as sympathetically as those of the people making their way to Fort Snelling, largely because these men were seen as murderous savages who committed heinous crimes against innocent, unsuspecting Whites. It is here that we as Dakota need to stand up most forcefully to call into question the innocence of Whites in Minnesota in 1862 and to declare that the violence committed upon the Whites in Minnesota during the war was not caused by the Dakota; it was caused by the Whites' own actions and the actions of their government. "Never in history has violence been initiated by the oppressed."

◄○►

In Governor Ramsey's message to the state legislature on September 9, 1862, he stated that the

Dakota "have themselves made their annihilation an imperative social necessity";[38] he appealed to the logic of vengeance for our assassination of White women and children. By Ramsey's own logic, though, what did the Whites in Minnesota expect would happen when they invaded our lands, watched or participated as we were defrauded of land, treaty money, and goods, forced us into starvation and subservience, and constantly attacked our way of life? No doubt they believed nothing should happen as a consequence of their behaviors, because in their minds they were morally justified. Why? Because they believed themselves to be superior civilized beings, while we were uncivilized savages. This alone decries White innocence.

Some have argued that friendships existing between the Dakota and White settlers demonstrate that there were innocent Whites in Minnesota in 1862 or that not all Whites were guilty of participation in the subjugation and/or extermination of the Dakota People. I would suggest instead that these relationships of friendship are more comparable to that of the exploitative relationship between a master and slave in the old South. By 1862, our Dakota ancestors knew that we were viewed as an inferior form of humanity—that our weapons, language, spirituality, housing, dress, food, and every other conceivable aspect of our culture were seen as inferior. By 1862 when White settlers were plowing and farming our old lands and destroying our resources, our ancestors also knew that there was a power imbalance. But more important, the Dakota People suffered constant trauma caused by invasion and colonization—the very survival of the Dakota Nation was at stake—and this trauma

played a major role in the formation of Dakota-Wasicu friendships.

Many other victims of trauma (such as those who are held hostage and suffer physical, sexual, or emotional abuse or are indoctrinated into cults) exhibit an emotional bonding with their perpetrators. This pattern of bonding is now referred to as the Stockholm Syndrome, named after a 1973 bank robbery in Stockholm during which the hostages became emotionally attached to their victimizers. Given this phenomenon of trauma bonding, it makes sense that victims of trauma caused by invasion and colonization may exhibit similar symptoms. Accordingly, many Dakota people in 1862 and in subsequent generations have denied the perpetration of tremendous violence by the invaders and have attempted to focus on what they (mis)construe as the positive benefits of colonization. Others rationalize the abusers' violence as a way to maintain an emotional and psychological bond with the colonizer in the face of ongoing colonization. Even more commonly, many of our Dakota People have been made to feel ashamed of our last attempt to strike out against the invaders, and so we resort to blaming ourselves for the colonizers' violence in an attempt to feel a sense of control. Sufferers of the Stockholm Syndrome often adopt such responses toward the perpetrators of their abuse and trauma. While these reactions might offer ways to overcome a sense of powerlessness or to maintain hope in an overwhelming situation, they nonetheless deny the violence of the perpetrator.

Yet the experience of Dakota people is different from that of other trauma victims. Whereas the dominant society presumably condemns acts of abuse, torture, and trauma, it still actively affirms the rightness of its invasion and conquest. Our Dakota people can find no larger community that offers shelter from the ongoing violence or safe haven for healing and recovery. Quite the opposite, the colonizer continues to benefit from the perpetuation of the historical relationship of oppression. Thus it is that each new generation is traumatized all over again, and the colonization of Dakota people becomes more deeply fixed.

In light of these realities, the Dakota-White "friendships" of this period are actually not true friendships at all but instead relationships born between a colonizer and the colonized, between the oppressor and the oppressed. We must be clear that no Whites in Minnesota believed it was wrong that we were removed from our lands and that our way of life was eradicated. If there had been Whites who advocated this, they would not have invaded. Furthermore, extensive research on this period has not uncovered evidence of such a view among any of the Whites. Even if some believed this in their hearts, they were nonetheless complicit in their actions.

◄◦►

It is true that a few Whites recognized what they deemed unfair treatment, such as the shameful behavior of the traders in swindling the Dakota out of treaty funds, the irresponsibility of the government in not fulfilling treaty obligations, or the injustices perpetrated in the trials of Dakota men. People such as Bishop Henry Whipple, Samuel Hinman, or the Williamson and Riggs missionary families raised these issues. However, even though these individuals were able to see gross wrongs in the situation, they would not deny that White people held a superior right to the land or that the Dakota way of life and spirituality had to be obliterated.

So, while there certainly were some White individuals who favored some Dakota individuals, we must ask if any of these "true friends" of the Dakota were willing to abandon their farms and return them to their rightful owners? Were they lobbying in Washington for the removal of White people from the state? If such sentiments had been expressed or actions taken, perhaps an argument could be made for some strain of White innocence. Yet this is not the case. In a situation of colonization, the colonizer realizes the benefits of subjugating other human beings. As Albert Memmi reveals about the colonizer:

> [H]e must also understand the origin and significance of this profit. Actually this is not long in coming. For how long could he fail to see the misery of the colonized and the relation of that misery to his own comfort. He realized that this easy profit is so great only because it is wrested from others.[39]

Every White person either came to Minnesota knowing that Indigenous people would be removed or killed to make way for them or learned this fact shortly after they arrived. Such knowledge did not prevent them, however, from making their homes on Dakota lands. Furthermore, they had a vested interest in keeping quiet or supporting Dakota dispossession, because to speak out would mean a loss of their own privilege. Even the most benevolent among them—those who believed merely in cultural and spiritual ethnocide—did not view the Dakota as human beings of equal value. We were valuable only because we provided an opportunity for them to save heathen souls. We must all be vigilant about our complicity in the injustices perpetrated around us.

Something must be said, though, about the degrees of culpability. Because some Whites may not have called for Indian extermination outright, as people like Ramsey did, or may not have physically attacked Dakota captives as they were paraded through the small towns of Minnesota, their degree of culpability might be lessened. However, claiming innocence would be a long stretch.

Some of the arguments made by scholars about the Jewish Holocaust during World War II regarding varieties of collaboration might be useful here. Andrew Rigby, for example, comments about countries of Axis-occupied Europe, "It was virtually impossible to be a neutral bystander."[40] He goes on to outline the various manifestations of political, military, social, and economic collaboration. Rigby stresses that collaboration may be offered willingly or reluctantly, and it may be motivated by degrees of individual self-interest and community interest.[41] Furthermore, as an advocate of a Truth Commission into Genocide in Canada, the Reverend Kevin Annett has invoked the Nuremburg Legal Principles to discuss complicity. These principles require that "citizens refuse to support, financially or any other way, institutions which committed or are committing genocide."[42] These are issues that must be explored.

—◦—

Though this discussion of the historical and ongoing injustice perpetrated against the Dakota will elicit reactions of anger and discomfort, it is time for us to stop denying the truth about our history to please our oppressors. Anyone who believes that oppression and colonization have ended need only drive down the road from my home reservation. In Redwood Falls, adjacent to the Lower Sioux Reservation, is Ramsey Municipal Park. Almost every day of their lives, Dakota people at Lower Sioux are reminded that Minnesota loves the man who called for the extermination of our People. This would not happen in a place free of oppression. A growing number of us will no longer be silent. We speak today carrying the burden of seven generations.

Frantz Fanon told us that decolonization is always a violent phenomenon, because it requires that the colonial structure be overturned.[43] Decolonizing our history regarding the events of 1862 will, therefore, be a violent phenomenon. The colonial structure established prior to the war that justified polices of theft, genocide, and forced removal is the same structure that denies justice to Dakota people today.

Furthermore, by not questioning or challenging their continued right to Dakota lands and resources, Minnesotans have sustained, generation after generation, all the rationalizations that supported our dispossession in the first place. No doubt it has been easy for them to do this, since "All the perpetrator asks is that the bystander do nothing. He appeals to the universal desire to see, hear, and speak no evil."[44] In 1862, citizens of the state were at worst direct perpetrators of genocidal policies of ethnic cleansing and at best complicit in those policies, but all of the citizens directly reaped the rewards of Dakota extermination and dispossession, as they continue to do today.

In recovering our forgotten history, we are seeking accountability from the perpetrators, and we are disallowing a claim of neutrality for the bystanders who watch and do nothing—from 1862 to the present day. The sense of a superior right to occupy our lands is so ingrained that fair reparations have never even been discussed. Furthermore, given the extent to which our Dakota people have internalized the colonialist mentality, the occupation of our homeland has not been significantly challenged since 1862. Just as Dakota people suffered the violence of oppression and colonization that led to the 1862 war, so too have we continued to suffer violence on our bodies and our spirits ever since. Only four tiny Dakota communities remain in our vast homelands of Minisota Makoce, and most of our People remain in exile. Our communities are still plagued by social ills stemming from generations of ongoing colonization.

More important, the means for us to most effectively heal ourselves—that is, to recover our Indigenous knowledge and ways of living—depend on our relationship with our homeland. Taiaiake Alfred describes the overwhelming reality of colonialism today as "the fundamental denial of our freedom to be Indigenous in a meaningful way, and the unjust occupation of the physical, social, and political spaces we need in order to survive as Indigenous peoples."[45] This is certainly the reality of colonialism that our Dakota people face today.

Not only will decolonizing the history of 1862 be a violent process, but challenging the master narrative about those events will be violent as well. For the Wasicu, the decolonization process in regards to 1862 will fundamentally challenge their right to exist on our land and their right to exploit our resources. This fresh look at 1862 bloodies the hands of the descendants of those who invaded our lands and called for our extermination or forced removal. The blood of our ancestors can no longer be washed away by appeals to White innocence or purity, as so often spew from the lips and writings of the colonizers.

For the many Dakota who have spent decades, generations, and lifetimes attempting to prove that they and their ancestors have been friends to the Wasicu, decolonization may be an equally violent experience. It will require calling into question their own actions and values, as well as any privilege they may have gained by carrying out the colonizers' objectives.

Those who are ready to stand up and speak the truth about the history of Minnesota will also face violence, since this is the usual response to threats to the status quo. Yet this group offers the greatest hope for the liberation of all. Referring to the fact that the task of liberation falls to the oppressed, Freire writes, "The oppressors, who oppress, exploit, and rape by virtue of their power, cannot find in this power the strength to liberate either the oppressed or themselves. Only power that springs from the weakness of the oppressed will be sufficiently strong to free both."[46]

While the consequences of war have hurt our People, so, too, have the consequences of complacency. We only need to look around our reservations today to see the poor social conditions affecting a once strong and healthy People, all of which is part of the legacy of colonization. Today, 144 years later, we must cultivate a critical consciousness that will allow us to shed the colonialist visions of our past—visions that have justified our extermination and expulsion from our homelands. We must organize a meaningful and essential recovery of what is ours.

Specialists in the area of trauma and recovery have noted, "Remembering and telling the truth about terrible events are prerequisites both for the restoration of the social order and for the healing of individual victims."[47] Once we make a proper account of the U.S.-Dakota War in the broader context of colonialism and thus achieve a wider recognition that our People have been subjugated, we will have taken a major step in our own healing and in restoring our dignity. To accomplish this, we must step forward and tell each other and our children that we do not need to make apologies for our actions and that we need to give one another the strength to tell our stories.

However, we need to take additional measures as well. In her excellent work on historical trauma, Maria Yellow Horse Brave Heart offers important strategies for addressing group trauma with group treatment—strategies that include "incorporating sharing experiences, the provision of hope, collective mourning, and social support."[48] Our Lakota relatives, for example, participate in a communal memorialization of the Wounded Knee massacre through the Big Foot Memorial Ride; so, too, must we as Dakota struggle with how to address the legacy of colonialism and historical trauma that we continue to face as a result of the forced removals of 1862.

-◄o►-

NOTES

1. This particular translation is offered by Chris Mato Nunpa.

2. Paulo Freire, *Pedagogy of the Oppressed* (1970; reprint, New York: Continuum, 2001), 55.

3. Desmond Tutu, *No Future without Forgiveness* (New York: Image Books, 1999), 106.

4. It must be noted that the treaty food provisions had arrived and were sitting in warehouses, but the gold also due had not arrived. The agent was waiting to distribute them together, while in the meantime, Dakota people were starving.

5. Samuel Brown, *In Captivity* (Fairfield, WA: Ye Galleon Press, 1996), 21. It must be noted that this is Brown's interpretation and translation of Little Crow's words. In Brown's translation, he reports that Little Crow said he was ashamed to call himself a Sioux, though it is much more likely that Little Crow used the term Dakota. It is also unlikely that Little Crow used the term "Indian," and he probably used "Dakota" here as well.

6. This strategy of divide and conquer is well documented. See, for example, Paulo Freire, who states, "As the oppressor minority subordinates and dominates the majority, it must divide it and keep it divided in order to remain in power." This must happen, he says, because unity of the oppressed would signify a "serious threat to their own hegemony." Freire, *Pedagogy of the Oppressed*, 141.

7. Gary Clayton Anderson and Alan R. Woolworth, *Through Dakota Eyes: Narrative Accounts of the Minnesota Indian War of 1862* (St. Paul: Minnesota Historical Society Press, 1988), 26.

8. Roy Meyer, *History of the Santee Sioux: United States Indian Policy on Trial* (Lincoln: University of Nebraska Press, 1967), 96–100.

9. Ed Red Owl, Minnesota Public Radio, September 26, 2002, "Execution and Expulsion" by Mark Steil and Tim Post in the MPR series *Minnesota's Uncivil War.*

10. Message of Governor Ramsey to the Legislature of Minnesota, Delivered September 9, 1862 (St. Paul: WM. R. Marshall, State Printer, 1862), 12.

11. Former governor of Minnesota Henry Sibley was chosen to lead this expedition because he had decades of experience trading with the Dakota, at one time even having a Dakota family. Though he

had no military experience, he was believed to be the best candidate for the job because he knew the Dakota so well.

12. See, for example, Harriet Bishop McConkey, *Dakota War-Whoop: Or, Indian Massacres and War in Minnesota, of 1862–'3* (1863; reprint, Minneapolis: Ross & Haines, 1970).

13. Ibid., 19.

14. Charles S. Bryant and Abel B. Murch, *A History of the Great Massacre by the Sioux Indians, In Minnesota, Including the Personal Narratives of Many Who Escaped* (Cincinnati: R.W. Carroll, 1868), iii.

15. Alexander Berghold, *The Indians' Revenge* (New Ulm, MN: Monument Press, 1891), 71.

16. Ibid., 72–73.

17. Elsie Cavender Oral History Project, conducted by Angela Cavender Wilson, Fall 1990.

18. Marshall had an excellent reputation among the White population for being "an officer without fear and without reproach," as one historian described him (see Buck, *Indian Outbreaks* [Minneapolis: Ross & Haines, 1965], 280).

19. Brown, *In Captivity*, 25.

20. Meyer, *History of the Santee Sioux*, 146.

21. The version here is based on the one appearing in Angela Cavender Wilson, "Grandmother to Granddaughter: Generations of Oral History in a Dakota Family," in *Natives and Academics: Researching and Writing about American Indians*, ed. Devon Mihesuah (Lincoln: University of Nebraska Press, 1998), 31–33, though it also includes some of the information edited out of that version.

22. Roy P. Johnson, *The Siege at Fort Abercrombie* (Bismarck: State Historical Society of North Dakota), 72, reprinted from *North Dakota History* 24, no. 1 (January 1957).

23. Brown, *In Captivity*, 26.

24. Bryant and Murch, *A History of the Great Massacre*, 454–55.

25. Brown, *In Captivity*, 25–26.

26. Bain Wilson, "My Great Great Grandmother," *Mahkato Wacipi* recording, American Composers Forum, 2001. Though Wilson states that this was in reference to the trip to Crow Creek, it appears that this story refers to the march to Fort Snelling. Elsie Cavender's account of her grandmother's experiences similarly placed the story in the context of the move to Crow Creek, clearly associating the first phase of this removal in November of 1862 with the removal out of Minnesota in the spring of 1863 and discussing it as one long event, rather than two separate events.

27. There is currently, though, a Letters Project in Flandreau, South Dakota, that has taken on the task of translating the letters sent back and forth among prisoners at Fort Snelling and Mankato. Perhaps they will uncover more specific references to these forced marches.

28. Sarah Purnell Montgomery, "Some Recollections of the Indian Outbreak of 1862," M582, Roll 2, Dakota Conflict of 1862 Manuscripts Collections, Minnesota Historical Society.

29. Duane Schultz, *Over the Earth I Come: The Great Sioux Uprising of 1862* (New York: St. Martin's Press, 1992), 253–54.

30. For this quote, see Isaac V.D. Heard, *History of the Sioux War and Massacres of 1862 and 1863* (New York: Harper & Brothers, Publishers, 1865), 240. It must be mentioned that while Heard places the date of the condemned men's departure from Lower Sioux on November 9, it is more likely that the group actually left on November 8. See Lisa Elbert's essay in this volume for further discussion on this topic.

31. Henry Hastings Sibley to his wife, Wednesday, November 12, 1862, Minnesota Historical Society, Henry Hastings Sibley Papers, M164, Roll 11.

32. Heard, *History of the Sioux War*, 243.

33. Buck, *Indian Outbreaks*, 222.

34. Montgomery, "Some Recollections of the Indian Outbreak."

35. John K. Glanville and Carrol G. Glanville, eds., *I Saw the Ravages of an Indian War: A Diary Written by Amos E. Glanville, Sr., Company "F" 10th Minnesota Volunteers, August 26, 1862 to July 29, 1863* (Leoli KS, 1988), 36–39.

36. Ibid., 44–45.

37. "Relates Unlikely Story: George Crooks, an

Indian Living at Morton Tells of His Experiences Following the Outbreak," *New Ulm Review,* February 10, 1909, no. 6.

38. Message of Governor Ramsey to the Legislature of Minnesota, 12.

39. Albert Memmi, *The Colonizer and the Colonized,* expanded version (Boston: Beacon Press, 1991), 7.

40. Andrew Rigby, *Justice and Reconciliation: After the Violence* (Boulder: Lynne Rienner Publishers, 2001), 19.

41. Ibid. 20.

42. Kevin Annette, *Love and Death in the Valley* (Bloomington IN: 1st Books, 2002), 163.

43. See Frantz Fanon, *The Wretched of the Earth* (New York: Grove Press, 1963).

44. Judith Herman, *Trauma and Recovery: The Aftermath of Violence from Domestic Abuse to Political Terrorism* (New York: Basic Books, 1992), 7.

45. See Taiaiake Alfred, "Warrior Scholarship: Seeing the University as a Ground of Contention," in *Indigenizing the Academy: Transforming Scholarship and Empowering Communities,* eds. Devon Mihesuah and Angela Cavender Wilson (Lincoln: University of Nebraska Press, 2004).

46. Freire, *Pedagogy of the Oppressed,* 44.

47. Herman, *Trauma and Recovery,* 1.

48. Eduardo Duran, Bonnie Duran, Maria Yellow Horse Brave Heart, and Susan Yellow Horse-Davis, "Healing the American Indian Soul Wound," in *International Handbook of Multigenerational Legacies of Trauma,* ed. Yael Danieli (New York: Plenum Press, 1998), 351. See specifically, Maria Y. H. Brave Heart-Jordan, "The Return to the Sacred Path: Healing from Historical Trauma and Historical Grief among the Lakota" (PhD diss., Smith College, School for Social Work, 1995).

Dakota Commemorative March

Thoughts and Reactions

CHRIS MATO NUNPA

◄o►

"How mitakuyapi. Owasin cantewasteya nape ciyuzapi do! Mato Nunpa emakiyapi. Damakota k'a Wahpetuwan hemaca. Mini Sota makoce heciyatanhan wahi k'a Pezihuta Zizi Otunwe hed wati."

"Hello, my relatives. With a good heart, I greet all of you with a handshake. I am called Two Bear. I am a Dakota and a 'Dweller In the Leaves' (one of the Seven Council Fires or Oceti Sakowin). I am from 'the land where the waters reflect the skies or heavens' (Minnesota), and I live in the Yellow Medicine Community" (in BIA terms, this is the Upper Sioux Community near Granite Falls, Minnesota).

For the past fourteen years, I have been an Associate Professor in Indigenous Studies and Dakota Studies (INDS) at Southwest Minnesota State University (SMSU). At the Eighth Annual INDS Spring Conference in April 2001, the first planning discussion occurred concerning a march to honor the Dakota women and children who were on the forced march in November 1862. We had a number of planning meetings for the Dakota Commemorative March at SMSU. On the march, I served as one of the Minnesota contact persons and as a "gofer": "go fer" this and "go fer" that. One of the Dakota communities located at Santee, Nebraska, donated a buffalo. This provided about 800 pounds of meat. So, I delivered one-hundred-pound chunks of meat to the various communities that cooked and fed the marchers.

The marchers who participated in the Commemorative March 140 years after the 1862 event came from South Dakota, North Dakota, from reserves in Manitoba and Saskatchewan, as well as from Nebraska and Minnesota. Most of the Dakota people had relatives or ancestors who were on these forced removals or were killed in the towns along the march or who were "murdered" in the concentration camp at Fort Snelling or were hanged at Mankato. For most of the participants, this march was an emotional and powerful experience.

My thoughts and reflections will be divided into three sections in this article. The first part will deal with some historical background, including the concept and policy of removal, forced marches, and/or "ethnic cleansings." The second part will highlight the backlash from some Euro-Americans, and the questions and issues they raised both in the planning and in the actual march. The last part will deal with personal issues—with personal emotions and the impact of the march upon me.

FORCED MARCHES, REMOVALS, AND ETHNIC CLEANSINGS

What happened to these Dakota civilians and non-combatants back in 1862 in Minnesota was not unique to the Dakota People of Minnesota. Many other Indigenous Peoples of the United States were forced to leave their traditional homelands—lands that the Creator gave to them according to their creation or origin stories—and be moved to strange lands where they would not be a bother or in the way of the Euro-American citizens of the United States. One major proponent of the concept and policy of removal was Thomas Jefferson, who is still regarded as a hero by many White Americans but as an enemy and Indian-hater by many Native Peoples. In 1803, Jefferson drafted a constitutional amendment that would allow the exchange of land that the Indigenous Peoples held in the east for other lands west of the Mississippi, though Congress did not give serious consideration to the draft amendment until twenty-seven years later.[1]

Then, in 1830 Congress passed the Removal Act. Andrew Jackson, elected in 1828, rapidly acted upon it. Although he is regarded as a hero by White Americans as well, Jackson was an Indian-hater, Indian-fighter, and an Indian-killer. Clifford E. Trafzer writes in his book that Jackson "pursued removal with unbounded vigor" and that he "treated Native Americans like dependent children who were too ignorant and savage to know that the time had come for them to move out of the way of progress and civilization."[2]

Andrew Jackson and his successor, Martin Van Buren, entered into over one hundred treaties of removal with individual Native nations. Dr. Russell Thornton, in his *American Indian Holocaust and Survival,* writes, "Indian removals and relocations became massive during the 1800s, following passage of the Indian Removal Act of 1830."[3] Thus, what happened to the Dakota People of Minnesota in 1862 has happened hundreds of times to other Indigenous Peoples. Francis Paul Prucha, in his book *American Indian Policy in the Formative Years,* writes, "It cannot be denied that the land greed of the whites forced the Indians westward and that behind the removal policy was the desire of eastern whites for Indian lands and the wish of eastern states to be disencumbered of the embarrassment of independent groups of aborigines within their boundaries."[4]

One of the more famous forced marches was the "Trail of Tears" of the Tsa-la-gi (Cherokee). According to Thornton, nearly 17,000 Tsa-la-gi were forcibly removed from their ancient and traditional homelands to land in what is now the state of Oklahoma. Thousands of Tsa-la-gi died. As with the Dakota People of Minnesota, the Tsa-la-gi were in "stockades," or concentration camps, where hundreds died before the actual march. In fact, Thornton says, "as a result of it [the forced march] the Cherokee may have lost almost one-half of their population of about 20,000."[5] Many people became sick, and little children died of whooping cough. The Tsa-la-gi died from depression, disease, starvation, and exposure. One minister remarked that, "our minds have, of late, been in a state of intense anxiety and agitation." This same source mentions "terrified children."[6] One could say that these Tsa-la-gi were indeed terrorized and terrified! I remember hearing one Tsa-la-gi man recount stories of their women being taken into the woods at night and raped by White soldiers.

Another forced march was the "Long Walk" of the Diné (Navajo) People in 1864–65. Christopher "Kit" Carson, a man famous to many White Americans and infamous to the Diné, was instrumental in the "taming" of the Diné, which then resulted in their forced removal. Kit Carson had been sent to Diné territory to demonstrate that "wild Indians could be tamed."[7] The Long Walk was a journey of 300 miles to Fort Sumner in New Mexico Territory, where the Diné were then confined. This site was selected "for the concentration and maintenance of all captive Indians from the New Mexico territory."[8] Here at this concentration camp, approximately 9,000 Diné people were held, "suffering from syphilis and probably other diseases, starvation, cold and harsh weather, and brutality."[9]

During this march, civilians—noncombatants—who fell behind were killed. Most of the Diné families have stories of relatives who were murdered by White soldiers on this march, as was the case with the hundreds of other examples of forced marches and removals—"ethnic cleansings." Many of the Dakota people who participated in the Dakota Commemorative March in the year 2002 have oral histories of their relatives, who were civilians or noncombatants, being killed by White soldiers on the forced march back in 1862. I had

a great-great-great-grandmother whose stomach was slit open with a saber by a soldier on horseback. Present-day Dakota do not know where the bodies of their relatives/ancestors who were killed are buried—or if they were buried at all.

◄○►

The genocidal and imperialistic mind-set present in the Euro-American population provides a context for understanding these "ethnic cleansings" of the Indigenous Peoples by the United States and its citizens. The United States was and is an imperialist country. Its citizens wanted Native lands, and they were quite willing to do whatever it took to get these lands and the natural resources upon those lands. Imperialism means that a foreign power penetrates, transforms, and defines another country and its people for the purposes of domination, exploitation, and subjugation.[10] Federal Indian policy is "true American imperialism" according to Dr. Angie Debo in the video *Indians, Outlaws, and Angie Debo*. Lenore Stiff Arm and Phil Lane Jr. state that by the mid-nineteenth century, "U.S. policy makers and military commanders were stating—openly, frequently, and in plain English—that their objective was no less than the 'complete extermination' of any native people who resisted being dispossessed of their lands, subordinated to federal authority, and assimilated into the colonizing culture."[11]

One of the questions or issues for me is this: when Saddam Hussein was in power, what if he had gathered up the Kurds who live in northern Iraq, force-marched them all to a concentration camp, and, eventually, forcibly removed them from Iraq? I suspect that there would have been an immediate outcry from the Euro-American public. They would have denounced this action as "ethnic cleansing" or as genocide—as a crime against humanity or as another corrupt and immoral action that plainly illustrated the "evil" of Saddam. Yet these same Euro-Americans would not see the hypocrisy in this attitude. They would be so self-righteously outraged. They would not be able to see the "ethnic cleansings" and "crimes against humanity" that their ancestors perpetrated not only upon the Dakota People of Minnesota but also upon all the other Indigenous Peoples of the United States in hundreds of horrific examples of forced removal and outright murder of civilians and noncombatants.

It never ceases to amaze me—but not to surprise me—that this country, the United States of America, actually had a policy of "ethnic cleansing" (the Indian Removal Act of 1830) of the Indigenous Peoples for most of the nineteenth century. This kind of genocidal thinking permeated much of Euro-American society, from top to bottom, from presidents such as George Washington, Thomas Jefferson, James Monroe, and Andrew Jackson, to the military and state officials, and down to the Euro-American citizenry and settlers.

BACKLASH AND ISSUES RAISED

As we began to plan the march and raise awareness of the ethnic cleansing of the Dakota People from Minnesota as well as the treatment of our noncombatants, our work also raised questions and backlash among the Euro-Americans we encountered. One of the questions raised by a Roman Catholic priest in Jordan, Minnesota, was, How would this—the Dakota Commemorative March—promote healing and reconciliation? Wouldn't this instead open up old wounds? Apparently, in his mind, things were going along smoothly for him and his congregation, so why bring up something so ugly from the past? As long as things were going well for him and his fellow Euro-Americans, he assumed everything must be going well for other people as well, including the Dakota People of Minnesota.

There are several points that we as Dakota People must make in response to the attitude of this Euro-American. For the Dakota People of Minnesota, these points are: the stealing of our land by the United States government and its Euro-American citizens; the violation of our treaties by the United States; the murdering of our people (genocide); the horrible events of 1862—mass executions, bounties, concentration camps, forced marches, and so forth; the trauma and tragedy of Dakota-U.S. War of 1862 itself; the forced removal (ethnic cleansing) of our People from our ancestral homelands in Minnesota, Wisconsin, Ontario, and other areas; and the fact that these horrible and catastrophic events are all still fresh in our minds. Thus, for us, the march was not reopening wounds. The wounds have never healed.

As a result of this priest's attitude, we never did get any help, aid, or assistance as we marched through Jordan. We, the marchers, never did get any food to eat, beverages to drink, or places to sleep in that town—we spent that night in Henderson, Minnesota. It reminded me of a line from a song about the "Dakota Trail"—the Commemorative March—that refers to "towns now stained with hate" (see Diane Wilson's essay later in this volume).

◄○►

Another incident involved another Roman Catholic priest who was offended by some remarks I had made that evening (Thursday, November 7, 2002) in Sleepy Eye, a town named after one of our Dakota leaders. Our marchers stayed overnight in their school gym. The Catholic church allowed us to use their school kitchen to heat up our buffalo stew and prepare other foods and to eat in their school cafeteria. That night, the marchers spoke about why they were marching and what it meant to them. Some of the parishioners of the Catholic church came that evening to listen and gave us gifts of socks, gloves, caps, and scarves. That was very heartwarming.

In my remarks, I discussed the parallels between what happened to the Dakota People of Minnesota in 1862–63 and what happened to the Jewish survivors of Nazi Germany during World War II. I pointed out that Hitler admired the efficiency of the U.S. genocidal programs against the Indigenous Peoples of the United States and viewed them as models for his own programs against the Jews. Hitler learned the techniques, methodologies, rationales, and terminology from the United States and Canada in their extermination of the Indigenous Peoples. I get excited when I talk about these things—I also have anger when I talk about this topic.

The Catholic priest and the school principal sent me a letter following the Commemorative March that conveyed the White response to this comparison. Concerned about the anger they sensed in my talk, they felt that as people who had come out to welcome us to the town of Sleepy Eye, they did not deserve anger for something that happened nearly 150 years ago. Furthermore, they felt that drawing a comparison between Hitler's atrocities and the White treatment of Dakota people in Minnesota was unwarranted and undeserved.

I responded with a letter in which I apologized for any offense I might have given them, and also I made it clear that my attempt was to inform and educate them about what really happened here in the state of Minnesota.[12] The concerns they raised, however, are concerns shared by many non-Natives, and thus it is important that they be directly addressed. Not only was it appropriate to make comparisons with Nazi Germany, but additional points must also be made about oppression and genocide. For example, Dakota people have a right to be angry about the "Great Commission," in which Jesus said, "go therefore and make disciples of all the nations"[13]—a statement that constitutes religious imperialism. Both Catholic and Protestant churches still practice this kind of imperialism by sending missionaries to other countries to proselytize peoples of color, to supplant their ancient religions, and to transform their cultures.

In addition, criteria five of the United Nations (UN) Genocide Convention of 1948, "the forcible transfer of children from one group to another group," was fulfilled by the U.S. government and the church when they perpetrated genocide upon the Indigenous Peoples of the United States, including the Dakota People, through their residential boarding schools.[14] Furthermore, many Dakota might still carry anger about the twenty-four million acres of land in southern Minnesota that was stolen from the Dakota and how the Bible was used to steal this land, namely, Manifest Destiny, which is predicated upon the "chosen people and promised land" of the Old Testament.

Thus, the fact that I "seemed angry" to these church members in Sleepy Eye is a reflection of a long history of oppression. This might be termed "righteous anger," which is "the emotional/psychological response of victims of racism/discrimination to the system of power that dominates/exploits/oppresses them."[15] Dakota People, as well as the other Indigenous Peoples of the United States, have a right to be angry about the stealing of some two billion acres of land; about the U.S. violation of nearly four hundred treaties; about the killing of millions upon millions of Native Peoples by western Europeans and Euro-Americans; about the suppression of our religious ceremonies, songs, prayers, and practices; and about so many other heinous, violent, and genocidal results of imperialism and colonialism.

Waziyatawin Angela Wilson, after reading the letter sent by the principal and priest at St. Mary's in Sleepy Eye, also responded to them. Some of the issues she addressed included what constitutes "proper" behavior for Dakota people and whether White people living in Minnesota today share a responsibility for what happened to Dakota people. In regards to this first point, Wilson stated,

> [I]t appears that these apparent acts of "peace" [giving the marchers socks, gloves, and other warming items] came with some strings, which is deeply offensive. You clearly had some idea about how we as Dakota people should be appropri-

« DAKOTA PEOPLE, AS WELL AS THE OTHER INDIGENOUS PEOPLE OF THE UNITED STATES, HAVE A RIGHT TO BE ANGRY ABOUT THE STEALING OF SOME TWO BILLION ACRES OF LAND. »

ately grateful to you . . . you seem to easily dismiss our right to feel and express whatever we feel is appropriate . . . you think your feelings are superior to ours.[16]

I agree with Wilson's statements. We, as Dakota People, have a right to be angry about the loss of our ancient homeland, about the forced marches, and so forth. Socks, gloves, and caps are not an even exchange for twenty-four million acres of rich farmland and do not even come close to compensating for the unresolved grief, anguish, and heartache of the Dakota People.

Wilson also addressed the issue of White responsibility. After stating that their failure to acknowledge their own responsibility for what happened was offensive, Wilson went on to state,

> While you look at the events of 1862 as "a long time ago," from the Dakota perspective, it is as though those events occurred last week, because no amends have been made in the last 140 years. . . . So every day that you have lived there, you have done so at the expense and suffering of Dakota people. To suggest that you can benefit from our dispossession and extermination, while not sharing in the responsibility for it, is a privilege only colonizers can enjoy.[17]

Over my thirty-plus years in education, and even over my lifetime of sixty-five years, I have encountered this attitude "I didn't do it," "other people stole the land," "this happened a long time ago," "get over it," "get a life," "let's go from here." Thus, Euro-Americans do not confront or admit the truth about what happened not only in this state of Minnesota but also in the country. The question raised by Wilson is appropriate: Who benefits from this twenty-four million acres of land? It certainly is not the Dakota People. The stealers and their descendants enjoy the land.

◄○►

Following the march, there was another exchange of letters with residents of another town along the route, this time to the editor of the *New Ulm Journal*. For brevity's sake, this discussion will be shortened. However, the letters and correspondence have been saved and are available for anyone who wishes to read them. The attitudes reflected in these letters correspond with what I, over my academic teaching career, have frequently encountered, especially here in southwestern Minnesota. The critical letters object to my mentioning topics such as stolen land, genocide, broken treaties, parallels to the Jewish genocidal experience in Nazi Germany, or to terms such as "ethnic cleansing" or "crimes against humanity." Other letters, more sympathetic or empathetic, were sent directly to me and not as letters to the editor, out of fear of being attacked publicly or out of fear of reprisals (for example, one woman was concerned about effects on her husband's business).

This exchange began as a result of the newspaper story about our stop in New Ulm during the Commemorative March. In the evening session, after a wonderful meal provided and cooked by some of the women of Turner Hall in

New Ulm, several of the marchers spoke, including me. Again, I discussed several topics, including parallels between the Dakota experience and the Jewish experience. A reporter from the *New Ulm Journal* was there and submitted an article, which was published the next day. This began the series of letters to the editor. Some of the issues raised in New Ulm were perspective, terminology, the term "Euro-American," and parallels between the Dakota experience in Minnesota and the Jewish experience in Nazi Germany.

Frederick Wulff, a retired professor from a local Bible college, wrote four letters to the editor of the *New Ulm Journal*. The letters are worth discussing here, because they reflect common claims made by Whites in Minnesota. In the first letter, Wulff stated, "I question that any speeches, writings, or correspondence of Hitler refer to his studying Minnesota history of the Civil War era and thus being inspired to practice genocide. . . . The native Americans do not need wild and inaccurate comparisons for their cause. Truthful history is on their side. The Dakota are a good and proud people who deserve healing that really heals."[18] The retired professor's statement about the Dakota being "a good and proud people" is a statement with which I most heartily agree. Also, I agree that "truthful history" is on our side, the Indigenous side. However, it is really a story that has yet to be told, and often when it is told, it is resisted vigorously by people such as Wulff.

In fact, there is evidence supporting the link between the treatment of Jews by the Nazis and the treatment of Indigenous Peoples by the United States. For example, John Toland's definitive biography of Hitler clearly illuminates this connection:

Hitler's concept of concentration camps as well as the practicality of genocide owed much, so he claimed, to his studies of English and United States history. He admired the camps for Boer prisoners in South Africa and for the Indians in the wild West; and often praised to his inner circle the efficiency of America's extermination—by starvation and uneven combat—of the red savages who could not be tamed by captivity.[19]

Hitler learned from the United States, and he viewed the U.S. programs against the Indigenous Peoples as forerunners for his own genocidal programs against the Jews, Gypsies, and other despised groups.

Indeed, Minnesota had two concentration camps, one in Mankato and the other at Fort Snelling.[20] In addition to the concentration camps and the warfare waged against the Dakota by the U.S. government and the Euro-American citizenry of Minnesota, there were other genocidal acts, such as bounties, mass executions, forced marches, forced removals, which could be considered not only "ethnic cleansing" but also crimes against humanity. So, though Minnesota is not mentioned directly by Hitler, what happened in Minnesota was part of the genocide perpetrated by the United States against the Indigenous Peoples, including the Dakota People of Minnesota.

In his second letter, Wulff stated, "My gripe is with the Southwest State professor who I feel did a disservice to the Dakota with irresponsible rhetoric. . . . The Southwest State professor which I cited contributes only rancor with talk about

Nazi concentration camps and Hitler's genocide techniques. The native Americans need better spokespersons who truly represent them."[21] I think I am in the business of truth-telling. Truth is, many times, unpleasant to hear. Genocide perpetrated by the U.S. government; Hitler learning genocidal techniques from the United States; broken treaties by the U.S. government; theft of nearly two billion acres within the continental United States; suppression of Indigenous religions and languages; and the general oppression of Indigenous Peoples in today's society are not pleasant topics to hear. So, I do not blame the professor for not wanting to hear these things and his desire to deny or diminish them by calling such statements "irresponsible rhetoric." The rancor that I see comes from Euro-Americans who do not wish to hear the truth.

In a third statement by Wulff, we see similarities with the letter from the principal and pastor from Sleepy Eye, especially regarding the complicity of today's inhabitants:

> The Nazi parallel is overdrawn. The Christianity of the Bible surely does not condone such things (that is, genocide). I have seen too often where academics are called racist because their findings do not always fit into a prescribed politically correct mold. None of my relatives were colonizers. I really don't think of myself as Euro-American, but as an American. All of my grandparents were born in Germany so none of them were in America in the nineteenth century to subjugate Native Americans.

The "Nazi parallel" has already been discussed above, but the reference to Christianity is worth exploring in more depth. In regard to the Bible and genocide, one needs only to look in the Old Testament (OT) and examine the dozens of references to "Chosen People/Promised Land" and to the OT God telling the Israelites to kill the Canaanites, Hittites, and others (genocide). Such verses were then used by the Euro-Americans to take the land and kill the Dakota People and other Native Peoples, the "godless Hittites." A few examples will suffice for the reader to get the general idea. One example regarding the concept of "chosen people" may be seen in the following Bible verse: "For you are a people sacred to the LORD, your God; he has chosen you from all the nations on the face of the earth to be a people peculiarly his own" (Deuteronomy 7:6). Another example regarding the "promised land" concept may be found in Genesis 12:6–7: "and Abram passed through the land unto the place of Sichem, unto the plain of Moreh. And the Canaanite was then in the land. And the LORD appeared unto Abram and said, Unto thy seed will I give this land."

One example of a Bible verse regarding genocide is found in Deuteronomy 20:16: "But of the cities of these people, which the LORD thy God doth give thee for an inheritance, thou shalt save alive nothing that breatheth." A second example is found in Deuteronomy 7:2, 16: "And when the LORD thy God shall deliver them before thee: thou shalt smite them, and utterly destroy them; thou shalt make no covenant with them, nor show mercy unto them: And thou shalt consume all the people which the LORD thy God shall deliver thee: thine eye shall have no pity upon them."

The preceding verses, and many others, provided a biblical rationale for invading, killing, stealing, occupying, and oppressing Indigenous Peoples here in the United States and in Minnesota. Such verses, especially those that talk about the "chosen people/promised land" notion, form the basis for Manifest Destiny, a concept that the Euro-Americans used to justify stealing Native lands and killing Native Peoples. The Euro-Americans saw themselves as "a chosen people" and our lands as "the promised land." The Euro-Americans perceived the Indigenous Peoples as the godless Canaanites who needed to be either exterminated or removed. Ramsey's call for "extermination or removal" is an excellent and relevant example of this attitude here in Minnesota. In taking the land and killing the Native Peoples, the Euro-Americans were merely fulfilling God's will.

In reference to Wulff's comment, "I really don't think of myself as Euro-American, but as an American," it has been my personal experience that Euro-Americans reserve the term "American" for themselves. Yet, when they refer to other people, especially people of color, they will say Native Americans, or Afro-Americans, or Mexican-Americans. So, it's okay for Euro-Americans to hyphenate other Peoples, but they wish to be referred to as "Americans," a double standard in my opinion. I prefer to be called a Dakota, or a Dakota man, or a Dakota person or individual. I am a citizen of the United States since the United States unilaterally imposed citizenship upon us in 1924, though this was done without consulting Indigenous Peoples or without a referendum vote to see if we wanted to be part of a nation that stole all of our land, broke four hundred treaties, and killed millions of us in the process of Manifest Destiny or westward expansion.

In his fourth and final statement, the professor commented:

> Professor Chris Mato Nunpa has made a good point that now the readers have a chance to see the difference between perspectives. Citizens should be informed about what is being taught in their tax supported universities. Professor Mato Nunpa is correct again when he states there is an emerging new perspective [the Indigenous perspective].
>
> Recently, I heard a speaker vigorously applauded by fellow professors at a major conference for denouncing the United States Constitution "as a white man's document. . . . Euro-Americanism was put on the defensive." Underneath the color of our skins we are all members of the human family, made of one blood to dwell on this earth.[22]

I was very pleased that the retired professor finally acknowledged that there is a different perspective from the Euro-American perspective—an Indigenous perspective. It should make sense that the original owners of a land who had their lands stolen will see history differently from how the stealers of the land will see it. For example, White Minnesotans will honor and revere Alexander Ramsey as a hero and as a "founding father" of the state of Minnesota, while the Dakota will regard Ramsey as an "Indian-hater" and as an "Indian-killer." Ramsey was the one who called

« IT SHOULD MAKE SENSE THAT THE ORIGINAL OWNERS OF A LAND WHO HAD THEIR LANDS STOLEN WILL SEE HISTORY DIFFERENTLY FROM HOW THE STEALERS OF THE LAND WILL SEE THE SAME HISTORY. »

for the "extermination or removal" of the Dakota from their own homeland, and Ramsey was the governor under whose administration there were bounties, warfare, concentration camps, the largest mass execution in the history of the United States, and ethnic cleansing of the Dakota People from their ancient homeland. The perspectives are definitely and dramatically different, if not diametrically opposed.

Wulff implies that once people find out what is being taught in "their tax supported universities," they will object to the "truth," as I see it, and then will attempt to have faculty such as me and programs such as mine removed. However, attempts to remove me and my program have been going on for the past fourteen years—since 1992. My years at Southwest Minnesota State University (SMSU) have been horrible. My program has been cut twice. My position has been cut twice. I have been denied tenure once. There have been two close votes and two grievance procedures regarding my program and my position at SMSU, in addition to many other instances of intimidation and harassment by two different administrations. I am not sure what would be different if taxpayers are "informed about what is being taught in their tax supported universities."

I certainly agree with the professor when he says, "we are all members of the human family." I will be glad and grateful when other Euro-Americans learn this truth.

◄○►

In the two letters (in contrast to the retired professor's four letters) that I sent in to the *New Ulm Journal,* I tried to make two basic points. One, there is definitely an Indigenous perspective, specifically, a Dakota perspective, through which the events of 1862–63 are and will be viewed. This constructed series of myths. Many Europeans whom I have met in my travels along life's road see the Indigenous perspective as "truth," as expressing what really happened in this country. Other Indigenous Peoples of the world, as well as other peoples of color, also see what happened in this country. However, our own Euro-Americans often cannot or often will not see the truth. They will not acknowledge what really happened. Our country is in big-time denial!

« What is "settlement" for the Whites is a struggle for . . . our homelands not only for the Dakota but also for other Indigenous People of the United States. »

perspective will generate differences in terminology. For example, where White male Ph.D. historians say that the Euro-Americans "settled" the land in Minnesota, the Dakota might say that our lands were stolen, legally and illegally. What is "settlement" for the Whites is a struggle for and defense of our homelands for not only the Dakota but also for other Indigenous Peoples of the United States. Where Whites might say that Dakota people died on the forced march, Dakota people might say they were "murdered" or "killed." Where Euro-Americans might say that the Dakota People were forcibly removed, Dakota people might refer to this as "ethnic cleansing" or "crimes against humanity."

I would like to further suggest that the Indigenous perspective is the "truth" about what really happened in this country and in Minnesota. What we all have been taught in what I refer to as "Euro-American history"—what is generally called U.S. history or American history—is a

I really appreciate the following statement by Russell Means about the myths and lies about the United States:

All my life, I've had to listen to rhetoric about the United States being a model of freedom and democracy, the most uniquely enlightened and humanitarian country in history, a "nation of law" which, unlike others, has never pursued policies of conquest and aggression. I'm sure you've heard it before. It's official "truth" in the United States. It's what is taught to school children, and it's the line peddled to the general public. Well, I've got a hot news flash for everybody here. It's a lie. The whole thing's a lie, and it always has been.[23]

The second point is that some of these issues raised in both Sleepy Eye and New Ulm will be raised again and again in the upcoming years, especially as the marchers resume the Commemorative March in 2004 and continue every other year right up to 2012, the 150th anniversary of the Dakota-U.S. War of 1862. Certainly the parallels between the Dakota experience in Minnesota and the experience of the Jewish survivors of Nazi Germany will be drawn again and again. Much attention will be given to the bounties on Dakota People; to the forced marches; to the two concentration camps (Mankato and Fort Snelling); to the forced removal or the ethnic cleansing of the Dakota People from their ancient and traditional homelands; to the hanging of thirty-eight Dakota men, the largest mass-execution in the history of the United States; to the genocide of the Dakota People; to the cries for "extermination or removal" from Alexander Ramsey, the governor, on down to the Euro-American citizenry of Minnesota; and, finally, to the Dakota-U.S. War of 1862 itself.

For the first time in their history, the International Conference of Genocide Scholars had two panels that focused on the genocide of Indigenous Peoples of the world at their gathering in Galway, Ireland, in June 2003. This was the beginning of studies on the genocide of Indigenous Peoples being included there, especially the genocide perpetrated by the United States and by the various states, including Minnesota. I believe that the attention that was given to the historical experience of the Dakota People of Minnesota with the Commemorative March is only the beginning.

In an interesting sidelight, three individuals who live in or near New Ulm contacted me and said they agreed with me and disagreed with the retired professor. When I suggested that they send in a letter to the editor expressing their views, they declined out of fear. One woman said her husband owned a business, and she was afraid what might happen to his business. Another person also said he was fearful. A third worked at a public institution and felt that she could not say what she thought. This probably said as much about the community of New Ulm as it did about the three individuals. It appears that the truth cannot yet be told in New Ulm for fear of attack—verbal or perhaps otherwise—by individuals such as the retired professor.

PERSONAL AND EMOTIONAL REACTIONS

Looking retrospectively, I consider my participation in this march to be one of the best things I have ever done in my life (I am now sixty-five "winters"). It was an intense and powerful experience. One of the things that was done—an idea from the Dakota women of Sisseton, South Dakota—was to place lathe stakes at each mile marker along the way. On both sides of the stakes were the names of our ancestors/relatives known to be on the march. When a stake was pounded in, the name would be read aloud. We wanted the spirits to know that we remembered them and that we honored them. When a marcher recognized a particular name as belonging to her or his relative, it was particularly moving. There were many tears shed on the march.

For example, one of our spiritual leaders, Clifford Canku from Sisseton, South Dakota, saw the name Canku on one of the stakes. *Cinye* (older brother to a man) Clifford was visibly moved.

When the name Duta Win or "Scarlet Woman" appeared on a stake, one of the Dakota women from the Wahpetun Reserve in Prince Albert, Saskatchewan, told us that she had just had a naming ceremony the past summer (2002) in which this name was passed on to one of her family members, a daughter. The name of one of my relatives (a great-grandmother), Haza Win, or "Blueberry Woman," is on a stake that was posted at a milepost marker between Sleepy Eye and New Ulm. I was not there, but my daughter, Tawapaha Tanka Win, or "Her Big Hat Woman" (or Dr. Angela Cavender Wilson) was, and it was an emotionally moving experience for her. Again, tears were shed. For the marchers, the trauma and tragedy of this forced march became very real through the emotions of hurt, sadness, and anger. I saw strong men weep unashamedly (I wept a number of times, too); never was I so proud of my Dakota people, of our women, of our children, and of our men! Never did I feel so close to my People!

These personal experiences remind me of a statement found in the book *Trauma and Recovery*. "Reliving a traumatic experience whether in the form of intrusive memories, dreams, or actions [for example, the Commemorative March], carries with it the emotional intensity of the original event."[24] The book goes on to say that, "because reliving a traumatic experience provokes such intense emotional distress, traumatized people go to great lengths to avoid it."[25] There were three Dakota women from Sisseton, South Dakota, at the Mankato ceremony held by the white buffalo statute who said they were going home the next day because they were not yet strong enough to face going to the concentration camp at Fort Snelling.

◄○►

Another important issue was that many of the marchers and Dakota people of today had relatives who were murdered along the 150-mile forced march, or were murdered in the concentration camps, or were hanged in the largest mass execution in the history of the United States in Mankato on December 26, 1862, or were murdered in the forcible removal from Minnesota to Nebraska and South Dakota, or were killed in the Dakota-U.S. War of 1862. We do not know where these relatives are buried, or if they were buried at all. There was no time to conduct our burial ceremonies and to grieve normally. Our ancestors were not sent off to the spirit world in a good way, in the Dakota way.

For example, in the town of Henderson, a baby was grabbed out of her mother's arms by enraged White people and dashed to the ground. The baby was killed. The mother put the baby in the crotch of a tree, and a brief ceremony was held; the mother had to keep marching on, never to see her baby again. One of my own relatives, mentioned earlier, had her stomach slit open with a saber by a soldier on horseback, and her body was eventually thrown in the creek. To this day, we, her relatives, do not know where her

> « FOR THE MARCHERS, THE TRAUMA AND TRAGEDY OF THIS FORCED MARCH BECAME VERY REAL THROUGH THE EMOTIONS OF HURT, SADNESS, AND ANGER. »

body and remains lie. Thus far, it is my understanding that we, the Dakota People, have been able to find, identify, and bury only three of the thirty-eight Dakota men who were hanged in Mankato on December 26, 1862, in the appropriate, ceremonial, and Dakota way.

Our relatives were not able to grieve in a normal way, our way. Our relatives were not able to bury their relatives in the Dakota way. The Dakota People of Minnesota, as well as of South Dakota, of Nebraska, and of Canada, still have a lot of unresolved grief!

In her book, *Trauma and Recovery*, Judith Herman, M.D., says of Jewish survivors of Nazi Germany,

> when survivors speak of their relatives who "died," she (the therapist) affirms that they were, rather, "murdered". . . . The Holocaust also robbed them, and still does, of natural, individual death . . . and thus, of normal mourning. The use of the word "death" to describe the fate of the survivors' relatives, friends, and communities appears to be a defense against acknowledging murder as possibly the most crucial reality of the Holocaust.[26]

As Dakota people, who are survivors of the trauma of the Dakota-U.S. War of 1862, we must begin acknowledging that our relatives and ancestors did not just "die." They were "killed," "murdered." We must begin calling a thing or act for what it is, to name the crime, and to name the perpetrator.

◄○►

One of the most inspiring sights for me was on the morning of the second day of the march, November 8, 2002, when we were going from Sleepy Eye to New Ulm. The marchers had slept in the school gym in Sleepy Eye. I was to deliver buffalo meat to two towns up ahead, to New Ulm and to Mankato. However, I decided that I would march with the marchers through downtown Sleepy Eye. If anything happened, if a violent incident occurred, I wanted to be there. Nothing did happen, thankfully—we marched through downtown, and I then left them to deliver the buffalo meat.

As I got into my car, I saw a brave sight. There they were—three adults and six children walking energetically and determinedly to the next town, New Ulm, with the eagle staff leading the way. With tears in my eyes, I went through a mix of emotions. An initial reaction was anger, "Where in the hell were our marchers?" We had about three dozen marchers the day before. That anger quickly dissipated. Then, my feelings turned to determination. My thinking was, "Well, if this is all who are going to be marching, then so be it. We'll do it!" And then, my thoughts turned to pride. There was my daughter, Dr. Angela Cavender Wilson, with her three children, my grandchildren! There was my niece, Ms. Marisa Pigeon, with her two children and her niece! There was my *tahansi* (cousin, male to male) from Canada, Leo Omani, who was carrying the eagle feather staff (our *toska*, nephew, Gerald Standing, was driving the little red car, our lead car). They were bravely walking down Highway 14, in spite of their few numbers, to New Ulm. I thought of how the 1,700 Dakota people back in 1862 were primarily women and children. I also thought of the town, New Ulm, the town to which our marchers were heading, the town where atrocities had been perpetrated upon our women, children, and elders as they marched back in 1862. I shall not soon forget this sight, and I shall not soon forget the pride I felt toward this small group of brave, determined marchers and that I felt toward our Dakota People, then and now!

―◦―

There were many wonderful things that happened along the way. Many examples of generosity, hospitality, and kindness were offered to the marchers—so many that we just cannot mention them all. For example, we would like to thank those who provided meals: various civic groups (for example, the Turner Hall ladies, with Richard Runck), campus ministries (for example, the Lutheran Campus Ministry at Mankato State University, with the Reverend Fred Fritz serving as head chef and the students cooking and serving), campus programs (for example, the Diversity Center at Gustavus Adolphus College, with Nadarajan Sethuraju, or "Raj"), and churches (for example, the United Church of Christ in Henderson, especially Arlene Busse for all of her hard work).

Many wonderful things also happened around and in the town of Henderson. There were many eagles and red-tailed hawks along the four-mile strip between Highway 169 and Henderson. They sat in the trees along the water on the east side of the highway. By this time, there were more marchers. Bill Means from the International Treaty Council and a member of the American Indian Movement had joined us. I took great strength and encouragement from his presence. Several of the marchers said that the eagles and the hawks were telling us that some of our People

had been killed in this area. These same marchers said that after the march, it would be good to hang some prayer ribbons or offer some tobacco in the area, which was done later.

When we marched from Mankato to Henderson on Sunday, November 10, 2002, we were fed hot beverages and lunch at the charter school, Minnesota New Country School, which all of us marchers greatly appreciated. We thank the director (Dee Thomas), the faculty (especially Jim Wartman), the staff, and the students for their great hospitality!

As we left Henderson on Monday, November 11, 2002, other animal Peoples joined and/or accompanied us. The horses pranced for us as we walked by them. A dog joined us for several miles and helped us by distracting a pit bull away from us to him, and we were able to walk safely past that yard. The same dog helped us to cross the busy Highway 169. In fact, no cars came until our whole caravan of marchers, Henderson charter school students, cars, trucks, vans, and our portable sanitation service wagon had crossed over the highway, so that we could then resume our march along 169 to Jordan, Minnesota.

As I mentioned, a number of students from the charter school in Henderson, the Minnesota New Country School, joined us for about eight miles from Henderson to Highway 169. These students honored us and gave us strength and encouragement by their presence and their interest. When it was time for lunch, they ate with us. I felt honored that we all could eat together. We had cold lunch meat sandwiches, cookies, and water. On the march, I learned the difference between eating for pleasure and eating for sustenance.

―◦―

The last night of the march, Tuesday, November 12, 2003, I, as the Minnesota coordinator of the March, did not know where we, the marchers, were going to eat, meet, or sleep. I had to turn this over to the Creator, Wakan Tanka (the Great Mystery). One of the marchers that I know about, for sure, made calls to the Shakopee Mdewakanton Dakota Community, and they agreed to house the marchers in their church and to provide an evening meal and a morning meal, and discounted rates at their Mystic Lake Hotel. Things worked out.

« ONE OF THE GREATEST SPIRITUAL GIFTS THE MARCHERS RECEIVED WAS THE APPROVAL AND PRESENCE OF THE SPIRITS, THE PRESENCE OF OUR GRANDFATHERS AND THE GRANDMOTHERS. »

Also, I did not know who was going to feed the marchers at the concentration camp at Fort Snelling on the last day, Wednesday, November 13, 2002. Again, I turned this matter over to the Creator and to Lisa Bellanger, a young Anishinabe women who is Director of Native Arts High School in Minneapolis, Minnesota. This young Native lady contacted programs and institutions and gathered other friends to help. The result was an outstanding feast. I am a diabetic, but I think I violated all the carbohydrate rules and just ate to my heart's content. I say a big "thank you" to the Native community of the Twin Cities!

Even though I had scouted the whole route and had driven the whole distance at least twice, I was not sure on the last day when we crossed the Minnesota River on the bridge how the marchers were going to find the path from the Mendota Bridge that leads to the concentration camp. Also, I was not sure how we were going to lead all the drivers of cars, trucks, and vans all the way around to the entrance of Fort Snelling State Park. Then, the Mendota Bdewakantun Club entered the picture—Bob and Linda Brown, Jim Anderson, Bear, and others—and they took over. It was like it was planned—only I did not plan it. They led our marchers down the path, and they provided a lead car for the drivers of vehicles. I am indeed thankful to Wakantanka for all the help and guidance and the Creator's working through the many individuals who helped to successfully conclude the 150-mile march.

One of the greatest spiritual gifts the marchers received was the approval and presence of the spirits, the presence of our grandfathers and the grandmothers. Several individuals, including Art Owen, one of our spiritual leaders from the Prairie Island Dakota Community, mentioned that they saw blue lights over the marchers as they approached the concentration camp at Fort Snelling. The spirits of the 1,700 Dakota women, children, and elders were saying to the marchers "thank you" for remembering and honoring us, "thank you" for your physical sacrifice. There were several marchers who marched the whole way, 150 miles, and who were there every day of the march.

A *wopida k'a woyuonihan wotapi* (a thanksgiving and honoring feast) was held in November 2003 at Fort Snelling. It was a wonderful gathering. Various marchers have indicated that this march will be done again several times beginning in 2004 and will be held every other year right up to 2012, the 150th anniversary of the Dakota-U.S. War of 1862.

To reiterate, this was one of the best things I have ever done in my life. I feel close to the marchers—those who were there every day or for most of the days. I have a debt of gratitude and feel close to all those who helped feed us, who provided lodging, or who gave of their own personal finances so that the marchers could have sandwiches, cookies, fruit, water, and so on, and to all those who helped in their own unique ways to remember and honor the 1,700 Dakota people and to thank the Creator!

Manipi kin hena wicunkiksuyapi! "We remember those who walked!"

‑‑◦‑‑

NOTES

1. S. Lyman Tyler, *A History of Indian Policy* (Washington, DC: U.S. Department of Interior, 1973), 54.

2. Clifford E. Trafzer, *As Long as the Grass Shall Grow and Rivers Flow* (Fort Worth, TX: Harcourt College Publishers, 2000), 149.

3. Russell Thornton, *American Indian Holocaust and Survival* (Norman and London: University of Oklahoma Press, 1987, 1990), 50.

4. Francis Paul Prucha, *American Indian Policy in the Formative Years* (Cambridge, MA: Harvard University Press, 1962), 224–25.

5. Thornton, *American Indian Holocaust*, 50.

6. Baptist minister Evan Jones, quoted in Trafzer, *As Long as the Grass Shall Grow*, 156.

7. Thornton, *American Indian Holocaust*, 183.

8. Ibid., 184.

9. Ibid.

10. Haunani-Kay Trask, *From a Native Daughter: Colonialism and Sovereignty in Hawai'i* (Honolulu: University of Hawaii Press, 1993, 1999), 251.

11. Lenore A. Stiffarm, with Phil Lane Jr., "The Demography of Native North America: A Question of American Indian Survival," in *The State of Native America,* ed. M. Annette Jaimes (Boston, MA: South End Press, 1992), 34.

12. Dr. Chris Mato Nunpa to Wayne Pelzel and Fr. Brian Ostreich, December 5, 2002, in the author's possession.

13. Matthew 28:19, St. Joseph Edition.

14. Jorge Noriega, "American Indian Education in the U.S.: Indoctrination for Subordination to Colonialism," in *State of Native America*, ed. M. Annette Jaimes, 381.

15. Trask, *From a Native Daughter*, 252.

16. Dr. Angela Cavender Wilson to Wayne Pelzel and Fr. Brian Oestreich, December 5, 2002, in the author's possession.

17. Ibid.

18. *New Ulm Journal*, November 13, 2002, 4A.

19. John Toland, *Adolf Hitler* (1976; reprint, New York: Anchor Books, 1992), 702.

20. Roy Meyer, *History of the Santee Sioux* (1967; reprint, Lincoln.: University of Nebraska Press, 1993), 137.

21. *New Ulm Journal*, November 14, 2002, 4A.

22. Frederick Wulf, "Letter to the Editor," *New Ulm Journal*, January 11, 2003, 4A.

23. Russell Means, American Indian Movement, October 12, 1992, quoted in Ward Churchill, *A Little Matter of Genocide* (San Francisco: City Light Books, 1997), vii.

24. Judith Herman, *Trauma and Recovery* (New York: Basic Books, 1992, 1997), 42.

25. Ibid., 42.

26. Ibid., 135.

Ties That Bind

Remembering, Mourning, and Healing Historical Trauma

MARY BETH FAIMON

—◄○►—

When I was asked to write about the Dakota Commemorative March, I needed to think about how I could organize my thoughts around micro and macro practice principles of social work as I comment on the event. I am a trained social worker and teach social work practice courses at a small state university in Minnesota. The university, as I like to describe it, is surrounded by five Dakota communities, three in southwestern Minnesota and two in South Dakota, and is located on Dakota land ceded to the United States government in the 1851 Traverse des Sioux Treaty. The Dakota-U.S War of 1862 occurred within thirty-five miles of where the university now stands. I have been teaching here for eleven years, and during that time have established close ties with several Dakota people.

Because of these relationships, I was asked to be one of the non-Indigenous logistical organizers of the Commemorative March. I am a Minnesotan. My great-grandmother was born in Marysville in 1861, just east of Jordan, Minnesota, near Shakopee. I have no idea what my ancestors' participation was in the 1862 events; no historical accounts were passed down. I do believe, however, that it is the obligation of every Euro-Minnesotan to share responsibility in the shameful history of the settlement of this state. It is a shared history.

—◄○►—

The Dakota War of 1862, as far as most Euro-Minnesotans are concerned, is a forgotten history. The event is given minimum attention in local history lessons in schools and is most commonly referred to as the "Sioux Uprising." Students come into college with little to no knowledge of how the state land was obtained from the Indigenous inhabitants and little to no knowledge of the history of treaties, specifically the contexts in which the treaties were made and broken with the Dakota People. Attention to the details would mean bearing witness to the horrible events that occurred before, during, and after the "Sioux Uprising." It would mean confronting the calculated colonialist, genocidal policies and strategies implemented by Washington, the territorial and state governments and their representatives, as well as the Euro-traders and settlers to remove and exterminate the Dakota People from the Minnesota territory and state. As represented in Washington, the United States' desire for land and economic expansion caused the Indigenous Peoples of Minnesota to be killed and removed. It is entirely predictable that intense denial and controversy would follow confronting truths that contradict the colonizers' defined "truth."

Indeed, are we not also the modern-day colonizers and perpetrators when we perpetuate and support the myths that have been created, when we keep silent, and when we reap the rewards of the governmental policies and actions that exterminated and removed the Dakota? Are we not also modern-day colonizers and perpetrators when we perpetrate and support current governmental policies and actions that continue to exterminate and remove Indigenous Peoples from their homelands? As Euro-Minnesotans, what is our share in the responsibility for and in consequences of the Dakota-U.S. War of 1862? What is our share in the responsibility for and in the consequences of the U.S. governmental policies in Indian Country today?

◄◦►

According to Judith Lewis Herman, a psychiatrist who specializes in trauma and recovery from domestic violence to political terror, "It is very tempting to take the side of the perpetrator. All the perpetrator asks is that the bystander do nothing. The perpetrator appeals to the universal desire to see, hear, and speak no evil. The victim, on the contrary, asks the bystander to share the burden of pain. The victim demands action, engagement, and remembering."[1] Leo Eitinger, a psychiatrist who has studied survivors of the Nazi concentrations camps, describes the conflict between bystanders and victims: "War and victims are something the community wants to forget; a veil of oblivion is drawn over everything painful and unpleasant."[2] Opposition from bystanders can change the perspective of the perpetrators and other bystanders. Ervin Staub, a psychologist who studies trauma and violence, states that "we must educate people about the 'bystander role': the insidious effects and moral meaning of passivity and the psychological processes by which people distance themselves from others in need."[3]

The aftermath of the 1862 war brought the forced removal of all Dakota in Minnesota and the confiscation of all their treaty lands. On March 3, 1863, the United States Congress passed a law entitled "An Act for the Removal of the Sisseton, Wahpeton, Medewakanton, and Wahpakoota Bands of Sioux or Dakota Indians and for the disposition of their Lands in Minnesota and Dakota."[4] This removal was accomplished through forced marches to concentration camps in Mankato and Fort Snelling and the subsequent forced removals to Nebraska. Extermination policies placed bounties on all the Dakota who remained, including men, women, and children. Thousands of Dakota fled into bordering states and Canada, while government policies rewarded the betrayal of relative against relative, brother against brother. Sisseton and Wahpeton scouts were recruited to serve General Sibley to hunt down and capture all "hostile" Dakota who had fled to the west and north with the order "take no prisoners."

Indescribable terror consumed the Dakota, and the legacy of that terror remains 140 years later, evidenced in the repression, dissociation, denial, alcoholism, depression, doubt and devaluation of self and culture, and helplessness that many Dakota descendants suffer today. "Traumatic events have primary effects not only on the psychological structures of the self," Herman argues, "but also on the systems of attachment and meaning that link individual and community."[5] An intergenerational legacy of shame, guilt, and distrust continues to overshadow the telling of stories that have been passed down through seven generations. Many stories have been lost and forgotten.

On February 19, 1867, a delegation of Sisseton Wahpeton leaders signed a treaty with the United States that provided for the establishment of two reservations, one at Lake Traverse in northeast South Dakota and southwest North Dakota, and the second one at Devils Lake (Spirit Lake) in North Dakota. These reservations were a reward to the Sisseton and Wahpeton bands that "in part remained loyal to the Government and furnished scouts and soldiers to service against their own people."[6] The signatories' descendents are familiar names on both the Spirit Lake and Lake Traverse Reservations today. Herman iterates that "traumatized people suffer a sense of alienation, of disconnection that pervades relationships from the most intimate familial bonds to affiliations with community and religion."[7] The Dakota People were traumatized not only by the United States government but also by their own relatives. The damage to the survivors' faith and sense of community is particularly severe when the traumatic events involve the betrayal of their own People.

─◦─

Addressing the historical trauma is an essential element of the recovery process, and remembering and mourning are critical. Recalling and retelling history from an Indigenous perspective bears witness to the experience and context of the events of 1862–67. The imposition of colonial ideas, knowledge, and historical accounts as well as the censorship of Indigenous knowledge have, for the Dakota, resulted not only in their doubting their own historical accounts but also in delegitimizing their own historical experiences. The experience has become literally unspeakable. The Euro-American historical chronologists have accomplished this in a very systematic way, which, according to Herman, is common for perpetrators to do:

> In order to escape accountability for his crimes, the perpetrator does everything in his power to promote forgetting. Secrecy and silence are the perpetrator's first line of defense. If secrecy fails, the perpetrator attacks the credibility of his victim, if he cannot silence [him or her] absolutely, he tries to make sure that no one listens. To this end he marshals an impressive array of arguments, from the most blatant denial to the most sophisticated and elegant rationalization. After every atrocity one can expect to hear the same predictable apologies: it never happened; the victim lies; the victim exaggerates; the victim brought it upon [himself/herself]; and in any case it is time to forget the past and move on. The more powerful the perpetrator, the greater it is his prerogative to name and define reality, and the more completely his arguments prevail.[8]

In spite of extensive literature on post-Holocaust and post-Vietnam War psychological trauma and its phenomena, Herman states that the debate still centers on the basic question of whether these phenomena are credible and real. The tendency is to discredit the victim(s). Applying these patterns of both trauma victims and traumatizers to the political and intrafamilial events that occurred 140 years ago will be criticized until the trauma is brought into public consciousness and a social context is created by relationships with friends, family, allies, and larger political entities that is powerful enough to counteract the processes of denial and silencing.

« ON A SOCIETAL LEVEL, THE PROCESS OF CONFRONTING HISTORICAL TRAUMA MUST INCLUDE OFFICIALLY ACKNOWLEDGING THE GENOCIDAL PROGRAMS AGAINST THE INDIGENOUS PEOPLES OF THE AMERICAS . . . »

On a societal level, the process of confronting historical trauma must include officially acknowledging the genocidal programs against the Indigenous Peoples of the Americas, as organizations such as the United Nations, human rights organizations, and other political entities are beginning to do. It includes establishing affiliations between Dakota academics and other genocide survival organizations and institutions. It also includes telling and retelling the stories and remembering what actually happened through rituals and ceremonies, educational lectures, and Web sites.

The Dakota Commemorative March tells a part of the story. The networking among individuals, community and church representatives, public officials, institutions, and the media that naturally occurred in the course of organizing the march forced a wider consciousness about the events of 1862. The march itself brought into public awareness a reminder of the historical events in the towns and surrounding communities where they occurred.

Psychological trauma is an affliction of the powerless, and the core experiences of psychological trauma are disempowerment and disconnection from others.[9] That being so, the first principle of recovery focuses on empowering the survivor. The Dakota People in Minnesota suffered enormously, and the governmental policies and forced humiliations to which they were subjected required that they surrender their culture, language, spirituality, and identity in order to survive. These policies promoted the destruction of Dakota community life by devaluing all forms of community that did not meet the institutional norms and ideals of the dominant colonizing culture. A process was set in motion that separated the individual from his or her group and standards of behavior, expectations, and support systems.[10] The traumatizing colonization efforts were nearly complete.

THE MARCH

In his article "A Model of the Effects of Colonialism," Dr. Michael Yellow Bird states that the antidote to colonialism requires that Indigenous Peoples create empowering definitions that help renew Indigenous spiritual values, beliefs, and meanings and introduce new ceremonies and rituals in order to renew relationships with the spiritual past.[11]

The Dakota Commemorative Marches are grassroots organized events, initiated and planned by Dakota women who are descendants of those on the 1862 forced march. To honor and remember the men, women, and children who were forcibly removed on those cold November days in 1862, the march organizers defined a route that would replicate the forced march route as closely as possible. Decolonizing efforts were made throughout the march. For example, at each mile marker along the route, a flagged stake was placed in the ground bearing the name of an ancestor who was on the original march. Tobacco and prayers were offered. An eagle feather staff was carried high, leading the walkers to the next highway mile marker for 150 miles. Each day began and ended with a ceremony.

This is a part of my personal account:

We were blessed with miracles. The Spirits were watching over us. In New Ulm we were joined by a small group of women from the Sioux Valley Reserve and Bird Tail Reserve in Canada, who had flown in that day from Winnipeg and driven down from St. Paul. They didn't know where we were, and when they stopped at a gas station in New Ulm, our sanitation unit driver was there and told them where to find us. New Ulm was a town of unspeakable horrors, where Dakota men shackled in wagons on the way to Mankato were murdered by local citizenry. Another group of Dakota from the Wahpeton Reserve in Saskatchewan had their car radiator overheat, and a New Ulm citizen who was walking with

us towed the car to his garage and had the radiator replaced.

When the walkers approached the Henderson cutoff from Highway 169 to Highway 93 on Sunday afternoon, they were wondering how they would get across the highway, since the traffic was heavy in both directions. Three highway patrol cars appeared and blocked the traffic. One of the highway patrol officers told the others that he would lead the walkers into Henderson. He also intervened with the patrol traffic engineer who was against the walkers using Highway 93 to enter Henderson and told him that the walkers had to go to Henderson; it was a part of their history. He had read about the Henderson area, and the significance of the town to the Dakota Oyate (People), how a baby was murdered, and others had died. Along the walk into Henderson, the trees along the river were filled with eagles, watching. This was thought to be the spirits of the ancestors and the people buried there who had died along the walk.

We were housed and fed in Henderson the following night and morning instead of Jordan. Several Henderson residents had ancestors who were in the Henderson area in 1862. They told stories of how their families had been warned by the Dakota, and their families left the area during that time. They were grateful for the warnings. When we left Henderson on Tuesday morning, we were accompanied by the students from the

Henderson charter school for eight miles along the Henderson Station Road across the railroad tracks on a gravel road.

I was driving ahead to see how far it still was to the intersection of Highway 1, and one of the walkers was taking a break and riding along with me. As we approached the asphalt road that is marked as County Road 51, a young, frisky, red dog greeted us. Now, I talk to animals, and I rolled down my window and greeted the dog and asked, "Are you coming with us?" not knowing what I really was asking. The dog joined the walkers, running in and out of the crowd, running ahead, and keeping all the other dogs away. When our headman carrying the eagle staff noticed a pit bull in a yard ahead, he became concerned, and the red dog distracted the pit bull while we walked past his territory. The dog accompanied us across Highway 169, and we were able to cross the highway as a group, not only the walkers, but the caravan of cars as well. There was no traffic either way. Then we all became concerned about the dog and his safety, but he was seen back in his yard when we drove back to Henderson to spend the night. Just before Highway 169, there was a horse ranch, and the horses lined up along the fencing and greeted the walkers. One of them, a beautiful black horse with a clipped mane began to prance, tail high in the air. The horse Oyate greeted the people. This was our walk to Jordan.

There are more stories that can be told. The laughter, conversations, and stories among the walkers bonded us. When the lathe memorial stakes were placed at mile markers with the names of the known walkers in 1862, the emotions and the tears were filled with grief. At least three stakes broke while being pounded into the ground, and the stakes belonged to descendants who were on the walk. It was interpreted to symbolize the mending that needed to take place in those families, and the stakes were retied with red strips of cloth. When the walkers entered Fort Snelling State Park on Wednesday, bright blue lights surrounded them. To the Dakota who walk the traditional spiritual path and who see these things, the Spirits were surrounding and supporting them.

◄o►

As I reflect on my experience, both as participant and observer, I am struck by the courage, strength, and resiliency of the Dakota people who marched. The numbers of those participating ranged from eight to thirty people on any given day, until the walk into Fort Snelling, when carloads of participants arrived to swell the crowd to well over three hundred. The largest group of walkers came from Canada for most of the march. One Canadian reserve conducted its own march in support of the walkers in Minnesota. I question why so few walkers came from Sisseton, the Lower Sioux and Upper Sioux communities, and other Minnesota Dakota communities, whose ancestors were murdered, hanged, and forcibly removed from Minnesota. Perhaps the resiliency of the Wahpetunwan Dakota and their political struggle for legitimate recognition in Canada has given them a strength and courage to find their historical connections and ancestral roots and to retell their stories.

The Sisitunwan, Wahpetunwan, and Bdewakantunwan of Minnesota, Nebraska, and North and South Dakota continue to live on the lands of memories and captivity, and for many, the remembering may be too painful. The policies that govern and regulate reservation life are still controlled by the colonizers and perpetrators. The profound disruption in basic trust, the common feelings of shame, guilt, and inferiority, and the need to avoid reminders of the trauma may still be evident in reservation life. A small group of walkers that came from Sisseton to the hanging site in Mankato were so filled with grief that they were unable to stay to continue the walk. They had not been with us long enough to experience the growing sense of community, laughter, and sharing of stories that mediated the shared grief among the marchers.

The core marchers—those who were able to share experiences and stories over a period of seven days—were able to recognize both the dire circumstances of the traumatic event (the forced march in 1862) and the moral dilemmas that their ancestors faced, given their severely limited choices. The issue of judgment is of great importance in repairing the connection between and among the descendants of the Dakota. In 1862, some Dakota chose not to fight in the war and fled; some remained during the war on their treaty land but did not act; some fought for their homeland, were wounded in battle, and died or were hanged in Mankato; some betrayed their own People; and some were killed by U.S. government forces. At the end of the war, though, it made no

difference; all remaining Dakota were forcibly removed, together.

SOCIAL ACTION AND SOCIAL JUSTICE OVERVIEW

Social justice is an action principle within the professional code of ethics for social workers. The principle is actualized through various forms of community-level practice. Community organizing is one form of practice and ordinarily implies action to address social needs by helping people gain access to goods and services that historically have been or are being denied them. Community organizing works to promote, for example, civil rights, access to equal education, and access to public services. Both community organizing and social action can be applied only in a broad sense to the activities related to the Commemorative March, but they are worth noting.

In social work, community organization has been somewhat mechanistic. In social action, confrontational tactics have classically been emphasized.[12] Jack Rothman, a professor emeritus in social work and community organizing, states, "Practitioners in the social action arena generally aim to empower and benefit the poor, the disenfranchised, the oppressed. The style is highly adversarial, and social justice is the dominant ideal."[13] It has been dependent on targeting an aggrieved or disenfranchised segment of the population that needs to be organized in order to make demands on the larger community. Some strategies used in classic social action include picketing, boycotts, demonstrations, civil disobedience, sit-ins, and marches.

A second approach to community-level practice is locality development. According to Rothman, "This approach presupposes that community change should be pursued through broad participation by a wide spectrum of people at the local community level in determining goals and taking civil action."[14] In this model, Paul Henderson and David Thomas, who write on community work, describe locality development as "putting people in touch with one another, and of promoting their membership in groups and networks. It seeks to develop people's sense of power and significance in acts of association with others that may also achieve an improvement in their social and material well-being."[15] The community is usually a geographic entity, such as a neighborhood, city, or village.

The traditional Dakota Oyate includes many communities. The geographic area encompasses Canada, North and South Dakota, Nebraska, and Minnesota. Where is the "community" as defined in social work community development literature? Community must be defined not in terms of geography but in terms of kinship and relatives. Puerto Rican educator and community activist Antonia Pantoja and her longtime partner Wilhelmina Perry describe this type of community as "a group of people who . . . are bound together by historical and/or contemporary circumstances; racial, religious, or national origin; and who share a common set of values, mutual expectations, and aspirations."[16]

The political and social structure of community will vary among Indigenous Peoples, and therefore the practitioner must understand that which defines "community." Among Dakota traditional Peoples, the political community is defined as the Oceti Sakowin, the seven council fires, and the social structure is the Oyate. The Bureau of Indian Affairs (BIA) defines the political community as the elected council, and the social structure is determined by tribal membership. Key leaders in the BIA structure would be identified as the council members, whereas in the traditional structure is defined as the heads of families. The family represents the cornerstone for the social and emotional well-being of individuals and communities.[17]

These are just two simplistic examples of the differences in the definitions of political and social "communities" within the Dakota Oyate. The social action arena is further complicated when the "demands" invoke listening and bearing witness to self-determination and cultural assertions to tell the truth about a forgotten history. Who is the aggrieved and disenfranchised population? What is the aim? Who is to be "organized," and who are the "organizers"?

According to Felix G. Rivera and John L. Erlich, both professors of social work, "a unique revitalization of cultural, social and economic survival strategies has emerged" in Indigenous communities.[18] They suggest that a new framework for defining, assessing, and organizing communities, particularly minority communities, is needed. They further argue,

> the primary cultural, social, political and economic interrelationships of such communities are of fundamental importance, because these qualities are seen as major determinants of life in them. We also conceive of them as "new" communities because we are identifying specific groups coming together in a new country or geographical area and attempting to salvage

their traditions in the face of a largely hostile existing social order.[19]

Organizing the Dakota Commemorative March, however, requires more than using the classic models of social action and locality development as organizing foundations. Further aspects must be addressed, namely: (1) the cultural uniqueness of the Dakota Oyate, (2) the roles of kinship, spiritual beliefs and practices, leadership networks, social systems, language, and the economic and political relationships within each community; and (3) the process of empowerment and critical consciousness.[20] Indigenous organizers play key roles in the success of this endeavor. In fact, the Dakota Commemorative March could not have been organized without the grassroots impetus of a kinship network and Indigenous leaders, who were involved intimately with traditional Dakota cultural and spiritual life and who operated from a traditional values base. Personal and political influence contributed to the successful actualization of the idea for a march to honor the women and children who were the silent victims of the traumas and atrocities endured by the Dakota Oyate in the aftermath of the Dakota-U.S. War of 1862.

Every year, beginning at midnight on December 25, Dakota men and women participate in a sacred relay run from Fort Snelling to Mankato, where thirty-eight Dakota warrior patriots were hanged in the largest mass execution in United States history on December 26, 1862. This relay run has been a tradition for nearly twenty years.

The idea of honoring the women and children arose from a summer institute in New Ulm in June 2001. Leo Omani, a former Chief of the Wahpeton Reserve in Canada, suggested that the two Dakota women, WakanIyotanke Win (Gabrielle Tateyuskanskan) and Tawapaha Tanka Win (Waziyatawin Angela Wilson), organize an event—an event from the heart. The women live in different physical communities but are connected to each other through Dakota tribal affiliations and shared ancestral histories. Each has unique talents and skills to offer as primary organizers. The goals have been simple: (1) to remember and honor the Dakota women, men, and children who were force marched to concentration camps in November of 1862, and, (2) to inform and educate Euro-Americans that the march would be passing through their communities based on a Dakota perspective of the historical events surrounding the forced march in 1862.

It is important to caution, at this point, that mechanistic, manipulative strategies and tactics for organizing communities are a wrong approach here. Classic strategies involve a more linear approach to organizing. Dakota strategies follow a circular path and are process oriented. The Dakota organizers of the marches have needed to develop their own approaches and responses within their own traditions for healing the historical trauma experienced by the Oyate on the forced march. Leaders have been recruited from among community members according to their recognized talents in particular areas. Leadership is shared. Those who have both the formal and informal sanction of their communities fill the major roles.

Myriad logistical details have needed to be worked out, and bridges have to be established with

Euro-American communities to arrange for housing and meals for the marchers. A few outsiders (two White allies, myself, and the Southwest Minnesota State University Lutheran campus minister, Steve Rasmussen) have been invited to serve as helpful technicians, approaching and confronting outside systems along with the Dakota organizers. Southwest Minnesota State University and the American Indian Studies and Dakota Studies Program have served as the clearinghouse for logistical and technical needs. Most of the planning meetings have been held at Southwest Minnesota State University and have been sponsored by the American Indian Studies and Dakota Studies program. The Dakota organizers use processes based on Dakota traditional community values in order to obtain the political, spiritual, and economic support and resources that are needed. These are Dakota events, not events organized by outsiders.

Historical ties bind together both the Dakota Oyate and the Euro-American communities in an ongoing struggle to remember, mourn, and regain a moral conscience concerning the events surrounding the Dakota-U.S War of 1862. There has been little discussion of the psychological consequences caused by political trauma on victims within the Minnesota communities affected by the war. How have these events touched descendents personally, and how have they touched the communities? New Ulm celebrated its 150th founding anniversary in 2004. What consideration was given to the political and psychological issues surrounding the community's history?

« HISTORICAL TIES BIND TOGETHER BOTH THE DAKOTA OYATE AND THE EURO-AMERICAN COMMUNITIES IN AN ONGOING STRUGGLE TO REMEMBER, MOURN, AND REGAIN A MORAL CONSCIENCE CONCERNING THE . . . DAKOTA-U.S. WAR OF 1862. »

WakanIyotanke Win refers to the need for reparation, reparation of the spirit, and how this march has sparked thinking within the Dakota Oyate—thinking about the psychological consequences of colonialism, about the desecration of those who were murdered on the march, and about those who died during the march. How are they to be treated when the oppressors have desecrated them? What ceremonies and rituals are needed for healing? How does one adequately mourn so massive a catastrophe as the genocide of a People?

The marchers created a "new community," a feeling of closeness to each other and a sense of revering each other. They formed ties that bind people together into a stronger voice to seek justice and a hopeful future for the children. The march evolved into a healing ritual, embodying the spiritual values, beliefs, and meanings of the Dakota People. As Gabrielle Tateyuskanskan stated on May 7, 2003, "We're attached to this land, our ancestors are a part of this soil, and we have a spiritual connection that no matter how much racism or psychological damage is done, we're tied to our homeland. It's the gift our ancestors gave us."

◄○►

NOTES

1. Judith Lewis Herman, *Trauma and Recovery* (New York: Basic Books, 1992), 8.

2. Leo Eitinger, "The Concentration Camp and Its Late Sequelae," in *Survivors, Victims, and Perpetrators,* ed. Joel E. Dimsdale (New York: Hemisphere, 1980), 127–62.

3. Ervin Staub, *The Roots of Evil: The Origins of Genocide and Other Group Violence* (New York: Cambridge University Press, 1989), 240.

4. Minnesota *Executive Documents*, 1862 (extra session), 11, Minnesota Historical Society, St. Paul, Minnesota.

5. Herman, *Trauma and Recovery*, 51.

6. Fifty-first Congress Session, Ex. Doc. No 66, Department of the Interior, Office of Indian Affairs, dated Washington, January 28, 1890.

7. Herman, *Trauma and Recovery*, 52.

8. Ibid., 8.

9. Ibid., 133.

10. Antonia Pantoja and Wilhelmina Perry, "Community Development and Restoration: A Perspective and Case Study," in *Community Organizing in a Diverse Society*, 3rd ed., ed. John Erlich and Felix Rivera (Boston: Allyn and Bacon, 1998), 218–41.

11. Michael Yellow Bird, "A Model of the Effects of Colonialism" (unpublished paper, Office for the Study of Indigenous Social and Cultural Justice, 1998).

12. Jack Rothman, "Approaches to Community Intervention," in *Strategies of Community Intervention,* 6th ed., ed. Jack Rothman, John Erlich, and John Tropman (Itasca, IL: F.E. Peacock, 2001), 27–61.

13. Ibid., 33.

14. Ibid., 39.

15. Paul Henderson and David Thomas, *Skills in Neighborhood Work* (London: Allen & Unwin, 1989), 4.

16. Pantoja and Perry, "Community Development and Restoration," 225.

17. Charles Etta Sutton and Mary Anne Broken Nose, "American Indian Families: An Overview," in *Ethnicity and Family Therapy*, 2nd ed., ed. Monica McGoldrick, Joe Giordano, and John K. Pearce (New York: Guilford Press, 1996).

18. Felix G. Rivera and John L. Erlich, "Organizing with People of Color, A Perspective," in *Tactics and Techniques of Community Intervention,* 4th ed., ed. John Tropman, John Erlich, and Jack Rothman (Itasca IL: F. E. Peacock, 2001), 169.

19. Ibid., 173.

20. Ibid., 173.

Wicozani Wakan Ota Akupi

(Bringing Back Many Sacred Healings)

GEORGE BLUE BIRD

—◄○►—

The years between 1849 and 1890 were the darkest for the three divisions of the Lakota, Dakota, and Nakota tribal nations.[1] We suffered through these years as White European people began moving through our lands, across the plains, over the mountains, and to the western seaboard. We suffered before and after this time, but never so harshly and inhumanely as we did between 1849 and 1890. A secret order of extermination for our leaders and warriors existed at all times. This order would later be put in place against our old people, women, children, our animals, and anything that moved in our camps. This order was authorized by different U.S. government and military leaders who were experts in corruption and cruelty.

When we look at the treaties that were made between our People and the U.S. government, we see that our ancestors were forced into believing that we would be given help and protection if we gave up our resistance in defense of our lands and accepted the reservation system. Some of our reservations were created on lands of our choosing, particularly our spiritual places of refuge, but others were created on lands around military forts or on lands not suitable for making a living. Our Dakota and Nakota relatives in *Mini Sota*

(one translation being "Smokey Water" because of the huge amounts of fog on the lakes and rivers in what is now called Minnesota) were the first of our three dialectical tribal divisions to feel the viciousness of the White people and their encroachment on our lands. The Dakota and Nakota nations lived in many dozens of traditional camps west of present-day Minneapolis, Minnesota, all the way to *Mini Sose Wakpala* (The River That Runs Fast or the Missouri River) in present-day South Dakota.

The Lakota Nation was next in line for the same experience of anguish and hatred. We received the same treatment: extensions of friendliness, sporadic intrusions onto our lands, threats of war, engaging in treaty-making, then actual war against our People, massacres of our people, and political assassinations of our leaders. Then we were left alone to live with the echoes of genocide. We were forced to watch our people die at the hands of the soldiers who outnumbered us and used a powerful arsenal of advanced weaponry.

All of the lands west of the Missouri River—south into what is now Nebraska, all around *Paha Sapa* (Black Hills, so named because as one approaches the area, the hills appear to be black), and far into what is now North Dakota—were occupied by the Lakota Nation. Our three divisions occupied our lands because it was intended to be that way from our Creator, who is named *Ate Wakan Tanka* (Sacred Father Who Encompasses All).

A majority of us were killed without mercy, some of us fled and became members of other tribal bands within our territories, and some of us fled in all directions and settled where we could. Many of us accepted the notion of peace and became dependent on the U.S. government for our general needs. Many of us were captured, forced to walk in long, agonizing death marches, and were put in military stockades where we were kept under threat of violence.

Our alliances with other tribes and our refuge with them played one of the major roles in our survival. The tribes in the high plains of present-day Canada and the tribes west of the Black Hills took us in and gave us protection until we were strong enough to make our way back to our homelands. On our return, we found our camps completely destroyed and our people nowhere around. We were strangers in our own lands.

All of the Lakota, Dakota and Nakota tribal prisoners incarcerated in the state and federal prisons in the northern plains are asked to remember the 1,700 Dakota people who were forcibly removed from their ancestral homelands in Minnesota and made to walk 150 miles from the Lower Sioux Agency to concentration camps in Mankato and Fort Snelling on November 7–13, 1862. The walk was very difficult and horrendous. The White people who lived on each side of the route tortured many of the Dakota by spilling boiling water on them, throwing objects of steel

and wood at them, whipping them with bull-whips, and inflicting many other acts of extreme cruelty. Many of the walkers died brutal deaths, and their bodies have never been found.

All of the prisoners are asked to remember the 350 Lakota people who began arriving in the first three weeks of December of 1890 at Wounded Knee. We arrived under various white flags of truce and under a promise that we would be kept in safety. Many of our Lakota people came to Wounded Knee out of fear, because the soldiers were killing our people on the Standing Rock, Cheyenne River, and Rosebud reservations. Many of our Lakota people believed that Wounded Knee was a place where food and water could be found. We did not know that Wounded Knee was a trap and, like our Dakota and Nakota relatives, we, too, were being marched to our own deaths. Wounded Knee on December 29, 1890, was a merciless slaughter of our old people, children, and women.

The prisoners are asked to remember all of the atrocities that have happened to our People and our ancestors. We ask for offerings of food, tobacco, tobacco ties, prayers, memorial songs, and ceremony. Our ancestors did not have to die that way, and because they did, we see the sacrifices they made so that we could stay alive and fulfill our natural right to live long and be prosperous. The reason the prisoners are asked to help is because they symbolize the spirits of our relatives who were kept in Fort Snelling and other stockades or concentration camps.

All tribal prisoners have a distinct way of thinking. We can survive anything, because we know that our ancestors paid for our freedoms by walking through the political fires of hate. The natural order of our ceremonies and our language worked for our ancestors while they sat imprisoned, and this same way of thinking is working for the tribal prisoners today. Our ancestors who did time in the camps did not have access to lawyers or other rights we have now. Their time in the camps was spent praying, knowing that on any given day or time, they could be taken away and killed.

We must study the weapons that were used to kill our people. There were rifles, pistols, swords, and whips. The deadliest and most feared weapon was the Hotchkiss machine gun. This weapon was capable of killing large amounts of people with precision accuracy and timing. The Hotchkiss machine gun was used against other tribes as well. It would be a time of healing for our People to be able to physically see these weapons. Do these weapons, especially the Hotchkiss machine gun, still exist, and can they be brought to our people for healing prayers? We want to perform these prayers for our own healing. Our people cannot rest until we know this has been completed. We want the smoke of burning sage, cedar, and sweetgrass to pass over these weapons as we pray for our ancestors.

We may never have control over our homelands again, but that will not stop us from returning to pray and to perform the *Oyate Ceyapi Wopakinte* (Wiping of the Tears) ceremony. This ceremony is very important, because it unites the spirits of our dead relatives and lets them pass on to the world up above. In this ceremony, we gather the family and the relatives of those who are deceased, and we release the dead through prayer, memorial songs, food, tobacco, and crying.

There were good White people on the killing grounds of our People who had nothing directly to do with the genocide and holocaust perpetrated against us. Some disagreed with what was going on. They could be seen moving our people away from killing areas, but no one said anything. They brought out extra portions of food for the hungry, bandaged the wounded, and comforted our children. They refused to enforce the sanctions that were put on us. They went out of their way to make sure that we were treated with some respect and compassion. These White people operated without anyone ever finding out that they helped to save some of our lives.

Our tribal women are very honorable. They fit into every category of our lives with a precious heart of wisdom and spiritual inspiration. All of our decisions to be who we are come from the power of our women. They encourage us to work hard and maintain a positive attitude in everything we do. Our decision to be an artist, singer, drummer, dancer, speaker, beadworker, or to pursue any kind of cultural teaching comes from the connection that we have with our women. They keep our families strong and united with a strict set of traditional values. This keeps our communities in balance with peace and dignity. They are mothers, aunts, sisters, and grandmothers, who are very loyal and highly motivated within all of our tribes, societies, bands, and everyday life.

We are nourished intellectually by our women,

> « OUR TRIBAL WOMEN ARE VERY HONORABLE. THEY FIT INTO EVERY CATEGORY OF OUR LIVES WITH A PRECIOUS HEART OF WISDOM AND SPIRITUAL INSPIRATION. »

and it is good to know this. We have some of the world's best cooks, quiltmakers, dreamers, storytellers, planners, and organizers in our homes and communities. Many of our women follow the ceremonies and are pipekeepers. They are very strong in their belief systems, and we appreciate what they do for us. All of our women are beautiful and carry themselves with honor at all times. They are bringing back many sacred teachings.

On November 7–13, 2002, 140 years after the 1,700 Dakota people were forced to walk to the concentration camp at Fort Snelling, some of the family and relatives of the ancestors organized Manipi Hena Owasin Wicunkiksuyapi (We Remember All Those Who Walked) or the Dakota Commemorative March. The march awakened the spirits of all those who walked in November, 1862. They were torn from their families, viciously attacked, beaten, and left to die. The march awakened them and prepared them for the journey back to the homeland up above. These spirits were glad to be awakened after 140 years of being asleep and lost.

They were reunited with their families and relatives, ate plenty of food, heard many songs and prayers, visited everyone, and then on the final day of the march went home up above. Six hundred Lakota, Dakota, and Nakota tribal prisoners from South Dakota's prisons gave prayers and made tobacco ties for the march. We sang some old warrior songs of hardship, unity, peace, and courage. We will do this every year.

Support is requested from the rest of the tribes for the march. All are welcome to contribute food, money, horses (with the means to transport and feed them), prayers, camping gear, letters, words of encouragement, and anything that will assist in the safety and endurance of the marchers and onsite organizers. The tribes are asked to bring people who are physically capable of walking the whole distance of the march, which is 150 miles. Please visit the Web site, http://dakota-march.50megs.com/index.html, for contact information or to learn more about the march.

The Big Foot Memorial Ride requests support for its annual ride, which is from Fort Yates, North Dakota, on the Standing Rock Reservation down through the Cheyenne River Reservation, in and out of the Badlands (The Stronghold) to Wounded Knee on the Pine Ridge Reservation. All contributions of support are welcome and appreciated. Please contact:

Arvol Looking Horse
Box 687
Eagle Butte, SD 57625
Phone: (605) 964-4807

Today we have teams of people—historians, lawyers, spiritualists, activists, musicians, writers, and organizers—who are educating the majority of tribal people and all people on the northern plains about what happened to our ancestors between 1849 and 1890. These teams of people stand ready to deactivate racism, injustice, violence, and inequality against all Indigenous people and to assist anyone who requests their help.

◄○►

NOTE

1. The date 1849 is used here because it signifies for the Lakota the difficulties leading up to the 1851 Treaty of Fort Laramie.

A Journey of Healing and Awakening

WAZIYATAWIN ANGELA WILSON

◄○►

Early on the morning of November 14, 2002, I boarded the plane with my family to head back to Arizona. It was the most painful departure from my homeland I had ever endured. I felt like I was tearing myself away from an amazing experience that was so powerful that I did not want to let go of it. I was beyond exhausted, but I did not want to sleep. Instead, I sat staring out the window of the airplane, aching to feel my feet touch again the lands I was leaving. I must have looked very serious. My son Talon reached up to put his hand on my cheek, and as he turned my face toward him, he said, "I want you to smile, Mom, we just did a good thing for our ancestors." Indeed, the heart of a seven-year-old boy was touched by the significance of what we had accomplished, as were the hearts of all of us.

In many ways the entire march was an exercise in faith. I don't think those of us planning the march understood the full significance of what it would mean—this is still revealing itself to us years later. The venture required an incredible amount of planning. We needed to raise funds, plan the route, figure out meals and lodging, cooperate with state and local authorities, and publicize the event. It required the help and coordination of many individuals, and in the planning stages, there were moments when the to-do list was overwhelming.

On one particularly difficult day at the end of summer, I was feeling bad because no tribal sources had yet responded to our request for financial support. I was worried about how we were going to feed the marchers and provide a warm place for them to sleep. Though canceling was an absolute last resort, I didn't know how we could keep publicizing the event without the means to provide for the people who would show up to walk with us. I learned a lesson in faith that day.

Out of the blue, I received a letter from an inmate at Jameson Prison in Sioux Falls, South Dakota. George Blue Bird had seen some of the announcements about the Commemorative March in the tribal newspapers, and he wrote to tell me about the support being offered through their Lakota/Dakota/Nakota Spiritual Group in the prison, stating:

> In a few more days, I and about 800 other
> Lakota, Dakota and Nakota brothers
> from prison will begin praying for the
> Dakota Commemorative March. We will
> load our pipes and smoke them in our
> ceremonies. We will sing and be with all

of the efforts that are being organized for the walk from Lower Sioux to Fort Snelling. We believe in what you're doing. We believe that it is right. Tribal justice and harmony are powerful thought processes, and we commend your heart and whole spirit for working to make the walk a reality. We hope that the strength from all of us will be with you as a reflection of sovereignty and tribal honor.[1]

With those words, I began to weep, and his letter marked a major turning point for me. From that moment on, I knew that everything was going to work out. With so many prayers being offered on our behalf for what we were trying to accomplish, it would not fail. While an incredible amount of hard work remained to be done, it was as if a huge burden had been lifted from me, and I could proceed with the planning without fear. Furthermore, what was so inspiring about this was the tremendous generosity of spirit exhibited by our tribal Peoples who have suffered so much trauma and hardship themselves. As George pointed out in the same letter, "As tribal prisoners, we carry the same spirit of many of our ancestors who were imprisoned in all of the earliest prisons. We know what it's like to survive the oppression and the inequalities."

Shortly thereafter, I received word that the Santee Nation in Nebraska was donating meat from a buffalo to the march. Finally we knew we could feed the marchers. Then Lower Sioux stepped forward with a generous monetary donation that covered the cost of the sanitation needs of the marchers. Other contributions soon followed from Upper Sioux and a variety of local church, student, and civic groups. Everything fell into place.

The day before the march began, my kids and I arrived in Minneapolis where my sister met us and drove us out to Lower Sioux. I was very pleased to learn that *inipi* (purification or sweat) ceremonies were already under way, food was ready to eat, and people were beginning to gather at the Eci Nompa Woonspe (The Second Chance Learning Center) in Morton, Minnesota. Many of us were both excited and nervous about what was to come. I was very happy when Gabrielle Tateyuskanskan, the co-coordinator for the march, arrived with her mother, Yvonne Wynde, to help with the last-minute planning and support for the event.

They arrived with a large bundle of wooden lathes, each one tied with a red strip of cloth and inscribed with two names, one on each side. The names represented the heads of families who were on the original march and who were then imprisoned at Fort Snelling. Because the march to Fort Snelling was primarily composed of women, most of the names were those of women. In all there were about three hundred such names, so two were written on each stake, and theoretically a stake was going to be placed about every mile for the approximately 150 miles between Lower Sioux and Fort Snelling. Yvonne had donated the stakes and cloth, and Gaby had worked with the children at Tiospa Zina Tribal School in Sisseton, South Dakota, to tie the cloth and write the names on the stakes. Gaby commented later about the experience of watching these innocent children taking on the morose task of writing the names of those who had suffered tremendous hardship and cruelty in 1862, but they did so happily, bringing a lightness and innocence to the project. Gaby and Yvonne brought half of the stakes to us that night at Lower Sioux and said they would bring the other half as soon as the stakes were ready and they could get them to us.

I awoke about 4:30 the first morning of the march. Knowing we would be sleeping in sleeping bags the next week, we had stayed at Jackpot Junction's hotel that night, and I was able to enjoy my last long hot shower for a while. By 5:15, I had our bags packed, and my kids and I were ready to go. I took a few moments to talk with them again about what would be happening. I explained that what we were about to do would be hard; it was meant not to be fun but to remember and honor our ancestors. I told them that when it got hard for them, they should call on the help of *Wakantanka* (The Great Mystery) and their ancestors, asking them for strength. My older son, Talon, who is very sensitive, began to cry. I assured him that our ancestors would recognize him and that they would be uplifted and proud of him—of all of them. Then we left.

The first breakfast was provided by Lower Sioux, and it was delivered to the basement of the old community center. It was an excellent and generous hot breakfast, and we each had our share of hot liquids before we began our long walk in the cold. A couple dozen people gathered with us that morning, most of them to walk with us. We had my deksi Leo Omani and ic'esi (cousin) Gerald Standing from Saskatchewan, a couple from New Mexico, some people from South Dakota, and more from Minnesota. At 7:15, we went outside and Ron Leith conducted our opening ceremony. At that time, he informed

us that the eagle feather staff for the thirty-eight Dakota hanged at Mankato wanted to make this journey with us. As keeper of that staff, he was sending it along under the care of Gerald Standing. We were honored to be carrying that staff, and it made sense that we should carry it, since the condemned men who had been sentenced to execution, including the thirty-eight who were finally hanged, also traveled this route, stopping at Mankato while the women and children continued all the way to Fort Snelling. Those who carried the eagle staff always walked quickly. Many said it was as if the eagle staff was pulling them along, giving them a strength and speed they did not normally have.

I was particularly moved by the presence of Kunsi (Grandmother) Naomi Cavender, a relative of mine who was there with her daughter, Judith Anywaush, and Judith's daughter Marisa. Along with their cousin Lindsay, Marisa's three children (Cody, Naomi, and Josh) were also present. From then on, we began to refer to them as the Four Generations. An ancestor of theirs, Wicanhpi Ota Win (Many Stars Woman) was several years old at the time of the forced march in 1862. After already losing her parents, she was walking with her grandmothers, who carried her on their backs for much of the way. The Four Generations family was walking to honor and remember that grandmother. As we watched Marisa with little Josh, many of us contemplated the difficulty an elderly woman would have had carrying a three-year-old on her back for the 150-mile journey. The starkness of the 1862 march came into focus. I was so grateful and happy to have them starting this journey with us. Kunsi Naomi planted the first stake in

Gerald Standing from the Wahpeton Reserve in Saskatchewan leading the marchers near St. Peter, Minnesota. Gerald took care of the eagle staff that led the Commemorative March from beginning to end.

the ground and walked the first steps of the march while she leaned on the stroller of her great-grandson. Our long journey had begun.

It did not take long before we settled into a routine. The sanitation truck driven by Dave Holm traveled in the rear, allowing marchers to leave the walk and use the restrooms whenever necessary. The system was so impressive and Dave was so kind and efficient that he quickly earned the nickname Super-Dave. Deksi Leo's little red car from Canada became the lead car, driving slowly a little ahead of the marchers for safety reasons and also to help mark the miles. Before we began using the green mileposts along the route, however, his lead car was clocking the mileage for us. We teased each other about the accuracy of the placement of the stakes, since it seemed he was occasionally using "Canadian miles"; his car's mileage gauge was calibrated only in kilometers. Though the plan was to place one of the wooden lathes every

mile, we were less than precise for this reason and also because we had to accommodate the landscape, the route, and safety requirements.

Each mile offered an opportunity for us to collectively stop and remember those who suffered through the forced march in 1862. When the lead car stopped, either Deksi Leo or Ic'esi Gerald would pull out one of the stakes from the bundle in their car and all of us would gather around. A speaker of our language would read the name aloud. Then one of the women present would hold the stake as it was pounded into the ground and offer the first prayer with tobacco. Everyone else could then come forward to offer their tobacco and prayers.

In many ways, our act of pounding each stake into the ground was also about reclamation. Mile by mile, we were physically reclaiming our memory, our history, and our land. We were also leaving a visible symbol of this reclamation. Some of the stakes lasted for months, marking our route of suffering and hardship, and a few are still standing today. Waving in the wind, the red strips of cloth on the stakes were important signifiers both of the blood that was shed in 1862 and of the blood in the

---

« MILE BY MILE, WE WERE PHYSICALLY RECLAIMING OUR MEMORY, OUR HISTORY, AND OUR LAND. »

---

life that still breathes—our blood as descendants of those who made this original painful journey. Those stakes were temporary only in the physical sense. Far beyond their initial purpose, they have begun a process of reclamation that will not be abandoned.

Planting the stakes was always a moving experience, but it was particularly moving when descendants who were present recognized their family names. Because I had so frequently heard the name of my great-great-grandmother Maza Okiye Win (Woman Who Talks to Iron) as well as heard the stories about her experiences, I fully expected that some time on the march I would see her name on one of the stakes. I was not prepared for what I did see. Just a few miles outside of New Ulm, my uncle pulled out a stake from the car with the name Haza Win (Blueberry Woman) on it. I was startled as I realized this was my relative— this was Maza Okiye Win's mother. My sister, Audrey Fuller, had just had this family name formally passed on to her in a name-giving ceremony the previous summer. My uncle and I put the stake into the ground and said the first prayers, but as I stood up with my hands still on the stake, a flood of grief washed over me, and I began to sob.

Leo Omani and Waziyatawin Angela Wilson planting the stake with Haza Win's name, Angela's great-great-great-grandmother.

I had walked in the path of these ancestors, my feet had retraced the path of their suffering, and in that moment I felt their grief and the grief of all the subsequent generations. Later when I gave it more thought, it made perfect sense that I would see Haza Win's name instead of Maza Okiye Win, as Haza Win would have been the head of the household at that time, especially after losing her own mother on the journey. This was one of the lucid moments on the journey when I felt the significance of our undertaking personally and powerfully. That was the second day of the march.

The first day of the march had been energizing and inspiring but also very difficult physically. In accordance with suggestion from the Minnesota Department of Transportation about walking only during daylight hours, at about mile fourteen we decided to split the group in two so that we could cover the miles more quickly before nightfall. One group was dropped off six miles down the road to walk from there to the twenty-sixth mile, two miles outside the town of Sleepy Eye. The other group, the one I was in, stayed behind to walk from the fourteenth to the twentieth mile. The plan was that we would all meet up again at mile twenty-six and walk the last two miles into Sleepy Eye together, where we knew a hot meal and hot drinks awaited us. Since many of the fast walkers had gone on ahead, some of us thought the first group might have completed the remaining two miles by the time we finished our stretch. We knew there was the big green school bus (donated by Lutheran Ministries for our use) waiting for us at mile twenty, and when we could see it off in the distance we were thrilled. When we finally got there, I told the young driver that I had never been so happy to see a school bus. He drove us to about mile twenty-six, where we saw the eagle feather staff still being carried. We got out of the bus but had to jog to catch up to the other marchers—no easy task after walking twenty miles. But we caught up and walked the last few miles in together. By the time we arrived in Sleepy Eye, those of us who had put in the miles that day were in a lot of pain. Several of us had large blisters that we would carry with us for the rest of the march. We slipped out of our shoes and moved very slowly around the cafeteria and gym of St. Mary's School,

grateful for the chance to sit down, rest, and have some hot food.

Though very difficult, the march had some aspects that presaged the long journey ahead of us. As we retraced the route our ancestors marched in 1862, many of our marchers in 2002 (especially those from Canada) had never set foot on these parts of our homeland. They were doing so now not just as children returning home to their motherland but as refugees facing the current occupiers who have since made our home theirs. While reconciliation with the White community was not a goal for this Commemorative March, speaking the truth to them about our historical memory was.

The night we arrived in Sleepy Eye, members of St. Mary's congregation came in to offer us gifts of warmth and comfort. They brought many handmade and store-bought items such as mittens, hats, scarves, socks, and even slippers. I picked out a pair of those handmade slippers and was thankful to have something else to put on my blistered and aching feet besides the hiking boots I had worn all day. In the evening meeting with the townspeople, we shared stories about why we were participating in this event, realizing immediately the difficulty of engaging in a dialogue with even the most well-intentioned White townspeople. All of us who had put in the miles that day were not only physically exhausted but also emotionally and spiritually exhausted. After shedding frequent tears throughout the day, many of us shed more tears as we offered our testimony about why we were participating. Life from this time and place was breathed into the stories of our ancestors, as we faced those who were now occupying the lands that once belonged to us. In many cases, they were the direct descendants of the settlers who had called for our extermination and forced removal.

Most of us were too emotionally drained to exhibit much more than the pain we felt. The irony of being welcomed into a town that was created because of our dispossession only compounded these emotions. However, my father, Chris Mato Nunpa, was better able to articulate the legacy of oppression perpetrated by Whites in Minnesota, which implicated even those present who had come to welcome us. He would later be criticized for those comments, but I think many of us present were thankful he had the energy to let people know that, though we were grateful for the gifts, the debt to be paid was much higher.

As I went to sleep that night with my children and the others in that huge gymnasium, I was filled with an overwhelming sense of gratitude. I was so thankful that we had made it through this first day and that we had begun this honoring of our ancestors that had become so important to me. However, I was in such pain physically that I had no idea how I was going to walk the next day. All I could do was pray.

The next morning I was up with my kids at 5:00, and I was pleasantly surprised. Although I was very sore, I didn't feel nearly as bad as I thought I would. My kids—two of whom had put in at least fourteen miles the day before—were also fine. Their little resilient bodies had little difficulty putting in the long miles and coming through blister-free and with only minor soreness. We ate another hearty meal and headed toward New Ulm, a landscape stained with much of our blood and carrying the difficult memories of a vicious cruelty to our People carried out by those who wanted our lands and resources.

New Ulm is a place that Dakota people rarely venture into today because the memories associated with the town are so painful—too painful for some to bear. The name of the town still inspires gasps and shudders when it is mentioned around Dakota people. This was the place where Whites (men, women, and children) lined the streets screaming and taunting our people while they showered us with rocks, food, sticks, and even boiling water. This is the place where our people were beaten until they looked like raw meat, some of them beaten to death. As we made our way there, we felt a growing sense of anxiety. It was on the way there that we placed Haza Win's stake in the ground. As this was a shorter distance (about fourteen miles), we arrived there in early afternoon and settled in at Turner Hall, with many hours to wait before the evening meal with White townspeople. Not surprisingly, only a dozen or so marchers actually stayed in the town. The rest traveled back to their homes to sleep, and several young people left to catch the evening session of a powwow. After they left, only three of us remained in the big Turner Hall, where we pulled out the mattresses and sleeping bags and set up our beds for the night. I experienced an intense feeling of sadness there, almost loneliness, perhaps because of the sickness of the place.

As in Sleepy Eye, we met with the White townspeople for an evening meal and discussion. The food was wonderful. The buffalo meat and many other dishes were prepared by local people who wanted to support our efforts. It was this night that I shared my grandmother's account about what happened to our ancestors as they walked through the streets of New Ulm in 1862. It was important to share that particular story with the people present, because it was about their town, their ancestors, and the atrocities they committed against our People in our homeland. My father again commented about the similarities with treatment of other oppressed Peoples. The local newspaper picked up our comments, which led to a series of editorials in the weeks that followed. These editorials demonstrated the strong sense of denial still prevalent in the area and rarely challenged.

Later that night, we were uplifted when more Dakota people arrived to participate in the march with fresh legs. Clifford Canku arrived, and he became an important spiritual leader for us during the march, offering prayers, carrying the pipe for us each day, and uplifting us by playing Dakota drum music in his car as he followed the marchers on the road. Another group arrived from the Wahpeton Reserve in Saskatchewan and another group from Sioux Valley. I was so thankful that we would be walking through the main streets of New Ulm the following morning with the strength of all these people.

The third morning of the march, the small crowd gathered behind Turner Hall, and after a brief ceremony, we headed out. A few supportive Whites from New Ulm joined us for the walk through their town, and a mother and daughter traveled with us all day. The town was still largely asleep as we walked down its main street, and few people were around to observe the passing of our caravan of walkers and vehicles. We were traveling unnoticed through the town that had waited with anticipation 140 years earlier for the oppor-

tunity to accost the procession of our ancestors. Now, with their occupation of our lands solidified and with no physical threat posed by our People, they could afford to ignore our presence.

This area of Minnesota, along the Minnesota River valley, is breathtakingly beautiful, even in November when the leaves have fallen and the landscape is dominated by shades of brown. While much of southern Minnesota is now flat farm country, along the river are heavy woods and rolling hills. For years, whenever I was in this portion of our river valley, even if I was only driving through, a heaviness would develop in my chest, and tears would inevitably come to my eyes. Walking each step on this journey, I realized that what I was feeling was grief. Connected with this land today is a tremendous sense of loss, made all the more painful because of its intense beauty. A profound longing emanates from the land, from the bones of our ancestors buried within the earth, all of whom are calling us home.

Numerous times along the way, we felt the spiritual presence of our ancestors and other relations. Things happened that could not have been planned. One example of this occurred with the wooden lathes. Gaby and Yvonne brought the first batch they had finished to Eci Nonpa Woonspe, the Dakota charter school in Morton, on the Wednesday evening before the march started. The lathes were blessed in the sweat lodge that night and then brought to the start of the walk the next morning. Gaby had said that they would bring the rest later, but we didn't know when, nor did we know exactly how many stakes we had and when the last one would be placed. We had thought the other stakes might arrive the first two days of the march, but when we hadn't received

Gabrielle Wynde Tateyuskanskan, co-coordinator for the march, arriving with the second bundle of stakes on the third day of the march.

them by the morning of the third day, we made another plan. We decided that we would use the extra red flags that Mary Beth brought and tie them to the mile-marker posts if the additional stakes did not arrive on time. That afternoon we planted the last stake we had. So on the next mile marker, we pulled out a red flag and were tying it to the mile-marker post when Gaby arrived with the next bundle of stakes. We were able to pull one out and place it there, without missing a single mile. It could not have been timed more perfectly. As we read each name out loud, the significance of what we were doing became extremely apparent. How often had the names of

these people been called out by our own Dakota people, and how often had they been remembered for the suffering they endured so that we could live? It was clear that they appreciated our efforts.

We had a moving evening at Mankato, which was not surprising given the historical significance of the concentration camp and hanging sites there. Once such a gross inhumanity has bled the landscape, I don't think the land ever forgets. After a wonderful hot meal at the Dakota Meadows School, we all drove to the site of the hanging of the thirty-eight in downtown Mankato. Once there, we gathered in a circle in front of the statue of the white buffalo, shared our thoughts about the march, and closed the day with a pipe ceremony. It was cold, and those of us who had walked all day were extremely weary and sore. But standing there with so many other Dakota people who shared our memories, our pain, and our love for our nation was probably the best way to restore a sense of warmth and well-being to each of us. We returned to the school, and those of us managing blisters bandaged our feet in preparation for the next day's walk. Then we slept.

The presence of the spirits was felt again the next morning as we left Mankato. Standing in front of Dakota Meadows School, Clifford Canku sang a pipe-filling song while Deksi Leo filled the pipe. As Gaby described later, during the song a mist quickly appeared from the east that had bumpy clouds like heads of people. It came overhead just as Leo finished filling the pipe and then SMACK, the stakes we had standing up by Clifford and Leo fell hard to the ground. It was our ancestors coming to let us know of their presence.

Clifford Canku (with the pipe) and Chris Mato Nunpa (with hand on the stakes) at sunrise in Mankato.

After we left Mankato, a palpable change in the march occurred. Though we initially envisioned this to be a march for women and children, the march did not begin at all how we expected. The male influence characteristic of the separate march of the condemned men from the Lower Sioux Agency to the concentration camp at Mankato quickly dominated our commemorative march shortly after it began. We did not immediately understand how or why that happened, but by the fourth day we understood quite clearly. The historical record is currently unclear about the precise route taken by these two groups, but we pieced together what we could. Though we know that the destination of the condemned men was Mankato, we do not know for certain whether the group of women and children who were headed to Fort Snelling traveled through Mankato.

In spite of this, because we had planned the march as a commemoration of the first phase of the Dakota removal from Minnesota, we felt it was necessary to stop in Mankato, as we knew the men were imprisoned there in the winter of

1862–63, while the others were hanged. When the eagle staff for the thirty-eight was presented to us to make the journey with us, it was as if the spirits of those thirty-eight and the other condemned men were leading the way. Thus, the first portion of the march to Mankato was more male dominated. Clifford Canku thankfully appeared as the male spiritual leader to help us through this portion of the journey, and other male participants played more prominent roles in getting us to Mankato. However, after arriving at Mankato, the female influence became stronger, and a shift occurred that would last through the remainder of the march, marked tangibly by the collapse of the stakes after the pipe had been filled. From Mankato to Fort Snelling, it was truly a march for the women and children.

We were on our way to Henderson, another town remembered for its particular brutality to the procession of walkers in 1862. It was important for us to walk through this town. During our many conversations with the Minnesota Department of Transportation, they had strongly urged us to avoid walking on Highway 93 for safety reasons, suggesting instead that we drive in caravans for that stretch and then drop the marchers off in town for a symbolic walk through the town. However, the day before, a man from the town of Henderson had caught up with the marchers on our way to Mankato and asked if it would be okay for them to meet us on horseback as we arrived in town. We agreed that would be appreciated. I believed strongly that we needed to make the walk into the town, despite the narrow shoulder on that stretch and the lower visibility.

While we had some disagreement amongst the coordinators regarding this change of plans, we eventually came to an understanding and agreed to make the walk to Henderson regardless of the department of transportation's recommendation. Besides extending what was already a long walk in terms of miles that day, our walk into the town of Henderson involved an incredible climb. Just as we were turning from the major and busy Highway 169, a very understanding state trooper arrived with assisting police vehicles to escort our caravan across the highway. As someone who had studied this period of Minnesota history, he understood that we needed to make the walk into town and volunteered to lead the walkers with his police car as long as the other cars drove on into the town and waited for us there.

The air was growing more damp and cold, and it started to drizzle as we began that slow uphill journey. Most of us who participated on the walk for that stretch into Henderson felt strong emotions, though they varied. My husband and children had arrived in the afternoon just after we left St. Peter and a lunch at Gustavus Adolphus College. My husband had arrived from Arizona

that morning, having cleared his work schedule so that he could walk with us the rest of the way. My children had been visiting their aunt and grandmother since Friday afternoon (the second day), and though their absence had made it easier for me as an organizer and participant, I was happy they had returned. Many others from the Twin Cities area came to join us that afternoon as well. It was wonderful to see both familiar and new faces of those who had arrived to walk for our ancestors. With my husband, children, and others there to make this journey, I felt uplifted and strengthened.

Because of the long distance between Mankato and Henderson (about twenty-eight miles), this was the longest day for us in terms of the actual walking time, which extended well into the evening. The previous night, we arrived at the Dakota Meadows School in Mankato at sunset, but this night we had to walk in the darkness. At dusk, we were walking along the river valley, and across the water we saw more eagles and hawks than many of us had ever seen in one place. Terri Yellowhammer, who had joined us for this portion of the walk, said she and her partner had counted at least eighteen. While a few were occasionally flying, most were perched in the branches of trees, seemingly watching us as our long caravan passed. Because these bird relatives frequently come when we gather, especially when we call on the spirits of our ancestors, their presence left me feeling very strong, despite having put in over twenty miles that day. It was as if they were welcoming us home and thanking us for our efforts. A few people had strong emotions of a very different nature. My cousin Gerald Standing shared with us later that night that he was overcome by a powerful, incredible sadness during that same stretch.

We were all curious about our reception in the town of Henderson. Though the group of riders was unable to meet us on horseback, as we entered the edge of town, we saw the same elderly White man who had approached me the previous day about meeting us. He opened the door to his house and shouted to the marchers, "Welcome to Henderson!" I don't think I was alone in shedding tears at that point, since our reception in 2002 was so very different from the one our ancestors experienced in 1862. We were welcomed with hot cider and snacks at the charter school there and then bused back to Gustavus, where we ate dinner and spent the night. This experience offered some hope for future relations.

In Henderson, there seemed to be a genuine yearning among at least some of the population to come to terms with the terrible history of that place—the brutality perpetrated against its Indigenous inhabitants. A large group of young people from the charter school walked the first half of the next day with us as we made our way to Jordan. We appreciated their youthful energy and commitment to supporting us. They were even appreciative as we passed out bologna and cheese sandwiches in the ditch along Highway 169 for our lunch break, and they said their thanks before heading back home.

When dinner was served for us at St. Paul's United Church of Christ in Henderson, they put a note of welcome in placards on each table, which also held the saying: "Over all the earth helpless and oppressed people wander." Recognizing the Dakota as an oppressed People necessarily means recognizing that oppressors are still oppressing. This was a refreshing awareness, and when we ate with the townspeople at dinner that night and shared our stories, I told them how much I appreciated this recognition, citing Paulo Freire's comment that "Violence is never initiated by the oppressed." Later someone affiliated with the charter school said he was happy to hear me mention Freire, because their school is based on his teaching principles. Rarely are White institutions of oppression recognized in small-town White America, and so any demonstration of critical consciousness is a sign of hope. To what extent these same people understood their own participation in our ongoing colonization and oppression is unclear, but I hope this will be explored and developed as we continue this discussion in the coming years.

It was on this same day that Alameda Rocha joined us on the march. We had not met before, but when we did, it was clear that she had come to help us. After receiving the message from water spirits the previous evening that she should join us, she had set out that day from Minneapolis to find us. After having no luck finding us according to the vague directions offered in the brochure, Alameda said she stopped to pray and ask for guidance. She then looked up and found us by following the eagles. We had been wondering who was going to serve as our spiritual leader when Clifford had to leave later that night, and the answer came with Alameda. She is a pipe carrier from Fort Peck, and her spiritual leadership would carry us through the last difficult stretch to the fort. After spending the rest of the day driving with us and helping to caravan marchers back to Henderson where we would spend the night, she offered to lead a women's pipe ceremony the next morning. We were very fortunate to have Clifford close that Monday (the fifth day) with a pipe ceremony and for Alameda to offer prayers with the pipe the next morning.

We were transported back to Henderson that night because we had been unsuccessful in finding lodging accommodations in Jordan. A very small town, Jordan had limited options anyway, but we received resistance from a priest there who was concerned that we were opening old wounds. Specifically, he wanted to know how this event would help heal Dakota-White relations. He was obviously unsatisfied with my response when I stated that the march was not about healing those wounds but about trying to heal our wounds, which have never been closed. His response to injustices is typical of those in power, for it is they who benefit from perpetuating the myth that peace can occur without justice or healing without acknowledging harms and making reparations for them. Anyway, this resistance meant that once the marchers arrived in the town, we had to be shuttled back to Henderson to spend the night.

The dozen or so marchers who slept in our sleeping bags in Henderson stayed on the second floor of their museum, which was a first for most of us. The museum had various exhibit areas and displays where each of us slept, one of which was a reconstructed tipi. The kids were thrilled about this, as they had slept in a tipi before but never one inside a building. My husband and I slept in a reconstructed land office from the 1860s, which ironically held a large portrait of President Lincoln, the person ultimately responsible for the mass hanging of our Dakota resisters.

Before sunrise at 4:30, my daughter Autumn and I awoke with Alameda for the women's pipe ceremony. We said our prayers for our ancestors and for the marchers and other participants and then enjoyed a hot breakfast hosted again by folks in Henderson. By sunrise we were ready to walk again, so we were shuttled back to Jordan where we picked up the walk and headed toward Savage, Minnesota.

By this time I kept thinking my body would have adjusted and that my muscles would have become strong enough for the soreness to diminish. Probably because my muscles never had an opportunity to rest and rebuild, this never occurred. Every day walking was painful, and every night I was so sore I wondered if I would be rested enough to complete the next day's walk. Even bending down was slow and arduous. One time I remember cringing when I dropped my Chapstick on the march and watched as it rolled away from me down the slight incline on the road. I quickly debated whether it was an expendable item; I decided it was not and knew it was going to be painful to pick it up. I was at least able to stop it from rolling further with one of the stakes I carried and then very slowly bent down to pick it up. As I looked up and smiled at the trailing vehicle right behind me, the driver chuckled at my slow and deliberate motion. Even minor movements were at times excruciating, but I always found the strength to keep walking.

We walked to Savage that night and then caravanned back to the Prior Lake Dakota Community, better known as the Shakopee Mdewakanton Sioux Community, where they provided the evening meal for the marchers and the basement of their church for sleeping quarters. To have our dinner, we were given a separate room in the

Little Six Casino that night. I remember it very fondly, because this was the only evening we had that was totally ours. No non-Dakota were there whom we were trying to educate. Those who were present were our strong allies and supporters and believed wholeheartedly in what we were doing; they were the people who had put in the miles with us.

These several dozen people comprised the core group of marchers. Some of them had not been able to participate every day, but they were the ones who had repeatedly come back. It was an opportunity for us to share among ourselves how this event had impacted us, and most of the people there took the opportunity to share a few words about their experiences on the march. It was a time of laughter and tears, and we were glad to feel that sense of closeness before the next day, when we knew many new faces would join us. We had become a close-knit community, regarding one another as family while facing hardship and unbounded grief over the previous six days. I took great comfort in knowing that, in this hardship and grief, our People were uniting and were taking important steps in healing ourselves and our nation. I knew that I would never forget all these people who had walked so many miles for our ancestors.

We awoke well before sunrise again for the women's pipe ceremony in Shakopee. With all our pleas for help and healing during the final stretch of our walk to the concentration camp at Fort Snelling, we also gave thanks. I was overwhelmed with gratitude that morning for how far we had come and for all that was accomplished. We knew that, emotionally, this last leg of the journey would be the most difficult, because we would

end at the site of imprisonment, where another estimated three hundred of our People had died that winter. We ate a good breakfast at the casino again and set off to the mile marker in Savage where we had ended the previous day. With traffic rushing past us and a larger group than usual arriving to march, we felt a different kind of intensity that morning as well as anxiety about this final stretch. We gathered together for Alameda to offer a prayer, and then we started to walk.

It seems now as if that day passed very quickly. So many people had joined us on foot or as part of the caravan of cars trailing behind us. I saw many familiar faces, including my Kunsi Carrie Schommer with interns from the Dakota language program at Shakopee. Students from the Dakota language program at the University of Minnesota and the Native Arts High School in the Twin Cities also came to join us, as did busloads from Tiospa Zina in Sisseton. Gaby Tateyuskanskan joined us again with her family, and I was thankful for a chance to visit with her while we walked.

Phyllis Redday, an elder from Sisseton, arrived on this day as well. We had expected her at the beginning, as she was going to help lead the women's prayers at the beginning of the march. When she called me over to the car and I saw her foot bandaged, I understood why she hadn't made it. She had injured her foot just before the march and so was unable to come. She then brought me around to the trunk of her car and showed me a beautiful sage wreath made by a group of elderly women in Sisseton, South Dakota. The sage wreath was wrapped in ribbons of our sacred colors and then tied with three hundred tobacco prayer ties, made for the families who were force marched in 1862. They made this wreath so it could be dedicated and left at the concentration camp site at Fort Snelling.

With all the people coming together, we felt a tremendous energy that helped us make it through the difficult stretches on the highway. On this day, we faced the problem of walking on major highways, the most difficult part being crossing the entrance and exit ramps as cars traveling full speed were forced to come to a halt. In spite of the clover leafs and spaghetti crossings constructed of concrete and asphalt, it felt really good to walk this portion of our homeland as our People once did.

It was on this final day that news reporters from the Twin Cities papers were around us, interviewing some of us and photographing others. Kunsi Naomi was back with us; she had come again to start us out on those first steps of our last morning. Later on, I watched as she sat in the passenger side of one of the trailing vehicles; a reporter was filming her as she talked briefly about her grandmother's experience on the 1862 march. I was holding her hand as the reporter walked away. A tear slid down the side of her face; she looked at me and said, "It still hurts to talk about it."

As we drew nearer to the fort, the tension increased. Deksi Leo announced that soon the men would step back and allow all the women and children to walk to the front, leading the way into Fort Snelling as they would have done so many years before. We were within two miles of the fort, and a stillness and weightiness overtook us. My body was convulsing under heavy sobs as I held my daughter and oldest son with my arms. My youngest son was riding on the shoulders of his father further back. When it came time for the men to step back, one of the men misunderstood a bit and instructed all the men and boys to move to the back in order to let the women and girls move up to the front. In that moment of deep grief, I shouted that the children needed to stay with us, and I clung tightly to the son by my side. At that moment, it would have been unbearable to have him separated from me. My comment was immediately understood, and he

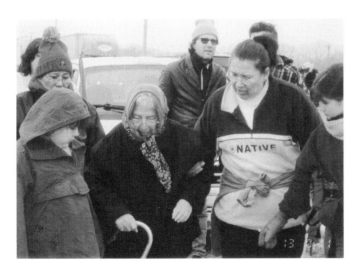

Pictured in the front are Naomi Pigeon, Naomi Cavender, Marisa Pigeon, and Autumn Wilson. In the back are Bev Waditaka and Craig Marsden. Dakota elder Naomi Cavender, her granddaughter Marisa, and her great-granddaughter Naomi Pigeon are all descendants of Wicanhpi Ota Win (Many Stars Women) who was on the original march in 1862. Naomi Cavender took the first steps for the marchers on November 7, 2002, as we left the Lower Sioux Reservation. She also started our walk on the last day of the march near Savage, Minnesota, where this photo was taken.

The front of the group as we headed toward Fort Snelling within a few miles of the Mendota bridge on the last day of the march. A quiet descended on the group at this point.

clarified that the women and children were to step forward and the men were to move to the back.

The movement of all the men to the back contributed its own effect in our reliving of this traumatic event. In that moment of vulnerability and in tremendous physical and emotional pain, the protective shield of our men was removed. We, the women and children, were made further vulnerable as we marched the final two miles to the fort, feeling waves, if only for brief moments, of the same loneliness and defenseless that our grandmothers felt before us.

We began the long walk across the Mendota Bridge, which goes right to the top of the bluff where Fort Snelling sits. The beautiful river valley spreads out below, and this was the first view we saw as we began to move across the bridge. Perhaps it was this beauty that made the harshness and cruelty of the imposing fort all the more apparent when it finally came into view. As I continued to weep and shudder, I kept thinking about this contrast.

For the Dakota, this area of Minisota Makoce is a sacred site. We refer to it as *Bdote* (now called Mendota), which literally means the joining or juncture of two bodies of water. There are many places where this occurs, but we were taught that the primary bdote is here where the Minnesota River joins the Mississippi River. Fort Snelling sits atop a bluff with an amazing view of this bdote. It is sacred because it is here that the Bdewakantunwan Dakota creation story places the origin of our first people, where thousands of years ago our first ancestors were created from the land. The irony of having a United States military fort located on one of our most sacred sites would not have been lost on the women and children who made this march in 1862. They, too, must have felt the love and power of this sacred land as they approached it on November 13, 1862. It must have been a source of strength, until they realized that this was where they would live and die in the coming months under cannons and within walls. The horror of a concentration camp imprisoning our own people on this sacred land hit me profoundly, marking me deeply as I made my way to the fort.

In the haze of my emotions on the bridge, I remember hearing the trilling (or li-li's as they were later referred to) of a woman below. I learned later this was Lisa Bellanger, who sent out four calls like this in support of the marchers. Hearing those sounds of strength and support intensified my emotions in a different way. They somehow conveyed a sense of endurance, resiliency, and hope amidst the grief and despair. As we continued to walk, I also felt a growing sense of strength emerging from our own fierce sense of survival. We were honoring not just the survival of those who were forced to walk in 1862 but also, seven generations later, the survival of Dakota people, the survival of our stories about 1862, and the survival of our commitment to reclaim our rightful place on this earth.

The walk down to the site of the Dakota concentration camp was slow, and the sound of women weeping was still prevalent. When we got to the edge of where the encampment would have been, Alameda broke down, and several of us stopped to offer her comfort and support. As we were the last group to enter the memorial area, I unfortunately missed the welcome song sung by Art Owen. Those who heard it said it was beautiful. I was happy, however, to see so many people now gathered in support of this commemorative event.

We kept the closing ceremonies brief, yet there were some things that we needed to take care of. One final stake needed to be planted, the sage wreath needed to be dedicated, and the pipestone marker made years ago by Amos Owen, Art's father, was to be rededicated. It was clear that the

spirits had followed us all the way to the end, as many people saw blue lights among us. Moreover, the way things came together at the closing indicated the spirits' presence as well. As I mentioned, we were less than precise in planting the stakes, especially at first, and the 150-mile figure was simply our best estimate. With two miles left to go to the fort, we realized that we had two stakes left. We could not have planned it more perfectly. So our first task after they placed the pipestone marker in its casing at the memorial was to plant the last stake and read the name aloud. Phyllis Redday, Gaby, and Alameda had gone to the front of the memorial site to help with these last tasks, and they were standing there when the last stake name was read: Anpetu Sa, the Dakota translation of Phyllis's last name, Redday (Red Day). As it had happened a few other times when stakes were planted in the presence of a descendent of the person named on the stake, this stake broke and had to be mended with an additional strip of red cloth. Phyllis was present to offer prayers specifically for her relatives. Then it came time to dedicate the wreath. It was placed on top of the circular pipestone marker, and it fit perfectly. Not only that, but it fit perfectly even with the cover of the display casing over it. These are things we did not plan—could not have planned—but they worked out.

After we said prayers, we had an honor song for our ancestors. Then we shook hands with everyone and enjoyed the wonderful meal prepared by women from the urban community. They had our traditional foods of corn soup with buffalo, wild rice, *wozapi* (fruit pudding), and fry bread. It was healing food, soothing to our cold and aching bodies. It was the last meal of buffalo I would have for a while. On this journey, we ate well with

The photo of the pipestone marker and sage wreath was taken in 2003 during our ceremony, feast, and giveaway at Fort Snelling. *(Molly Schoenhoff)*

buffalo soup, buffalo stew, buffalo hot dish, buffalo meatloaf, and even a buffalo Hungarian goulash, which was a first for me. We were all appreciative of the Santee Nation for the privilege of having this traditional and nourishing food every day of the march and for the buffalo who gave his life to feed our people.

We ended the march with a final discussion and closing prayer, primarily among the core group of marchers, which was facilitated by Art Owen. An eloquent speaker and mediator, he gracefully solicited comments and wrapped up with encouraging and supportive words. It was important for many of us to have this opportunity to offer our final comments about the march in a meaningful way and to say good-bye, at least for a while, to those with whom we had shared so much.

While I was looking forward to the hot shower and the rest I had been dreaming about all week, I was also incredibly sad that the event had come to an end. I have since had time to contemplate

that sadness and to clarify the significance of the Commemorative March for me on a personal level. More than anything, I think this experience was about empowerment. We were honoring our ancestors who had not been honored in this way or publicly grieved over; our ancestors had been dismissed in the history books as unfortunate casualties resulting from Dakota violence against White settlers. Despite the physical and emotional hardship—or maybe even because of it—we were taking a hold of our past and controlling our history in a powerful, public effort. We were beginning the process of reclamation, steeped for seven generations in the memory and strength of our ancestors.

◄○►

NOTE

1. George Blue Bird to Angela Cavender Wilson, September 7, 2002, in the author's possession.

A Written Response from Canada

LEO J. OMANI

—◄o►—

Why would someone, a Dakota from Canada, suggest such an honoring of our late Dakota relatives who were force marched 140 years ago from the Lower Sioux Agency in Minnesota to a concentration camp in Fort Snelling, Minnesota? The following comments will provide an insight. It may take a bit of time to read it, but we as Dakota People now have to begin telling our side of the story, so that our Dakota children and grandchildren can truly begin to understand our own Dakota history. The information in this article may appear repetitive at times.[1] This repetition, however, modeled on the traditional Aboriginal style of storytelling with its cyclical learning and communication, is intended to make the information more meaningful, understandable, and accessible to the Dakota people.[2] In addition, I intend to provide an emic, social scientific perspective, referred to as the "insider's" or "native's" perspective of reality.[3] The information I provide is based on the fundamental principles of social scientific inquiry, which includes both oral Eastern Dakota history, specifically the Dakota bloodlines of M'dewakantonwan, Wahpekute, Wahpetonwan, and Sissitunwan, as well as previous written documentation. Thus, the story

of the Dakota Commemorative March is provided from a Dakota perspective.

—◄o►—

First, one needs to know that after the Dakota-U.S. War of 1862, while many of our Dakota relatives were force marched from the Lower Sioux Agency to a concentration camp in Fort Snelling, many others moved back north of the 49th parallel, to the country now known as Canada. Written documentation and Eastern Dakota tribal history reveal that this land has always been a part of the Indigenous tribal homelands of our Dakota People as members of the Oceti Sakowin, or Seven Council Fires.[4] Further, many of our Dakota First Nations in Canada have Pre-Confederation Treaty Medals with the British Crown received in 1763, 1779, and 1812 from King George the III.[5]

Second, through oral history that has been passed down from our Dakota parents, grandparents, and great-grandparents, and more recently through written documentation found in the national archives of Canada, as well as in Minnesota, many of our Dakota People of Canada are now just beginning to find our relatives across the border.[6] For me, I can truly say that this would not have happened if it were not for my tahansi Chris Mato Nunpa, who along with his daughter, my niece Angela, and their families, came from Minnesota to Canada in 1996 looking for their Dakota relatives. To me, this showed courage, for they had done this from their hearts.

Yes, I can say with pride that Tahansi Chris Mato Nunpa, his children, and their families truly understand and have lived up to the Dakota saying *Mitakuye Owasin.*[7] I now understand why my late uncle, Deksi Ernest Goodvoice, passed on the Dakota name Wambditanka[8] (Big Eagle) to me. I say *pidamayaye do* (thank you) to my tahansi and his family for showing me where one of our Dakota heroes, Wanbditanka, is buried adjacent to the Upper Sioux Reservation in Minnesota.

« Yes, the oral family history of our Dakota people passed down from generation to generation is powerful, and what is said is true. »

Yes, we as Dakota do have heroes. In my numerous trips to Minnesota since then, I always stop and offer tobacco at the burial site of my namesake, Wanbditanka (Big Eagle).

Because of my tahansi Chris Mato Nunpa and his family encouragement in seeking out surviving Dakota relatives in Canada, and based on family oral history passed down from my late uncles Robert Goodvoice and Archie Waditika and my late mother, Mahpeya Ku Winyan (Edith Omani), I was able to locate written documentation about my late great-grandfather Anpetu Wasicu, also known as John Sioux, in the national archives of Canada, cited in the 1901 Canadian Census as a U.S. Sioux Indian. Further, I was able to locate written documentation about him at the Minnesota Historical Society, cited in the 1853 M'dewakontonwan and Wahpekute Dakota Treaty Annuity Pay List. Yes, the oral family history of our Dakota People passed down from generation to generation is powerful, and what is said is true. This documentation verified that the bloodline of Anpetu Wasicu is Bdewakantunwan, just as the family oral history indicated. I also want to note that Bdewakantunwan is the Dakota pronunciation and spelling of the English version of the word cited as *M'dewakantonwan* in many Euro-American and Euro-Canadian documents.

Having provided this family history, I can explain why I recommended an honoring of the women and children. I had heard numerous stories of the honoring provided annually for our thirty-eight Dakota men who were hanged in Mankato, Minnesota, on December 26, 1862, in the largest mass execution in United States history, after the Dakota-U.S. War of 1862 was over. This was discussed again at the April 2002 conference held at Southwest Minnesota State University. At that time, it became clear to me that nothing was ever done to honor specifically our Dakota women and children as well as our Dakota grandparents who were force marched 140 years ago from the Lower Sioux Agency in Minnesota to a concentration camp at Fort Snelling. I suggested that perhaps it was time to do something to honor them. After some discussion, it was agreed that we would walk in their honor, thus the Dakota Commemorative March, held November 7–13, 2002, became a reality.

Once the Dakota Commemorative March

began in November of 2002, many stories were told along the way about how our late Dakota relatives, specifically our Dakota women, our Dakota children, and our Dakota grandparents, were treated. It was told by some of the descendants of our late Dakota relatives that many died before reaching Fort Snelling and many more suffered not only from the cold but also from hunger, from beatings, and from having boiling water and rocks thrown at them while traveling through the various towns along the way to Fort Snelling.[9]

This Dakota Commemorative March was also a sacred journey, for we were led by an eagle staff, offered to us by one of the members of the Lower Sioux Reservation. For each of the 150 miles, we planted a stake with a red ribbon tied to it; written on each stake were the names of two of our late Dakota relatives who had made the journey and were held at the concentration camp at Fort Snelling. The women and children of the Sisseton-Wahpeton Sioux Tribe, Lake Traverse Reservation, in South Dakota provided these stakes with red ribbons tied to them. I say "pidamayaye do" to them and to Clifford Canku of the Lake Traverse Reservation for the use of his sacred pipe. For those who participated on this walk, we started each morning with a prayer, and each evening we completed the day with a prayer.

It was an honor for my toska Gerald Standing from Canada to be offered tobacco and given the responsibility to care for the eagle staff, and it was an honor for me to be provided with tobacco and given the responsibility of caring for the stakes with red ribbons tied to them and of ensuring that each was planted for every mile walked on the 150 miles of the Dakota Commemorative

March. For each mile that we planted a stake with a red ribbon, we prayed and called out the name of our late Dakota relatives whose names were written on the stake.

Yes, it was a very sacred journey. In addition to the walkers, I say "pidamayaye do" also to the Redtail Hawk who traveled with us. I say "pidamayaye do" to the Eagle Nation, the Horse Nation, and the sacred little dog, all of whom came to honor us and to protect us from any harm on this walk. I am so proud of everyone who participated in our Dakota Commemorative March. I never previously could bring myself to participate in other commemorative rides and/or walks because there was still too much pain in my heart—in the memory of our Dakota ancestors of Minnesota. I also participated in this Dakota Commemorative March, however, in honor of our late Dakota relatives, originally from Minnesota, who passed away in Canada.

As each stake was planted and a prayer said, I sang a short little song in Dakota, asking Wakan Tanka, our Creator, to take the tobacco being offered and to allow our late Dakota relatives to now go home into the spirit world. Yes, this has truly been a healing journey for me, and I know that my children, Jason, Carla, Terrance, and Charles Omani, as well as my grandchildren, will also be blessed because of our Dakota Commemorative March that we completed. The words on the CD entitled *Tell Your Children: 140th Anniversary of the Dakota Woman's March,* composed by David and Diane Wilson and recorded with the support of the Bird family at Featherstone Studios in South Dakota, does capture the true meaning of the Dakota Commemorative March (see Diane Wilson's essay, "Dakota Homecoming," in this volume).

◄◦►

NOTES

1. Eben Hampton, "Toward a Redefinition of American Indian/Alaska Native Education" (unpublished papers, Saskatchewan Indian Federated College, University of Regina, 1989); Leo J. Omani, "Developing a Process for Conducting Educational Research with the Dakota People of Wahpeton" (master's thesis, University of Saskatchewan, 1992).

2. Omani, "Developing a Process."

3. David M. Fetterman, *Ethnography Step by Step* (Newbury Park, CA: Sage, 1989), 27–139; Omani, "Developing a Process."

4. Gary Anderson, *Little Crow: Spokesman for the Sioux* (St. Paul: Minnesota Historical Society Press, 1986); Gary Anderson, *Kinsmen of Another Kind: Dakota-White Relations in the Upper Missippi, 1650-1862* (St. Paul: Minnesota Historical Society Press, 1997); Peter D. Elias, "The Dakota Documents" (unpublished manuscript, Lily Plain, SK: The Dakota Association of Canada; Prince Albert: Saskatchewan Indian Federated College, Northern Campus, 1980); Peter D. Elias, *The Dakota of the Canadian Northwest: Lessons for Survival* (Winnipeg: University of Manitoba Press, 1988); Sam Buffalo, a total of four (4) documented oral interview transcripts of the late Sam Buffalo, Wahpeton Dakota Indian Reserve, Saskatchewan, Canada, Saskatchewan Archives, Indian History Film Project, Saskatchewan Archives Board, Regina, 1977; Robert Goodvoice, a total of ten (10) documented oral interviews of the late Robert Goodvoice, Wahpeton Dakota Indian Reserve, Saksatchewan, Canada, Saskatchewan Archives, Indian History Film Project, Saskatchewan Archives Board, Regina, 1977; Simon Hanska, *Summary of one (1) documented oral interview transcript of the late Simon Hanska, Birdtail Dakota Indian Reserve, Manitoba, Canada*, in *The Canadian Sioux*, by James H. Howard (Lincoln: University of Nebraska Press 1984); George Bear, *Summary of one (1) documented oral interview transcript of the late George Bear, Birdtail Dakota Indian Reserve, Manitoba, Canada*, in Royal B. Hassrick, *The Sioux: Life and Customs of a Warrior Society* (Norman: University of Oklahoma Press, 1964); Howard, *The Canadian Sioux*; Gontran Laviolette, *The Dakota Sioux in Canada* (Winnipeg; DLM Publications, 1991); William K. Powers, *Oglala Religion* (Lincoln: University of Nebraska Press, 1975); Allen Ross, *Mitakuye Oyasin, "We are all related," America Before Columbus, based on the oral history of 33 tribes* (Wiconi Waste, Box 48005, Denver, CO 80248, 1989).

5. Robert S. Allen, *His Majesty's Indian Allies: British Indian Policy in the Defense of Canada, 1774–1815* (Toronto: Dundurn Press, 1992); Elias, "The Dakota Documents": Elias, *The Dakota of the Canadian Northwest*; S. Antal, *A Wampum Denied: Procter's War of 1812* (Ottawa: Carlton University Press, 1997).

6. The National Archives of Canada, *The 1901 Census, Anpetu Wasicu, also known as John Sioux, noted as a U.S. Sioux Indian*; Minnesota Historical Society, *Anpetu Wasicu/John Sioux cited in the 1853 M'dewakontonwan and Wahpekute Dakota Treaty Annuity Pay List.*

7. A. Ross, *Mitakuye Oyasin.*

8. The name of Big Eagle can be spelled several different ways in Dakota: Wamditanka, Wambditanka, or Wanbditanka. We have chosen the latter here because it is consistent with the orthography used in the rest of the collection.

9. Angela Cavender Wilson, "Grandmother to Granddaughter: Generations of Oral History in a Dakota Family," in *Natives and Academics: Researching and Writing about American Indians*, ed. Devon A. Mihesuah (Lincoln: University of Nebraska Press, 1998).

A Living Memorial

MOLLY SCHOENHOFF

━◦━

Last November, on my first visit to the state of Minnesota, I spent several hours in the corner of a small antique shop in downtown St. Paul sorting through wooden boxes of random postcards, old family photographs, and discarded tourist ephemera, most of which depicted images and information about regional sites. There was an oversized postcard presenting a map of "MINNESOTA ARROWHEAD COUNTRY, THE GREAT MID-CONTINENTAL RECREATIONAL REGION OF AMERICA—FOR THOSE WHO SEEK THE TONIC OF THE WILDERNESS." There was a brochure promoting the Mount Rushmore National Memorial, indicating the monument's proximity to a road named for General Custer. Another brochure beckoned the reader to "ENJOY MYSTERY CAVE, MINNESOTA'S LARGEST CAVE—ALWAYS 47 DEGREES—A NEVER TO BE FORGOTTEN MEMORY FOR THE WHOLE FAMILY—SEE THE FASCINATING MARVELS OF NATURE'S HANDIWORK AS COURTEOUS AND INFORMATIVE GUIDES ESCORT YOU THROUGH THE SPACIOUS, ELECTRICALLY LIGHTED CORRIDORS OF MYSTERY CAVE." One of the family photographs depicted a man posing before a war memorial; another group portrait appeared to have been taken at a summer picnic.

The women sat next to one another on chairs, hands folded neatly across their laps, stocking-clad legs crossed at the ankles. The men stood behind them, wearing straight ties and cardigans and smiling through spectacles. An impression on the back of the photograph indicated that the picture was taken in 1946.

At one time these artifacts might have evoked in me a certain nostalgia, an appreciation for their narrative tone and their reference to the trappings of the early American Midwest. Today, however, they evoke a range of sentiments, including betrayal, confusion, dismay, and disgust. The maps and photographs, the brochures and the tourist attractions they promote—all tell stories about a stolen land and a place contrived by White settlers and their descendants, of whom I am one, and with whom I am connected.

I had come to Minnesota to witness and participate in an event commemorating the removal of Dakota People from their homeland after the U.S.-Dakota War of 1862. The event was called Manipi Hena Owas'in Wicunkiksuyapi, which means "We remember all those who walked." It would end at Fort Snelling, yet another historic site: a military outpost from the 1820s that also served as a postwar concentration camp for Dakota people.[1] In preparation for the event, I read about the war of 1862 and learned that many Minnesotans have called it the "Sioux Uprising" in keeping with the popular myth that the uncivilized bring their troubles upon themselves. Some historic accounts conveyed the familiar sense of entitlement that often accompanies patriotic messages. They carried a didactic "lest we forget" message to those White descendants presumed to inherit the land. Other accounts acknowledged the abuse of power by early White settlers, but did so in a way that tended to excuse those of us who reside in the present. They conveyed regret and remorse along with a sense of distance.

This arms-length acknowledgment makes sense to me. Confronting the realities of my own cultural heritage is complicated by my desire to divorce that heritage and extricate myself from the legacy of the White settler. Western concepts of time and place make this selective attachment seem possible. In dominant White culture, place is objectified through maps and representations. Land is property and spectacle. Time is a series of events, and the past is as malleable as our record of it; images and artifacts evidence the truth. We tend to display that which affirms our existence, and hide, disown, or detach from that which degrades us. We have a contrived orientation to time and a selective orientation to ancestry.

> « In dominant White culture, place is objectified through maps and representations. Land is property and spectacle. . . . We have a contrived orientation to time and a selective orientation to ancestry. »

In November of 2002, a group of Dakota, friends, and supporters gathered together and walked the 150-mile trail that Dakota ancestors walked as prisoners in 1862. The stories about that commemorative march suggest a collapsing of time; those living in the present walked with their ancestors in a gesture of acknowledgment and reclamation that transcended temporal boundaries. At the commemorative event in 2003, a circular memorial suggested inclusion and continuousness. Individual wooden stakes marked with red tobacco ties identified those who had died in 1862. People stood on sacred ground near the source of two rivers for a collective recognition of lives lost and spirit that endures.

The removal of Dakota People from their tribal home altered the course of history, yet it is scarcely recognized in the American public. Few schoolchildren learn that the largest mass execution in United States history was that of thirty-eight Dakota warriors, convicted by white commissioners and sentenced to death by President Lincoln. Relatively few United States citizens are aware that the Dakota were and are a People; more familiar is "Sioux," the name given to Dakota, Nakota, and Lakota nations from the derogatory French and Ojibwa word *nadouessioux*, meaning "little snakes."

It is all too easy to maintain ignorance. Vestiges of the Dakota past are obliterated by signs of progress in present-day Minnesota. The path that Dakota prisoners traveled in 1862 winds alongside the Minnesota River through farms, small towns, and residential subdivisions, on state routes and highways littered with gas stations, garden centers, industrial parks, and strip malls. Commercial and municipal signs tell the story of what this place has become: yankee doodle road, the laura ingalls memorial highway, brooks automotive, little saigon restaurant, the pizza ranch, commerce avenue, welcome to new ulm. Nowhere along the way is this site recognized for what it is to the Dakota People. No postcard or brochure indicates its proximity to other memorials or national sites of interest.

I propose that we honor the Dakota legacy by creating a living memorial that indicates the path of removal. One concept for this memorial involves marking the 150 miles (from the Lower Sioux Agency to Fort Snelling) with Native plants. The primary color of the plants would be red. Red is a sacred color in the Dakota tradition, representing lifeblood and the life of the People. It is always present at Dakota ceremonies, and it is the color typically selected for ceremonial prayer ties. In this memorial, red would also signify bloodshed and loss of life. Red foliage, berries, stems, and leaves would consistently contrast the natural landscape and built environment, but they would change seasonally, referencing the dynamic aspects of both life and memory.

The change in the earth's surface would acknowledge the cultural and physical genocide that accompanied the establishment of the United States. Moreover, it would be a gesture of recla-

mation for the Dakota People—a means of expressing their heritage and deep connection to the place they know as Minisota Makoce. Rather than marking one spot, it would move through space and time. The strand of red would become a part of everyday life for some residents of the Minnesota River valley as they conduct the business of their lives. Travelers would take notice of it and inquire—an action that would encourage the retelling of a story that has long existed in the shadows of dominant narratives about the West. In time, the memorial would attract visitors from other places; over time it would be cared for by generations of people who believe that this is a story worth remembering and preserving.

The story of the ethnic cleansing of the Dakota People challenges the integrity of nationalistic propaganda by acknowledging injustices committed on behalf of American nation building. Planting red Native plants would be an acknowledgment that offers the possibility for a more honest relationship with our past and would be a step toward amending the colonial legacy of which we are all a part.

◄◦►

NOTE

1. The "Historic Fort Snelling" Web site, administered by the Minnesota Historical Society, reads: "The story of Fort Snelling is the story of the development of the U.S. Northwest. While surrounded today by freeways and a large urban population, Fort Snelling was once a lonely symbol of American ambition in the wilderness." (http://www.mnhs.org/places/sites/hfs/history.html, accessed July 18, 2004).

Voices of the Marchers from 2002

WAZIYATAWIN ANGELA WILSON

◄○►

When you start it with a vision, every step that you take should be for a relative . . . every step you take is mitakuye owas'in. [1]

◄ Art Owen (November 13, 2002) ►

The Commemorative March in 2002 transpired through the efforts of hundreds of individuals: those who helped in the planning; those who supported the march either through prayers, monetary, or food donations; those who contributed their time and energy; and those who participated in the commemorative event. Many of these individuals shared their perspectives either while on the march or shortly afterward at one of the gatherings held to discuss the event. While some of these people might not have felt comfortable enough to write an essay to include in this collection, their voices are nonetheless equally important and extremely valuable.

The majority of comments contained in this chapter were transcribed from the tapes I made along the course of the journey, and others came from transcriptions from video or audio recordings of meetings held after the walk. A few others are from newspaper clippings or comments people wrote to me after the event was completed. We felt it was important to try to document as unobtrusively as possible the thoughts and feel-ings of participants, as most of us were deeply affected by our participation and felt transformed by the end of the experience.

WHY WE CAME

Most of the people who ultimately participated felt called to the event, or at least drawn to the event, for a variety of reasons. For some it was because they were distinctly aware of their own lineage and knew they had ancestors who were on the forced march in 1862, or because they were descendants of the condemned men who were moved to Mankato and kept in the concentration camp there. For example, Neil McKay, the Dakota language teacher at the University of Minnesota, commented the evening in New Ulm that it was an honor for him to participate and stated, ◄ *"I'm descended from Sleepy Eye and Cloudman's people. So I have relatives who were on the march and relatives who were on the run during the war also. But I'm doing this also because I'm Dakota, and I know our relatives who went on before us are* proud of what we are doing. And also, so I can tell my children about this, in Dakota." ▶

Marisa Pigeon also had a direct connection to the Dakota on the forced march of 1862. Through tears toward the end of the march, she shared with the group why her family decided to participate: ◀ "We got ready and we knew we wanted to be here for my great-great-grandma. Her name was Wicanhpi Ota Win [Many Stars Woman], that's who my daughter is named after. She was three years old at the time of the march. She'd already lost her parents, so she was with her grandmothers. They carried her most of the way. . . ." ▶ Marisa's voice then trailed off as she was overcome with emotion.

Others were not certain whether they had direct ancestors who were part of the forced march in 1862, but that did not dim their desire to participate. For example, Carol Noel from Beulah, Manitoba, in Canada commented upon first arriving that evening in New Ulm: ◀ "My grandparents were here also. I don't know if they were involved in what happened here. All I know is that they were from here and I want to support them. I want to be here for all those people, the people who had to walk." ▶

Because of the diaspora of our exiled population after 1862, there has not been a way to collectively maintain the body of knowledge surrounding events from this traumatic period in our history. In addition, whether or not an individual today is a direct descendant of someone on the march, Dakota people still have a sense of connection with the sufferings of all our People, the entire Dakota Oyate. The intergenerational trauma and deep feelings of empathy that have perhaps even unconsciously been transferred through the generations became apparent in comments during the march.

Yvonne Bearbull, from the Birdtail Reserve in Manitoba, shared with the group that she was hoping to learn more about the history and possible family connections through her participation in the Commemorative March. She also stated, ◀ "My niece did a presentation at one of the schools. She picked this subject [of the forced march], and when she was talking about what happened to the people who were on the walk, she said she broke down and she didn't even know a lot about it. So she said she wants to interview me when I get back." ▶

Yvonne must have put in close to fifty miles walking during the several days she participated in the march, walking in the footsteps of our ancestors. I am sure she had much to tell her niece upon returning to Canada. Furthermore, in support of our efforts in Minnesota, immediately upon returning to Canada, Yvonne and some of her community members quickly organized a short walk that was held on Saturday, November 13, 2002, the day our group arrived at Fort Snelling. Chris Mato Nunpa read a message that evening from Doris Pratt and Yvonne, who is a councilor for the Birdtail Sioux First Nation, which stated: ◀ "We the students and staff of the Birdtail Sioux School, Birdtail Education Authority, will be walking on November 13, 2002, in support of the Dakota Commemorative March from Lower Sioux to Fort Snelling. Our local march will be from the nearby community of Beulah, Manitoba, to our home community of Birdtail Sioux, a distance of approximately eight kilometers or five miles. The walk will commence at 1:00 P.M. We commend you on your dream of realizing the march of Dakota relatives and supporters." ▶

Our Canadian relatives were with us in spirit on this journey. Eunice Bear also organized a walk on the Standing Buffalo First Nation Reserve in Saskatchewan to support our commemorative efforts in Minnesota.

Overall, we had a strong Canadian delegation on the walk. Four of the eight Dakota Canadian Reserves were represented. Their commitment to their ancestors was apparent in their devotion to participation in this march. Doris Pratt, from the Sioux Valley Reserve in Manitoba, came with Carol Noel and Yvonne Bearbull. She clearly identified with this as a women's march, stating: ◀ *"A lot of them were women who were on that march. It was a long and tortuous and painful journey for them, and November is not the nicest month. Often it is cold and you just don't know what to expect from the weather, but we wanted to come and take part in that. . . . We are women and we have children and grandchildren. I thought it was fitting that women should come."* ▶

Others made the long trip from Canada, even from the Dakota Reserve the farthest away. In addition to Leo Omani and Gerald Standing, who were there from beginning to end, another delegation from the Wahpeton Dakota Reserve outside of Prince Albert, Saskatchewan, also made the journey back to Minnesota for the march, including Bev Waditaka, Dale Standing, Bernice Waditaka, and Yvonne Waditaka. Like many of us, they had little idea about what to expect once they arrived and experienced some anxiety regarding the march. Bev explained to those present in Mankato after her first day of walking: ◀ *"I didn't know what to expect when we came . . . on this walk. I've heard it before. I met Chris and Angela many times prior to this, and I was glad when*

I came in. When I first came through the doors, the first people I saw were from back home. My brother Leo and my nephew Gerald were sitting there. And it gave me a good feeling at that point, and then this morning I was kind of feeling weary about going on the walk. I'm not a physical person at all. I was kind of scared, I guess. I was starting to walk, and I started running and stuff because I had to catch up to you guys already, first thing this morning. And by the time I caught up with you, my heart was just racing, really racing hard. And I was thinking in my mind, I don't know if I'm going to be able to do this. But as we started walking, I started calming down. I started feeling the serenity of the things around me. At that one point, I really thought there was something mysterious about this walk." ▶

Dale Standing also commented that he was participating to get more information about where his family came from. It was clear that for many of us, the desire to connect with our People and to achieve a sense of unity was and is a powerful driving force.

Many who participated were seeking greater understanding. David Wilson, for example, and his sister Diane were part of the core group of marchers. With David's long legs and quick pace, we gave him the eagle feather staff to lead us when we needed to make good time with the miles. David and Diane's great-grandmother was from Lower Sioux, a Dakota woman married to a French-Canadian man. Together they have been working on a family history that Diane is writing. As David explained, ◀ *"What we're trying to do is tell my mother's story, and by doing that, by making these miles with these people here, it gives us a sense of who our relatives are, who we're really*

Dale Standing (carrying the eagle feather staff), Bev Waditaka, and Bernice Waditaka, part of the Canadian delegation from the Wahpeton Reserve near Prince Albert, Saskatchewan.

talking about. . . . *The walk these past five days or so has really given us a feel for the kind of people our family lived with, dealt with, cried with, and ate with."* ▶

Diane commented further, ◀ *"One of the things I've tried to understand is what it would be like for a Dakota woman married to a white man with mixed-blood children, with family inside the fort and family outside—what that would be like in the middle of the war."* ▶

Because of the factionalism within the Dakota community, many of our People today have ancestors on all sides of the war: those who fought against White oppression, those who fought alongside Whites against their fellow Dakota, those who fled, and those who were forcibly removed. As a writer, Diane was particularly concerned with the devastation this factionalism wreaked on the Dakota community. In that context, the march takes on new meaning. She explained at the end of the seven days, ◀ *"For me this march has everything to do with healing that rift, that division that occurred in the 1862 war and everything that followed it."* ▶

The loss of extended family because of the events of 1862 was an issue that Leo Omani from the Wahpeton Reserve in Saskatchewan also addressed. In the last several years, he has made connections to family from whom he has been separated by a huge geographical distance. This is the legacy left for all of us—for all the descendants whose divided People have not known one another for several generations. In the last few years, Deksi Leo connected with Naomi Cavender, a relation of his through his grandfather John Sioux. At the end of each day, he frequently talked about various topics as the marchers gathered, but one evening he spoke specifically about this newfound relative and how he felt about sharing the experience of the march with her. He described his reaction when he came out of the sweat lodge Wednesday night before the march began: ◀ *"We come out and I saw my relative there, Kunsi Naomi, 88 years old.[2] One of her great-grandchildren was sitting here, going to camp outside. Oh it's cold this time of year, it's cold. . . . When we were leaving, we noticed the daughter and granddaughter loading stuff into the pop-tent, and we thought she was going to go camp far away, you know, go back home to Granite Falls. Showed up the next morning, you* wouldn't believe it, an 88-year-old woman slept in that pop-tent. That's to honor her relatives. When we got to Thursday morning [the morning the march started], she was the first to lead in honor of her relatives. Her grandmother was out there at Fort Snelling. . . .

"And I got kind of lonesome for my relatives over here, her daughter and granddaughter and great-grandchildren when they left yesterday.[3] I went around all day, wondering when they were going to come back. Then when we were going into this last town here where our people suffered [Henderson], all of a sudden a mile or two off the interstate, a big van came, and there were my relatives. I had to give her a hug, I was so happy to see her here. Those kinds of things are important. For us, our families have been torn apart. We don't know where they are, a lot of us don't know or are scared to ask. A lot of times growing up, we were punished for wanting to learn our language, wanting to keep our traditions alive, so we've held that inside, and that pain is hard to bring out. And this is what's happening to us." ▶

Thus, while it was clear that we were all participating to remember our ancestors and the suffering they endured on the march back in 1862, it was equally clear that the sense of hurt and pain from that event was intertwined with all the hurt and pain we have felt from the loss of connection to our relatives, to the suppression of our stories and culture, and the distances we now have to travel to come together. However, when we do come together, the strength that we gain from one another is also apparent.

After we arrived in Henderson on the evening of November 10, 2002, we shuttled people back to Gustavus Adolphus where we had our evening meal. Once there, Bill Means (Lakota) shared with us one of his reasons for participating on the march: ◀ "And when you say, why do you come here? I have a good reason. I have a grandson now who is from the Lower Sioux Reservation. His grandma is a Wabasha and his grandpa is Barry. And so I'm representing him here today. His name is Mato Itancan, and he received his name in Lower Sioux about two years ago, a year and a half ago. So that's the reason why I'm here." ▶

Bill then told the group of marchers and faculty, staff, and students from Gustavus who were all gathered there: ◀ "But also because throughout my lifetime I've been on a few walks and marches, rides, and takeovers, so in case you didn't know . . . we're not leaving here!" ▶ Given Bill Means's history with activism and take-overs, this comment was greeted with much laughter by the audience.

As organizers of the march, we also had our reasons for participating and for sharing our stories with one another and with the non-Dakota people along the way. After explaining to those gathered at Gustavus that they were all participating in a historic event, given that it was the first time in 140 years that Dakota people had come as a group to meet with people from Henderson and talk about the events of 1862, I also explained the rationale behind the organization of the march: ◀ "The current social crisis (we have high rates of alcoholism, we have high rates of abuse, we have high rates of depression, high rates of suicide, high rates of chemical dependency), from our perspective, is a consequence of colonization. These things are a consequence of having our lands invaded, of being dispossessed from our lands, and having a policy of genocide or ethnocide perpetrated against us in a very systematic way. . . . And so when we were thinking about all of these problems, our thinking was that we need to do some healing ourselves, and we need to come to terms with some of these injustices. We need to come to terms with the violence that was perpetrated against us, because I think many of us today carry a great deal of what we might call historical grief—pain that hasn't been reconciled for all of the injustices perpetrated against us. So we were talking about 1862. How much has been left unsaid? How many stories have been untold? And we thought it was important that we get our People together to talk about these stories, talk about them openly in an honest way with one another, most importantly, but also as a secondary consideration, with the non-Dakota public in Minnesota. And so it was my uncle's idea here to have a commemorative march for the women and children, primarily, who were forcibly removed." ▶

Kathryn Akipa from Sisseton, South Dakota, also recognized the importance of our People telling our stories. When she joined us at the end of the day in Mankato, and we said prayers down by the hanging site of the thirty-eight, she appealed to all of us there, saying, ◀ "Anybody who has a story in their family to tell, please don't forget to pass that down to the young ones, because if we forget our traditions, our culture, our language, all those things that make us who we are, then what do we become if we have nothing to pass on?" ▶ Rather than becoming like Wasicus with brown skin, she went on to state that it was very important that we pass these things on while also giving honor to our ancestors.

Many people commented that they knew as soon as they heard about it that they wanted to participate. For example, Dottie Whipple first heard about the Commemorative March at the Morton Powwow. She said, ◀ "When I heard about it, I thought this is something that I need to do." ▶ Dottie participated as often as she could, given her other commitments, and she made our hearts glad whenever she and her husband, Harlan, joined us. Dottie emits a sense of serenity and quiet strength, which was a blessing on our long walk. This painful period of removal is one that Dottie had contemplated before. In a letter she sent to me after the march, she told me that she and her son Alan had previously retraced the route taken on the second phase of removal from Fort Snelling to Crow Creek, South Dakota. Dottie and Harlan understand the importance of this connection to our past and to our ancestors.

In other instances, whole families participated together, and this was beautiful to witness. Sharon Odegard from the Upper Sioux Reservation in Minnesota joined the march with her mother, Irene Howell, and her daughter, Samantha Odegard. They were another three-generation family, all women, who spent as much time with us as their work schedules would allow. Sharon commented after it was completed, ◀ "It had to be done, and it was a good time for it to be done so that we don't forget who we are or where we came from." ▶

In addition to the Dakota people who participated in the march, many non-Dakota came to walk with us or to support the march in some way. As the march was still being conceptualized, those of us who were organizing it knew that there were some key issues to address. One of the issues we examined was to what extent we wanted to attempt to heal relations between the Dakota and Wasicu communities in Minnesota. Chris Mato Nunpa would remind non-Native people about our history and why we were walking. He frequently would open the evening with remarks such as these from New Ulm: ◄ *"For the benefit of our Euro-American relatives, this is a commemorative march in honor of the 1,700 Dakota, primarily women, children, and elders, who were force marched from the Lower Sioux Community to the concentration camp at Fort Snelling. That's a hard word to listen to, concentration camp, because it brings up images of Hitler and Nazi Germany, but that's what they did here in the U.S. We've got two concentration camps here in Minnesota, one at Mankato and one at Fort Snelling. Politically and militarily, we were conquered in the 1862 Dakota-U.S. War, but spiritually we still feel that we are owners of this land."* ►

In our Commemorative March of 2002, these were things that needed to be said, but our saying them so clearly perhaps distinguished the event from other reconciliatory events. For example, a major goal of the Year of Reconciliation, declared in 1987 by then-governor Rudy Perpich, was the healing of Dakota-White relationships in the state of Minnesota. Marking 125 years since the U.S.-Dakota War of 1862, the Year of Reconciliation was designed on the belief that, through a series of workshops, symposiums, public dialogues and events, the hurt and anger surrounding the memory of 1862 would at last be laid to rest or at least that significant strides would be made in that direction. Perpich stated, "We discover by reconciling our past, we find ways to build our futures together." Nearly twenty years later, it is apparent that the Year of Reconciliation did not meet this goal. At the conclusion of the 1987 activities, some people recognized how much these efforts fell short of what was needed.

For example, David Larson from the Lower Sioux Reservation near Morton, Minnesota, stated that he and others on the reservation were glad the year was finally over, since they continued to feel angry and bitter that White history was still blaming Indians. Similarly, Vernell Wabasha expressed that the whole idea was "a farce."[4]

Even the Dakota Studies Committee (DSC), chaired by Chris Mato Nunpa (then Chris Cavender), which had conceived of the idea of the Year of Reconciliation and sponsored many of the activities, ended the year on a discouraging note. The committee had passed a resolution, along with many other organized groups, requesting an apology from the Minnesota Historical Society (MHS) for their shameful treatment of the remains of Chief Little Crow, the leader of Dakota resistance in 1862, which they displayed and held at the museum for 108 years before finally returning them for reburial in 1971. The DSC believed that in the spirit of reconciliation, 1987 provided an opportune time for the MHS to redress this wrong and perhaps even erect a special monument to Little Crow. The MHS had participated in other Year of Reconciliation activities, including a series of public programs they cosponsored with the Dakota Studies Committee. In spite of this outward sign of support, the request for an apology revealed how little the Historical Society was willing to take institutional responsibility for their part in the oppression of Dakota People. The MHS adamantly refused to issue an apology and, in fact, was so angered by Chris Mato Nunpa's efforts to advocate for an apology that he remains persona non grata at the society.

We kept these issues in mind as we began planning for the Dakota Commemorative March, and we realized that healing with the White community was a long way from realization. We also discussed the fact that reconciliation can occur only if a peaceful, solid relationship existed previously and if oppression was not current. Elizabeth Cook-Lynn's question regarding the ongoing celebration of L. Frank Baum, the author of the *Wizard of Oz* who advocated the complete extermination of Indigenous Peoples in 1890–91, is directly applicable to the situation in Minnesota, where perpetrators of genocide are still celebrated: "With genocide the historical answer to the question of the unwanted presence of the first occupants of this country, why would anyone think that 'reconciliation' would be easy or even possible in our time?"[5]

In discussing the events of 1862, those of us organizing the march agreed that the notion that peacefulness or a solid relationship of friendship had been created between the Dakota and the non-Dakota prior to 1862 was a myth. While we all will ultimately strive toward peaceful relations with the non-Dakota community, we realized that our first goals must be reconciliation among our own people as well as healing our own people and that these goals must necessarily occur independently of our interactions with the non-Dakota community. With this in mind, we felt we needed an opportunity to gather together, to share our stories with one another amidst an environment of support and love, and to bridge the distances separating our People, both temporally and ethereally.

At the same time, however, most of us involved in the planning felt that education would be a powerful instrument in achieving reconciliation among our own people and, eventually, in finding healing with the non-Native community. Thus sharing our stories about the 1862 Death March would help us educate one another about our collective history as well as provide an opportunity for the Wasicu people present to share our pain, to feel a sense of empathy with our people, and perhaps to move them toward taking responsibility for their part in the ongoing subjugation and oppression of Dakota people.

This is not to suggest that the non-Dakota population of Minnesota today is responsible for the actions of White Minnesotans in 1862, including the ethnic cleansing of the state. In no way can they be penalized for the actions of the people of 1862, even if they are direct descendants of those early invaders and settlers. Every Minnesotan today, however, has benefited from the policies of extermination and ethnic cleansing that occurred during 1862 and the subsequent years, and no restitution has been made to the Dakota People. In fact, Minnesotans today participate in the ongoing celebration of Dakota extermination and dispossession, if only through their silence and complacency. Until there is justice, there can be no true peace.

When the issue of injustice arises, people often make the claim, "I didn't know." Desmond Tutu described this phenomenon among the White population in South Africa who benefited from apartheid but at the same time claimed ignorance of its horrors and injustice. After the Truth and Reconciliation Commission of South Africa revealed the heinous crimes perpetrated under the system of apartheid, he stated, "No one in South Africa could ever again be able to say, 'I did not know,' and hope to be believed."[6] We must bring the same attention to the injustices perpetrated against the Dakota as well as to how the colonization process is still implemented and enforced. Through education, we want to remove ignorance as a justification for a lack of justice. This we cannot achieve without the assistance of non-Dakota people.

Two key non-Dakota individuals were instrumental in the organization of the Commemorative March, and both are people who have embraced the history and past and now see the pursuit of justice as a necessary part of their own privilege. Mary Beth Faimon and Steve Rasmussen are both faculty members at Southwest Minnesota State University (SMSU) in Marshall, Minnesota, and worked ceaselessly with us to arrange food and lodging. As campus Lutheran minister, Steve used his connections with the church communities to find lodging for us in the small towns along the march, and Mary Beth helped to follow up on a lot of his leads. In addition, Mary Beth mobilized students on their campus, the social work students in particular, to help make lunches for the marchers. In many ways, people like Mary Beth and Steve served as conscientious and ethical models for the White population with whom we were trying to negotiate. This did not always place them in a good position.

For example, when making arrangements in the town of New Ulm, Steve received an email from a fellow clergyman who seemingly wanted to help but expressed concern about the planning of the march. For example, one man had contacted someone from the Lower Sioux Reservation, and because that person did not know about the

« THROUGH EDUCATION, WE WANT TO REMOVE THE EXCUSE OF IGNORANCE AS A JUSTIFICATION FOR A LACK OF JUSTICE. »

march, he raised the question of whether or not the event was being talked about sufficiently inside the Dakota bands. In addition, the group at New Ulm was concerned about the "lack of clarity about who is driving the project." They felt they had the "ability to show hospitality," but they also expected that at the end of the weekend, an understanding and reconciliation between American Indian Peoples and the people of New Ulm would have been achieved. Steve forwarded these concerns to the Dakota members of the planning group for suggestions on how to address them and then continued to serve as the liaison with that community. He had far more patience in addressing these issues than some of us.

We first had to make very clear that the focus of this march is on the healing of Dakota people, not on the White townspeople. Our feeling was that we would appreciate it if they wanted to support the march, but we would not accept their contributions at the cost of the truth. We needed to address racism and oppression where we were seeing it. I pointed out to Steve the absurdity and ignorance involved in assuming that any Dakota person they talk to should be aware of the event. Would they assume that they could call any White person in Minnesota to find out about any given activity taking place within the state? Furthermore, would they expect every Minnesotan to support an event? Those expectations would be considered ridiculous, but when they are applied to a whole nation of people, they are also racist.

In fact, we had notified all the tribal councils

in Dakota communities in the United States and Canada about the event, and some were better than others about getting the word out to their own communities. In addition, in various communities on the Dakota powwow circuit over the summer, we put brochures on all the vehicles, made announcements, and had planning meetings. Furthermore, announcements were made in many of the tribal newspapers. Lower Sioux, in fact, was the first community to come through with a major monetary donation, and their donation remained our largest. We are all extremely grateful to them. In the future we hope to create more publicity for the event and do a better job of getting the word out, but we did the best we could for the 2002 event with the resources we had. Fortunately, Steve was able to take my response to these concerns and patiently and kindly filter them to keep negotiations as productive as possible. This was one example of the ways in which Steve and Mary Beth intervened on our behalf, diffusing tensions and serving as trusted mediators.

During our evening discussion in New Ulm, Steve shared with us how he viewed the situation, saying, ◀ *"The history that we share in this Minnesota River valley is a joint history. It is not a history that is just White, it is not a history that is just Dakota, it is a history that is our history. Though we stand on opposite sides, there are within us, and within those who surround us, deep memories. How we shape ourselves in the future is determined by how we understand ourselves in the past. In the book that I spend a lot of time reading, it says 'The sins of the fathers are visited upon the children to the third and fourth generation.' Now we are in the seventh generation, but oftentimes, if*

we do not deal with those issues, they continue and continue and continue." ▶

Though advocating a healing among all of our People, Steve was clearly aware that issues must first be addressed. He further commented on the spiritual aspect of the march that was so important to those of us who were walking for our ancestors, ◀ *"It is important that we pray that there be divine space for healing in the midst of this and that those spirits that surround us might be appeased and might be themselves brought together in peace."* ▶

As a social worker dedicated to social justice, Mary Beth came at the issue from a slightly different perspective. Modeling an honesty and openness about her own family's participation in Dakota subjugation, she told the group at New Ulm: ◀ *"My great-grandmother was born in Marysville, which is near Jordan, in 1861. I don't know any stories, but they weren't newcomers to Minnesota, and my great-grandmother was born here in Minnesota. The point of that is that I'm the fourth generation from there, and I think that does play a part in why I'm doing this, more than I've given thought to before—how important it is for German people with German ancestry to acknowledge, to admit, to look to the past in this shared history."* ▶

But Mary Beth was also aware of her role as a social worker and the significance of the Commemorative March from that perspective. "Dealing with and understanding historical grief and the healing that is necessarily important—addressing that is a part of my profession." She then went on to explain that part of the code of ethics she sees for the profession includes justice, mercy, and charity.

As a non-Dakota, Mary Beth could also share an insight with other non-Dakota that would be difficult for Dakota people to bring to their attention. She described to the townspeople gathered at New Ulm that a few years earlier she had traveled to Australia with colleagues and students from SMSU. She happened to be in Alice Springs when they were having an "I'm sorry" Day. She described how all of the stores had books in which White Australians could sign their names attesting to the fact that they were sorry for what their ancestors had done to Aboriginal Australians. This is an important idea, and one that is a necessary step in seeking justice and establishing peace between the Dakota and non-Dakota Peoples. Mary Beth then commented, ◄ *"I think all of us have an obligation, and this is my belief, that this is a shared history, and to deny the perspective of another person's history is just wrong. We need to listen better. We need to get rid of the ways that close our ears and say it didn't happen that way, because we don't want to hear how it happened."* ►

Similarly, one of the social work students, Deb Bottelberghe, explained: ◄ *"I don't know if any of my relatives were directly involved with anything that took place in 1862, but I just feel that being a Euro-American, if I don't take some sort of stand and come to terms with things myself and let people that I'm in contact with and my family know about all the lies that we've been taught in history, you know, from the government and our educational systems, I am just as guilty as the people who actually were there and involved in it."* ►

Once non-Dakota have come to this place or have achieved this understanding, we have a basis from which to work. Continuing on about the relevance of Dakota accounts regarding this event, as well as the way the truth is often covered up by governmental officials, she stated, ◄ *"I*

don't want to just sit and not do something about it. I feel like I need to be involved in things and just speak the truth." ►

Lisa Elbert, a non-Dakota who has developed proficiency in the Dakota language through the program at the University of Minnesota, participated in several days of the march, walking, driving, and helping to shuttle people back and forth between stops. At the end of the event she commented, ◄ *"A lot of problems come from people just being ignorant. I'm Wasicu. I don't have any Dakota ancestors. I don't have ancestors who were ever oppressed as far as I know. I've grown up with White privilege, and Wasicus take that for granted. I wish more Wasicus would know about this kind of history."* ►

For many of the people who heard our stories during the Commemorative March, it was the first time they had heard this history. Their reaction was often one of shock. Donna Nieckula, faculty at SMSU, stated, ◄ *"The biggest part of the experience was learning—not knowing the history and that sense of being denied the knowledge—and finally starting to piece things together and realizing how much more I don't know."* ►

When experiences are purposely suppressed, it is because those in power benefit from their suppression. It seems that it is difficult for many White Minnesotans to conceive of themselves as a privileged class or as people in power, preferring instead to think of themselves in humbler terms. However, as they remain the colonizing class in a place where Dakota people still face subjugation, whether they realize it or not, they have become complicit in that subjugation, taking for granted their occupation of Dakota homeland. As Michel-Rolph Trouillot points out, "The ultimate mark of power may be its invisibility; the ultimate challenge, the exposition of its roots."[7] Thus, our job is to relentlessly seek to expose those roots.

Some of the people who came out to join us in the evenings also told stories about the war. Some of them reveal the complexity of Dakota-White relations in the mid-nineteenth century. For example, Darla Gebhard, who joined us at Turner Hall in New Ulm, relayed that her Aunt Hilda told her that ◀ *"Dakota people came and warned us [about the start of the 1862 war], and that's what saved our lives."* ▶ Darla then proceeded to thank us, as descendants of those Dakota people, for that. She shared another more painful story as well, this one from her Uncle Albert: ◀ *"My Uncle Albert said my great-grandfather, his grandfather, used to take him fishing down by the river. And he said one time when we were fishing, Grandpa said, 'I still have nightmares from the Dakota War.' The nightmares came because he came with Flandreau from St. Peter and was involved in the second battle. And he said the nightmares came from picking up the dead bodies off the fields. And as an old man he still had nightmares."* ▶

Darla went on to say that she hoped we could find some common ground and common understanding so that relations could improve among all of our Peoples. Others, like Tom Sanders who has had extensive interaction with Dakota people through his position at the Jeffers Petroglyph site, stated enthusiastically, ◀ *"It's making me a new person at the end of the day. That's why I'm here, because I knew it was going to happen and knew I* just wanted to be part of a good thing. I was supposed to do this, no other reason than that." ▶ Tom and his daughter Sara spent several days walking with us that week.

THE SPIRITS

Clifford Canku, our spiritual leader on the march, was very important to us, continuously lifting our spirits with his strength and kindness. His humble description of his role in the march captures the tone he helped set through his prayers and his assistance: ◀ *"On this walk I felt very, very privileged, whatever I could do, I just made myself helpful wherever I could. There are certain things that happened. When we started out, I brought my pipe, and we had a pipe ceremony asking for a safe journey, that nothing would happen, but we asked for the spirits of our ancestors to commune with us, to be with us. That was good, because I walked and I drove and I walked and drove. I felt joyful. I felt real good."* ▶

In spite of the long miles on a chilling journey, most of us who participated were uplifted and strengthened through the experience. Many of us would attribute this to the power of prayer and the presence of our ancestors along the way. We were fortunate in that we completed an intensive and arduous event without any serious injuries or problems. We were blessed.

The offerings we made, the tears we shed, and the prayers we said were for the spirits of our ancestors, with the belief that, by helping them, we

> « THE ULTIMATE MARK OF POWER MAY BE ITS INVISIBILITY; THE ULTIMATE CHALLENGE, THE EXPOSITION OF ITS ROOTS. »
> MICHEL-ROLPH TROUILLOT

would also be helping ourselves and future generations. As contemporary Dakota people, we have a major challenge in trying to heal our fractured nation. We viewed this Commemorative March as an important step in that larger process, as we were attempting to repair the cultural damage resulting from our conquest and colonization. On the march, this meant addressing the murder of our women and children by White soldiery and citizens in Minnesota in 1862. Clifford Canku gave an important statement at Henderson about the importance of these events, reminding us that we have a lot of healing and grieving to do. He connected the need for this healing with the interrupted grieving process of 1862, which never allowed our people, either alive or deceased, to go through the appropriate processes: ◀ *"When a person dies, we have a ceremony after one year. After one year, we have what you call a giveaway, we give away all kinds of beautiful things. The reason why we do that is because we give thanks to God for all the blessings and experiences we have here in this realm called Unci Maka, earth. We give thanks and also we release their spirits, so that they could go back to God and to the place where all of our ancestors are, a beautiful place. And so we do that, but we haven't done that with all these relatives who suffered back in 1862–63. And especially along the way, some of them were killed, our relatives were killed. And we still haven't gotten in touch with them personally. So this journey is really a getting in touch with those people who have died and also paying homage to them. So that they would realize that we remember them."* ▶

Chris Mato Nunpa followed his comments. Using post-911 terminology, he reminded everyone that the women and children who suffered in 1862 were civilians and non-combatants: ◀ *"Like in New Ulm, scalding hot water was poured upon our people, some of them were beaten badly, others were beaten to death. Or over here at Henderson, an enraged Euro-American woman took a baby from a Dakota mother's arms and smashed the baby on the ground, and the little baby died. But since they were being force marched, they didn't have time to properly bury the little baby, so they placed the baby in the crotch of a tree, sang a brief song and prayer, and then they had to go, never to see the relative, that little loved one again. I myself had a great-grandmother whose stomach was slit open by a saber by a soldier on horseback, and again, our relatives never saw that body. Things like that happened. My koda[8] Clifford Canku was talking about that. We didn't get a chance to properly send them off to the next time and place. We didn't get a chance to say the appropriate prayers, or the songs, or the ceremonies, so some of this that we're doing is related to that kind of thing. It's related to part of the healing for us as Dakota People."* ▶

Dakota people today carry the grief from the terrible suffering endured by our ancestors leading up to 1862 and continuing to the present day, and so we are now trying to resume that interrupted grieving process. The descendants of those who died without having the proper ceremonies performed for them faced ongoing distress and anxiety. This is echoed by what we see as the distressed spirits of our ancestors. Thus, the healing that must occur for Dakota people transcends the boundaries between the living and the dead and between the present and the past. The healing must occur between our ancestors from 1862 and all the subsequent generations, including our own.

The presence of spirits was thus an important and consistent part of the Commemorative March. Right from the beginning, we had to find our own way. We were unsure about how things would work out, since this 2002 event was the first one. Deksi Leo Omani commented later about the huge responsibility he shouldered after he was asked to take care of the stakes, ◀ *"They gave us some candi [tobacco, saying] 'Every mile we want you to stop.' Wo-ho! I was going to fall over then. With the clutch, eh? We didn't have any Wasicu hammer . . . really unsika [pitiful]. All of a sudden this tunkasida [grandfather] came, right? That beautiful stone, every mile it made it here and it's going home with us to Canada."* ▶

We consider the stones to be our relatives, our grandfathers, as we recognize them as ancient spiritual beings. The stone he found at the beginning was used to pound in every subsequent wooden lathe each mile of our journey. That stone does have a new home in Canada today.

Alameda Rocha, the woman who would serve as our spiritual leader for the second part of the march, was told to come by the water spirits, with whom she shares a special relationship. Clifford, who served as our spiritual leader for the first part of the march, had to leave, and we needed someone to help us. Alameda was the one who was sent, saying later, ◀ *"I knew I had to come."* ▶ However, she wasn't sure exactly where to find us, so she simply headed toward where we were supposed to be traveling that day according to the flyer we had distributed. She conveyed this experience to the group gathered at Henderson with her wonderful sense of humor: ◀ *"I came and I looked for them, and I couldn't find them. What kind of Indian am I? So I said, 'Okay, we'll*

start over again. Grandfather, where are they?' There's an eagle, there they are. Okay. I start going. They're nowhere around. All of a sudden, I felt somebody staring at me. I looked up and there's another eagle, and I followed it. Took that road, come around that bend, and there they were. It was good."* ▶

Operating from a place of compassion and love, Alameda then described what she was generously offering our group, ◀ *"I come to bring myself and my prayers, my support, the love that I have in my heart for my People, for mankind."* ▶

Alameda was not the only one drawn to the march because of the connection to spirits. In Mankato, Kathryn Akipa described the connection many of us feel to our ancestors, ◀ *"It is like we know all of our grandmothers and our grandfathers like people of our family today, but we have never seen their faces, face-to-face."* ▶ She told us her great-great-grandfather Pezi Skuya was one of the Dakota men originally sentenced to execution, but he received a reprieve and was then sent to Davenport, Iowa, where he was kept for a long time. As we were gathered near the hanging site, she said, ◀ *"That's why I'm here tonight—at this place here."* ▶

Leo Omani also had a connection to the thirty-eight who were hanged in Mankato. He shared with us his family's story about an aspect of that tragedy: ◀ *"I come from the oldest bloodline back home. There's seven brothers, and the middle one, he was really small. He was sixteen years old, and the story in the family is that he was one of those who was supposed to be hanged, from the thirty-eight. But there was an old Dakota warrior who stepped forward and took his place. From that point on, my relatives who came down from Wahpeton, they carry that name. The name is Waditaka, Brave. So that's the story we have back home. An old Dakota warrior took the place of this young boy."* ▶ We were all grateful to hear these stories, especially because many of them have been unknown to our Dakota people spread throughout the various reservations and reserves.

On the second day of the march, Doris Pratt, Yvonne Bearbull, and Carol Noel flew in from Canada, arrived at the airport in Minneapolis, and then rode down to New Ulm with Neil McKay. However, they didn't know where we were staying in New Ulm or how to find us; all they knew was that we were somewhere between Sleepy Eye and New Ulm. Doris stated later that evening: ◀ *"We drove here not realizing that none of you have cell phones. In Canada, we can't go without a cell phone. I said, How do you get a hold of them? We're here, but we didn't know where to go and so we went on and on and on. We finally went to Sleepy Eye, then back we came, but we didn't have a clue about where to go. We went driving round and round, but . . . the Great Spirit, he helps us in everything we do, and we just stopped at this hotel, and we went in. And this gentleman over there was standing there getting registered, and we struck up a conversation."* ▶

The gentleman they ran into was "Super Dave" Holm, owner of On-Site Sanitation. Dave was staying at one of the local motels and just happened to be at the front desk when Doris and the others arrived. He was able to direct them to Turner Hall, where we had our evening meal and where some of the marchers spent the night. She said that as they had pulled up to the motel, they had all just been joking about how convenient it was to have a septic and washroom in a

truck so that after dinner they could just head in there and wash their hands. Little did they know that the truck was his and that he was part of our Commemorative March.

Many of us walked farther during the seven days of the march than we ever thought we could walk and certainly farther than we had ever walked before. The women on the march were really quite amazing. Yvonne and Bev Waditaka, Yvonne Bearbull, Dottie Whipple, Diane Wilson, Naomi Pigeon, and I were, I think, all surprised at the distance we walked. Some of us walked from sunup to sundown, putting in over twenty miles a day. Looking back now, it seems that we were existing in another reality. At the follow-up meeting after the march, Clifford described this condition: ◀ *"There are a lot of things I guess we could center on, but whenever we do something together, the spirits of our ancestors, God's spirit, is always there. But a lot of times, it happens when we do things after the third day, because our bodies get tired. The rationalism that predominates in our minds begins to subside, and our natural intuitive ways of doing things begin to take shape, and that's when spiritual things begin to happen to us in a way that unifies us as a group.*

"I've experienced that many times in the sundance. I sundanced nine years, and it's always the third day when everyone uses up their natural strength and then they begin to depend on the spirit to strengthen them. This was no exception, when you walked and everyone began to [do that]; they always say, 'Let go and let God,' or 'Go with the flow,' or whatever words we use in order to try to explain what happens. But we have that ability to work in a good way. So that really happened on this walk." ▶ Indeed, walking for more than twenty

miles the first day sapped our natural strength. We relied on the power of our prayers to keep walking.

The morning of the fourth day, we were leaving Mankato and heading to Henderson. That was a very special day, not only because the women's portion of the march began in earnest, but also because this was the day that we felt the presence of our ancestors powerfully. At sunrise, we gathered in front of Dakota Meadows School and began with a loading of the pipe ceremony. As Gaby Tateyuskanskan stated later, ◀ *"A mist came in and when it reached directly overhead of us, Leo finished loading the pipe just at that moment and then the flags of our relatives fell facing the direction north [the direction we were heading]."* ▶

When the bundle of stakes with the red flags and the names of our ancestors fell, they crashed to the ground with a loud clap. To us, this signified several things. Deski Leo perceived this as a signal that the women now needed to take the lead for the march. He said, ◀ *"Today I was getting really scared, you know, the last number of days the men were kind of carrying this, and I was getting really worried, because the intent was to honor our women and children. . . . But it was very powerful, the ceremony he mentioned while we loaded the pipe, all of a sudden [he clapped], we had those stakes there, moving. Oh, oh. It's got to be the women now. That's what we said."* ▶

During the first portion of the march, we had been tracing not only the path that the women and children walked on the way to the concentra-

> « IT'S BEYOND WHAT YOU CAN UNDERSTAND. IT'S VERY POWERFUL, THE SPIRITS THAT GO WITH YOU. »
>
> LEO OMANI

tion camp at Fort Snelling but also the route that the condemned men had traveled, shackled and in wagons, on their way to the concentration camp in Mankato. On the fourth day of the Commemorative March, we were leaving the place where our men were imprisoned in 1862, and the last leg of the journey retraced the route of the women and children.

Clifford described how we had summoned the spirits with the pipe ceremony, saying, ◀ *"One of the things that happened this morning is that we sang a song and loaded the pipe, a long peace pipe. When we sing a song, if our relatives are still in the earth realm, they come, they come to us. . . . So this morning, as we had the pipe ceremony, they came. My koda here was filling the pipe while I was singing, and they came in a real powerful way, up to the pipe."* He went on to explain, *"We load the pipe, and then we also have an eagle fan, an eagle feather, and we journey with that all day. And at the end of the day, we smoke it, and we thank our relatives for being with us. All along the day, there are signs that tell us that our relatives are with us as we walk and as we drive."* ▶

At times, this was revealed to us in the animals who came out to guide us or protect us, as in the way Alameda found us along the route or in the way that the eagles and hawks came out in large numbers as we traveled through the Henderson area. After describing how we seemed to be getting stronger each day, Deksi Leo explained how the animals helped as well as the sacredness of the walk: ◀ *"It's beyond what you can understand.*

It's very powerful, the spirits that go with you. We met a red-tail hawk that's come with us all the way, even from Canada . . . scouting ahead. And that honor that the horse nation gave to us, oh that was a beautiful horse. He saw our people coming and was just a-dancing. It was very special. It really touched my heart and gave us a good honor. And that sunka, that dog, was very special, he looked after our people. . . . He was only a pup, blood-hound, only a pup, but he'd chase these bigger dogs all away. At this last house, there was a pit bull, oh that pit was coming, and I was ahead of our people, and the people were catching up. That pit-bull was just a-coming, but that little puppy was busy playing with my little grandchild here, "Kuwa wo, Sunka! Come on and help out here!" He came running, just when the pit-bull was about here. He showed up and took the attention away from our people. A small young dog just pushed those dogs back in the yard, that's how powerful it was. All that protection that we got. . . ." ▶

The children along the march were particularly comforted by the presence of all the animals who had come out to support us. Twelve-year-old Autumn Wilson, for example, stated later, ◀ *"I felt connected to my ancestors, especially with all of the animals, the eagles and the dog and horses."* ▶

All of the discussion of spirits along the march was not without humor. About the eagles we saw on the way to Henderson, Chris Mato Nunpa later remarked, ◀ *"These guys would get into these real serious profound discussions about what that all meant. It was beautiful. Then pretty soon one of them said, 'You know what those eagles were saying? 'Where did all these ugly guys come from?' It [the conversation] just went down hill after*

that." ▶ With these comments, he got a chuckle from everyone at Fort Snelling.

The pounding of each memorial stake into the ground also offered a time to commune with the spirits of our ancestors. Clifford commented, ◀ *"Every time we stake one of those down after a mile, we shout their names, and we say 'Mitakuye, our relative, we recognize you, we acknowledge you,' and we remember them. Sometimes it's emotional, because you really get in touch with your own relatives."* ▶

This was the case with a number of participants in the march. Diane Wilson discussed how, though she has recovered a lot of information and learned a great deal through her family research, participating in the march deepened her understanding, ◀ *"The family names on the stake . . . these people are not just names on your genealogy chart; they are relatives, and they appreciate that you walk and that you read those [names on the stakes]."* ▶

On the day we walked to Jordan, the name Canku was on one of the stakes, which means "Road," Clifford's family name. From reading the list of names of the prisoners at Fort Snelling, he already knew that he had nine family members under the name of Canku (as head of household) who made the walk in 1862. Yet, the act of remembering and honoring those family members when that stake was placed in the earth was overwhelming. As he later recalled this moment, ◀ *"Oh, wow. I said a prayer. Geez, this is really something very real that is happening to me. I thank God for the opportunity to be a representative there for my family. Then we came back and had a ceremony at the church. . . . I really felt a sense of them [the spir-*

its] connecting with us. It was really good. I had a real good spiritual feeling." ▶

At another point he described this process of remembering our ancestors, ◀ "Symbolically, as we stake this down, we put tobacco on it, and everybody touches it. Being in touch with our relatives, we're letting them know, 'We remember you. We haven't forsaken you. We remember you with fond memories, and also spiritually we recognize and acknowledge you in terms of the sacrifice you have made for us.'" ▶

Similarly, in Mankato, Bev Waditaka shared with the group, ◀ "One of the stakes that was staked in was my older sister's name . . . and right away I felt her strength because she's a pipe carrier. So I was proud of that." ▶ The connection she felt with the spirits of our ancestors and the commitment she felt to the purpose of the march came through that day too. Bev continued, ◀ "But I was more proud when my sister walked twenty-three miles today. I walked quite a bit too, because I was really feeling it myself. I walked fourteen miles today. . . . I think I know what it is about now. . . . For me as an individual, I now know what it is for me." ▶

Bernice Waditaka had an ancestor she identified as Tootawe (Red Woman)[9] on the original march, and she commented later in their tribal newspaper, ◀ "In some places it was really emotional for most of our people because some of them had names; they were related to those people that were on those stakes that we put down." ▶[10]

Doris Pratt is a direct descendant of Dowans'a, one of the men executed by hanging on December 26, 1862. As we came across the name Dowan on one of the stakes, Doris stated, ◀ "I know that these were our relatives, and I felt that this was a very important event. . . . I feel that in coming here . . . their spirit is here. The physical form dies, but spirit is there, and they all know when we do things like this and that we are remembering them." She went on to state, "So tomorrow as we walk, I can't guarantee that I'll walk all those twenty-eight miles, but I can walk two." ▶

Chris Mato Nunpa commented in New Ulm about the connections he was making to place, based on the oral accounts he heard as a child. A few months earlier, he had taken a tour of New Ulm with Darla Gebhard while making route plans, and he was shown the buildings along Minnesota Street, the town's main street. It is likely that one of the two building sites toward the end of the street housed the women and children who poured scalding water on our Dakota ancestors. He said, ◀ "I heard that story when I was little growing up in my home. I heard that many times . . . there would be screaming, and hollering in pain." ▶ Clearly those family memories became more stark for Mato Nunpa when he was confronted with the physical site where they took place.

Kathryn Akipa carried the same story in her family: ◀ "Our great-grandmother Emma Ortley, Wasicu caze [English name], she was a little girl during that time. She was one of those children who had hot boiling water thrown down on her when she was walking. Her mother had been killed in the uprising. Her mother's little sister was like a teenager, and she saved her little niece, Kunsi Emma. When they were force walked like that, she had hot water thrown on her. She remembered all of that. She healed from her wounds, but she still carried that scar. So we're here, my mother, she's with us here, her prayers are with us. And we're here as representatives of our *families who were touched by this uprising and the forced march and the hanging."* ▶

Kathryn highlighted an essential point: our people can recover from physical wounds, but it is the emotional and spiritual wounds that are more difficult to heal. They are also the wounds that are transferred from one generation to the next. Unless we can heal those wounds, they will be carried indefinitely.

At the end, Mary Beth Faimon commented, ◀ *"It was a spiritual walk and the spirits took care of us, and that's not something we had plans for. One doesn't control that at all. We only have some control about where we are going to sleep, where we're going to stay, who is going to feed us, and it all fell into place, in places we didn't expect it to."* ▶

Everything did fall into place, and all of us who participated felt uplifted and strong. The morning when we left Mankato, during the pipe-filling, Clifford said he received a message telling us, ◀ *"Be happy. We sacrificed for you. We did this for you. You are free. So be happy being Dakotas. We did these things for you so that you could be happy and have a beautiful life."* ▶

EDUCATIONAL MESSAGES

> *Politically, militarily, we were conquered in the 1862 Dakota-U.S. War, but spiritually we still feel that we are the owners of this land.*
>
> ◀ Chris Mato Nunpa ▶

After we made each day's destination point, we gathered for dinner—a meal of buffalo meat in some form—which was followed by an evening of oratory. We used this time to share comments with one another about the day's experiences as well as to fulfill an educational purpose. It gave Dakota people an opportunity to hear stories about our People's past, forging a collective Dakota consciousness about the forced march, but it also allowed us to share our pain and sense of grief with the non-Dakota people who gathered to support our efforts. The stories we shared were unpleasant, and the perspective from which we were speaking at times caused discomfort, even among those who thought of themselves as our allies. It was very important for us to create a space where our voices and our experiences would be validated and supported rather than discredited and demeaned.

Chris Mato Nunpa emceed this portion of our event, and he usually began by placing the forced march within a broader context and connecting the Dakota experience in 1862 with the experience of the Jews in Nazi Germany. In one town he stated: ◀ *"If you read about Minnesota history, you'd learn . . . about bounties on us—$25, $75, $200—you'd learn about the two concentration camps that we had here in Minnesota at Mankato and at Fort Snelling. And that's where we're going to end up on Wednesday. You'd learn about the largest mass execution in the history of the United States here at Mankato where we out-Texased Texas that year in capital executions. And of course you'd learn about the warfare that occurred and the forced removal and in general the genocide that was committed upon the Dakota People, not by Sadaam, not by Osama, or not by Adolf, but by the United States of America and the Euro-American citizenry of Minnesota, right here, right here. Those are things that eventually* *are going to have to be acknowledged. They are going to have to be looked at, put on the table, and eventually taught in the curriculum. So all these things in our mind are related. All of these things go through our mind as Dakota People as we go along the march."* ▶

While many certainly may have felt that this was an acrimonious way to begin our discussions in the small towns along the route, causing immediate discomfort among White members of the audience, it was also necessary. Too often, Dakota suffering has been dismissed as an unfortunate consequence of our own violence. It was necessary for us to clearly articulate that U.S. brutality, which had systematically worked to subjugate the Dakota People, was the cause of the violence in 1862. Our People would not have gone to war if we had not been invaded and oppressed. We needed to make sure that in the course of our discussions, these facts were never forgotten.

During our evening on the Gustavus Adolphus College campus, we had a large crowd gathered consisting of march participants, faculty, staff, and students. Many in the room were non-Dakota. Thus, the conversation that night was decidedly educational. Clifford Canku stated early on in the evening, ◀ *"Since 1800 a tremendous amount of life and land has been lost and the curve came to a bottom about 1972. But now we're making a comeback. The population of our Dakota People is rising, we're buying back land. So these two things are returning, our land and our lives that we have lost."* ▶ It is easy in moments of despair to forget these facts, so these words on the fourth night of the march were particularly empowering.

There was also a great deal of good-natured bantering. As Chris Mato Nunpa introduced Bill

Means, he couldn't resist a few jokes explaining to people the difference between the Lakota and the Dakota: ◀ *"I'd like to call upon somebody that to me has been a champion of Indigenous Peoples, of Native Peoples, and he's one of our cousins from the West, Lakota. We say Dakota, they say Lakota. And there is a lot of good-natured kidding, and sometimes it's pretty sharp too. Like they'll say to us, 'You Dakotas, you were exposed to the White man first, and you got exposed to his missionaries, and you had the L preached out of you.' And we might say something like, 'Well, you notice it's not North Lakota or South Lakota, it's North Dakota and South Dakota.' You know, we go back and forth like that. The gentleman I'd like to have say a few words is Mr. Bill Means. He's with the International Indian Treaty Council working with treaties, Indigenous Peoples issues, at the United Nations, and he came today to join us in this march. I, myself, am very grateful, very gratified that this champion of our Peoples would come and help us and support us in our Commemorative March."* ▶

Bill Means rose to the occasion and took the opportunity to continue the educational process. He began by explaining, ◀ *"We don't tell you these stories to make you feel guilty; we tell you these stories so that maybe you can hear the truth, because in public school you don't have the opportunity. . . . So that's the reason why we have to bring these things up to you about babies getting their heads smashed on the road, or women getting cut open by a sword, or that on the same day that President Lincoln signed the Emancipation Proclamation, he also signed the order to hang thirty-eight of our relatives right down the road here at Mankato."* ▶

Indeed, these topics are rarely taught through

the dominant society's educational system. It is only through the narratives of resistance, often passed on orally, that these things are remembered. Bill went on to say: ◄ *"We didn't get our sovereignty, or our self-determination, for nothing. It came at a heavy price. That's why we're walking. Seventeen hundred people marched so we could have a little bitty casino down here to help the people. We gave up millions and millions of acres right here in the state of Minnesota. . . . Maybe sometime when you have children, you'll be able to say you know what happened here in the state of Minnesota in 1862 and what has happened to the Dakota People."* ►

The fruits of years of cooperative projects and educational programs were apparent in Mankato. For years now, the Mdewakanton Club has worked with various Dakota individuals and families (such as the Amos Owen and Eli Taylor families) to sponsor an annual powwow, the *Mahkato Wacipi,* with accompanying educational programs. By the time our group came through Mankato for the Commemorative March, there was a base of support for our project. While in Mankato, we stayed at the Dakota Meadows School, a name decided upon by the student body when the school opened a few years earlier. Bruce Dowlin, a long-time member of the Mdewakanton Club, came to join us the evening we arrived in Mankato, and he shared with us the history of the school: ◄ *"Out of all the names they could have chosen, they chose to honor the Dakota heritage and named it Dakota Meadows. . . . This whole school is engulfed in Dakota names, so all these kids go down these hallways with Dakota names. These kids chose to do that . . . and I wanted you to know*

that. You have a lot of friends in this area—among the children and all ages." ►

This was not the only warm reception from young people. The students from Minnesota New Country School in Henderson—a school with a nationally recognized program—walked with us until lunchtime on November 11. It was a chilly day, and with the number of miles put in, I'm sure more than a few students developed soreness and blisters, but they wanted to show their support for us nonetheless.

On the sixth or seventh day of the march, as we were getting closer to the Twin Cities, we had stopped along the Sioux Trail to have our lunch. As we did nearly every day, the vehicles trailing us just pulled into the ditch, and we either distributed our sack lunches to the marchers or made the sandwiches right there. Marchers and drivers would find a seat on the ground, and we would rest our bodies for a period before resuming the march. On this day, we were feeling disheartened and stunned, as a clergyman from a church there came to ask us—with some hostility—what we were doing. When we told him, he said, ◄ *"I just wanted to find out what people were doing here on our land."* ► Those of us who heard his comments showed what I thought was remarkable restraint and told him we were just stopping to eat our lunches and that we would soon be on our way. His comments exemplify the colonizer's mentality, and apparently he saw no irony or insolence in telling a group of Dakota People that we were on his land.

The sting from this man's comments was diminished, however, by the support shown from an unexpected source. A teacher or administrator appeared from the Sioux Trail School and told us they wanted to bring their students out to honor our People, but they weren't sure what would be respectful: clapping, shouting, waving, or just standing silently. As Bernice Waditaka later recalled for her tribal newspaper, ◀ *"When we got close to that school there were [students from] five or six classrooms all lined up just waving as we were going by. It made us feel real good."* ▶[11]

We were all appreciative of this gesture of support, and in spite of the clergyman's comments, we left that area believing there was tremendous hope for the future.

The evening we stayed in Henderson also demonstrated at least a willingness of all parties to talk about the events of 1862. I commented positively about the placards on the tables, which read, "Over all the earth, helpless and oppressed people wander," placing this phrase in the context of the history of the Dakota: ◀ *"When we finally went to war in 1862, it was in response to that oppression. It was reacting to oppression. We couldn't take any more and so our People struck back. And it meant very severe consequences. It meant dispossession from our homeland, exile for many of our People for a long period of time, and for some permanent exile; it meant losing that connection to the land; and it meant continuing physical assaults on our People that were implemented with the policies of genocide created by Governor Alexander Ramsey, implemented by Sibley and Sully and other people who were part of that. And it was supported by White citizens of Minnesota in 1862.*

"One of the things I've realized when talking about 1862 in Minnesota is that very few White Minnesotans are willing to acknowledge their part in the oppression of Dakota People. Because we had this wonderful meal prepared for us, I want to thank all of you for hosting us, because we're tired and we're hungry, and these things that you have provided to us mean a lot. But for me, what means even more is an acknowledgment of these assaults upon our People because our People are still suffering." ▶

Similarly, invoking the Bible to find some common understanding, Chris Mato Nunpa also educated the citizens of Henderson about Dakota understandings: ◀ *"There's a phrase in Dakota and it comes from some of our ceremonies, one of the most sacred ceremonies, the sundance, it goes 'Heun oyate nipi kte!' 'Therefore the People will live,' or 'That the People may live.' So some of what we're doing here is that, remembering that . . . their death, their strength, their sacrifice, their spirit is making it possible for us and young ones like this. . . . And the other thing just in the plain physical sense, I read this in some old book, it says, 'When I was hungry, you fed me' and I'm thinking about that now. We're hungry and you fed us. The master says, 'In as much as you have done this unto the least of these my brethren, you have done it unto me.' You know now, when Euro-Americans first came to this land, we had the land, they had no land. Now they have the land, and we are strangers on our own land. We are truly indeed among the least. So in a way, too, you could take that teaching that is in your Bible and you've implemented that, at least today, in a physical sense."* ▶

The mayor of Henderson, Keith Swenson, was among those with us at the meal that evening. He ended the evening with a story from

Leo Omani carrying the eagle staff as we edged closer to the Twin Cities metropolitan area.

his own family's history: "My great-grandfather was born in 1857. . . . My family, on the advice of some Indian friends, fled to St. Peter during the Sioux Uprising. We think of it as so long ago, but I remember in the '50s sitting at family reunions, and for them it was a real event. This was my great-grandfather, only four generations back. If I leave the valley for four days, I get homesick. I understand a little bit the way you feel, and like I said before, we want to say, 'Welcome.' You really have been away too long."

We very much appreciated being welcomed to a town that had previously been so hostile to our People, yet at the same time the evening was bittersweet, because we were now the visitors in our ancient homeland.

EXPERIENCES OF THE MARCHERS

By the last few days of the Commemorative March, we were able to begin reflecting on the signifi-cance of the march for each of us personally as well as for our nation. I stated quite emotionally to the core group gathered at the evening meal in Shakopee on the sixth day of the march, ◀ *"I just want to say . . . that when I look at everyone sitting here, this core group, the group that's made a lot of the miles, I'm just really proud of all of you, proud of what we've done. We're almost at the end. All of you have made me proud of being Dakota, proud of the strength of our People, and I want to thank you."* ▶

Because we were experiencing so much indi-vidually, it was also important for us to make sense of what was happening collectively. Every once in a while, one of the stakes would break as we were trying to hammer it into the ground. When that happened, we would use red strips of cloth to bind the two pieces together and then ham-mer the longer stake into the ground. About this Deksi Leo later commented: ◀ *"People were won-dering sometimes about those stakes that would break—oh, they felt bad—then we'd have to mend it. It didn't dawn on me until after it happened, it's the beginning of that healing process. We need to mend our hearts. We're only human, and we need to let go of the bitterness. We were torn apart. It was beyond our control. All of our People got torn by the Wasicu religion in our way. And it's hard to talk about those things. I believe that, in time, this walk is going to heal all our communities. . . . It was tough, I know for all of us, it was tough when we put those stakes in, because we know our relatives, which side they were on, and we honored them. No matter which side they were on, it doesn't matter." ▶*

These connections and understandings were important for all of us who participated. We all have mending to do as a consequence of the events of 1862, but not just as Dakota people who suffered at the hands of the oppressors. Deksi Leo's comment reveals how deeply divided our People were. Among those who were forcibly removed in November of 1862 were those who fought to protect the Dakota way of life and land as well as those who worked to protect the White population and compromise the strength and unity of the Dakota, thereby betraying the resistance movement. Some of the mixed-bloods who could not be trusted by those who had gone to war against the Wasicu had been taken captive and were released only at the end of the war.

The fractionated relationships among the surviving Dakota have been transferred from generation to generation, and this has created a lingering resentment among our own People. This factionalism is a consequence of colonialism; colonialism is the real culprit, but as a People, we have often directed our hurt and anger toward one another.

Reverend Steve Rasmussen, one of the organizers of the march, later invoked a familiar Bible story to convey what this meant on the march: ◀ *"The experience of a walk like this is significant on many different levels. But the one obviously for me, being a religious person or spiritual person, was the spiritual aspect of the walk. The story of the first fractricide, the violence, speaks of Cain's brother's blood crying out from the ground, and there is this image of the earth weeping over the violence that brother has against brother. That was part of the walk."* ▶

In spite of this intergenerational fractionation, as we came together to recognize the suffering of our ancestors, a sense of compassion overwhelmed us, and we were able to acknowledge our common suffering. As a result, a deep sense of unity was created amongst the marchers; we were bonded together in a very profound way. As Mary Beth Faimon shared at Fort Snelling: ◀ *"I think that because of that connectedness, everyone shared in the pain and in the mourning, and everyone shared in the stories and the laughter. People who came and didn't stay long enough only experienced the sorrow and the pain. They weren't there to have that other part of that healing with the bonding and with each other and the joy that came with that connecting. It was a very powerful experience for me."* ▶

The good feelings were present even the night before the march began, thanks largely to all the efforts of Tim Blue and everyone at the Eci Nompa Woonspe school, which he directs. Not only was it a wonderful way for us to begin, but it was also good for the students at the school. As Tim explained later: ◀ *"Part of my undertaking with this event was to present it to the students in my school, looking into your past and looking into your extended family in the present, and all the connecting that we have to look forward to. I think it was really good at the school. We got everybody together there and launched it off in a good way. We blessed the stakes at the sweat that night and fed the people, and I think the students really enjoyed that."* ▶

Even those who had no expectations regarding the march could not help but be moved by the experience. We were very fortunate to have "Super Dave" Holm, the owner of On-Site Sanitation, accompany us the length of the journey, and we really couldn't have asked for anyone more kind and supportive. There were only a handful of people who were there every day of the march—all of the 150 miles—from before the sun rose until well after it went down. Dave was one of those people. He had become such an important part of the group that he even made new family ties. By the time we reached Shakopee, he was referring to Bernice Waditaka from Prince Albert, Saskatchewan, as his older sister, because she had spent much time riding in his pick-up and he had developed a closeness to her. That evening, he told all of us how much he had learned along the route and ended his comments by saying, ◀ *"I can't be more proud than to be associated with you. . . . I just want to say thank you for accepting me."* ▶

As people who suffered together and mourned together, we also developed a profound love for one another. By the time we had arrived at Mankato, this love and sense of connection were apparent. Standing near the site of the hanging of the thirty-eight Dakota, I said, ◀ *"One of the things that strikes me listening to people talk and listening to people's stories is that it's nice to be*

among people who understand these things and who understand the pain, who understand the history that we can share together. We can carry that burden together. It's really important to me, again, to have all of you here with us to go through this." ▶ The opportunities for addressing this experience among people who hold this memory in common, along with all the accompanying emotions, allowed us to develop shared memories surrounding the original march.

Diane Wilson has since been contemplating how to transmit this experience into writing, music, and art, so that others can begin to understand the event on an emotional level. A few weeks after the 2002 March, she commented about how her understanding of colonization and decolonization had developed on the march, ◀ *"Since then, I've thought about what we do with this, having drawn together this absolutely incredible group of people who are now bonded together on such a profound level. How do you take that back out into the world and make change with it?"* ▶ She has been working on organizing a gathering of artists (and maybe a few academics) who have created work surrounding the forced and commemorative marches.

Diane's brother, Dave Wilson, was one of those who immediately began to transform the experience of the walk into an expression for others to appreciate. While on the march, a song came to him, and within a few weeks of the march he had created a music CD with the help of the Gordon Bird family. By the time the meeting of artists was held later in the month of November 2002, he had completed the project, saying, ◀ *"This walk was a real emotional thing for a lot of us. I still feel it today. It's one of the reasons that the spirits and the Creator compelled us to make this music tape. It was the only way we could express our feeling."* ▶

Part of creating this understanding of what our ancestors suffered in 1862 was experiencing our own suffering during the Commemorative March. Most of the walkers commented on the new understandings we gained from this physically demanding event. We knew that when we were experiencing difficulties or hardships, feeling tired, and getting blisters or cramps that we could draw strength from remembering the far more intense suffering of our ancestors. As Bev Waditaka commented later, ◀ *"I thought about my ancestors every step of the way—how hard it was for them and how easy it was for us to make this trip."* ▶[12]

However, participation in the Commemorative March was not easy, especially for those who already suffer physical ailments. For example, Irene Howell from the Upper Sioux Reservation suffers from arthritis in her back, making even driving in the caravan difficult, yet she wanted to support the marchers. She commented later, ◀ *"I got thirsty, but I had water. I wonder how they [our ancestors] were. I got tired myself, but that was from sitting because I have arthritis in my back. But I thought, well, they must have gone through a lot. My little suffering isn't that much."* ▶

Judith Anywaush talked about how the realization of our ancestor's suffering hit her the night before the march began. Describing their night camped in a pop-up tent at Lower Sioux, she said, ◀ *"My nose got a little cold, but you know we had sleeping bags, pads so the cold wouldn't come up out of the ground, tent shelter, food, everything was there. We might have felt we were suffering a little bit there, but that was nothing."* ▶

Judith's daughter Marisa Pigeon also commented on this: ◀ *"The first night we camped out with my grandma, and I was thinking the same thing about all the kunsis who were there and how they must have been cold with all the little ones. As I rolled up that night with Josh [her three-year old son] in our one sleeping bag keeping warm, I thought about how they must have been cold and hungry, and how much pain and suffering they must have gone through. And I thought about those things the whole time we were on the trail, my tiny blisters, and I thought about how little that pain must be compared to theirs."* ▶

Because the original forced march from Lower Sioux to Fort Snelling had consisted primarily of women and children, the children's participation in the march brought that reality home to us. Yet on the Commemorative March, they were amazingly resilient, and like the children from Tiospa Zina Tribal School who made the stakes we planted along the way, they were eager to participate and support the event. Twelve-year-old Autumn Wilson later wrote about the march, ◀ *"After a while, I accepted the fact that we were going to have to get up before the crack of dawn, and then I started to look forward to it. We had a long way to go. I came to understand that we needed to get up that early because the marchers in 1862 probably got up a lot earlier and under worse conditions. We got up from a warm bed and a heated room, among people who supported us instead of people who were throwing stones at us."* ▶

Crossing the Mendota Bridge that leads to Fort Snelling was particularly emotional. At that time the fort finally came into sight, and we could look down upon the site where the concentration camp stood. All we could do was continue to put

At Fort Snelling monument site, which reads "Wokiksuye k'a Woyuonihan" (Remembrance and Honoring). The final ceremony for the 2002 Dakota Commemorative March was held here with a (re)dedication of a pipestone marker made by Amos Owen, the dedication of the sage wreath from the women in Sisseton, and the placing of the last wooden lathe at the site.

one foot in front of the other as grief overtook us. One of the young girls broke down, and we stopped walking across the bridge to help warm her, comfort her, and pray for her. The last portion was difficult for all of us. Sharon Odegard recounted her experience, ◄ *"Coming across that bridge I was thinking of the women and children, and what they were thinking about . . . the fear they had, not knowing what their fate was going to be. It was really strong, really powerful for me."* ►

Marisa Pigeon expressed the same thought, ◄ *"Coming over the bridge—I think that was the most powerful time for me. . . . I came across the bridge, and I was carrying Josh. The emotion that came up, I couldn't even look over the side of the bridge, because the moment I did, the emotions that came up from there were so powerful that it was really something."* ►

The event was moving to our non-Native supporters as well. Steve Rasmussen shared with us later: ◄ "I think probably the most powerful part of the walk was, for me, walking across the bridge as a White person in the midst of all these Dakota, and my son, who is part Mohawk on his mother's side, walking with me. And hearing the drum group singing as we walked across the bridge and knowing that the songs that they sang were not just their songs but the songs of the ancestors who were joining us there. It was so incredible. . . . I've been across that bridge many times before, but it had always been driving a car, in a hurry to get somewhere, and it became just a place that was in the way until I got to where I wanted to be. This gave a whole different feel to the earth and what is built over there." ►

During our discussion at Fort Snelling, I explained why it had been so important to me to fulfill this dream of a commemorative march to remember and honor our ancestors. I described how I grew up hearing about this event and how that had left a significant impression on me and affected my life in important and lasting ways. I also described how the work that I carry out weighs heavily upon me, especially since there are few opportunities to release the emotional burden that focusing on these difficult topics can cause: ◄ "Because I study these things all the time, I write about them all the time, I teach about them all the time, it gets really hard and I feel it all the time. So especially when we were coming across the bridge and we started getting close, I could feel it, and it was all coming out." ►

In many ways we were cleansing ourselves through tears. As difficult as that was, I believe it was a necessary part of the experience: ◄ "Our hope is that by remembering them, by remembering their suffering, by coming to terms with just how hard it was, just how much they suffered, just how long that walk was, just what it meant when they came to Fort Snelling, we can begin to come to terms with the truth about our past and work towards healing for the future generations." ►

Strong emotions were a regular feature of the walk, but in spite of this, we were compelled to keep going. Dave Wilson shared with us later, ◄ "I was honored to be there, but a lot of times I asked myself: 'Why are you here? Why are you carrying this staff?' There was a reason I was supposed to be there, because to me this was a spiritual walk. It was very powerful. It still affects me a lot, and I think the emotions are still kind of raw." ►

Mary Beth Faimon was able to sum up this emotional experience by saying: ◄ "The walk was in remembrance, but it also was a walk of mourning, and it seems to me that the mourning for all that was lost 140 years ago and since has been denied. So there has been this denial and forgetfulness. And yet, it has just stopped—trapped—the emotions inside without any sense of hope. So I think this has triggered and opened up a mourning period and a remembering [for the Dakota], as well as an ownership for those of us who are White who are here now and who were there then." ►

The emotions triggered for some of our Canadian relatives were also connected to the sense of disconnection that they have experienced from being so far away from Minisota Makoce. Like Leo Omani, Bev Waditaka commented about the reconnection to relatives and lands. She explained that the current generations did not start learning about who they were and where they came from until they attended the Dakota summits in recent years. Since then, they have been able to start relocating relatives, learning their names, and identifying places. Their road has been a difficult one in Canada. Bev relayed: ◀ *"To this day, we are struggling; we're a nonstatus band, nontreaty band and we're trying to get the whole treaty process going for our People. . . . Part of our history is coming out here and there. It's really interesting to see that happen. I guess one of my reasons for coming down here was to find some truth, the truth about our People, about us, about how we got way up there in Canada."* ▶

This truth has been hard to come by with the diaspora of our People, even in regards to our own experiences. Bev elaborated on this topic later to the reporter from their tribal newspaper: ◀ *"It was hard to accept all these stories when we were walking. When I took this walk I realized that, yes, it did happen to our People. And I never believed that our people were ever put in concentration camps. I never thought it ever happened to our People, and now I have a new perspective on the history of us as a Dakota People. I have a better understanding and acceptance of it than I had before."* ▶[13]

We all felt a sense of understanding and reconnection. For those of us whose families returned to our homeland after the late 1880s, it was pure joy to have relatives coming home. The experience helped all of us. As Diane Wilson commented about a conversation she had with Clifford Canku, ◀ *"One of the reasons for that [strong sense of connection] is that people are working to put the puzzles of their lives back together, and that whatever those problems are, whatever those pieces are, one of those pieces is ob-*

«TO ME, THIS IS JUST A SEED THAT WE'RE PLANTING. IT COULD BLOSSOM INTO SOMETHING; IT COULD FOLLOW MANY DIFFERENT DIRECTIONS. »

CLIFFORD CANKU

viously, I think, connected to the march for them. The way that we connect to history is part of that total." ▶

For many of us, it was a life-changing experience. Chris Mato Nunpa later stated, ◀ *"It was probably one of the best things I have ever done in my life, and it was like the words Diane used in an e-mail, 'It was an intense, powerful, and spiritual experience.'"* ▶ His statements were echoed by others who said this was the most important thing they'd ever done.

When the march had been completed, rather than feeling as though something were over, many of us felt like it was just the beginning. Clifford Canku captured this sentiment well: ◀ *"To me, this is just a seed that we're planting. It could blossom into something; it could follow many different directions."* ▶ He reminded us again later, ◀ *"I believe that this opens up a new era for us to do things in a way that would help our People. We're just opening the door."* ▶

We agreed almost immediately that we would march again, and we would seek the support and participation of more people, so they too could experience the power of the understanding and healing that emerged from this event, as well as the connection to our ancestors and the sense of unity. But there was also a sense among all of us that there was more we needed to do.

When the Commemorative March of 2002 ended, the power of truth-telling had affected us all. In the meeting held a few weeks later to discuss the experience, Clifford Canku reminded us of the need to educate ourselves and our children about our history. He closed with some powerful words: ◀ *"We don't need to be complacent anymore. We can speak out and be proud of who we are as Dakota People. It is okay to do that. I think many of us grew up with parents and grandparents who felt very intimidated by the White person. They felt a sense of staying in their place and saying the right thing, not yet realizing that the right thing is to be who you are, coming out with appropriate words that would be true to us as Dakota People and not to surrender our freedom to somebody else who maybe will say 'This is what you need to say.'*

I think it's time that we risk bravery and say this is what we feel, this is what we need to do, and get it done, do it. . . . We're living in exciting times, and we need to vision for our People. We need to have more visionaries. If you have anything that comes into your mind that really speaks out, you need to share that. We really need to share those things." ▶

◀o▶

The next Dakota Commemorative Marches will be held November 7–13 of 2006, 2008, 2010, and 2012. We hope you will join us.

◀o▶

NOTES

1. *Mitakuye owas'in* means "all my relations," a prayer in this instance.

2. *Kunsi* is the Dakota word for grandmother.

3. Naomi's family had to leave the march for a brief period to go home before they returned the next day.

4. For these comments on the Year of Reconciliation, see "Area Indians Say Year Failed to Mend History," *Free Press*, 26 December 1987.

5. See Elizabeth Cook Lynn's chronicle in *The Politics of Hallowed Ground: Wounded Knee and the Struggle for Indian Sovereignty*, ed. Mario Gonzalez and Elizabeth Cook-Lynn (Urbana: University of Illinois Press, 1999), 88.

6. Desmond Tutu, *No Future without Forgiveness* (New York: Doubleday, 1999), 120.

7. Michel-Rolph Trouillot, *Silencing the Past: Power and the Production of History* (Boston: Beacon Press, 1995), xix.

8. *Koda* is the Dakota word for friend.

9. In the orthography used throughout this collection, we would spell this Duta Win.

10. Ron Merasty, "Wahpeton Members Take Part in Dakota Commemorative March," *Prince Albert Grand Council Tribune* (vol. 3, no. 4, November 2002), 4.

11. Ibid., 4.

12. Ibid.

13. Ibid.

Signatures of a letter of support from the Lakota/Dakota/Nakota Spiritual Group at the Jameson Prison in Sioux Falls, South Dakota.

Dakota Homecoming

DIANE WILSON

—◄o►—

In the morning my left hip aches so that it hurts to stand, hurts to walk to the kitchen for my coffee. In the two days that I have not walked with the march, leaving the group at a community center in Henderson after a long day that ended with several bone-chilling miles in the sleeting rain, the pain has grown worse, as if I walked all night to make up for the lost days. At night I would fall asleep and dream of the eagle staff moving steadily down the road ahead of the group, my legs following behind with strong, sure steps. In the morning I woke tired, my knees sore, my hip aching.

When the flyer went out announcing the Dakota Commemorative March, it was the first time in 140 years that the original march in 1862 had been publicly acknowledged, much less grieved. How many people saw it, read it, and tossed it away, while others felt those words immediately begin to stir something in the blood, a heartbeat that echoed across the country as a small group of marchers recognized a call, a summons to be present. History was about to repeat itself as we retraced the original 150-mile forced march from the Lower Sioux reservation to a prison camp at Fort Snelling. For many of us, the march would become one of the most significant events in our lives.

I could feel the marchers moving closer, feel their presence as they approached Prior Lake, now a sprawling urban city. The group had grown larger with each passing day as more marchers arrived from the Santee reservation in Nebraska, from the Sisseton Reservation in South Dakota, from reservations across Canada where Dakota people had fled in 1862 rather than risk hanging or imprisonment. This was their homecoming, the return of the Dakota so many generations later to land that was their heritage.

The March followed the original route as closely as possible, passing through the towns of Sleepy Eye, New Ulm, Mankato, and Henderson— names made infamous by the townspeople who had battered the original marchers with sticks and rocks and scalding water, channeling their own grief into a murderous hatred of all Indians. But this march is relatively peaceful, passing through these towns without incident. The route grows more arduous as the long caravan of marchers and cars leaves behind the bucolic back roads near the Lower Sioux Reservation and is forced to walk on the shoulder of increasingly busy highways.

On the morning of the seventh and last day of the march, the day when we would arrive at the original site of the Fort Snelling prison camp, I woke at 5:00, drank my coffee, burned sage with a prayer for strength for the marchers, swallowed four ibuprofen, and drove through the pre-dawn morning to the Little Six Casino in Prior Lake. After breakfast, the marchers regrouped at the mile marker where they had ended the previous day's march. The woman who offered the morning prayer wept as she spoke. Already the mood of the group had begun to shift, feeling the weight of six days of remembering, of sharing stories with other descendants, combined with the sense that we were about to arrive at the final destination of this long, exhausting journey. The march was approaching what had been a prison camp at Fort Snelling, the winter home where many more would die of disease and broken hearts.

We walked along the shoulder of the highway with red prayer ties braided in the women's hair, tied to the antennas of a long line of cars and vans, wound around the arms of the men who carried the eagle staff at the head of our procession. The wind was strong and cold that morning, rising up to meet this group with its own challenge; the air whipped by the passage of fast-moving cars and trucks. We crossed freeway entrances by stopping traffic. My brother, Dave, and the husband of one of the organizers, Scott, became the shepherds of this ungainly caravan. They wore orange plastic vests and stood at the top of the freeway entrances, waving their arms at cars that hit their brakes suddenly, surprised at the unexpected presence of a long line of people walking along the highway. Some drivers seemed to clench in frustration at having the morning

commute made even longer, their fingers tapping the steering wheel while they looked away rather than face this band of marchers, this motley group who must be protesting God knows what; why don't these people just get over the past and move on? Others honked and waved in support, waiting patiently for the long line to cross safely.

We continued to stop each mile and place a stake with a red prayer tie that carried the names of two of the original marchers. One of the elders would read the names out loud in Dakota and then translate them into English, and we would all offer prayers and tobacco after the stake was pounded into the ground with the "Canadian hammer," a large stone that had presented itself to Leo on the first day of the march. Leo and his nephew, Gerald, had traveled 1,200 miles from a Canadian reservation to drive at the head of the procession in the "red pony." It was Leo's original idea that had brought us all together, when he suggested at a conference that the women and children who made this journey in 1862 needed to be remembered, their suffering and courage recognized and grieved by their descendents. The march was named Manipi Hena Owas' in Wicunkiksuyapi, or "We Remember All Those Who Walked."

Sometimes one of the marchers would turn away in silence, wiping away tears after recognizing the name of a relative who had been part of the original march. I carried the heavy knowledge that my great-great-grandmother Rosalie Iron Cloud, a full-blood Dakota woman, had escaped this fate by taking refuge at Fort Ridgely with her French-Canadian husband, Louis LaCroix. She may have survived as a result, but I have often wondered what it cost her to be separated from her family and community, to have witnessed her sons and husband fighting against her Dakota relatives.

In the afternoon we stopped again to place a stake at one of the mile markers. When it was brought out, Leo said, "This one is easy to understand, no translation is needed as it is not an Indian name." When it was my turn to say a prayer and place tobacco at the base of the stake, I read the names, Narcisse and Louise Frenier. I felt an electric shock of recognition travel down the length of my arms, all thoughts of prayer momentarily suspended. These names belonged to my family. Narcisse and Louise were relatives of my great-great-grandmother on the other side, Rosalie Frenier, or Iron Lady, from Sisseton.

« WHEN PEOPLE COME BACK TO THEIR HERITAGE . . . THEN THEY ARE SLOWLY PUTTING TOGETHER THE PIECES OF THEIR LIVES, LIKE A PUZZLE. »

In that single moment, all of the research I had done about the 1862 war and the following displacement, the reading, the writing about my other grandmother's experience, even walking and hearing the names of the original marchers, it all came together in a single, deep feeling of grief. Where I had felt compassion and a strong interest in the events of the march, suddenly it became personal; it was my family who was abused as they passed through the towns of New Ulm, Henderson, and Mankato. It was my relatives who were hit by bricks, stones, and scalding water, who were spat on, taunted, hated. I felt stunned by this realization, watching as each one in the group took their turn in offering tobacco and prayers to my relatives, to my family. How many others had I missed in the days I had not marched?

An hour later I was walking next to Clifford Canku, a spiritual leader from Sisseton. As we walked we exchanged our stories, telling about our relatives and what had drawn us to this march. I told him about my grandmothers and finding my relatives' names on the stakes a few miles back. I told him how I had felt, for the first time, a powerful sense of grief for the original marchers, that in mourning for my own family, the march had become personal as well as for the Dakota People. Clifford nodded his head as he listened.

After I stopped talking, Clifford paused for a moment in thought. He said, "We are all part of the collective unconscious, and the people's connection to it is growing stronger, partly because of events like the march. When people come back to their heritage, when they learn their language, when they march to reconcile a part of history that has never been acknowledged, then they are slowly putting together the pieces of their lives, like a puzzle."

In the mid-afternoon, when we had marched almost fourteen miles, we turned onto Old Highway 13, also known as the Sibley Memorial Highway. At one of the last mile markers before we would reach the Mendota Bridge and cross to Fort Snelling, Leo stood in front of the group and announced that it was time for the men who had led the march with the eagle staff to step aside. "This March is to acknowledge the women and children and elders who made this journey, and they need to go ahead of the men. They are the givers of life," he said. "The men will walk beside them and behind them."

As the men moved in silence to walk along both sides of our small band of women, a palpable wave of grief settled in as the history that we had re-created began to blur the distinction between past and present, and the sense that we were not alone on this journey grew even stronger. I was near the back of the group of women and children, and I could see how we had been transformed by Leo's words. Waziyatawin Angela Wilson, the woman who was the "heart" of the march, one of the primary organizers and the only person to walk the entire 150 miles, became the lightning rod for the dark feelings that washed over the women. She was the first to begin weeping with deep, shuddering sobs, her head bowed while she continued to walk with her arms wrapped tightly around two of her children. One of the women waved an eagle feather around her head, while others patted her gently on her back. Clifford filled a tiny bowl with sage and moved through the group, stopping briefly to allow each woman to wave the smoke into her face, hair, and breath. It became difficult to continue walking, as my limbs grew heavy and weak, and I was filled with an absolute sense of despair that deepened the closer we came to the bridge that would lead us to the prison camp below. The pain in my left hip had returned, and my entire right arm and shoulder ached as if I had been carrying something I could not set down, a baby perhaps, or the weight of an elder leaning on my arm.

As we continued to walk, the pavement beneath the women's feet began to fade and disappear, the rigid layer of tar and gravel slowly giving way to the prairie beneath. Long-stemmed grasses

dusted with a layer of snow now bent beneath the hems of the women's dresses as we began to move in our own private landscape. The wind no longer carried the fumes of truck exhaust and fast-food grease. I could smell the rich scent of leaves decaying on moist earth, crushed by the slow rolling of the wagon wheels. The fields had been turned under for fall, a thick layer of pungent manure spread across the black soil, its neatly furrowed rows a testament to the white farmers who owned it, who subdued it with their plows and horses. Even the land had lost its freedom, lost its wild mane of prairie grass and sumac bushes.

The men disappeared, leaving the women guarded by a long string of soldiers on horses. Our small group swelled until it stretched into four miles of women and children walking, with a few wagons that carried the elders, the meager possessions we were allowed to bring, children too young to walk, and those who were already ill. I could turn back and see the long train that snaked slowly behind us all the way to the horizon, pointing the way back to the land that had been stripped from the Dakota People.

We had been forced to march over twenty miles each day, and sometimes one of the women stumbled, their legs giving way in exhaustion. "Get up," was the order, as a musket was pointed at the prostrate figure on the ground. "Get up or plan to stay here," the soldier would say with an ugly laugh, his small eyes lingering on the hip of the younger woman who bent quickly to help, to pull her aunt to her feet, to whisper in her ear that she must, she must get up quickly, we will rest soon. Her aunt looked up at her and her niece could see the surrender in her soul, her willingness to go no further, to have her life end beneath the broad sky of the prairie she had always known, leaving her bones unburied, her memory lost to her family. Her aunt rose slowly and painfully, her life now a gift to her niece. She leaned her weight on her niece's arm while the crowd of women flowed slowly around them, murmuring, come auntie, patting her arm and her shoulder as they walked past on sore, swollen feet.

The sky was gray and heavy with snow, the wind gusting in swirls of leaves that danced around their legs, as if mocking them, knowing that some of these women would never dance again. Women pulled their blankets tightly around their shoulders to keep the wind from finding their hearts, from tearing the children from their grasp, especially the little ones who coughed and lay in their mothers' arms without crying, their eyes already focused on the horizon.

Come please, auntie, I said, feeling the urgency of the soldier whose horse paced restlessly nearby, his muzzle level with my head, feeling his eyes on my hip, my leg. I placed my arm under hers, felt her weight heavy against my shoulder, felt my hip ache and threaten to give out. But I am young and strong and I can bear that much pain and more; I have untold depths of rage for my People. If I had my knife, I would remove this soldier's staring eyes, cut his insolent tongue from his mouth and feed it to the crows that circle overhead. I would cut the hair from his head and I would dance for my aunt, for my mother who is already dead, for my father, who is in a prison in Mankato, accused of killing a man when he was miles away. I would dance for my People, who are treated as less than

> « I STARED AT THE GROUND AND HELD MYSELF IN PRAYER, KNOWING THAT AS LONG AS I PRAY, NOTHING CAN MOVE ME, NOTHING WILL HARM MY SPIRIT. »

animals, who are spat on and beaten. My face is bruised from a rock that a White woman threw as we passed through Henderson, her face twisted in hate, her soul aflame in her eyes that were so terrible I could not face them; I could not look into that dark place and survive. I felt the blood trickle down my face, but I did not flinch or wipe the blood from my chin. I stared at the ground and held myself in prayer, knowing that as long as I pray, nothing can move me, nothing will harm my spirit. My aunt stumbles and pulls hard on my aching arm. I feel my hip clench but it holds; we will make it, auntie. I'm not sure where we will end, but we will get there.

We stop at the side of the wide river where there is a ferry waiting to take the first group of women across. I can see the stone fort on the hill, its windows watching us like little eyes set in its walls. I can see the heads of soldiers who stand guard with their muskets. It's good they have such a large, strong army to protect themselves from these women. I spat quietly to one side, filled with disgust for such cowardly men, who threaten women, who shoot the ones who could not keep walking, women who closed their eyes, willing to die rather than to live any longer this way. I saw them crowd around an elder and I could not watch; I had to bury my face in my blanket. But nothing could keep the shot from ringing in my ears, from waking me at night when I dozed, too cold to sleep deeply, woken by the rumbling in my empty stomach. I wondered where her body lies; is she still at the side of the road with no one to bury her, no one to mark her grave, no one to carry her memory forward for her family? I could not even weep for her, my tears all used for my family and now I was dry as a bone. I was the cornhusk left in the field, useless and empty.

Only my anger kept me moving, kept these two bloody feet walking, one step after another, kept my auntie upright by the sheer force of my will. I felt my anger, my sorrow rise in my chest and burst out as a fierce ululation that took the other women by surprise. They looked back and I could hear another voice and another rise as we said, "We are Dakota and we will not be defeated." But a stinging blow to my head snapped it forward, cutting off my voice, and for a moment the world around me went dark. It was my auntie's strength then that held me up, kept me alive while the soldiers called harshly for silence, threatening to shoot the next woman who opened her mouth.

It was a slow ride across the river with the cold wind whipping the blankets around our legs. We could see the first few teepees already set up under the watchful eye of the fort. This was our prison, our land reduced to this patch of woods where we would live on handouts from the government. The first few flakes of snow began to fall, softly and gently laying a white blanket on the fallen leaves. We had little food and none of our own medicines, while many of our People were already ill. I could see in their eyes that some had already given up, were ready to make their last journey. I looked around our frigid camp, teepees rising up ghostlike in the woods, no sign of a welcoming fire where we might warm our hands and feet at the end of this road. I wondered then if this would be the last home of the Dakota People.

◄◦►

Our small group of marchers had grown in the last few miles to at least fifty or sixty people, a long line that covered most of the bridge as we moved slowly across to our final destination. Women walked in silence, heads bowed, weeping quietly. What despair we all felt as we moved forward, what a sense of hopelessness, of grief, of uncertainty about the future. We had to stop once when one of the young girls, who had been walking with her arms wrapped around her mother, simply stopped, weeping, unable to go on. Again, the other women came to her and wrapped a red scarf about her head, shielding her face from the view of the river, wrapping a blanket around her shoulders. As we approached the far end of the bridge, we could hear the ululations of some of the women who had reached the camp ahead of us. At that same moment, the sun broke through the clouds, brightening the bridge with the first rays we had seen all day, warming the hills above the river with a soft golden glow.

I walked next to Clara Strong, who told me she had just turned sixty-three, and had originally moved to Minneapolis from Canada. We followed the paved path from the end of the bridge that led down to the park, to the site of the concentration camp. The path turned downward at a steep angle and Clara grabbed my arm while I steadied the two of us all the way to the bottom of the hill.

As we moved slowly downhill, we could hear a solitary male voice begin to sing as he welcomed us with a traditional song, a poignant end to an exhausting journey. The singer was Art Owen, son of Amos Owen, and he was singing a welcome song that his aunt had recently given him. He would tell us later that he had not known why she had given it to him until he sang it as the marchers entered the park. He also said that when he saw the group crossing the bridge, he got choked up; he felt tears on his face. Those are the spirits, he said, pointing to his cheeks. "When you were crossing the bridge," he told the marchers, "I could see blue lights surrounding the group. Those were spirits traveling with you."

After a ceremony to honor the 1,700 original marchers, dedicating a commemorative plaque, an honor dance for this group of marchers, and a feast, we were told that there would be a closing ceremony with testimonials from people who had been part of the march. Chris Mato Nunpa, Angela's father, a self-confessed "worry wart" and a fierce advocate for the historical and political necessity of remembering this 1862 march, moved through the group inviting everyone to stay and be part of the ceremony. Many of the marchers would leave immediately after the feast to begin the long drive home. Chris came to me and said, "We would like to hear a testimonial from you, if you're willing. People think you're a Wasicu but you have Dakota relatives."

When we were all seated in a large circle, Art Owen talked about the emotion of the day and the importance of the march in healing and reconciling the past. He talked about his own experience marching, how beer bottles were thrown at them, people yelled out swear words and racial epithets. He said that as long as you're in prayer, nothing can stop you. Each step you take on a march should be for a relative. When something gets in your way, you don't go around it, you go through it; otherwise it might become an obstacle next time. The feelings that came up when you were crossing the bridge were the spirits, he explained, and their presence meant that the healing had begun. He told us that what we had brought to the march, the words that had been spoken, were all together, like a bag that has been filled and then closed, and that we would all take part of that with us when we left.

Other testimonials followed with many of the marchers telling his or her story, explaining what it meant to them to be part of this event. These seven days had drawn together a group of strangers from across this country and Canada who would leave this night feeling like family, like we had formed strong bonds of community in what we had shared.

When it was my turn to speak, I offered a poem I had written during the days when I could not be part of the march, as a way of giving something back to the group, of offering my thanks for an experience that had changed my life. Somewhere in these seven days I had stepped fully into my Dakota heritage, feeling my ancestors gather round like prodigal family. As a witness to my family's experience, and that of the Dakota People, I learned how much we are our own history, how our daily lives are only the tip of the iceberg that peaks above hundreds of years of generations whose experience, acknowledged or not, has everything to do with the people we become.

◄○►

Tell Your Children

We hear your voice, grandmother
We hear your whisper in the grass
We hear you asking why no one remembers
What has happened in the past

One hundred and forty years ago
Dakota warriors made their stand
They said our children are starving
We've lost our ancestors' land

When the war was over
Thirty-eight men sang one last song
Women and children began to march
No one asked if this was wrong

Tell your daughters, tell your sons
Tell the little ones yet to come
That we will always remember
The Women's March on the Dakota Trail

By day they walked, a four-mile train
In blankets thin, feet worn with pain
Mothers held their babies tight
Too many died on cold November nights

One hundred and fifty miles they walked
Through towns now stained with hate

Today your children walk this road
We follow footsteps carved in pain
We mark each mile we pass
With a stake that bears your name

Step by step we reclaim this land
In cars and trucks and caravan
Eagles' feathers pointed high
As we march together we remember why

Through the stories that we hold dear
Our voices keep the ancestors near

Tell your daughters, tell your sons
Tell the little ones yet to come
That we will always remember
The Women's March on the Dakota Trail

◄O►

Photo by Craig Marsden.

2004 Commemorative March Commentaries

◄○►

Commemorative March Photo Collages

CRAIG MARSDEN

◄O►

of thirty-eight

ember 26   1862,

While the remains of many Dakota have been repatriated to their ancestral homelands, the remains of many more are still awaiting repatriation and burial in a respectful manner with proper Dakota ceremonies.

and agony of our history. We will be freed from all future oppressions that will be encroached upon us by governmental forces and influences that will want to control us.

What happened to our Dakota relatives in Minnesota was one of the greatest injustices that ever happened to our people. Thanks to all of you for working to make everything successful.

In The Blessings Of Freedom,

George Blue

Telly Stand

Raymond Grey

Chris Feather

Larry Black Bear

Blaine Bring

Dave Jensen

John Top Bear

David Red St. (LAKOTA)

Walter New Holy

Richard St.

Clayton Creek

Bring Plenty

Ted Thornton, Sr.

The Terrible Truth of a Beautiful Landscape

The Dakota Commemorative Walk of November 7–13, 2004

GABRIELLE WYNDE TATEYUSKANSKAN

◄o►

Wocekiya Odowan

Wakan Tanka tokaheya cewakiyedo
Wakan Tanka tokaheya cewakiyedo
Mitakuye ob
Wani kta ca
Tokaheya
Cewakiyedo

This narrative is a continuation of the Dakota oral tradition of telling the story. It is also about the importance of story, of love and heartbreak, happiness and sorrow, beauty and destruction, as well as the value of understanding what it is to be human and to give voice to the heart. It is about the stories that come from the oral tradition and songs of Indigenous People that explain the spiritual and emotional connections we make on our life-journey. As this story continues in the present, it is no longer being told solely as oral narrative. It has become a written story. It is also a family history, a tribal history, and American history.

The heart of the ancestral homeland of the Dakota Oyate (Nation) encompasses what is today called the Minnesota River valley. It is an aesthetically beautiful valley as well as a sacred place. The sacred earth is a spiritual gift to the Oyate from the Creator, and it is the birthright of every Dakota. This belief is affirmed through the Dakota oral tradition. The oral narratives explain how the Dakota People came into existence and were given the responsibility of caring for the sacred earth. On this land the Oyate honors and lives with a spiritual connection to Ina Maka or Mother Earth. Our spiritual and cultural ideals connected us to the land, enabling the Dakota to sustain our lifestyle. Our ancestral home is a land rich in natural resources. South of the river valley lies twenty-four million acres of some of the richest farmland in Minnesota. Natural resources like timber, water, and wild game were abundant. For these reasons our homeland was coveted by Euro-American citizens.

In August of 1862, the Dakota Oyate was experiencing life-threatening hardships. Dakota people were starving because of the loss of our land base, natural resources, and an unfulfilled treaty payment. By promoting a policy of Manifest Destiny, the American government had already acquired extensive Dakota land through previous treaties. The Dakota Oyate could no longer sustain themselves with a diminished land base. Moreover, the growing Euro-American presence was having a negative impact on the environment; their much larger human population was increasing the demand for natural resources. The Civil War was also occupying the attention and finances of the American government. America was unable to make the promised treaty payment to the Dakota Oyate on time, yet Euro-American citizens were benefiting from the unpaid land and resources. It was for these reasons that the Dakota People were suffering and were experiencing life-threatening hardships.

For a country that has ideals in its constitution that purport to promote equality and justice, it is disturbing that these ideals have not been applied to all of humanity, namely, to Dakota people. The American government was consistent in maintaining a deplorable pattern of violating treaty obligations to Native Americans. As a result of multiple negative experiences, the Dakota People had developed a deep distrust of the American government, and they were suffering from malnutrition. The treaty payment was crucial to prevent the Dakota Oyate from dying of starvation.

As the leader Taoyateduta stated, "Hungry men will help themselves." Taoyateduta declared war in August 1862. In September 1862, the governor of Minnesota, Alexander Ramsey, stated, "The Sioux Indians of Minnesota must be exterminated or driven forever beyond the borders of the State."

Near the end of the U.S.-Dakota War of 1862, approximately 1,700 primarily women and children were taken as prisoners by the American Army. The defenseless Dakota were noncombatants. Separated from their male relatives and protectors, they were forced to walk from what is today Morton, Minnesota, to a concentration camp located at Fort Snelling. The American Army did little to protect the vulnerable four-mile procession against angry mobs of Euro-American citizens. Numerous Dakota died along the way due to the violence and brutality of both American soldiers and citizens. Private American citizens collected some of the bodies of those who perished for museum collections. The location of the remains of most of the Dakota who disappeared during the forced march is unknown.

« THIS NARRATIVE IS . . . ABOUT THE IMPORTANCE OF STORY, OF LOVE AND HEARTBREAK, HAPPINESS AND SORROW, BEAUTY AND DESTRUCTION, AS WELL AS THE VALUE OF UNDERSTANDING WHAT IT IS TO BE HUMAN AND TO GIVE VOICE TO THE HEART. »

—◦—

To remind humanity of the terrible annihilation of a People because of the American citizens' desire to acquire our Dakota homeland, the first Dakota Commemorative March was organized and held on November 7–13, 2002. The organizers of the march were those of Dakota ancestry and their allies who honored and remembered the men, women, and children who had surrendered to the American Army in 1862 and had been forced to walk from the Lower Sioux Agency to a concentration camp at Fort Snelling. The spirit of generosity demonstrated by the walkers created unity and a profound sense of kinship. Those who participated in the events surrounding the march's organization and in ceremonies held in memory of Dakota ancestors felt this unity and kinship grow. Many non-Dakota friends walked in support of the Dakota Oyate; they learned about the traumatic events in Dakota history and understood the need for healthy social change in American society. Their participation stands in sharp contrast to the vicious and malevolent behavior of the American soldiers and Euro-American citizens in 1862 toward Dakota people. The cooperative spirit established among the Dakota Commemorative March participants continues to strengthen and touch the lives of those who have become involved in these events.

The following year, November 13, 2003, a ceremony was held at the Fort Snelling concentration camp site to remember those Dakota ancestors who were incarcerated by the American Army in 1862. During their imprisonment, the Dakota people were denied religious freedom. This is an unjustifiable action by Americans who founded their nation on principles of religious freedom. The Dakota prisoners were deprived of the con-

solation of their spiritual life that was such an integral part of Dakota culture. A bonfire was built, and the prisoners were instructed to burn their pipes and sacred bundles. The medicine bundle of the Wabasha family was recently discovered hidden within the walls of Fort Snelling. Many Dakota prisoners were coerced into becoming Christian. They were also encouraged by missionaries to learn to read and write the Dakota language. At one point, accounts state that Dakota prisoners sent over one hundred letters a day. The concentration camp site is located near the confluence of the Minnesota and Mississippi rivers. This is a sacred site to the Oyate. Dakota oral narratives explain that this sacred space marks the place of emergence and creation of the Dakota Oyate. For many of the present-day walkers, this site has become a symbol of reclamation, reemergence, and rebirth.

◄○►

During November 7–13, 2004, the second Dakota Commemorative Walk was held. The walkers gathered at 6:00 A.M. on Sunday morning to share breakfast at the Lower Sioux Community Center in Morton, Minnesota. The prayer to bless the meal symbolized the beginning of my spiritual journey to return to the beauty of the sacred Dakota ancestral homeland, reunite with a community of my relatives, and reaffirm my spiritual inheritance. The walkers of 2004 traveled a route using present-day roads that follow approximately the original route that vulnerable Dakota women and children were forced to walk from present day Morton, Minnesota, to a concentration camp at Fort Snelling in November, 1862.

The Dakota Commemorative Walk of 2004

began with words of support from David Larson of the Lower Sioux Community. I also spoke on behalf of the Dakota Commemorative March Committee, thanking the participants for their generosity, encouragement, and support of the walk. Then a prayer flag was held up and a Dakota elder read two Dakota names and translated the names into English. This ritual began the long journey to Fort Snelling. Each red prayer flag had a Dakota name written on each side to represent two families imprisoned at Fort Snelling. The prayer flags were placed every mile along the 150-mile journey. As a prayer flag was planted into the earth, Leo Omani of Saskatchewan, Canada, sang a Dakota prayer song. Then each walker offered tobacco and prayers to the relatives. At times a walker recognized the name of an ancestral relative. It was heartbreaking to observe the emotions expressed when individuals reconnected with their relatives intimately. Individuals openly displayed their most painful and heartfelt grief for their ancestors. The reality of how close we are to those horrendous events was difficult to witness.

The procession of walkers was led by Leo Omani, who drove with the prayer flags in his car. In 2002, a walker carried the eagle feather staff of the thirty-eight hanged at Mankato, Minnesota. In 2004, a woman walker carried the sacred bundle of the Dakota Commemorative Walk Women's Society. The group support and spirit of generosity enabled individuals to tell the traumatic narratives of their families. The weight of their private testimonies of disappearance, murder, viciousness, and horror was not easy to hear. The truth of human cruelty and the disturbing lack of moral response in 1862 are hard to understand. Yet these Dakota narratives give hope to the living descendants, because they demonstrate the strength of the human spirit and the miracle of survival. This endurance has given strength to the Dakota People, enabling us to walk on this journey and to tell our family narratives today.

As I began my own personal journey on that first day early Sunday morning, my sense of the sacred world became heightened in appreciation of the beauty of the earth around me. I observed the warming glow of early morning sunlight slowly illuminating the corn stalks in golden fields. I wondered about the spirit of the land and our Dakota ancestors. Does creation remember their relatives, the Dakota Oyate? Has creation been waiting for the reappearance of visible prayers and songs, the eagle feather staff, and the return of the People? The feel of the fresh cold autumn air and the sounds of the birds in the nearby trees and fields increased my gratitude for the goodness in the world. My heart fluttered, the palpitation a sign that I had come home. It was a bittersweet feeling to be walking in the beauty of the Minnesota River valley, the Dakota place of origin, however, because the prayer flags were grim reminders of the brutality, oppression, injustice, and human suffering that took place during and after the U.S.-Dakota War of 1862.

Dakota families were torn apart and endured horrific atrocities. This devastating mistreatment was in extreme opposition to the Dakota ideal of respect for life. In the Dakota language, the root word *ni*, which is translated as "life" or "to live" in English, is an important cultural value. *Mini* means water in the Dakota language, and this word contains the root word *ni* meaning "life." The Dakota understand that life could not exist

Tiyomaza Win, American name Alice Onihan, and her son, Louis Tiona, Jr. *(Family photograph.)*

without water. One of the Seven Sacred Rites of Dakota ceremonial life is the *Inipi* or the Rite of Purification. The ceremony affirms gratitude for all life on earth and the human responsibility to actualize the sacredness of life.

My contemplation took me to a personal place, reminding me that my great-great-grandmother, Tiyomaza Win or Alice Onihan, was born at Cansayapi or present-day Redwood Falls, Minnesota. She was probably three years old when Taoyateduta declared war in 1862. Her father disappeared during the chaos of war. Alice and her mother fled from Minnesota and the fighting. In spite of their loss, they considered themselves among the fortunate ones, as Alice was an only child. Her mother, as a widow, did not have to

worry about protecting and feeding many children during the turmoil of war. They were able to escape and survive. Alice experienced great loss during the U.S.-Dakota War of 1862 and after. She worried throughout her life about the well-being of her departed Dakota relatives. Alice instilled in the generations to follow a deep respect for the spirits of Dakota ancestors, which has been practiced, for example, in the Dakota ritual of preparing a spirit plate. The plate contains offerings of food and tobacco to feed the spirits. This ritual of honoring ancestors remains an important part of Dakota spiritual life. To this day, our family does not know what happened to Alice's father. He remains among the disappeared.

The self-sacrifice of Dakota fathers, uncles, and brothers in time of war and their intense desire to protect their beloved relatives demonstrates their profound love of family. Alice was robbed of her father's presence in her life. As a result, he did not experience his daughter's life passages. Her father did not live to see her leave childhood and become a young woman. He was absent from her adult life of marriage, children, and grandchildren. All the intimate celebrations that are important to family and Dakota society were taken from them. Family stories describe how Alice would sit near the shore of present-day Enemy Swim Lake with other female relatives and through her tears describe her loss.

Family oral narratives also tell the story of another ancestor, Tawakanhdiota or Jacob Eastman.

During the U.S.-Dakota War of 1862, my great-great-great-grandfather Tawakanhdiota was incarcerated at the concentration camp at Fort Snelling with his sons. Governor Ramsey's policy of ethnic removal was carried out, and they were later imprisoned at another concentration camp located at Davenport, Iowa. One of his sons became literate. He wrote to his maternal grandfather, Captain Seth Eastman, a White soldier in the American Army. In his letter he tells his grandfather that they are starving. The letter was never answered. It is difficult to comprehend a grandfather's inhumanity. Jacob's other children fled from Minnesota with their paternal grandmother and uncle to live in exile in Canada. They were so fearful of the U.S. Army and the atrocities they committed that they traveled to British Columbia to escape the soldiers.

During their flight, a child was given away to another tribal group. Their hope was that no one would know the child was Dakota and the child's life would be saved. My family does not know the fate of this child. The youngest of Jacob's sons, Ohiyesa or Charles Eastman, would later in life write about his experience in exile in his book *Indian Boyhood*.

Many of the walkers, descendants of the Dakota prisoners, shared powerful narratives of heartache. As we walked in the beauty of the Dakota landscape, their stories of anguish and grief stood in sharp contrast to the beauty of our surroundings. Solemn voices related the malicious killing of relatives by soldiers and crowds of angry Euro-American citizens. Dakota relatives suffered beatings; they had boiling water poured on them and rocks hurled at them by ruthless, angry mobs. People were murdered during the

Jacob Eastman (*Reprinted from Charles A. Eastman (Ohiyesa),* From the Deep Woods to Civilization, *with permission from the University of Nebraska Press.*)

forced march and in the concentration camp. Many died on the way from their injuries. Those imprisoned at Fort Snelling died of exposure, disease, and starvation. Today many Dakota still do not know what happened to our relatives. There is no known burial site to mark the final resting place of those who died on the walk or at Fort Snelling. One measure of our humanity is a civilized culture's practice of respect for the dead. The living Dakota relatives are left to wonder whether our relatives were given a burial at all.

All human beings despair when beloved

relatives disappear. The faces of lost children on present-day milk cartons show the fierce determination of families to find their loved ones. The human mind craves the peace that comes with finally knowing the fate of a loved one. It is difficult to realize that the perpetrators and murderers have gone unpunished. The worst human crime is to deprive families of the knowledge of the fate of the disappeared, since wondering about lost beloved relatives causes ongoing anguish for the human heart.

It is troubling when high ideals such as equality and justice are not applied to all human beings in America. Where are those individuals who believe in moral accountability? Are their numbers so small, or are their voices silent? Why is there no dialogue in academia about the double standards in America in regard to human rights, atrocities, and political oppression? Where are the theologians who speak of the struggle against evil in the world? Is everyone a bystander to inhumanity in the modern world? American history includes many examples of atrocities committed against human beings other than Dakota people, and the majority of Americans stood by and did nothing.

Does it matter that millions of Indigenous people have been massacred, starved, or allowed to die of disease? Who mourns the death of African slaves brought to this country to provide free labor? What about the thousands of Mexicans who were killed for the purpose of conquest? Who grieves for the Black men who were lynched?

« AS WE WALKED IN THE BEAUTY OF THE DAKOTA LANDSCAPE, THEIR STORIES OF ANGUISH AND GRIEF STOOD IN SHARP CONTRACT TO THE BEAUTY OF OUR SURROUNDINGS. »

What is to be done about the mistreatment and internment of Japanese Americans during World War II? The country that committed these acts believes that its society is progressive and civilized and that it demonstrates high levels of cultural achievement and respect for human life. In spite of these beliefs, however, America has blood on its hands.

Tolerance of atrocities is too terrible a price to pay for any society where progress means failure to practice human ideals. Will America's crimes against humanity go unresolved? The dialogue cannot begin if people are uninformed and history textbooks only lightly address the issues of the inequality, atrocities, and oppression that have taken place in diverse communities throughout the country. Double standards need to be erased, and diversity needs to be acknowledged. In a diverse world, America must have this internal dialogue in order to promote a healthy society. Collective denial does not support the well-being of a nation. It is the obligation of thinking people to protest injustice. We must face up to our responsibilities as human beings to walk on this earth.

⏤◦⏤

Each step of my spiritual journey during the Dakota Commemorative March is a reminder that the 150-mile walk is a war crime scene. The names on the red prayer flags belong to the victims. The political oppression and human rights violations committed against our Dakota relatives must be acknowledged. This Dakota narrative is not finished. The bones of our ancestors need to tell their truth. Forensic anthropologists must assist the Dakota Oyate in the truthful inquiry to document the victim's story. I believe goodness can come out of terrible events. This does not, however, excuse the perpetrator or the bystander who watched and did not act. As human beings, we must recognize the suffering of others and respond to it. Healing from the evil and terror of war can begin only if the truth is spoken. My historical grief will not find peace until the crimes against the 1,700 vulnerable prisoners find justice.

Until this happens, I will continue to walk in the beauty of the Minnesota River valley, acknowledge my spiritual tie to the earth of Dakota origin, work for social change by seeking recognition of Dakota historical trauma, and bear witness to the disappeared. As the story continues to the present, questions arise: How has this painful history affected subsequent generations? Are contemporary social ills linked directly to our past? Challenges exist today, such as poor mental health, poverty, alcohol abuse, suicides, and homicides. One way I choose to contribute is to educate others by continuing the Dakota oral tradition of telling the story, but others must be willing to listen.

« COLLECTIVE DENIAL DOES NOT SUPPORT THE WELLBEING OF A NATION. IT IS THE OBLIGATION OF THINKING PEOPLE TO PROTEST INJUSTICE. »

The account of the U.S.-Dakota War of 1862 is a story that has been told numerous times before in many cultures as a consequence of the human obsession with pursuing material possessions. It is a theme often found in classic literature, such as Homer's *Iliad* and *The Odyssey*, Steinbeck's *The Pearl*, and Hemingway's *The Old Man and the Sea*. In the twenty-first century, the story is America's pursuit of oil resources in the Middle East and Alaska.

Many times in my life, I have been told by teachers, college professors, and other Euro-Americans, "Why don't you just get over it?" or "That was the past, forget about it," when I have attempted to have a dialogue about the genocide and forced removal of Dakota People from our ancestral homeland. These Euro-Americans were unable to comprehend the gravity of the injustice that happened to the Dakota in 1862. Humanity must meet the challenge of learning from the stories of past generations in order to uncover the flaws and uncomfortable truths about human character. The heartbroken and shattered lives of Dakota people need to be healed from the trauma of our historical grief. Validating the story and recognizing the human spirit will bring the light that will finally allow the healing to begin.

◄○►

Reconnecting Past and Present

My Thoughts on the 2004 Dakota Commemorative March

MYLA VICENTI CARPIO

◄◦►

About two years ago, Waziyatawin Angela Wilson had just returned from the Dakota Commemorative March. She described it as a life-changing week and added that the march would take place every two years until the 150th commemoration of the original march, which would be held in 2012. When the time of the march returned, she asked me if I wanted to go.

I decided to participate in the Dakota Commemorative March for several reasons. First, I had lived in Minnesota for a year, teaching at Carleton College. I really liked it there, and while living there, I developed an attachment to the landscape. Second, I also understood the history behind the Dakota forced march. Some of the people I knew were Dakota and descendants of the people who were forced marched to Fort Snelling. Third, I primarily went to support the descendants by placing myself there physically. It was not enough to just say, "Good luck, and have a good time." I needed to actually participate and support them by walking with them on this weeklong journey.

I also had my own connection to a similar event that took place hundreds of miles away. I am Jicarilla, Laguna, and Isleta. The Jicarilla People were also forced marched. In 1883, the United States government forced men, women, and children to walk, with only a few wagons, from northern New Mexico to southern New Mexico (approximately 400 miles) to live with the Mescalero Apaches. We were not placed in a concentration camp, but we were forcibly removed from our homelands—the place of our origin and the location of our religions and spiritual connections. Our confinement lasted as long as we stayed; slowly, then more rapidly, many of us returned home. In fact, the Jicarillas did their own commemorative march to Mescalero some time back. Some of them walked; others actually took wagons and horses.

Although the events leading to the forced march for the Jicarilla were different from those for the Dakota, both events are indicative of the United States' imperialist war against the Indigenous Peoples over lands and resources that the U.S. government sought to appropriate for White settlers. These are but two examples of the violence committed against our People in the attempt to possess our lands and resources. The Dakota Commemorative March was a result of the U.S.-Dakota conflict and the attempt of the U.S. Army to silence any resistance through genocide. In the Southwest, the Jicarilla Apaches confronted the overlapping legacies of Spanish and U.S. empires. The Spanish army and their consorts, the missionaries, sought to displace and dominate the Indians in the Southwest region ever since the fifteenth century, until they lost their territory in the Mexican revolution. The United States government, having defeated Mexico in the 1848 Mexican-American War and having dispossessed the Jicarilla of our lands, sought to relocate us onto a reservation. Yet whenever they were about to create a reservation, the Spanish settlers—who then considered themselves "natives"—would find out; soon some would squat on the land and claim it was theirs in order keep the Apaches out of the area.

The U.S. government, not wanting to offend the Spanish settlers and assuming that all Apaches were alike, then thought to move the Jicarilla onto the Mescalero lands. This solution was inherently flawed, because the imperial logic was based on ignorance: simply placing together two groups of people who use a common language did not mean that the two groups were culturally the same. Moreover, the U.S. government had no sense of the spiritual connection Indians have with the land. Over time, many of us returned to the land of our origins. Given this history of my nation, I understood empirically the meaning and significance of a commemorative march.

A commemorative march is about community memory—what a community chooses to remember and why. For Indigenous people, maintaining

« FOR INDIGENOUS PEOPLE, MAINTAINING OUR COLLECTIVE MEMORIES AND HISTORIES IS FUNDAMENTAL TO WHO WE ARE AND WHO WE CAN BE. »

our collective memories and histories is fundamental to who we are and who we can be. Since the colonizers have written many of our histories, these histories have been distorted through the colonizers' own perspective, based on what is good for them and what is bad for them. Whereas the Pueblos, for example, sought to organize and protect our land, religious ceremonies, and People, the Spanish settlers' perspective was that we were attacking and betraying them. So, too, whereas the Dakota saw themselves being destroyed and slaughtered, the U.S. government, soldiers, and citizens justified this violence by claiming they were "civilizing" the western territory. Honoring our own history and reclaiming our own perspectives remind us of what our People went through in our fight to survive. The commemorative march is part of that process.

What makes the march important is that, by reclaiming this history and these past experiences, we also change the present. We walked into towns that are so ready to forget the past, to forget the atrocities their ancestors committed against our ancestors, and ultimately, to forget how what they are doing today is tied to the past. The commemorative march brings the past into their faces and into their towns, so that the past is not forgotten. At the end of the day, in the evening, the Dakota shared the oral stories that had been passed down with the townfolks who had come to listen. These stories of people dying, how the townspeople treated the Dakotas when they came through, and how brutal the townspeople had been are the stories they usually do not hear. While many White townspeople might come to greet the marchers, they may not be familiar with the Dakota perspective. Even if they have read published histories, most of those are written from an entirely different perspective. Hearing the stories face-to-face through the oral tradition is very different, because listeners can hear the hurt in a person's voice. These are the connections that were made on the march.

It is curious that some people are not able to understand the purpose of the commemorative march and question why Indigenous people would want to bring attention to something in the past, especially something so painful. Yet there is something essentially human about remembering the past. After all, what is the difference between the marchers and the people who reenact the Civil War? They also participate in remembering their past. Those of us on the march are trying to acknowledge a past and to learn from that past, to heal from that past, and to (re)create our own histories. We have the right to retell our own histories in our own ways, which is even more important given how our histories have been denied for so many years. Why is it that so much attention is paid, for example, to the anniversary of 9/11 in the United States? In remembering 9/11 or the Civil War, Americans are seeking to create a common history and a community. The difference is that, whereas these events celebrate a national identity, the Commemorative March challenges that national identity. From the American nationalist perspective, that can be painful.

For us, however, it is very healing to acknowledge what was done to us, to acknowledge our own ancestors who endured all of this, and to acknowledge our survival. The march is a reminder for me not only of what the Dakota went through but also of what my own and other Indigenous ancestors went through. It reconnected me with them and reminded me that I should remember their experience and safeguard their sacrifices. They sacrificed themselves for our survival. We cannot take our survival for granted. We still need to survive, so that our nations will continue for future generations, but we also need to heal, so that we do not continue just to destroy ourselves and do the colonizer's work. We must not become what the colonizer wants us to be—nothing. To ensure our survival and our healing, we must take the young people with us, so that they understand their own histories and do not lose their connection to them. The march is part of a cycle of history, so that we can go forward and our children do not lose what our ancestors have worked and sacrificed for.

One of the things I learned on the march was that, even though I could talk about the march, write about it, read about it, or have somebody tell me about it, actually walking that distance myself was a very different story. On the Commemorative March, we were walking voluntarily, and we were fed along the way. But we always were cognizant of the fact that those who walked before

> « What makes the march important is that, by reclaiming this history and these past experiences, we also change the present. »

us were held at gunpoint and had little food or good water. I developed a greater understanding of the environment and how awful it must have been for them to walk and walk and not know where they were going, day after day after day. Our bodies were exhausted, and it was difficult to walk each step. But it is not until you walk in their footsteps and understand what it means to walk twenty miles a day that you understand how the spirit can drive the body. The spirit to survive is much stronger than could ever be expressed in words.

> « WE WERE SACRIFICING OURSELVES TO HONOR THEM. IT WAS ABOUT ACTUALLY PUTTING OURSELVES IN THAT POSITION AND TAKING RESPONSIBILITY FOR UNDERSTANDING OUR ANCESTORS' SACRIFICES ON A DEEPER LEVEL. »

When I was actually walking step by step by step, walking all those miles, my body hurt and my heart hurt, and I realized that the walk was also about sacrifice. This is very different from reading a history book for an hour about forced removal. Too often, you can read about something tragic and still maintain an intellectual distance. On this march, we were the ones walking. We were walking in their footsteps. We were walking, and we were going through our sacrifice—and it *is* sacrifice. We were sacrificing ourselves to honor them. It was about actually putting ourselves in that position and taking responsibility for understanding our ancestors' sacrifices on a deeper level.

I came away from the march with a completely different understanding of history. As academic scholars, we read and read and read, and some things move us or provoke a reaction, but we are still at a distance. Though I may feel empathy or empathize, I still feel distanced from the historical event. Walking the same path that the Dakota were forced to walk in 1862 revealed the little things that written history does not usually capture, like needing to go to the bathroom, the amazing recuperative powers of the body, and the absolute power of the spirit to survive and to keep going, even when the body hurts and tells you not to go any farther. I learned how your mind and belief systems can drive you and how our Peoples survived.

Going on the march also brought me to a whole different understanding of the Indigenous view that there is a direct connection with the past no matter what happens. We know that just because somebody died and is buried does not mean that we have no connection with the person or that our powerful relationship with their place of death and with the spirit of that person disappears. We have a direct connection to our past—be it through our memories or our bodies—that is very strong. In walking that distance, I realized how those connections gave me strength. My ancestors were with me in ways that cannot be seen or heard in the Western sense; on the march, there was a point for me where the past and the present came together.

Somehow in Western society, there is a belief that our past is past, and we should let it go. For us, however, the past is the present, especially when it comes to the wounds that were inflicted upon us on all different levels—the loss of land, loss of religion, loss of ceremonies, loss of language, loss of our loved ones. When the past and pres-

Ron "Bear" Cronick,
John Provost, and
Edward Valandra

ent come together, we are reminded of the loss of a way of living that was based not on oppression but on relationships. Walking in the present was a way of healing some of those wounds, because following the path of the original Dakota march created a relationship with the past. Walking with them and understanding what they went through healed some of the hurt. It allowed me to acknowledge some of the choices that people (including some my ancestors) made in the past in order to survive, and it provided me with a better understanding and more compassion for people whose choices are limited by oppression.

Participating in the march also gave me a whole new understanding of what the men from 1862 must have gone through. I understood not just how the women must have felt losing their male protectors and being forced to walk while they were so vulnerable, but also how the men must have felt when all that they loved was taken away, including their ability to protect and help their women and children. They lost the sense of power that comes from being with their own community, and they had to watch the people they loved leave. They were not able to do anything about it or fulfill their primary responsibility as protectors. How awful that must have felt.

As all the men, women, and children walked together in 2004, we became stronger and more connected. I had known Edward Valandra from a few years earlier, but on this march we had opportunities for many conversations, jokes, and laughter. On the last day, we made it to the Mendota Bridge, and at that point the men had to leave the women and children to cross the bridge to Fort Snelling. Alone. I watched as the men I had grown close to expressed their painful goodbyes to the women and children. For the first time, I saw how awful it must have felt. I watched Ed and cried for his pain. As we walked across the bridge, an overwhelming sense of pain and loss came over me. The emotions I felt were distinctly male and female. I began to understand how it must have felt to be a woman crossing the waters of the Mississippi River, facing an unknown present and future. In those same steps, I began to understand the enormous loss, anger, and uncertainty that the men must have endured. I will always be grateful to Ed and the other men for teaching me compassion. To understand what the men lost gave me a greater sense of compassion for men and an ability to better understand choices made in the past and present.

From these experiences, it became clear that this march is an example of the process of decolonization. Decolonization is about understanding our own history—where we come from. It is also about understanding how we have been affected by colonization, so that we may re-envision and relive our lives outside the colonization context. Understanding colonization will allow us to empower ourselves and to fully embrace what we ourselves possess. By reliving the histories that have been spoken in our communities, we can reclaim, retell, and relearn our stories and experiences of the past.

Decolonization is also about the empowerment that comes through reconnecting to the land, reconnecting to what it means to walk, reconnecting to our bodies, and reconnecting with others. Everybody is so busy going as fast as they can from A to B, not even touching the earth. We either fly or we drive. Our feet are not physically in contact with the earth for long periods of time, or if they are, it is only when we are sitting in our house.

Reconnecting with the environment—especially the environment to which we are culturally connected—helps strengthen and reconnect us to who we are as Indigenous Peoples outside of this colonialist system. The reconnection is not only physical through our feet and bodies but also emotional: we reconnect emotionally with the land, and we reconnect emotionally and spiritually with our ancestors. So decolonization is not just about reconnecting with historical events; it is also about reconnecting the past and the present. That reconnection reminds us of our relationships and our obligations to our Peoples, our cultures, our religions, and our lands. That reconnection also allows us to strengthen our bonds with those who have gone before us as well as with those who are still here.

◄○►

Oyate Kin Unkanikupi Pelo

(The People, We Are Coming Home Bringing You All)

EDWARD VALANDRA

-◄o►-

It is my nation, my People, who have been subjected to this horrific act—genocide—by violent Americans. By retracing our ancestors' steps, I wanted to show my ancestors that, unlike these Americans, we had not forgotten them after all these years. I also wanted to remind the Americans that, despite their torturous efforts to justify their acts of genocide against the Dakota in November 1862, the Oceti Sakowin Oyate and others will not let them forget either.

MY MOTIVATION: *WACEWAKIYE* (REVERING RELATIVES)

Like others who, for one reason or another, chose to participate in the 2004 Dakota Commemorative March, I decided to walk the 150-mile journey for many interrelated reasons. For one, I am Sicangu Lakota, and that alone situates me within the *hocokata* (center) of the Oceti Sakowin Oyate (herein Oyate).[1] It is not a stretch to say that the Dakota children, women, and men who, under the American soldiers' "protection," were forced marched through hostile American communities in November 1862 are my relatives. Though born and raised on the Rosebud Sioux Reservation, I, like many people of my nation, have deep historical roots connecting me to others throughout our homeland. My Dakota roots are on my mother's side. In the mid-1800s, my ancestor, a Sisitunwan Dakota called Tawapaha Sa, and his tiospaye, Tisa Oti, would often visit the Sicangu and other Tituwan Lakota in the Missouri River country. Not surprisingly, these frequent gatherings led to inter-tiospaye marriages amongst the Oyate and, as a result, members of the Tisa Oti Tiospaye eventually became part of the Sicangu Lakota.

These roots come from the easterly direction of our homeland now called Minnesota. Little did I realize as a youth growing up on the Rosebud Reservation that I would be returning to the place of my mother's Dakota ancestors. After participating in the Run to Remember in December 2003 and the Commemorative March in November 2004, I now realize that my ancestors were calling me back, but why? To be sure, a generation had passed between the time of my first arrival in Minnesota as an undergraduate student in 1974 and my subsequent return in August 2000 as an assistant professor at another Minnesota state university. Reflecting on why I felt drawn to participate in the march, I began to understand that kinship renewal with my Dakota relatives was the reason. Several years ago during a New Year's Wacipi at the old St. Francis Indian School gym located on the Rosebud Reservation, the late Father Noah Broken Leg told me, "As long as we have our kinship system [the tiospaye], the People will not perish." As I write this essay, I feel the power of his words and realize that my journey has come full circle.

> « AS LONG AS WE HAVE OUR KINSHIP SYSTEM [THE TIOSPAYE], THE PEOPLE WILL NOT PERISH." »
> FATHER NOAH BROKEN LEG

A second reason for participating in the march arises from my post-secondary education choices, in particular, where I decided to attend university. After graduating from a South Dakota public high school on the reservation, I attended Mankato State University (now Minnesota State University at Mankato) in the fall of 1974. Of course, Mankato, Minnesota, is infamous for having conducted the largest mass public execution in American history on 26 December 1862. On that day, the Americans hanged thirty-eight Dakota patriots for the simple act of defending their families and their homeland. People may wonder why I, a Lakota, would choose to attend this university in the first place. Didn't I know about the hanging and the other ethnic-cleansing acts perpetuated by the Americans against my People in Minnesota? If so, why did I choose to go there?

To be honest, many an Oyate youth like myself who attended White-run schools during the 1960s and mid-1970s had not been exposed to our own People's history. So much of the Dakota Oyate voice surrounding the 1862 American-Dakota War that we now know was not part of our public school education. Unaware of our Dakota relatives' stories about their experiences in Minnesota—such as the Americans' role in compelling my nation to take up arms in 1862, the Dakota refugees who fled in terror to Canada to escape the ensuing White bloodlust, the 150-mile Death March, the internment of mostly Dakota children and women at Fort Snelling during the 1863 winter, and the Dakota's subsequent exile in late spring of that year to the Crow Creek Reservation in Dakota Territory—speaks volumes about what happens when the education of an Oyate youth is left in White hands. Had I known and appreciated the Dakota experience, would I still have gone to Mankato? Perhaps not, but then again, another reason influenced my decision.

I decided to leave South Dakota in large measure to escape the Indian-hating climate that prevailed and still prevails there. During the 1970s, a Lakota's decision to attend a college or university within South Dakota was not merely a matter of choosing the best school academically or the most compatible environment socially. The question on many college-bound Oyate minds was, "Can a Native attend a state college or university in South Dakota without the constant fear of being harassed?" After all, I graduated from high school at a time when the Oyate's political resistance against colonization had reached a critical level. Conflicts had developed within our homeland and, thanks to the media, had spilled over into White "awareness." Whites in the state and their Native collaborators (the colonizers' always handy tool) were reacting violently to the Oyate's demonstrations of national solidarity (e.g., Wounded Knee II and the establishment of Lakota independence). As our political solidarity transformed into an even stronger national will, Whites reacted with a reign of White terror against the Oyate. Numerous murders of Lakota by Whites and other vigilantes would not be given justice. Either White perpetrators would be acquitted by all-White juries or, if Native collaborators were the culprits, no criminal investigation would occur at all.

These atrocities sparked outrage among the Oyate, who directly challenged this lethal form of colonial repression. The White norm of Indian-hating and Indian-killing had resurfaced with a vengeance in South Dakota. Perhaps the clearest example of this White norm was William Janklow, the Whites' poster boy of the modern-day Indian Fighter. A notorious colonizer and blatant racist, Janklow rose to power on his image as a gun-carrying public official, who stated publicly that the most effective way to end the Native resistance taking place was to put a bullet in the head of each of its leaders. His unabashed racism had (and continues to have) much appeal in South Dakota. Indeed, his virulent Indian-hating vigilantism earned him enough loyal gratitude among Whites to elect him as South Dakota's attorney general (1974–78), as its governor four times (1978–82, 1982–86, 1994–98, 1998–2002),

and most recently as its representative in Congress (2003–2004), until he was forced to resign for killing another White male. With the benefit of hindsight, I realize that my choice to attend a Minnesota university at a time when White terrorism against the Oyate in South Dakota went unchecked—even though Minnesota had such a notorious reputation among Dakota people—made sense: Minnesota appeared to be the lesser of two evils.

The third reason—and the one that made my participation in the march especially significant to me personally—concerns the time and the place of the birth of my son, Wanbli Wanblake. He was born on 22 September in Mankato, Minnesota. His birth time placed him within the period (17 August–23 September) during which his ancestors fought against the White colonizers in 1862. Wanbli's birthplace is where 2,000 of his ancestors, including the 307 Dakota POWs (out of nearly 400) who had been tried in a military court and who received death sentences, were interned after being force marched from the Lower Sioux Agency in November 1862. In fact, I could walk a very short distance from the hospital where my son was born, look down into the river valley, and locate the spot of the mass execution of these Dakota patriots.

At Lower Sioux, the Dakota POWs were separated from the children, women, and elderly. The families of the POWs were marched through hate-filled White towns on their way to Fort Snelling, only to be detained once again and later exiled to Dakota Territory. The Dakota who did not survive this excruciating ordeal and made the journey to the spirit world look with pride, perhaps even vindication, whenever an Oyate baby is born in a place filled with such horrendous deeds. For three years while he was being raised in Mankato, the spirits of Wanbli's ancestors enjoyed watching this little Sicangu boy grow before his return to the Rosebud Reservation. This cultural understanding of my son's arrival is not unique among our People, since all our children are sacred beings. Given the circumstances of how I returned to the eastern part of my homeland combined with my greatly expanded knowledge of my nation's history, my son's birth at this place has assumed far more significance than I realized when I was a much younger father.

WOKIKSUYE K'A WOYUONIHAN (REMEMBERING AND HONORING)

When I returned to Minnesota in August 2000, my decision to participate in the Commemorative Walk was set in motion. Whenever I traveled home to the Rosebud Reservation from the Twin Cities, I would stop in Mankato where our thirty-eight Dakota men died (there is now a "historical marker") and sometimes leave sage and/or tobacco, sometimes sing a song, or sometimes remain silent with my thoughts. I did these small personal acts so that the spirits would know that they are remembered. Little did I realize when I performed these acts of remembrance that I would later participate in a run from Fort Snelling to Mankato to honor our thirty-eight Dakota heroes as well as in a walk from Lower Sioux Community to Mankato to Fort Snelling.

In the fall of 2002, I read a brief write-up in one of the local Native newspapers published in the Twin Cities about the first Commemorative March that was to take place in November. I did not walk in this commemoration but instead made plans to welcome my relations, the Dakota marchers, and their supporters in a show of Oyate kinship when they arrived at Fort Snelling. As the marchers arrived, I could feel the emotional and spiritual heaviness from their weeklong journey and see the physical stress on those who had walked the farthest.

These feelings were not unfamiliar to me, because I had experienced them twelve years before when the *Si Tanka Oyate Wokiksuye* riders finished a 175-mile journey at Wounded Knee. On a bitterly cold day in December 1990, the Oyate welcomed the many riders as they rode their horses and gathered with the people at the mass gravesite. At that moment, many people let their tears fall freely, as though the massacre had just occurred. We sent our voices to our ancestors who suffered physically during their arduous winter journey from the Standing Rock Reservation to the Pine Ridge Reservation a century before, only to be ruthlessly murdered a few days later. Most of all, we knew that by honoring and remembering this one-hundred-year-old national tragedy and wiping our collective tears, we were helping to heal our nation, the Oceti Sakowin Oyate. It was healthy and normal for us to be able to feel deep bitterness and intense hatred toward the Wasicu colonizers, who not only allowed this butchering of defenseless people to happen but, even more egregiously, immortalized their genocidal deed by officially describing the massacre as a "battle." Once again, I found myself participating in the wiping of our nation's tears over the terrible loss of my relatives' lives and the inhuman treatment they received by the Americans fourteen decades earlier.

A year passed, and on 8 November 2003, the community of people who had either organized or participated in the first march held a wopila ceremony at the interpretative center at Fort Snelling. I arrived at the center where the walkers and their supporters were feeding the people and other guests. Those who had something to say about the Commemorative March went up to an open microphone and told their moving stories or personal observations. Ironically, a few days prior to the wopila, Minnesota's White Commissioner of Education, Cheri Yecke, stated in a Minnesota Public Radio interview "that children should not be taught Native-American views of Columbus because he was not responsible for the genocide of indigenous peoples."[2] Her comment was driven by the cultural war that was raging over a draft of social studies standards to be used in the Minnesota public school system. For a White official to make such a claim proved to the Oyate that she and many other Whites could completely excuse the genocidal conduct of individuals such as Columbus and Governor Ramsey. In 1862, Ramsey ordered that every Dakota child, woman, and man be exterminated or forever exiled from our homeland. Native Peoples and their supporters organized a press conference at the Department of Education building to challenge Yecke's assertion about Columbus and to demand that she either apologize or resign. She refused to do either.

This controversy surrounding the White edu-

« . . . I TOLD MY DAKOTA RELATIONS THAT THEY WERE NOT ALONE, THAT EACH FIRE OF OUR NATION WAS—AND WOULD ALWAYS BE— WITH THEM WHENEVER THEY MARCHED IN REMEMBRANCE OF OUR PEOPLE. »

cation commissioner's position on social studies standards reaffirmed to those of us at the wopila gathering that little has changed in twenty-first-century White America. It seems a waste of our time to try to convince Whites that their horrific master narrative is truly colonialist, truly racist, and truly genocidal. Indeed, from what I can gather in talking with other Native Peoples, Blacks, Chicano/as, Hawaiians, Peoples from the African continent, Arab Peoples from the Middle East, and Asians (American and otherwise), 11 September has given the White colonizers all the license they need to cash in their politically correct ticket for two painfully familiar tickets: White supremacy and the racial hatred of non-Whites.

Rather than trying to establish relations with the many Whites consumed with asserting their supremacy and their hatred of non-Whites, the Oyate is reestablishing relations among ourselves. Commemoratives or remembrances, such as the Dakota Commemorative March, and cultural and political summits sponsored by our communities bring each of the Seven Fires together. While at the November 2003 wopila, I experienced the strong pull of Mitakuye Oyasin—our time immemorial call to hold each other in a caring and thoughtful relatedness. As we ate our food, laughed at our crazy jokes, prayed for our relatives, and mourned our losses, I wondered if all Seven Fires were present. Yes, Father Broken Leg and other Oyate Elders are indeed correct when they say that losing our kinship system leads to our cultural and spiritual death as a People—to the demise of our nation. It was in this context that I spoke at the gathering. In my remarks, I told my Dakota relations that they were not alone, that each Fire of our nation was—and would always be—with them whenever they marched in remembrance of our People.

A few weeks after the wopila, there was a ninety-mile relay run from Fort Snelling to Mankato to honor the thirty-eight Dakota who died for our People. Rather than return home to the Rosebud Reservation as I usually do for our New Year's Wacipi, I decided to stay and participate. For me to run was to show solidarity with my Dakota relations. Fortunately, I had been running somewhat regularly by then and physically felt up to the effort. It was the sixteenth year of the run. It started at midnight on 25 December and finished in the early afternoon of the next day. I anticipated that it would be very cold as we ran, but the weather was unusually mild for December. Having run in bitterly cold weather before, I was very grateful.

As several runners and supporters gathered at Fort Snelling, the organizers opened with a pipe ceremony. We were told that a fire was being lit at Mankato and that it would burn the whole night as we ran. After the pipe ceremony, the run commenced with the first leg of the relay. The runners carried a staff that would be passed from runner to runner. Throughout the relay run, several cars followed the runners. One car in particular followed closely behind each runner, playing Native songs on a CD or tape player. Six hours later, in the early morning hours before the sun's light, I took the staff from Emmett Eastman about half a mile or so north of Belle Plaine on what was to

be a six-mile leg of the relay. I was tired from the lack of sleep. A couple miles into my run, a long gradual hill loomed ahead of me. Now I was feeling my forty-eight winters. Fortunately, at points along the route, a drum group sang traditional songs as runners passed by them. I made some distance going up the hill, but its crest was still far away and I felt exhausted. I could faintly hear the drum group as I inched closer to the top. The road was in a valley and a traditional song was reaching to me, giving my tired body the needed lift to make it to the top. As I went by, I waved the relay staff toward the drum group in their honor as well as thanks.

The song and the drum reminded me of why I chose to run at a time of year when it is usually the coldest and at hours when most people along the route were sleeping comfortably in their warm beds: to remember the sacrifices our ancestors made so that we may live. I am sure that the Native runners who heard these traditional songs sung by the drum group felt as I did and that whatever hardships they may have been experiencing were made a bit more bearable, too. After finishing my six miles, I handed the relay staff to a Dakota youth. I gave him some words of encouragement and then climbed into a waiting van that was part of the caravan.

About two miles north of Mankato's city limits, I received the staff again. Around noon a young woman handed it to me, and as I passed by the Happy Chef restaurant, three or four young Dakota male runners joined me. The relay staff was maybe a good three miles from the Land of Memories Park (our final destination), but these young runners were obviously energized. I struggled to keep up with what was clearly an easy pace for them, but after about two miles, I was so exhausted that I could not run any longer and had to walk while the relay staff continued on. After a few paces, a car slowed and a young man in the passenger seat offered me water; the driver directed me to get in the back seat. As I collapsed on the seat, I was so grateful to the driver. I learned that he came all the way down from the Red Lake Reservation in a show of solidarity. I remember thinking it was so good that our Anishinaabeg neighbors were part of this memorial run.

The runners gathered at the park's entrance so that we could proceed together with the relay staff and now with an eagle staff. As we jogged toward the wacipi grounds, we could see the fire lit in its center. We entered the grounds and formed a circle in front of the tobacco ties on individual willow branches that circumscribed the wacipi grounds. The supporters and runners shared words of encouragement, ceremonial and traditional songs were sung, and prayers were offered. Then our relative, the bald eagle, came to partake in the gathering. As we watched our relative, I thought of my son, Wanbli Wanblake. I had wanted him to be connected to this run for the obvious reason that he is a Lakota born in Mankato, and I decided that the way to make this connection would be to wear the eagle feathers that he has earned for his educational and other achievements.

After the ceremony, I returned to St. Paul, recuperating from the aches and pains of having run but nonetheless feeling a better person for the experience. After all, I had participated in one of the most time-honored ways of my People, namely, renewing my relations on my mother's side of our nation's hoop. Even though I resumed my daily routine, I knew that in another eleven months, I would share another difficult experience with my Dakota relatives. This time we would be walking to remember the horrific Death March that our ancestors took in the fall of 1862.

MANIPI HENA OWAS'IN WICUNKIKSUYAPI

On Sunday (7 November 2004), the day when the 150-mile march was to start, I and Denise Breton, a Wasicu and friend, left the Twin Cities at 4:00 in the morning. We left early both because the Lower Sioux Community is a couple hours' drive and because it was the time of year when it stays dark longer. Our route was simple: head west on Interstate 494, then turn off on the Highway 212 exit going west, and, when we arrived at Olivia, Minnesota, turn south on Highway 71 until we reached the visitors' center. Despite our best-laid plans, though, we missed the first mile or so of the march, and for several reasons.

First, because of highway construction and a poorly marked exit, I missed Highway 212 and realized we were traveling in the wrong direction (Highway 12 instead of 212). As the driver, I knew turning south on any road would eventually intersect Highway 212. Second, I was speeding 20 mph over the posted speed limit so as not to be late for the start of any ceremonies before the march and the march itself. As might be imagined, a White law enforcement officer stopped us. I immediately assessed this routine stop for speeding by a White cop as a formula for disaster and, as the events unfolded, I truly wondered if I was going to make the march at all. Our colonizer's system was conspiring against me, as racial profiling in White society is a social reality for men of color.

Once the White cop realized that I was a dark male with long hair pulled back in a ponytail traveling with a White woman in the early morning hours when it was still dark and in a hurry, the only question in the cop's mind was, "What crime was I guilty of—that is, besides being Native?" I felt the separation of time between 1862 and 2004 collapsing. After all, part of the ethnic-cleansing legacy of Minnesota's White history was the bounty put on Dakota scalps. As the White cop was coming toward the driver's side of the car, he easily could have been any one of the scores of Wasicu who were out hunting down my Dakota relatives. And as it was for my relatives back then who had to negotiate as best they could to avoid being either killed outright or, if not killed, beaten—some within the inch of their very lives—or forcibly hauled off by Whites to be confined, the resolution of this tense situation between me and the cop rested squarely on my shoulders.

When the White cop asked for my driver's license, it turned into a major problem. Although I knew my license was among the gear we had packed for the march, finding it required informing the cop that I would have to step outside the car to locate the bag it was in. To complicate matters, Denise opened the trunk of the car and, of course, I had placed some sage in the trunk in case it was needed for ceremonial purposes. I had eagle feathers in with the sage as well. I tried finding the bag with my license while calmly talking to the White cop, so he would not become more excited as he saw the sage and eagle feathers. He moved back a few paces while placing his hand on the gun's holster, which indicated to me his excited behavior—perhaps he thought I was searching for a weapon rather than my license. Realizing this scenario was deteriorating, the best I could now do was to calmly and deliberately follow whatever the White cop asked of me. He commanded me to move away from Denise's car and stand next to the police car. I complied with his order. He then asked me what my name was, and at this point I used my professional title, replying, "Dr. Edward Valandra."

> « WHAT CRIME WAS I GUILTY OF—THAT IS, BESIDES BEING NATIVE? »

Next, he went over to the car and asked Denise what my name was (and other questions). As he was returning to his car, he ordered me to get into the backseat. While I sat there, he entered my name into a computerized database to run a check on me: Were there any outstanding warrants in my name? Might there be an all-points bulletin for my apprehension? Or was I using an alias? Of course, during the moments when he waited for the information on me, he wanted to know what we were doing, given that everything thus far did not fit into the category of a leisurely Sunday drive. I used the opportunity to explain that we were headed to Lower Sioux Community for a commemorative march but had gotten lost and were making up for it in order to get there on time.

While I was doing what I could to resume our trip by talking with the cop, the spirits came to our aid. The White cop never closely checked the license plates on Denise's car. Maybe thoughts danced in his mind that he might have a real fugitive in his grasp instead of a professor at some small urban university. Had he checked, though, he would have found out we were driving with expired tags—another profile "checkmark" alert, making our circumstance perhaps even more tenuous. After answering all of the White cop's questions to his satisfaction (and maybe a little disappointment) and having been "declared" clean by the computer, the cop finally let us go, but not before telling me how to get to Highway 212 from where we were. However, for several miles thereafter, I could not help but feel the great chasm of colonized and colonizer between me and Denise, respectively. Yes, colonialism, at very adverse moments, does indeed stretch even the best of friendships and, I might add, relationships between the Oyate and our Wasicu colonizers.

We arrived late. The marchers had already walked at least a mile. We drove ahead and waited. As the women carrying the canunpa and a few others walked past, I joined the marchers, while Denise joined the rest of the car caravan following us. From this point on and each mile we walked thereafter, my initial desire to participate in the walk as a show of solidarity with my Dakota relations grew into an understanding of why the men of our nation need to join in this commemorative march. In large part, I owe this understanding to my friend Myla Carpio, an Apache woman who had traveled from Arizona to participate in the walk. A few months after the walk, I saw Myla at a February 2005 Native Studies gathering at Arizona State University. After our initial greeting, Myla told me that at the Mendota Bridge (a span of about a mile towering above the concentration camp site), she could see how pained I looked, and, in a humble manner, she thanked me for helping her to see how the forced march had impacted the men of my nation.

I was taken aback and overwhelmed with emotion, because she had touched on what I and, I am sure, other Dakota/Lakota/Nakota men were thinking throughout the march: "If only our men had been there to help, to comfort, or to defend in any way our mothers, our aunties, our sisters, our grandmothers, our wives, our women cousins, our children, and our elderly as they were being routinely tortured and brutalized by Wasicupi." This thought became more poignant as we marked each mile with the two names written on a wooden stake wrapped with a ribbon of red cloth. The people whose names or whose tiospaye's names appeared on a wooden stake were said out loud. Prayers were offered as we placed tobacco at the base of each stake, and, sometimes, an oral story was told about one of our ancestors who died on the 1862 Death March.

This statement of our feelings as Oyate men reflects our thought and philosophy about kinship. Ella Deloria, an Ihunktunwan Dakota, speaks eloquently about how our People value one another as relatives:

> Kinship was [and still remains] the all-important matter. . . . By kinship all Dakota people were held together in a great relationship that was theoretically all-inclusive and co-extensive with the Dakota domain. Everyone who was born a Dakota belonged in it; nobody need be left outside.
>
> This meant that the Dakota camp circles were no haphazard assemblages of heterogeneous individuals. Ideally, nobody living there was unattached. The most solitary member was sure to have

Dakota families

at least one blood relative, no matter how distant, through whose marriage connections he [or she] was automatically the relative of a host of people.[3]

Throughout the march, I frequently heard many Oyate invoke various kinship terms in acknowledging each other as, I am sure, our ancestors did while they marched in 1862. Acknowledging relations reaffirms more than a White sociologist's or anthropologist's contorted views of tribal societies, as are found in university texts or academic journals. Neither is our experience of kinship captured by the New Age mantra that the four colors of the medicine wheel represent harmony among the four races. Our bond as a People is profound

John Provost holding his daughter Jennifer at an evening gathering at Henderson, Minnesota. Henderson was the town where a White woman grabbed a nursing Dakota baby and dashed the baby's head to the ground. The baby died a few hours later.

beyond these Wasicu views. Kinship within the natural world is deeply rooted in our origin story, and, as Deloria further notes, is to be valued above all:

> [I] can safely say that the ultimate aim of Dakota life, stripped of its accessories, was quite simple: One must obey kinship rules; one must be a good relative. No Dakota who has participated in that life will dispute that. In the last analysis every other consideration was secondary—property, personal ambition, glory, good, *life itself*. Without that aim

and the constant struggle to attain it, the people [Oceti Sakowin Oyate] would no longer be Dakotas in truth. They would no longer even be human.[4]

I cannot speak for all Oyate men, yet I personally witnessed how emotionally painful the 2004 walk was for the males. Moreover, as I read our oral tradition now presented as a written narrative of the original 1862 march (first published in the *American Indian Quarterly* and now republished in this volume), I was deeply moved by the stories of the descendants—my relations—who had walked two years earlier in 2002. It was excruciating for me to imagine that our men during that initial march could not perform their fundamental responsibilities of kinship for the most vulnerable of our nation.

Indeed, for the men who accompanied the children and women on these commemorative marches, our reason for participating, though simple, was profound. During the initial forced march, Dakota men were separated from the women and children, forcibly removed from Lower Sioux in wagon-trains and imprisoned at or near Mankato, Minnesota, leaving mostly children and women to fend for themselves during their 150-mile ordeal. Though about three hundred Dakota men were condemned to die, their pending execution paled in comparison to the pain of knowing that the most vulnerable of our People—women and children—would be at the mercy of Whites filled with hatred. Our oral tradition proved what the Dakota men most feared: helpless women and children suffered and many perished at the hands of Whites during their forced march from Lower Sioux to Fort Snelling.

One hundred forty-two years later, we—Dakota/Lakota/Nakota men—had the opportunity to do what is ours to do as grandfathers, as fathers, as uncles, as brothers, as male cousins, and as male in-laws for our women and children. Thus, when these descendants of the women and children of 1862 wept because of the hardships endured by those on the first forced march, their grief and pain was almost unbearable for me. I experienced deep sorrow at the inexcusable loss of innocent life as well as deep anger that made me ask: "What are these Wasicu that they can do such things to innocent people?" At the same time, I experienced deep compassion as I tried to find words that might console my grieving relatives. I would soothe them with hugs or, in many instances, just share my tears with theirs.

Of course, what is a Native event without the all-to-be expected encounter with our White colonizers? Much like the stop by the law enforcement officer that I encountered on my way to the Lower Sioux Community, we encountered a White Minnesota highway patrol officer a few miles north of Jordan, Minnesota. Once again, the decades separating the original 1862 March and the 2004 Commemorative March collapsed. The officer informed us that planting the stakes was not permissible under state law, because the stakes diverted attention away from other "legally" posted signs. He also made it clear that there would be consequences if we persisted in doing this ceremonial activity. The hypocrisy

« TODAY, THE DAKOTA MEN IN THE SPIRIT WORLD . . . KNOW THAT THEIR MALE DESCENDANTS ARE NOW TAKING THE JOURNEY THAT THEY COULD NOT. »

was obvious. In plain sight all along the route of the march, we saw many unauthorized signs: campaign posters for political candidates, advertisements for real estate showings or sales, directions to other gatherings, and even non-Indian memorials for loved ones who died at a particular spot along the highway. Clearly, these "unauthorized" signs littering the highway also fell within the highway patrol officer's pale and were far more distracting than our wooden stakes with a single red ribbon. Yet I suspect that the individuals or groups who placed these signs did not get a visit from the authorities informing them of their violations, as we did.

In spite of the White officer's threatening tone, the women marchers firmly informed him that we would continue with our ceremonies and that he was free either to cite or to arrest those "violating the law"—that we would continue to place our unauthorized "signs" that might detract from the signs and billboards authorized (or simply allowed) by our colonizers. After this incident, my emotions were mixed. On one hand, the men present were willing to extend ourselves at the women's request, and the White cop knew it—about that I felt certain. On the other hand, because the men were separated from the people during the original march, this feeling of certain support—that no matter what the circumstances, both the women and men would endure it together—was precisely what the marchers of 1862 were denied. Not being able to endure the hardships of the original march together anguished my male ancestors, and I and the other male marchers could feel their anguish.

COMPLETING THE HOOP

There is no doubt that the walk renewed my kinship—indeed all our kinships—within the Hocokata Oyate. There is also no doubt that the walk has fundamentally called into question the Whites' role in this horrific event. The march has even created a healthy way for Whites and other non-Indians to ally with us, the Oceti Sakowin Oyate. When I reflect on the march, I know that the many moments that the marchers recall will eventually fill volumes. But there was a moment, in addition to Myla's insight, that made it possible for me to find the words to write this essay. During the final stretch of our march, we stayed at Mystic Lake. Gabrielle Tateyuskanskan, one of the organizers and a walker, came from her Dakota homeland and told us what the spirits were saying in our ceremonies. Our people in the spirit world were very grateful that their descendants did not forget them. At one point in her talk, she mentioned that the spirits were glad that the men were walking with the women and children this time, since they could not do so before. I was moved by what our spirits had said, because I realized that my participation had much more to do with being in solidarity with my Dakota relatives. I walked for those Dakota men who, because of the circumstances of that extremely difficult time, were absent during this horrendous 150-mile journey.

The Oyate have walked a full circle. The first march denied that all Dakota would endure this journey together—that our men could be with their loved ones at a time of such terror and suffering. Today, the Dakota men in the spirit world (with their loved ones) know that their male descendants are now taking the journey that they could not. *Hecetu welo.*

◄○►

NOTES

1. Oceti Sakowin refers to the People of the Seven Fires. These terms describe our socio-political organization. We comprise the Sisitunwan, Wahpekute, Wahpetunwan, Mdewakantunwan, Ihanktunwan, Ihanktunwani, and Titunwan. The first four Fires reside in the eastern part of our traditional homeland and speak Dakota. The next two Fires reside in the central portion of our homeland and speak Nakota. The last Fire resides in the western part of our homeland and speaks Lakota.

2. Paul Spies, "Action Education: On the Front Line in Minnesota's Social Studies War," *Rethinking Schools Online* 19(1) <www.rethinkingschools.org>

3. Ella C. Deloria, *Speaking of Indians* (1944; reprint, Lincoln: University of Nebraska Press, 1998), 24–25.

4. Ibid., 25, emphasis mine.

Pazahiyayewin and the Importance of Remembering Dakota Women

RAMONA STATELY

◄o►

On November 7, 2004, I decided to partici-pate in the Dakota Commemorative March. We gathered before dawn, had a feast together, and began our walk. It was an especially moving experience for me for two reasons. First, my own research on my family history had led me to my great-great-grandparents. My great-great-grand-father Mazaadidi (Walks on Iron) was one of the men imprisoned for his participation in the war, and my great-great-grandmother Pazahiyayewin (She Shall Radiate in Her Path Like the Sun) was on the original Death March in 1862. Second, I was greatly moved because it didn't really occur to me at first that I, too, was modeling the col-onizer's patriarchal worldview by focusing my research on Mazaadidi rather than on Pazahi-yayewin. We called our family reunions in Santee "Mazaadidi" family reunions. We made and wore jackets with his name on them in his honor, be-cause he was the eldest member we could find at that time.

One of the biggest negative stereotypes peo-ple have about Indigenous people is that they do not value women. The European culture has not valued their own women, and therefore they have undervalued Indigenous women. The

reality is that women play—and have always played—a significant role in Indigenous societ-ies. They are known as the carriers of the culture, and the Dakotas are matrilineal. True, contact with Europeans altered Indigenous women's roles. Colonialism weakened the women's role, and the missionaries reinforced that by introduc-ing the notion that God is male and that women are inferior like Eve. To the Dakota and many other Indigenous Peoples, women are thought to provide sustenance to the tribe and to hold the power of creation. Because the Europeans have been the writers of history and have not rec-ognized the contributions of women or valued their opinions, an important part of the history of the U.S.-Dakota War has not been recognized, namely, the story of the wives and families of the condemned warriors. Seldom do we hear what happened to them.

After speaking briefly with Mary Beth Faimon at the Granite Falls powwow, however, I real-ized that it is the women we should be honoring. This was a lightbulb moment for me, and it was powerful. I was filled with many emotions. I was sad and ashamed that I hadn't made the connec-tion sooner, but I was also happy and rejuvenated

Mazaadidi—Walks On Iron, 1834–1892
Mazaadidi was one of the 300 Dakota Warriors condemned to death by hanging by a U.S. Army tribunal for his part in the Dakota War of 1862. He and other prisoners were sent to a concentration camp, Camp McClellan (Davenport, Iowa). He was pardoned by President Lincoln in April 1864 and rejoined his tribe, which had been removed to Crow Creek, Dakota Territory. Later the tribe was removed to Santee, Nebraska, where Mazaadidi lived as Dennis M. Kitto.

Pazahiyayewin—She Shall Radiate in Her Path Like the Sun, 1839–1918
Pazahiyayewin was the wife of Mazaadidi. She survived the Army's seven-day forced march from Lower Sioux Agency (Morton, Minnesota) to Ft. Snelling (Minneapolis, Minnesota) in November of 1862. *(Photo printed with permission from Reuben Kitto.)*

that I finally realized the power of the Dakota women. Little did I realize how much I would be impacted by that conversation.

—◦—

From that moment on, I became involved in the Dakota Commemorative March, as did my entire family. One of the first things I did was to call my dad and order a new jacket. Now, instead of Mazaadidi on the back, mine says Pazahiyayewin! He thought that was a great idea. Then we got on the moccasin telegraph to spread the news that we had to really support this next event. We organized a meal to feed the walkers who stopped to rest one evening in Shakopee. They were so

weary, as they were more than halfway into their 150-mile walk. It was a great honor to be able to provide some comfort to them.

As I walked, I thought of Pazahiyayewin, and I felt her there. This was my way of walking in her path, acknowledging her suffering, reclaiming my identity, and teaching this to my children, who walked by my side. Our friend Carolyn Anderson had found Pazahiyayewin's (aka Mrs. Ellen Kitto) obituary in the *Iapi Oaye–The Word Carrier,* a bimonthly newspaper printed by students at the Santee Normal Training School on the Santee Reservation, volume 48, number 1, January–February 1919. This is how we knew so much about her. There were two obituaries written for

Pazahiyayewin (Ellen P. Kitto), center; her daughter Lucy Kitto; and granddaughters. According to family records, this photo was probably taken in Oklahoma in 1909. No information on the names of the children is available. *(Photo printed with permission from Reuben Kitto.)*

her, one by her daughter and one by a "Miss Collins," who was on the staff at the Santee Normal Training School. Miss Collins states:

"It was in 1862 when the Indians were driven out of Minnesota, and Mrs. Kitto and her children were among the unfortunate ones. Her husband, a non-combatant, was taken by the soldiers and cast in prison. Dr. Stephen Riggs and Dr. Thomas Williamson, missionaries, succeeded in securing a pardon from President Lincoln, but it was after long imprisonment. He had taken no part in the trouble, which was afterward proven to the satisfaction of the President. The very night that he was torn from his home and family, and his home destroyed, his wife gave birth to a baby.

"The families of three hundred pris-oners were driven from the state. Only a few old men were allowed to accompany them. Mrs. Kitto with her new born babe in her arms and three little ones at her side, with her old mother too, to care for, started on the long journey from Minnesota to Nebraska. There were not enough men to supply game to feed the flock. Mrs. Kitto's children were crying with hunger, and the brave mother's heart could not endure that. She took a gun and went out to help hunt for meat. This is a thing that Indian women never do. But, she was successful and would take her share of the burden of supplying the camp with food, notwithstanding the heart sorrow because of not expecting to ever see her husband again, the burden of carrying one child all the time, the care of the others, and the old mother."

As a Dakota woman, I believe in carrying on the art and culture of my nation. I have been given a gift of making moccasins. I never really knew where this gift came from, but I have always kept an open mind to my sixth sense or unconscious self. I did know that I was guided by a spirit who gave me this particular talent. I knew for sure who guided me when I read Pazahiyayewin's obituary written by her daughter Eunice Baskin. It said, "no one at Santee could make a better moccasin than she" and also that "she taught us [the sisters] how to do beadwork . . . and how to make a good moccasin." The moment I read that, I understood what Waziyatawin Angela Wilson meant when she said, "stories handed down from grandmother to granddaughter are rooted in a deep sense of kinship responsibility, a responsibility that relays a culture, an identity, and a sense of belonging essential to my life."[1]

Today, in an effort to unite nations, women are gathering together and taking back their traditional roles as leaders. Although we have conflicts between the White world we live in and the tradition ways, we must maintain our culture to survive. Indigenous women are taking these responsibilities to heart. As Indigenous women, we must reclaim our identities by creating relationships with other women and by maintaining and teaching the culture that we know. It is our responsibility as Native American women to tell the stories we know and to listen to others.

The purpose of the Dakota Commemorative March is to tell our stories. Dakota women are now the voices of our grandmothers. As we come together to touch the earth of our ancestors and walk the same path that they did in what must have been their darkest hours, we remember and honor them. In this way, we can take back the spirit of our identities and begin healing for our future generations. It doesn't matter where the stories come from. Some are passed down through the generations; others must be found amongst piles and piles of papers. The important thing is that we discover them and share them.

« DAKOTA WOMEN ARE NOW THE VOICES OF OUR GRANDMOTHERS. AS WE COME TOGETHER TO TOUCH THE EARTH OF OUR ANCESTORS . . . WE REMEMBER AND HONOR THEM. »

At the end of the march, everyone gathered for a pipe ceremony, and I was honored to have my father to my right and my daughter to my left. Three generations standing together in unity and love, and there was a lot of healing that day. I realized that right there I was the link, linking the past with the present, honoring history and creating it—all at once.

―◦―

NOTE

1. Angela Cavender Wilson, "Grandmother to Granddaughter: Generations of Oral History," *American Indian Quarterly* 20:1 (Winter 1996), 7-14.

Tracing Their Footsteps

The Dakota Marches of 1862

LISA ELBERT

◄o►

"Wamasicu esta Dakota oyate takuwicawaye ka tewicawahinde. Hena oyate wastepi. Taku ota unspemakiyapi ye. Manipi kin hena owasin wicaweksuye ye."

"Even though I am non-Indian, I cherish the Dakota people and consider them my relatives. They are good people. They've taught me a lot. I remember all those who walked."

INTRODUCTION

This paper is part of ongoing research into the Dakota March of 1862, begun in 2001 in preparation for the first Commemorative March.[1] As Waziyatawin Angela Wilson suggested earlier, until more Dakota accounts come to light, "additional insight may be gleaned from the plethora of Wasicu first-person accounts detailing their experiences." The purpose of this chapter is to describe what I have found in the way of Wasicu first-hand accounts of the marches and to speculate on possible routes taken by the two groups of Dakota prisoners. This is not intended to be a definitive history of the march. Details of the atrocities committed against the Dakota People are elsewhere in this volume.

My sources were primarily letters and diaries of soldiers who guarded the prisoners, letters of missionaries who ministered to the Dakotas, news-paper accounts, and nineteenth-century maps of Minnesota. Thus far I have been able to identify seven enlisted men who served as guards on the march to Mankato and who either kept diaries or wrote letters home from the field. There is scanty direct material from the women's march, though the research is ongoing. To date I have not been able to find any diaries kept by soldiers who were on this march to Fort Snelling. Existing known accounts of the march do not go into enough specifics to allow historians to pinpoint the exact route, although educated guesses can be made. I have also considered the published histories of Isaac Heard and Stephen R. Riggs, who were on the march with the condemned Dakota men.

Given the descriptions I have been able to find, and taking geography into account, I will attempt to make some guesses as to which roads the Dakotas may have traveled, which towns they may have passed through (besides New Ulm and Henderson), and even possible camping sites. Readers should keep in mind that much of it is guesswork and sometimes the sources contradict each other.

THE WOMEN'S MARCH

Most sources state that the forced march of women, children, and elders to Fort Snelling took place from November 7–13, 1862, but there is conflicting evidence about this date of departure. For example, according to Samuel Brown, son of the trader and Indian agent Joseph R. Brown and author of the oft-cited account about his experiences in the war and its aftermath, the group left on November 9.[2] He also reported that the two groups—the women's group bound for Fort Snelling and the condemned men bound for Mankato—left Lower Sioux at the same time. Isaac Heard, however, the self-designated official historian of the war, recorded that the women's group left on November 7.[3] Most subsequent historians have cited Heard.

Although not part of the guard for the women's group, two soldiers mentioned their departure, suggesting that the date the group left might have been November 6 or 7. On Wednesday, November 5, Charles "Herb" Watson in the Sixth Minnesota Regiment wrote to his father, "[T]he Squass are going to leave here tommorow to go below somewhere[.] they are dealing out crackers to them."[4] The following day, Thursday, November 6, John Wood noted, "most of the squaws started to day for St. Paul[.] they had rations delt out to them before starting the Red Wing band getting their rations."[5]

Aside from these soldiers' references, there is very little documentary evidence of this march to Fort Snelling. According to Dakota oral accounts, the four-mile-long train of women and children passed through New Ulm. This would have them traveling for at least forty miles along the south side of the Minnesota River between Lower Sioux and New Ulm, until at some point they would have had to cross the river to reach Henderson, which is on the western/northern side of the Minnesota. The November 15 *Mankato Semi-Weekly Record* reported, "Lieut. Col. Marshall passed down a few days ago, with fifteen hundred squaws, children, and 'friendly Indians.'"[6] This could have meant that the group passed through Mankato, or possibly "down" in the general sense of the direction of the river toward Henderson and Fort Snelling. This route would have the group following the Minnesota River the whole way, on one side or the other. John Williamson traveled with the group from Lower Sioux to Fort Snelling and mentioned "stones and curses" being hurled at the Dakota people along the way, but his letters provide no clue as to what route they took or what villages they passed through.

Another possible route is suggested by this report of the *St. Paul Press* from November 13:

> Lieut. Col. Marshall is expected down to Fort Snelling to-day, with twelve or fifteen hundred Indians, principally women and children, who are to be quartered there until the intentions of the Government respecting them shall have been made known. They have marched all the way *from Red Wood, via Fort Ridgely and Henderson.*[7]

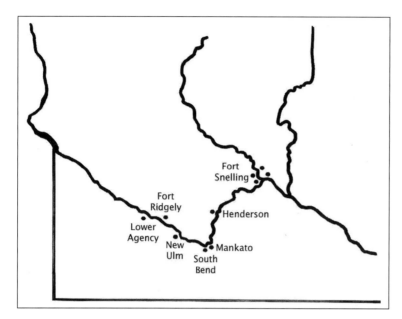

Map 1:
Southern Minnesota showing the Minnesota River, with key towns and forts.

In 1862 the Henderson-Fort Ridgely Road was an important supply road. It cuts overland, more or less directly east-west, across where the Minnesota River makes a V-shape with Mankato at its point (see map 1).

The statement "they marched via Fort Ridgely and Henderson" implies that they traveled on this road. This is one of Minnesota's original "highways" that generally followed the higher ground north of the Minnesota River. Some of the trail was eventually built up and paved; in Sibley County, State Highway 19 follows much of the original course of that road. The history of this trail is well documented in a Sibley County Historical Society publication.

Although little can be said with certainty, the women's group must have crossed the Minnesota River at least once. The Lower Sioux Agency and Fort Snelling are on opposite sides of the river. No bridges over the Minnesota River existed in

1862. As the river was normally sufficiently wide and deep enough to admit steamboat traffic, it would have been a significant obstacle. In dry periods the river might have been low enough to ford in places, or it could be crossed when frozen. Further research may reveal whether either of these situations was the case. The only other way to get wagons across the river was by ferry. Photographs of river ferries from the 1860s show crafts that could *maybe* hold two wagons at a time, if they were small. This should be kept in mind when imagining ferrying a four-mile train of people, wagons, travois, and livestock across the river.

If they went, as one newspaper said, "from Red Wood, via Fort Ridgely and Henderson," it would mean they would have crossed the Minnesota River either by the Lower Sioux (Redwood) Agency or by Fort Ridgely. If, as oral accounts state, they went via New Ulm, they probably bypassed Fort Ridgely on the opposite side of the river. In any case, this is the route the men's group most likely took: there would be no reason to cross the river to the northern side (where Fort Ridgely is) if they were going straight from Lower Sioux to New Ulm (see discussion below). The only scrap of written evidence we have is the newspaper account, which indicated that the women's group went via Fort Ridgely, and this obviously conflicts with other accounts. The only thing we can know for sure is that at *some* point they would have had to cross to the Henderson side of the river. Where they did this is unknown.

The story whereby ten-year-old Mazaokiyewin witnessed the stabbing death of her grandmother is recounted in more detail elsewhere in this volume.[8] The older woman was stabbed in the stomach by one of the soldier guards for moving too slowly as the group crossed a creek. The family tells this story like it happened last week; unfortunately, they do not know precisely *where* it happened.

One element of the story was a bridge. Smaller streams could be forded or crossed by log bridges or culverts. Maps can show us which streams the road did cross. The Henderson–Fort Ridgely Trail crosses four creeks: Eight-Mile Creek, Little Rock Creek, Rush River, and Fort Ridgely Creek. The latter one was crossed via ford, the others by bridge.[9] Little Rock Creek flows through Mud Lake in Cairo Township, Renville County. As it has a rather steep valley, the bridge near the south end of Mud Lake was one of very few places where wagons could cross this stream.[10] East of Swan Lake, the trail crosses Eight-Mile Creek in Severance Township, Sibley County. Moving eastward, in Dryden Township, Sibley County,

the trail crosses the north branch of Rush River. Today Eight-Mile Creek and Rush River look more like irrigation ditches than streams, and the only creek a person is really conscious of crossing is Little Rock Creek. I have yet to explore the streams and creeks on the southern route.

Mazaokiyewin also told her granddaughter about a canpahmihma kawitkotkoka, (crazy cart) that some of the children rode in. The cart's wheels did not have spokes, just one big round board that was not sufficiently greased. It squeaked terribly and added to the misery of the journey. "You could just hear that noise about a mile away," she said.[11] Such carts were not uncommon at the time. Sometimes referred to as "Red River carts," they are described in Sibley County Historical Society's *Henderson to Fort Ridgely Trail*:

> Some settlers also made crude two-wheeled carts for their use. The axles were made of hard wood like maple or oak, and had no iron skeins, nor did the wheels have iron liners in their hubs. It was wood rubbing on wood as the wheels turned. This created quite a screech and growl when running dry of lubricants. Mineral greases and oil were not yet too available, and greases from animal and vegetable fats were used. . . . A bit of humor that "old timers" would like to tell of long ago was that one early morning shrill sounds came from the west and the people thought that Indians were coming to raid. So a scout was sent to investigate if there was such danger. When the scout returned, he reported that an old man was riding his ox-cart on his way to Henderson.[12]

Although there are too few clues presently available to identify where the group might have camped most nights, we can guess which towns they went through. Oral history identifies New Ulm and Henderson. In addition, along the Henderson–Fort Ridgely Trail about seven miles west of Lake Titlow was a small town called Eagle City, just south of where the town of Winthrop is today. In 1862 Eagle City was large enough to have its own post office and hotel, as well as a tavern and other businesses. Eagle City was approximately halfway between Fort Ridgely and Henderson and a popular stopping place for travelers. One or more of the buildings there was burned during the war in 1862.[13] Although the town of Gaylord was not established until the 1880s, the trail passed a small travelers' way station (the nineteenth-century rest stop) on the southeastern side of Lake Titlow, where Gaylord is today.[14] About one-third of the way from Lake Titlow to Henderson is a tiny town called New Rome; it was first settled in the late 1850s and at the time was known as Prairie Mount Village.[15]

In Henderson, the trail from Fort Ridgely comes into town on the west side, descending a steep grade called Fort Road, which is still there today. The Fort Road runs into town and becomes Main Street. Although few, if any, buildings remain that would have been there in 1862, the street would have been lined with storefronts and houses, from which townspeople threw things at the Dakotas as they passed through. Gabriel Renville remembered,

[T]he whites were very much angered and threw stones at the Indians, hitting some of them, and pulled the shawls and

blankets off the women, and abused them much. But they finally got through the town without anyone being killed, and formed a camp beyond the town, in an open prairie.[16]

However, contrary to Renville's assertion that they made it through Henderson without anyone being killed, there was at least one death. Samuel Brown recounted the story of an enraged White woman tearing a baby out of its mother's arms and dashing it upon the ground. The baby died a few hours later, and "[t]he body was quietly laid away in the crotch of a tree a few miles below Henderson and not far from Faxon."[17]

Most likely the journey continued north out of Henderson and stayed on the west or northern side of the Minnesota River.[20] Gabriel Renville mentioned that they formed their camp "beyond the town, in an open prairie." On early maps of the area, about two miles north of Henderson is an open area designated "prairie" (see map 2). This could be the camping place that Renville mentioned. Another thing to consider is that this whole area was then known as the Big Woods. Westward it was largely prairie and oak savannah, but this part of Minnesota around Henderson was once thickly wooded. If one considers that the most likely trail is going to be the path of least resistance, going over prairie would be easier than through forest. On the northern/western side of the river, between the river and the hills that wall the river valley, was a narrow strip of prairie—ideal for a road.

Faxon village, also known as Walker's Landing for its steamboat landing, was once located about four miles north, or down-river, of Hen-

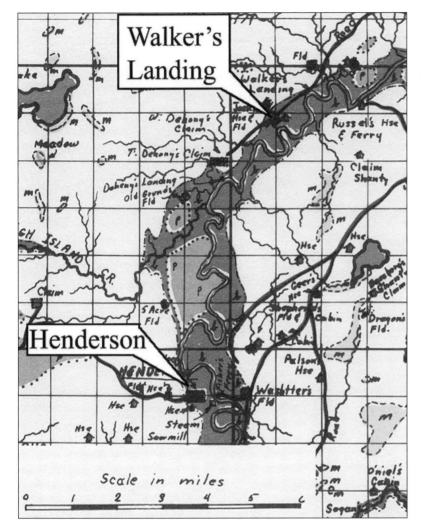

Map 2:
Area along Minnesota
River between Henderson
and Faxon (Walker's
Landing), ca. 1855.[18]

derson. Today nothing remains of the town but a road out of nearby Blakeley called Faxon Road. There is, however, some visible evidence remaining of the road between Henderson and Faxon. In places an overgrown track is visible along the base of the hill, and some barely discernable wagon ruts in the woods hint where Faxon and Walker's Landing once stood. Today this road

that leads north out of Henderson is Fifth Street, which becomes Sibley County Road 6, then Highway 40 in Carver County and continues through the towns of Carver and Chaska.

According to John P. Williamson, they arrived at Fort Snelling on the afternoon of Thursday, November 13.[21] Two weeks later he summarized the journey to his superior:

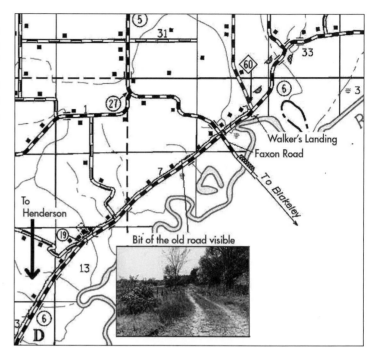

Map 3:
Modern map showing area around what was once Faxon.[19]

Map insert:
Probably part of the original road.

I accompanied the Indian camp from the Lower Agency to this place [Fort Snelling] where we arrived a week ago last Thursday. We were under the escort of three companies of soldiers in charge of Lieut. Col. Marshall. . . . [T]hey performed the march with much fear, and notwithstanding the guard of soldiers, they received sundry salutations in the form of stones & sticks, to say nothing of the curses which were heaped upon them from the doorways & hillsides.[22]

Not knowing their own fate or the fate of their husbands, fathers, brothers, and sons, the 1,700-some Dakota prisoners were moved through a series of concentration camps in the vicinity of

Fort Snelling to wait out the winter. Many of them did not survive.

THE JOURNEY OF THE CONDEMNED MEN

According to most published histories, the military entourage with the condemned Dakota prisoners left the Lower Sioux Agency on November 9, 1862. However, diaries of soldiers on the march suggest they departed the day before. With the eagerness of bored soldiers in camp anticipating a move, many of them mentioned in their entries for Friday, November 7, that they had received marching orders for the next day.[23] John Kingsley Wood noted in his diary for Saturday, November 8: "we got up at 2 and got started at 6."[24]

Amos Glanville wrote for November 8, "Saturday morning, at half past three A.M., we fed and saddled our horses, ate breakfast and reported ourselves ready, one hour before sunrise."[25] With the wit that characterizes his diary, Glanville described the scene that morning: "The sun rose most beautifully and lit up a scene I never saw before, an army in motion. A rather small one, of course, but it is the largest I've seen as of yet. I have never caught sight of the rear end when under way."[26]

The condemned men were carried in wagons, shackled two-by-two at the ankles, "the wagons containing each ten prisoners, flanked by a strong force of mounted men."[27] There were also some Dakota women and men with them who were not chained. According to Glanville, "There were very few squaws with us. What few there were, trudged by the side of the wagons or out in the grass on either side."[28] These were employed as cooks, laundresses, and nurses for the Dakota prisoners. According to Samuel Brown, there were seventeen women, four infants, and four men.[29] A roster dated December 31, 1862, gives their names and jobs (see appendix).

From the front of the column, John Nelson wrote at the end of their first day's march, "up before daylight, struck tents and comensed our march before daylight. marched *about* 25 miles. camped within 9 miles of New Ulm."[30] The Seventh Minnesota, including Corporal James Ramer, brought up the rear. He wrote for Saturday, November 8, "We was on the march at sunrise. we had a very pleasant day. We passed Fort Ridgley at noon. we pitched our tents at six oclock. the distance traveled to day is 23 miles."[31]

Although Ramer mentioned passing Fort Ridgely, it is likely that they passed the fort on the opposite side of the river. As the Lower Sioux Agency, New Ulm, and Mankato were all on the south side of the river, they would have no reason to cross it (see map 1). Another member of Ramer's regiment indicated in his diary that they traveled down the south side of the river.[32]

On the first day, they marched twenty-three to twenty-five miles, by soldiers' estimates, traveling for about twelve hours.[33] They camped eight or nine miles west of New Ulm.[34] Glanville wrote of their campsite,

> We camped tonight, eight miles west of New Ulm, in a field belonging to a man who had a very narrow escape from the Indians. They had shot his wife through the window. He went down in the cellar. They didn't follow him, but set his house on fire expecting to see him come out. The cellar ran out beyond the house under the shed. Here, he made his way out and ran, in the smoke, to the woods nearby and thus made his escape.
>
> On the other side of the road stands a house in which an old man and his two daughters were killed. . . . A son, about fourteen years old, was there at the time and fought his way out with a hatchett. . . . This same boy told us that the citizens of New Ulm were intending to kill our prisoners as we passed through the town.[35]

This description, examined next to survivors' reminiscences, suggests the location of the farm where they camped that night. Historians of Brown

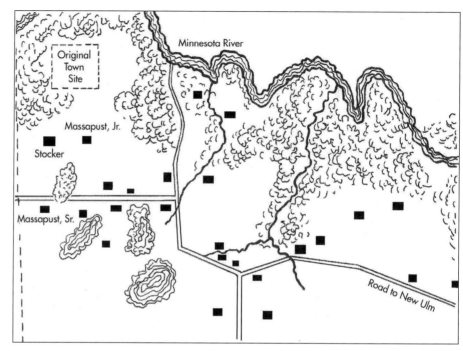

Map 4:
Farmsteads
in Milford
Township,
Brown
County,
ca. 1862.[37]

Minnesota River

Original
Town
Site

Massapust, Jr.

Stocker

Massapust, Sr.

Road to New Ulm

County believe this to have been the Stocker farm, and the farm across the road where the fourteen-year-old boy escaped was probably that of John Massapust. This land is in the northwestern corner of Milford Township, Brown County, north of Brown County Road 29 and southwest of Horseshoe Lake.[36]

Sunday, November 9, 1862, was the fateful day that they passed New Ulm. Sibley wrote afterward to his superior officer, Major General John Pope,

As I approached the town of New Ulm on my march, I was met by two persons, one of whom, representing himself as a major in the State Militia, and in full uniform, presented to me a very extraordinary document from one Roos claiming to be Sheriff of the County of Brown, in which

he forbade me to march with any Indian prisoners through the County and especially through the town of New Ulm, on pain of being resisted, etc.[39]

On this day the citizens of New Ulm were re-interring those who were killed and hastily buried during the battles of New Ulm from that August.[40] Sibley responded that he "was a United States officer in command of U.S. forces, and in charge of U.S. prisoners, and if any attempt was made to resist any passage through any part of the United States, or to fire upon the prisoners, [he would] repel it with the whole of [his] command if necessary." He added, however, that he would respect their wishes as far as to go *around* the town rather than through it.[41]

Most of the accounts from Wasicus on the

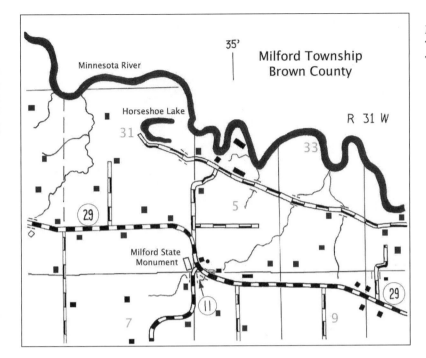

Map 5:
The same area of Milford
Township today.[38]

march mention this detour. John Wood wrote, "passed New Ulm about 10[.] did not go through town because the inhabitants were down on the indians."[42] Herb Watson wrote to his father, "we did not come through town because we heard that they were going to kill the Indians[.] they had barrels of hot water to throw on them to scauld them."[43] Sibley reported,

> [U]pon gaining a point about half a mile from New Ulm, I halted my column, threw out a company on either flank of the wagons containing the Indian prisoners, to strengthen the mounted men on guard, and I directed them to load with ball [and] cartridge, which was done. I then advanced and avoiding the town of New Ulm entirely, the main column was about opposite the center of the town when it was assailed by a crowd of excited people of all ages and both sexes.[44]

Glanville, from the perspective of the mounted infantry on either side of the prisoners' wagons, described the scene thus:

> About a mile from town, we came to a halt and a guard of infantry was placed between us and the wagons containing the Indian prisoners. We again moved forward and orders were given to allow no man to come within the lines. Instead of going through town, we were marched around it. We had gained the rear of the place when the people found it out and came rushing across the lot presently.[45]

The column was assailed by the townspeople, using any weapon or blunt object they could get their hands on or carry in their aprons. Amos Watson recalled later,

We passed the town about one mile to the south of it; however, the citizens were out there, women with their aprons full of brickbats. There were two rows of guards on each side of the wagons. I was guard on the side next to the town. The first I knew, one very large German woman slipped through in front of me, and hit one of the Indians on the head with a large stone. Well, he fell backwards out of the wagon, he being shackled to another Indian that held him, so he was dragged about five rods. Then myself and comrade picked him up and put him back in the wagon.[46]

The soldiers were hard-pressed to keep the mob back, especially when most of them probably would happily have stood aside and let the Dakotas be torn to pieces. These were Minnesota boys; most of them sympathized more with the White townspeople than with their prisoners, and none of them had been trained to strike a White woman. Finally, Sibley invoked the threat of steel. The bayonet was designed to be intimidating, and most soldiers hoped that their adversary would have enough sense of self-preservation not to actually run into a wall of bayonets. This tactic appeared to work in New Ulm:

The row was finally stopped by a company, being drawn up, with fixed bayonets, at a halt, across the road, which stopped the crowd and allowed us to go through. Eight out of ten Indians in the wagon that I was guarding were hurt.[47]

How did this happen? Ostensibly the troops were there to protect the prisoners and keep off civilian mobs. Some say Sibley let it happen. Letters from Sibley suggest that a Major Brandt of the state militia was instrumental in inciting the attack.

Sibley arrested some men who apparently were under Major Brandt's command. Sibley clearly had doubts as to the authenticity of this "major," as he tended to put question marks after the man's rank in his correspondence. Major Brandt wrote to Sibley on the evening of the attack, stating that the men Sibley had arrested were due to be mustered into the state cavalry the next day and asked that they be released. On the back of this letter, Sibley had written,

I replied to the Major ? that I had good evidence of his direct encouragement of the attack, and should report him to Gov. Ramsey he claiming to be a State Officer. That as to the release of the arrested

« THE COLUMN WAS ASSAILED BY THE TOWNSPEOPLE, USING ANY WEAPON OR BLUNT OBJECT THEY COULD GET THEIR HANDS ON OR CARRY IN THEIR APRONS. »

men he claimed, I should consult my own judgment in the matter and not his wishes.[48]

Sibley stated in his report to General Pope,

[S]everal of the State Militia were active [in the attack], and some arrests of them were made. They were subsequently released by me after a proper admonition. No attempt was made by any of the citizens, so far as I am informed, to restrain this disgraceful assault, and I have the best reason to know that Major ? DeBrandt [sic], the individual before referred to, not only did not discountenance, but encouraged it.[49]

This Major Brandt apparently also had a hand in the attempted mob attack on the Dakota prisoners in Mankato a month later. After Colonel Miller successfully turned aside the mob, General Sibley wrote to Governor Ramsey to describe the troubles they had been having with the local populace, asking that this Major Brandt be arrested:

Conspicuous among these agitators and disturbers of the peace, is Major Brant [sic], who has been brought to your notice heretofore as unfavorably connected with the attack upon the prisoners and their guards near New Ulm. He is now reported by Col. Miller, and by Capt Williston commanding a company of U.S. troops stationed at New Ulm, as one of the leaders among the German

population at New Ulm, in inciting and encouraging them to defy the authority of the U.S., by direct assaults upon the guard having in charge the Indian prisoners. Major Brant [sic] claims to be an officer of the State Militia, holding a commission from you, and among those who are said to be active in prompting and abetting the secret combinations against the public peace, are many members of the corps under his command, enrolled as State Militia.[50]

Sibley seemed to feel that if any soldiers were problematic, they were in the state militia rather than United States forces. According to the writings of some of his own troops, however, they hardly needed any encouragement. The soldiers themselves were largely sympathetic with the Whites and were extremely reluctant to intercede between them and the Dakota prisoners. Glanville described what happened when a soldier did consider striking back at a White woman:

An infantryman, who had been struck, was about to bayonet a woman when [another man in the company] leveled his carbine at him and swore he would blow his brains out if he did. The woman was left alone. I confess my sympathies were with the people, and so were those of every man in the Company.[51]

The sentiments and intentions of the following soldier are even more clear. In early December, a large mob attempted to get at the Dakota prisoners in Mankato. Infantryman Eli Pickett wrote to his wife describing the incident. Upon hearing the alarm in camp that a mob of citizens was approaching the prison,

> My first business was to put on my straps and prepare to kill as many Indians as I could[.] this I had resolved to do, in face and eyes of the oath I had taken to obey my officers and in this detirmination I was not alone, for nine tenths of the soldiers present had openly anounced their purpose never to fire on the citizens but on the other hand to pitchin to the Indians.[52]

After the attack at New Ulm, Sibley wrote to his wife,

> The assailants were finally driven back by a bayonet charge and fifteen or twenty men who were among them, were arrested, and made to march on foot, twelve miles to the spot, where we encamped for the night, where after being reprimanded for the insult to the U.S. flag committed by them, and their female associates, they were released, and compelled to walk back the entire distance to New Ulm.[53]

They arrested some citizens, mostly men (although the attack had largely been carried out by women), and brought them along to that night's camp. That is to say, the New Ulmers were made to walk with the rest of the army some twelve miles. At that night's camp, they were lectured and released. Their punishment was to walk home. There was no mention of assault, just an "insult to the U.S. flag." Sibley seemed more offended that civilians, or some "Major" in the state militia, would presume to tell him what he could or could not do—it was an affront to his authority. There is little indication that he felt any humanity for the Dakota men who were the ones assaulted.

The train of prisoners and guards continued past New Ulm and into Blue Earth County. Again, they made camp about 6:00 P.M., probably somewhere in what is now Cambria Township. Members of the Seventh Regiment wrote, "we pitched our tents at six oclock. To day we marched twenty miles" and "Camped 18 miles from South Bend."[54] According to Glanville, "Some of the Indians died that night from wounds received during the day."[55]

The following day, Monday, November 10, 1862, they reached South Bend and Mankato. The army was then dispersed for the winter, a few companies staying in Mankato as guards for the prisoners. Again, this was—in theory—more for the prisoners' protection. On the night of December 4, a mob attempted to break past the guard to kill the Dakota prisoners. The commanding officer, Colonel Stephen Miller of the Seventh Minnesota, had received word of this and had the troops ready. Corporal Henry Mills remembered later, "They came prepared, having guns, pistols, bludgeons, ropes & for the business in hand."[56] Pickett wrote of the incident to his wife,

> [Colonel Miller] now made a few remarks to the soldiers and ordered them to be ready to defend his most precious pets, to which I heard many reply they would see him damnd first[.] he wound up by telling them that he would shoot the first

man that refused to shoot the citizens that dared to attack us. . . . [A]fter surveying us a short time, and being assured of our determination not to give up the red skins[,] they quietly retired to the mutual dissatesfaction of all parties interested except a few of our principle squaw loveing officers and the Indians themselves[.][57]

Mills remembered that the colonel "made the crowd a little fatherly speech and dismissed them."[58] The attitude Pickett and his comrades held toward their prisoners is blisteringly clear. With guards like these, it is no wonder that prisoners died. One of the companies of soldiers that escorted the women and children to Fort Snelling was the very same Company B, Fifth Minnesota, that had been ambushed at Redwood Ferry in August. They suffered heavy casualties, including the death of their captain. Given the assignment to "guard" unarmed women and children, it does not require much imagination to see them taking the opportunity for some revenge.

CONCLUSION

Much of this paper, in terms of the actual routes taken by the Dakota prisoners, is conjecture. The women's march in particular is significantly lacking in documentation. Information that does exist about the march is contradictory.

As with any chaotic, traumatic event, details of exactly what happened are difficult to pin down. Dakota oral accounts tell of boiling water being thrown from upper-story windows onto the Dakota people in the wagons as they went by. There certainly is a suggestion that the citizens of New Ulm had boiling water at the ready. The soldiers state that the chained prisoners in the men's group went around the town rather than through it, but this does not address the route of the women and children. Written accounts of the women's march mention going through Henderson but are vague on any other towns along the route. There are no known Wasicu accounts naming any of the places where the women's group was attacked.[59] A number of Dakota families have it in their oral history that this attack with boiling water thrown from windows occurred in New Ulm, and this evidence should not be dismissed.

The Wasicu way has always been to believe the written records and discount the oral. But it does not do scholarly justice to summarily dismiss any sources. I am Wasicu, and it is true that I was raised to put my faith in written documents, but I also know writers can make mistakes or omissions. On the other hand, special training, akin to an apprenticeship, went into Dakota oral history as it was passed from one generation to another. According to Waziyatawin Angela Wilson, because of this training, the Dakota oral tradition is not the same as a Wasicu grandmother telling old family stories.[60] Going through New Ulm would have meant a detour, but the Wasicus demonstrated in other instances that they were willing to go out of their way to harm Dakota people. Readers will have to consider the evidence at hand and come to their own conclusions.

NOTES

1. A slightly longer version of this paper was submitted as partial requirement for my M.A. in U.S. History, December 2005. I wish to thank Arlene Busse, Darla Gebhard, and Waziyatawin Angela Wilson for all their help.

2. Samuel J. Brown, *In Captivity: The Experience, Privations and Dangers of Samuel J. Brown and Others While Prisoners of the Hostile Sioux during the Massacre and War of 1862* (Washington, DC: G.P.O., 1900[?]), 25.

3. Isaac V.D. Heard, *History of the Sioux War and Massacres of 1862 and 1863* (New York: Harper and Brothers, 1863), 240.

4. Charles H. Watson, Lower Agency, to Father, 5 November 1862, Charles H. Watson letters, 1862–1865 (St. Paul: Minnesota Historical Society [MHS] Manuscripts Collection). In transcribing handwritten letters and diary entries, I have tried to preserve, as best as I could make out, the original spelling, although I added some punctuation.

5. John Kingsley Wood Diary, 1855–1865, 6 November 1862 (St. Paul: MHS Manuscripts Collection).

6. *Mankato Semi-Weekly Record,* 15 November 1862.

7. *St. Paul Press,* 13 November 1862, emphasis added.

8. See Waziyatawin Angela Wilson, "Decolonizing the 1862 Death Marches," *American Indian Quarterly* 28 (2): 195–98.

9. Sibley County Historical Society, *The Henderson to Fort Ridgely Trail* (Henderson, MN: Sibley County Historical Society, 2003), 53. Hereafter referred to simply as *The Henderson to Fort Ridgely Trail.*

10. Ibid., 50.

11. Elsie Cavender, quoted in Waziyatawin Angela Wilson, "Decolonizing the 1862 Death Marches," *American Indian Quarterly* 28 (2): 196.

12. *The Henderson to Fort Ridgely Trail,* 6.

13. Ibid., 27–28.

14. Ibid., 25.

15. Ibid., 19.

16. Gabriel Renville, *A Sioux Narrative of the Outbreak in 1862* (St. Paul: Minnesota Historical Society, 1905), 610.

17. Brown, *In Captivity,* 26.

18. Detail from J. William Trygg, "Composite Map of United States Land Surveyors Original Plats and Field Notes," Minnesota Series, Sheet 6, Ely, Minnesota, 1964.

19. Map of Sibley County (detail), with comments added by the author; photo insert by the author, October 2005, Minnesota Department of Transportation, Mn/DOT Office of Transportation and Data Analysis: County Maps, 2005, http://www.dot.state.mn.us/tda/html/counties.html.

20. The river flows more or less northeast from Mankato to Fort Snelling, so either the "north" or the "west" side of the river refers to the same side.

21. J. P. Williamson, Fort Snelling, to Father [T. S. Williamson], 14 November 1862, Thomas S. Williamson Papers, 1839–1939 (St. Paul: MHS Manuscripts Collection).

22. J. P. Williamson to S.B. Treat, 28 November 1862, ABCFM Papers (St. Paul: MHS Manuscripts Collection).

23. Though not quoted here, it is clear from their diaries that they had been in camp for a week or two already (depending on the unit). Most entries read along the lines of "drill," "mustered for pay," "wrote home," or "nothing of importance." Of the five diarists who made entries for 7 November 1862, all five of them noted that they had received marching orders to leave the next day.

24. John Kingsley Wood Papers, Diary, 8 November 1862 (St. Paul: MHS Manuscripts Collection).

25. Amos E. Glanville, *I Saw the Ravages of an Indian War: A Diary,* August 26, 1862–July 29, 1863 (St. Paul: MHS Manuscripts Collection), hereafter referred to as the "Glanville Diary," 8 November 1862.

26. Ibid.

27. H. H. Sibley to his wife, 12 November 1862, cited in Harriet Bishop McConkey, *Dakota War Whoop: Or, Indian Massacres and War in Minnesota of 1862–'63* (1863; revised 1864; reprinted, Chicago: Lakeside Press, 1965), *fn 83*, 241.

28. Glanville Diary, 8 November 1862.

29. Brown, *In Captivity*, 25.

30. John Nelson Papers, Diary, 8 November 1862 (St. Paul: MHS Manuscripts Collection), emphasis in the original.

31. James Ramer Diary, 8 November 1862 (St. Paul: MHS Manuscripts Collection).

32. John Danielson, *History of Company G, of 7th Minnesota Volunteers, War of the Rebellion, Aug. 12, 1862–Aug. 16, 1865* (St. Paul: MHS Manuscripts Collections).

33. Ramer Diary (8 November 1862).

34. Nine miles according to John Nelson's diary, eight miles according to Glanville's and Eggleston's diaries, Hubert N. Eggleston Papers (St. Paul: MHS Manuscripts Collection).

35. Glanville Diary, 8 November 1862.

36. Darla Gebhard, Brown County Historical Society, personal communication, 30 August 2005, in the author's possession; Christ Spelbrink reminiscences, *New Ulm Review*, 19 August 1937.

37. *New Ulm Review*, 19 August 1937.

38. Minnesota Department of Transportation, *http://www.dot.state.mn.us/tda/html/counties.html*, Brown County.

39. H. H. Sibley to Gen. Pope, 11 November 1862, Alexander Ramsey Papers (St. Paul: MHS Manuscripts Collection).

40. William Folwell, *A History of Minnesota*, vol. II (St. Paul: Minnesota Historical Society, 1924), 200.

41. H. H. Sibley to Gen. Pope, 11 November 1862, Alexander Ramsey Papers (St. Paul: MHS Manuscripts Collection).

42. Wood Diary, 9 November 1862. Ramer in the Seventh Regiment also mentions reaching New Ulm about 10:00 in the morning.

43. Charles H. Watson, Camp Lincoln [Man-kato], to Father, 14 November 1862. C. H. Watson Letters, 1862–1865 (St. Paul: MHS Manuscripts Collection).

44. Sibley's letter to Gen. Pope, 11 November 1862, Ramsey Papers.

45. Glanville Diary.

46. Amos Watson, "Reminiscences of the Sioux Outbreak," [undated], microfilm, #M582, reel 3, frame 590, (St. Paul: MHS Dakota Conflict Collection).

47. Glanville Diary, 9 November 1862.

48. Major Brandt to Sibley, 9 November 1862, Ramsey Papers.

49. H. H. Sibley to Gen. Pope, 11 November 1862, Ramsey Papers.

50. H. H. Sibley to Gov. Ramsey, 8 December 1862, Ramsey Papers. Williston was captain of Company G, Seventh Minnesota, stationed at New Ulm for the winter (see *Minnesota in the Civil and Indian Wars 1861–1865*, Minnesota Board of Commissioners on Publication of History of Minnesota in Civil and Indian Wars (St. Paul: Pioneer Press, 1889).

51. Glanville Diary, 9 November 1862.

52. Eli Pickett to his wife, 4 December 1862, Eli K. Pickett Papers, 1861–1865 (St. Paul: MHS Manuscripts Collection).

53. Sibley's letter to his wife, 12 November 1862, quoted in footnote 83, McConkey, *Dakota War Whoop*, 241.

54. Ramer Diary, 9 November 1862; Danielson, *History of Company G,* 9 November 1862.

55. Glanville Diary, 9 November 1862.

56. Henry L. Mills and Family Papers, 1894 reminiscences (St. Paul: MHS Manuscripts Collection).

57. Eli Pickett to his wife, 4 December 1862, Pickett Papers.

58. Henry L. Mills Papers.

59. Although they served on the side of the Wasicus in the war, the three men who wrote accounts of the attack in Henderson—Thomas Robertson, Gabriel Renville, and Samuel Brown—were part Dakota.

60. Personal communication, in the author's possession.

Decolonizing Restorative Justice

DENISE BRETON

◄○►

When I first heard about restorative justice, I remember feeling liberated and inspired by a movement that advocates responses to harm other than inflicting more harm. What a concept! It gave me hope that the untold harms in this world could be addressed in healing ways—ways that addressed why harms were happening in the first place. We could put our energies and resources into repairing whatever needed mending and changing whatever was generating hurt.

If, for example, a square peg was not fitting into a round hole, hitting it harder, denigrating square-ness, or locking the peg in a drawer for a few years was not going to solve the problem. According to restorative justice, harms alert us that we need to look deeper into our relationships and how we are going about life. If we respond to harms in a good and open way, they can help us live better with a greater understanding of those around us and the nature of our worlds. Because there is no part of our lives where conflicts, hurts, and harms do not arise, restorative justice can be revolutionary to virtually everything we do. The concept seemed so simple yet so profound.

Restorative justice still gives me hope, but I have had more time to think about it, and I have

since been on the 2004 Dakota Commemorative March. I still believe that restorative justice holds huge promise for helping us learn how to coexist as people, but I now think the very essence of restorative justice as a philosophy and way of life calls us to expand our focus to include more than person-to-person harms. What about our history—how we got to where we are as Peoples? How did we end up with this "round pegs only" pegboard, and at what cost?

These are the more fundamental questions—those that make us look at the roots of harms. As we do, we are challenged to apply what restorative justice practitioners have learned about healing harms between people to healing harms between Peoples. This is the direction restorative justice must go, I believe, or it will fall short of fulfilling its promise. Indeed, it will risk joining the other side and becoming part of the institutions that not only deny the greatest causes of suffering but also actively perpetuate harm.

◄○►

For those new to the concept, restorative justice is about intervening on painful plotlines and exploring how to shift those plots, so that people's lives can move in more healing directions. It is about responding to harms not with knee-jerk forced removals to detentions, suspensions, jails, or prisons but with concerted efforts to work things out and make things right. At its core, restorative justice is about coexistence: How can we make coexistence work—not when things are easy but when they are hard? Precisely when hurts occur and where harms exist, restorative justice poses the questions:

- What happened?
- Who was hurt?
- Who caused the hurt?
- What amends could and should be made now?
- And what might it take for those harmed to feel whole?

When all those affected, including communities, come together to address these questions in open, honest, and heartfelt ways, healing generally follows. With time, effort, and resolve, people change, relationships blossom, and communities grow. Possibilities open for addressing harms that before seemed impossible.[1]

Central to the restorative justice process is listening. It begins with listening to others and hearing stories different from our own. Before long, we start listening to ourselves in different ways as well. Listening more than speaking and listening with the heart as well as with the head

are things that I, like so many others who have come into restorative justice, am learning and finding transformative to all my relationships.[2]

By creating spaces for people to share their stories, restorative justice processes also bring to light how the individual and the collective overlap. Interconnected as we are, we each face realities not of our making but which affect us nonetheless. Put simply, other people do things that affect us, and we often do not have a say in what they do. Every action occurs in a context of relationships, cultures, and histories. As we reflect on the larger contexts in which harms have occurred, we inevitably ask: How did we arrive at a point where harms like this happened—and will happen again if we do not change?

―◦―

Initiated in the 1970s with victim-offender mediation programs, restorative justice is basically new to the dominant society's criminal justice system, yet its core concepts are ancient. Many Indigenous Peoples' teachings and traditions distill generations of experiences about coexistence as a way of life and therefore about how to mend relations when they break down.[3] As a White person, I do not know these ways firsthand, but what has been explained to me makes huge sense and certainly challenges to the core my society's power-over, hence punitive, ways of responding to harms.

As I understand a more community-based approach, which is closer to an Indigenous approach,

« HOW DID WE ARRIVE AT A POINT WHERE HARMS LIKE THIS HAPPENED—AND WILL HAPPEN AGAIN IF WE DO NOT CHANGE? »

for people living in closely knit communities to react to the surface event of harm without addressing the deeper dynamics that led to it is neither logical nor practical. The realities of connectedness suggest that hurt is not an isolated event; it comes from somewhere, and because of connectedness, it affects many if not all people in the community.

In fact, those most affected serve to protect the well-being of the community, much as the canaries who died in the mines warned the miners of bad air: one person's harmful act or another person's suffering signals an imbalance that could be harming everyone. If one community member is behaving hurtfully, the rest of the community wants to know why. Where is the urge to harm coming from? To effectively heal a hurt, those involved need to consider how it arose, and to do that, the whole community needs to participate in some way. The goal is not retribution but to repair broken relationships for the good of all. When harms occur, the most practical question is: What does it take for the community to come together and feel whole, so that the community and everyone in it are stronger, healthier, and less susceptible to similar harms in the future?

There are many ways of doing this, and those affected must simply come together and decide how they want to work things out. Haudenosaunee scholar Michael Cousins explains that some Indigenous traditions do not rule out taking a life in extreme cases, such as murder, though banishment is more common. If killing the perpetrator of harm is chosen, though, it is generally not done to punish or deter. As he explains, other reasons are given, such as to appease the aggrieved so that retributive violence does not escalate, or to make it possible for the soul of the murdered to work things out with the soul of the murderer by sending the latter to the life beyond. The aim is healing, repair, restitution, and making whole, so that the community heals.[4]

Dakota linguist and scholar Ella C. Deloria provides an example of this determinedly reparative approach from her People, the Ihanktunwan Dakota. In an article, Ms. Deloria shares her notes from a 1936 interview with Simon Antelope.[5] Mr. Antelope was well into his seventies at the time of the interview and was considered a man of standing among his People. Mr. Antelope explained to Ms. Deloria four methods that a Dakota community might use to respond to murder—a crime that rarely happened. Though Mr. Antelope considered one of these methods as more exemplary than the others in terms of its moral and spiritual demands, he said that any of the four responses was considered effective for community healing.

The first option was for a relative of the murdered person to kill the murderer: a life for a life. This option ended the matter. No further acts of retribution would follow.

The second option was to convene a council. The most peaceful men would approach both the murderer and the one who had been appointed to avenge the death to see if peace could be made. The whole community would contribute fine gifts for this process, because it was in everyone's best interests that peace be restored. When the two antagonists accepted peace, the gifts were divided equally between them.

The third option was considered the most powerful and by far the most exemplary response, though it was the most difficult to do. It was for the family of the murdered person to adopt the murderer as a relative to take the place of the one killed. If this path was chosen, the murderer was not treated as a despised slave to the family but was given the finest gifts and treated with all the kindness and respect that the dead relative would have received. By so doing, both the family of the murdered person and the murderer would spend the rest of their lives committed to healing a harm that might otherwise have divided the community. "Such a man usually made a far better relative than many a natural relative," Mr. Antelope observed, "because he was bought at a high price."

Putting the murderer through ordeals of physical endurance was a fourth possibility. If the person failed the test, he was killed instantly by the arrows of onlookers related to the person who was murdered. If he passed, he was either taken in as a relative by the kin of the murdered or allowed to go free, exonerated.

◄○►

The challenge for restorative justice today, I believe, is to apply this determinedly reparative, healing approach to addressing harms between Peoples—harms that go back generations. Yet the choice to engage in this process remains a hard sell, and many objections are raised to dismiss it. We have all heard them, and those of us who are White are rigorously programmed to have them:

All this awful stuff happened in the past. I didn't personally do it. Why should I pay for what my great-great-great-uncle did or didn't do—or for people I'm not related to at all? People are just using the past to avoid taking responsibility for their lives

now. My grandfather came here with two pennies in his pocket and built a good life; why can't others do the same? We should put the past behind us and start fresh—let's make it a clean slate. We're all equal now. In fact, people of color get favored over the rest of us. Does the past really affect us all that much? Even if we wanted to, fixing the past is impossible, so why waste our time trying? Our ancestors won, and yours lost. That's just the way it is. Get over it! Move on! Stop whining and blaming others for your problems! Pull yourself up by your bootstraps! Blend in! In any case, how do we know you're not exaggerating? Our historians don't tell us about these terrible events. Stories of atrocities aren't in our written records. When Columbus landed, there probably weren't more than one or two million Indians here anyway. I can't help it if their immune systems couldn't handle European diseases. Whatever happened, it's no one's fault; it's just progress. If it hadn't been us, it would have been someone else. Let's focus on today's harms; we'd be lucky to put those right. You can't go forward by looking back. Face it: you're better off now than your ancestors were before we came. You've got TVs, computers, cars, music, refrigerators, cell phones—tons of stuff you didn't have. And look at TV sitcoms and all the news anchor people of color: there's no racism anymore. We like everyone. I do anyway. Some of my best friends . . .

As Whites, we are programmed from birth to have these and similar reactions, because that is how we play our part in maintaining the status quo. These familiar responses keep how we got to where we are off our collective radar as well as off our conscience. Thanks to our programming, our time frame extends no more than a few decades into the past and into the future. If it were comparable to how we live personally, it would be like refusing to think one minute ahead or behind "now." How could we sustain relationships or any serious endeavor? How could we learn to act responsibly?

To expand my perspective and to help loosen the hold of my White programming, I imagine how I would feel if I were watching a movie about our history on this land:

The scene opens on a People who are human in every way—families, desires, differences, good years and hard years, close relations with some neighbors, more difficult relations with others. Over countless generations, they have worked out respectful relationships with all the beings who people the land. Indeed, as a People, their traditions teach them from their earliest moments of life how to be a good relative to each other and that all of creation is their relative. Respect and being generous out of gratitude for the generosity that sustains them are values that pervade their way of life. They are raised to be mindful of how we are all related, not because they have always done this perfectly, but precisely because they remember times in their history when they have forgotten to do this and have lived in unbalanced, disrespectful, or ungenerous ways. The costs, first

paid by others, came back on them and proved too great. Having learned through hard experiences how to be a good relative, they have lived as a People on the land since time immemorial, and their ancestors are buried there.

Then the scene shifts. One day, a different sort of People arrives. At first, they seem friendly, but it quickly becomes clear that the newcomers are there because they want what the Original People seem to have, namely, not only the land but also control of everything within the land. It is also clear that the newcomers do not place much value on "being a good relative." Seeing the newcomers hit and yell at their children, saying "spare the rod, spoil the child," the Original People wonder why the newcomers don't like their own offspring. It worries them, because if people treat their own so harshly, why would they treat others better? When these children grow up, where in their lives would they have learned how to treat others with respect, integrity, or kindness?

As the film moves on, the Original People's worst fears come true. The newcomers, now settlers, become insatiable about claiming land without regard for those who live there and taking resources without noticing how it upsets the Natural World. They seem to stop at nothing to gain control of the place where the Original People have lived for generations. Inequitable agreements wildly favoring the settlers are made under fraudulent and deceitful circumstances, and even then, the settlers ignore the meager terms afforded the Original People. The settlers give the Original People blankets infected with smallpox, so that huge numbers of them get sick and die. Dispossessed of their lands and livelihood, betrayed by governments that ignore their commitments, homeless and starving—we know what happens next.

But the conflict between the two Peoples simply provides a pretext for the settler's original agenda to go into full swing: to exterminate the Original People, either by killing them outright, causing their death through starvation, disease, exposure, or torture, or forcibly removing them beyond their borders. The genocide that follows, openly mandated by the settler's governor and executed by every crime against humanity, is perpetrated not by a few in government divorced from the will of the citizens but as a direct response to the will of the settlers, so that the settlers and their descendants can live where the Original People have always lived. In fact, the settler population actively carries out genocide against the Original People, murdering men, women, and children, even babies to collect a bounty, which for a single murder amounts to a year's income.

As I watch this movie, I wonder how on earth it is going to work out. It's as if I am watching *The Godfather*, only it's much worse—more like *Schindler's List* without a Schindler. Depressing as it is, I decide to fast forward.

A century and a half later, the settlers have now become firmly entrenched as the colonizers, the ones who hold the power, call the shots, arrange things for their own benefit, and don't consider the cost to others. At any point, they could have changed their relationship with the Original People, but they haven't and have no thought of doing so. In fact, having done everything they could to kill the Original People or to drive them away, the colonizers have achieved their goal of never having to think about the Original People. Colonizer life goes on as if the Original People never existed on the land.

True, the land retains many of the place names used by the Original People, but many counties, roads, and public facilities are now named after the most virulent settler leaders of genocide. Colonizer children born only decades after the holocaust occurred have been taught nothing about what happened or how they came to live on the land. They encounter very few if any of the land's Original People as they go about their daily lives. The region becomes known as the "Whitest state in the Union," yet no one asks how this came to be so. Instead of explaining the infamous history, schools, museums, clergy, books, magazines, and newspapers promote a story that celebrates the settlers' occupation, while dismissing the Original People—their language, traditions, knowledge, relationship with the land, even their competence as humans—as minor footnotes buried in the past.

Not surprisingly, the colonizers live well: they are mostly landowners, they have nice homes, most of them do not worry about food, they have good jobs, their children enjoy promising futures, and they have full representation in their colonial governments. They are told and believe that they live in a just, fair, and equitable society. They assume that when conflicts occur, everyone involved will receive "due process." "The law of the land" is assumed to be basically good, and the system is assumed to be trustworthy and reliable. Though injustices occur, the colonizers are raised to believe that these are the exception rather than the rule.

True, there are problems, yet the problems these descendants face as a People are those they themselves have created, and in large part because they have not questioned the means that were used to get them where they are. "Might makes right" has continued as an unfortunate but inevitable way to conduct business and government. The colonizers spend most of their waking hours in institutions that are authoritarian, hierarchical, competitive, and driven by money. "Being a good relative" is not a value in this environment; instead, doing what it takes to succeed and maximize profits are the priorities. Not only does the Natural World suffer as a result, but also the ruthlessness once reserved for the Original People overshadows the colonizers' working relations. Though the colonizers have been raised to accept this way of life, many are unhappy. Heart attacks most commonly occur on Monday mornings. Addictions are epidemic, as is the use of antidepressant drugs. Many of their children are unhappy as well. Staggering numbers of them must be medicated in order to attend school, and some become vandalistic, violent, or suicidal.

Nonetheless, the colonizers view themselves as good people, and they consider their society the pinnacle of human evolution. They see themselves as superior humans living in a superior culture. Their ethic is to get an education, work hard, go to church, and be conscientious in childrearing, even questioning their ancestors' harsh treatment of children. Some volunteer to help the needy through their religious institutions, while others are active in civic and political life. Precisely because their schools and institutions still promote win-lose ethics and competition as the way to find one's place in the world, the colonizers feel they have earned whatever they have and that they deserve a good life. Their self-image is that of a wholesome, dedicated, God-fearing, and generally righteous People. They have no sense that the good life they enjoy came through the suffering and genocide of their neighbors—indeed, of those whose ancestral lands they inhabit. Neither do they realize how profoundly their genocidal history shapes their society as well as their character as a People.

As I sit and watch this familiar self-characterization, it is hard to view the movie's colonizers as they obviously view themselves, and it is clear how much the colonizers' self-image and way of life depend on keeping their history of genocide off-screen. In fact, when a few of the colonizer characters learn a little of the history, they go through a predictable sequence of mental and emotional turmoil. The ones who persevere through the stages of denial, defensiveness, self-justification, and anger find themselves plunging into identity crises: self-doubt, shame, guilt, grief, loss of the otherwise solid sense of themselves as good people, depression, and despair about what to do.

As a movie-goer, I think about what I would want these "good citizens" to do. What would feel satisfying to me as their response to this history? What would I like to see happen? And how would I feel if the movie ended here?

When the scene shifts to the descendants of the Original People, I see how differently they live:

> Several hundred years after the newcomers arrived, many Original People do their best to maintain their traditions, for it is through them that they have maintained the will and the means to survive. "Being a good relative" has not been forgotten, and its attending values of respect, honor, and generosity continue to be taught to their children through practice more than words. A sense of community and identity as Original People remain.
>
> Yet despite the positive force of their traditions and values, these descendants struggle under the realities of multigenerational trauma created by the core conflicts between the Original People and colonizer society,

which remain unresolved centuries later. The crimes of genocide and massive land theft have been made invisible. In fact, they continue, but under bureaucratic, corporate, economic, social, political, religious, scientific, legal, or institutional guises. For the colonizers, it is as if the deeds of genocide never happened; for the Original People, they never stopped happening.

> As a result, the Original People do not share the colonizers' belief that the prevailing colonial order is just, good, or reliable. "Due process" is not something they experience, either as victims or offenders or as a People. Quite the opposite. They have been forced to live under the constant threat of annihilation, since the colonizers have never questioned their state's official policy of genocide. It is as if post-World War II Jews had to live in a place called "Hitler County," and when they went to some of the finest restaurants where the monied and powerful go, they saw pictures of Hitler hanging on the walls; how safe would the Jews feel? Would they feel that the society was committed to their safety and well-being or to reversing the genocidal policies of the past?
>
> So, too, the Original People find no grounds for regarding any aspect of colonizer society as trustworthy. For example, when a group of them broke into a colonizer headquarters a few decades ago in political protest, they discovered that the "health care" provided by the colonizers had been routinely sterilizing their women without their knowledge or consent.

Billions of dollars that treaties guaranteed them in payment for access to resources on their lands have mysteriously disappeared. Through centuries of such experiences, the Original People have come to realize that no aspect of colonizer society can be trusted to defend or promote their best interests. Instead, *every* aspect encroaches, invades, threatens, undermines, and altogether works to destroy the Original People—both as people and as a People.

Those who venture into colonizer society to make a living find that what it takes to become a "successful" person in colonizer society—willingness to win at all costs, willingness to embrace colonizer language and self-promotional ways, willingness to swallow racist treatment, and willingness to disregard community good or respect for the Natural World in order to achieve material gain—goes against Original People teachings. Original People face a dilemma: to survive "well" in colonizer society, they are pressured to go against who they are as Original People, yet to do so intensifies their genocide.

As if this dilemma were not challenge enough, the racism that was used to justify the extermination of Original People persists, so that Original People descendants are largely excluded from getting good jobs, obtaining loans or mortgages, or gaining opportunities for their children. They remain the "degraded Other," "those people." This makes it exceedingly difficult for them to break the cycles of poverty that began when the settlers invaded and destroyed their means of livelihood. Denied their traditional ways and unable to afford good colonizer food or medical care, their health deteriorates.

Retraumatized daily by having to cope with a society whose values are so antithetical to those of their ancestors, many seek to anesthetize their trauma of dislocation through addictions. Suicide rates are high, especially among young people. Confronted daily with messages that denigrate, marginalize, and dehumanize who they are as a People, the descendants of the Original People manifest a range of behaviors. Some are unhealthy and damaging—violence under intoxication, property violations, or domestic abuse—though nothing of the order of the organized crimes against humanity that the settlers and now colonizers have perpetrated.

Other behaviors are clear assertions of identity and sovereignty as Original People but which colonizer authorities (teachers, bosses, police, administrators, and government officials) find threatening. A young boy, for example, writes "Original People Pride" on his notebook, whereupon a colonizer teacher thinks he must belong to a gang and interprets the student's subsequent conduct through this filter. Teens weaned on settler-colonizer racism pick fights with the boy for being proud of his People, yet he is the one labeled a troublemaker by the school authorities. He no longer enjoys school, and so truancy goes on his record. Before long, his parents are charged with neglect, and the authorities use their institutional might to forcibly remove the son from his parents' home. He grows into adulthood in a colonizer boarding school, juvenile facility, or foster home far away from his family and community. He is told that his forced removal is for his own good. Given such "opportunities," colonizers expect him to "make good," and so when grief overcomes him to a paralyzing degree, some of the colonizers conclude that he is from an ungrateful, lazy, no-good People.

As an adult, it does not take much for this man to find himself in court. Continuing the original policy of forcibly removing those who do not conform to settler society, the colonizers systematically remove large numbers of Original People, especially men, to prisons. Some go for life because they cannot afford adequate legal representation. This "solution" of forced removal fits with the colonizers' historical response to conflicts with the Original People. The colonizers' "law enforcement" system uses force, intimidation, punishment, and imprisonment to maintain control. Instead of facing the history, the settler descendants continue to define "the problem" in ways that blame the Original People. "'Those people' have a problem; we have nothing to do with it." The ones in prison are just "bad apples" and "need" to be locked up. After all, look at the "successful" Original People! Hard feelings are planted to divide Original People against each other, while the colonizers' role remains unnamed.

All this is supported by the colonizer's origin story—the story told to new generations about how the settlers came to this land. The story describes the settler population and culture as superior and the Original People as quaint, savage, and destined to go extinct. "Why be concerned with the plight of those who can't 'make it'? The best we can do is put them in prison where they're fed and have a place to sleep—but can't reproduce."

Watching this movie is incredibly painful—certainly for the descendants of Original Peoples but for many colonizers like myself as well. Even for colonizers who have known only the colonizer narrative, witnessing this origin story told to include the experiences of the Original People can be "unsettling."

Of course, I know this is one of many movies I could watch. I could, for example, watch a movie about a time and place several millennia earlier where my ancestors were the Original People and faced a similar invasion and colonization. In that story, the physical differences between the settlers and the Original People were not so marked, and so assimilation and hence loss of culture occurred more completely as the centuries passed. Even so, millennia later, vestiges of my Original People ancestors' teachings and traditions remain.

I could also watch a movie about the traumas my ancestors suffered in Europe as a result of their colonization—the social, economic, religious, and political traumas that drove them to find new homes, to treat their children as they did, and presumably to behave so savagely to the Original

Peoples when they came here. By the time they arrived, my settler ancestors were apparently unable to conceive of coexistence as an option. Whereas Native Peoples largely operate from a "me and my relatives" paradigm—and "relatives" includes all of creation—my ancestors largely operated from a "me and not-me" or "us and not-us" paradigm. Everything that is "not me" or "not us" is viewed as a threat—the reaction of a People for whom trauma (and traumatizing) is a normal, everyday way of life.

Given this outlook, they evidently had no knowledge or experience of what it means to work out relationships with those who seem different but whose needs are much the same. They assumed coexistence was impossible: one People or the other could survive but not both. "Not me," "not us," had to go. Given current events, from the Iraq war to the torture of political prisoners in Abu Ghraib to global warming, this paradigm of engaging trauma as a way of life remains very much in force.

◄○►

Participating in the Dakota Commemorative March was like seeing the Original People–colonizer movie for a week, only I was in the movie and living it, and I still am. It is a painful movie to live in, to be sure, but it keeps me focused on harms that, from a restorative justice perspective, I and my fellow colonizers need to address if we care about our dignity and self-respect. Whether I personally committed these crimes or not, I benefit from them. They were planned and executed precisely so that I could live here now in one of the Whitest states in the country, Minnesota. And I perpetuate these crimes by

continuing in the colonizer habits—the mental, emotional, behavioral, social, political, economic, religious, scientific, racial, institutional, and systemic patterns of power and privilege—that have been my way of life since birth.

These colonizer habits include, for example, ignoring the history, acting like it never happened, not holding myself and my People accountable for immense harms done, and escaping to a comfortable, consensual, racial amnesia. The colonizer mind-set carries an automatic presumption of superiority and rightness—that the way I and my fellow colonizers see and do things is the "right" way. Even if we become fascinated with other Peoples and learn their ways, we still hold ourselves apart as "above;"[6] we are the default mode, because we represent the dominant social order. These habits reinforce the biggest colonizer habit, which is to regard the land I live on as legally, legitimately mine. After all, everything that happened was done for land. The Dakota had it, and the settlers wanted it. Once they exterminated the Dakota to get it, the Minnesota colonizers finished the job by passing laws that made the entire land-grab through genocide seem legitimate, lawful. The land is now "legally" ours: this is the epitome of colonizer thinking.

Participating in the march is about breaking these habits. If I am here, how I came to be here matters. The history directly affects me, and on more levels than I ever realized. Most fundamentally, I live on this land—land gained through mass murder. Yet not only do I benefit materially from being a descendant of the people who did these things, but also I am shaped by my People's collective character, which has been formed through this history.

My Euro-American history tells me, for example, that if my position affords me the power to harm another for my own benefit and to get away with it, then I should do this, and I should never question whether I did something wrong, much less worry about making it right. If this were not so, Congress and corporations would not behave as they do and have done. Corporate ravaging and "preemptive" wars to conquer other Peoples and to control their lands and resources are not an aberration in American history; they are how Native Peoples have experienced us from the start.

These classic colonizer habits are programmed into me, and my fellow Americans consistently vote into office those elected officials who will most vigorously enforce and extend colonization. It is hard to imagine a politician anywhere in America winning an election on a platform of land return and reparations to Native Peoples and other Peoples on whose suffering this nation has been built. Moreover, even if I work every day to question and challenge my internal colonizer programming, its ways of hooking me are continually reinforced by the colonizer society, which is everywhere now. I will do my work of decolonizing myself and my life, but I also know that this work will never be "done."

◄○►

One of the things that keeps me going in doing this work is the movie. Once I have seen it and seen how I am living it, I can no longer escape asking myself if this is the kind of person I want to be. More, is "colonizer" the kind of People in whom I can take pride? The movie is still playing, and, although I am not its director, I have some

say in how it goes. Keeping the painful movie in front of me helps me to remember the programming, to name colonization for what it is, to name my role in it, and to attend to its dismantling. I no longer see myself or my fellow colonizers only as we see ourselves but also in the light that our People-to-People history sheds. I need the pain to help me do my work and not get lost in the mesmeric forgetting, which every nuance of my programming would have me do.

To be clear, it is not that I enjoy the pain of putting my hand on a hot burner; it is rather that the pain reminds me to pull my hand away. The burner in this analogy is not the Dakota People or even the history; it is the settler-colonizer programming that set horrific cycles of pain in motion and then tried to build a "good" society on this foundation.

The pain is also useful, insofar as it marks the first movements toward learning what it means to be a good relative. I cannot imagine healing a relationship that has been so broken by so many for so long without experiencing pain in the process. If I believe in the restorative justice process—if we as a People want to find our way to being good relatives to those whose ancestral homeland we inhabit—we have to be willing to feel the pain of what has been done and our ongoing roles in keeping that history going.

As useful as the pain can be, though, it is also good to be living in a movie whose plot we can alter. Obviously, there are some things about this movie that we cannot change. We cannot change that genocide happened, for example, but we can change denial of this fact. We can begin to acknowledge the magnitude of harm and its ongoing effects. We can acknowledge who did what to whom, and then we can work to heal these harms in whatever ways are possible—and much is possible. We can begin to intentionally imagine coexistence in ways our colonizer programming has kept off-screen.

◄○►

Minnesota's colonizer society has responded to this history and its effects mainly through social service programs or, if those fail, through the criminal justice system, in other words, by imprisoning Native people. Yet neither of these responses addresses the roots of harm. Quite the opposite, they keep the movie's plot going in its original genocidal direction, because the aim of both institutions—social services and criminal justice—is forced assimilation into colonizer society. They are not designed to honor the Dakota People or to rectify longstanding harms against them. As Dr. Waziyatawin Angela Wilson so clearly explains in her introduction to this book, a social service mind-set further blames the victims of genocide, racism, and colonization; it does not promote decolonization by challenging these realities as the roots of harm.

Restorative justice could offer a more appropriate response, because it requires acknowledging that at the root of these harms lies a criminal act—indeed, immense crimes against humanity. The issue between Minnesota's colonizer population and the Dakota People is a criminal issue first. All the social, economic, and political issues that Native people face today follow from this central

> « WE CAN ACKNOWLEDGE WHO DID WHAT TO WHOM, AND THEN WE CAN WORK TO HEAL THESE HARMS IN WHATEVER WAYS ARE POSSIBLE—AND MUCH IS POSSIBLE. »

truth: crimes have occurred that have never been rectified or brought to justice.

As with any victim-offender situation, restorative justice processes begin when the perpetrators of harm acknowledge guilt and take responsibility. Acknowledging the crime and rectifying its effects are central to helping both the victim and the offender recover and be able to live good lives. Only when the crime is addressed to the victim's satisfaction can the victim and the offender begin to explore whether or not they are able to be in a good relationship with each other.

If, however, the crime is not even acknowledged much less repaired, victims are continually re-victimized. In fact, they are often blamed for the harm, as if they deserved to suffer or as if it were their fault; they are blamed for failing to "bounce back"; or they are blamed for the dismal condition that the crime left them in. The assumption is always that something is wrong with the victim. In the meantime, the offenders not only go scot-free with the booty but also continue to harm their victims by not holding themselves accountable for the ongoing suffering they are causing.

If the restorative justice movement fails to address the People-to-People issues and the crimes embedded in our history, it will risk losing credibility in this country, as it seems to have already done in Canada. Many First Nations now reject restorative justice, and precisely on these grounds. The core vision of going to the roots of harm and doing what it takes to make things right is experienced as empty rhetoric, invoked only when colonial power structures deem it advantageous to do so. Instead of working toward wholeness for Peoples, restorative justice functions as another tool of colonizer institutions, whose goal is not healing but for one People to justify and reinforce their domination of another People. Restorative justice is simply used to make the violence of the criminal justice system—the colonizers' control-by-fear fist—seem more humane. Instead of addressing the wider contexts that generate harms, the focus stays on trying to fix person-to-person conflicts. Individuals, families, or communities are viewed as "the problem," while the larger reasons that individuals, families, or communities have problems remain invisible.

« If restorative justice embarks on People-to-People healing, the systemic issues causing suffering to Native Peoples will begin to be addressed and rectified. »

This does not mean that we as individuals—colonizers or Original People—should not be held accountable for the harms we do. Yet here in Minnesota, we colonizers have not been held accountable *at all* for state-sanctioned, citizen-supported crimes against humanity—and yet we describe ourselves as international leaders in restorative justice. How could Dakota people—or anyone else who knows the history—take restorative justice seriously if we diligently hold this or that offender accountable for drug possession or stealing a car or even doing graffiti while we fail to hold ourselves accountable for genocide that we committed so we could steal an entire state's worth of land? If we were to apply our own laws about murder and stolen property to this case, we would have to rule that every time we sell a house in Minnesota, we commit a felony, and every Minnesota realtor should be imprisoned for dealing in stolen property gained through murder.

Restorative justice does not have to be hijacked into being an accomplice to colonization, for its roots are not there. If restorative justice embarks on People-to-People healing, the systemic issues causing suffering to Native Peoples will begin to be addressed and rectified. Together as Peoples, we can acknowledge the massive harms done, name racism as it operates to hurt Native Peoples, arrange substantive land return, honor the inherent sovereignty and self-determination of Native Peoples, make restitution and reparations, return the billions of dollars missing from trust funds that have been accumulating from the White use of Native resources, respectfully cease behaviors that denigrate Native Peoples (such as using them as sports mascots), and teach everyone the full history of this land.

These steps of healing justice give us an agenda to work on, yet we do not have to wait for local, state, or federal governments to begin this work. If we are committed to seeking restorative justice between Peoples, we can also do a great deal as individuals. First and foremost, we can expand our awareness of how we have been programmed to be racist and of how we now function as colonizers, not only by benefiting from past harms but also by justifying them, so that the status quo that secures our advantage remains unchanged. Talking to other Whites and finding ways to educate each other about our history and our internalized programming is something we can all do. This is not personal; virtually all of us Whites have been subjected to it—but it hurts persons, ourselves included. Parents in particular can work on exposing the racist and colonizer programming and one-sided histories presented in children's books and school curricula.[7]

And we can take action. For example, many Whites who have no children, such as myself, might consider returning the stolen land we live on to the Dakota People in our wills. My mother and I have made such land-return arrangements for the home we now live in, and my sisters, both of whom *do* have children, agree and support us in this personal step of land return.[8] Many religious congregations are finding their numbers dwindling and are deciding to fold and sell their church property. This land could be returned as well. These individual and group actions by no means reduce the necessity of People-to-People, nation-to-nation rectification of harms; quite the contrary, they contribute to building the public and collective will to do so.

All such efforts contribute to healing our People-to-People relationships by grounding them in economic, social, political, and basic human justice. It may take decades or even centuries to rectify harms of this magnitude. But with this work, as far as criminal justice issues are concerned, it is reasonable to postulate that many if not most person-to-person harms done by Native people—committed largely against themselves or each other, not against colonizers—would likely disappear. It is also reasonable to postulate that both Peoples would benefit by taking the journey to coexistence.

◄○►

Indeed, the benefit to us White colonizers is another reason why I hope that restorative justice will embark on People-to-People healing. A core tenet of restorative justice—something practitioners have come to believe because of extensive experience in this work—is that holding the perpetrators of harm accountable is essential not only for fairness but also for the perpetrators' healing and transformation. When offenders experience accountability, they are transformed.

In restorative justice, being held accountable is not about punishment or revenge. It is about connecting and becoming more real—connecting with more of reality than the narrow sphere in which inflicting harm made sense. To start, it means becoming acquainted with the effects of their harms, which usually involves listening to victims. Offenders meet the human faces of those whose lives they have damaged. They hear the pain in the voices of their victims as they tell their stories. Harm is not abstract or "over there"; the person who has suffered is sitting in the same room and telling the offender face-to-face how life has changed as a result of the crime.

Being held accountable leads to honest soul-searching: Why did I do this? What was I thinking or feeling, and where did these thoughts and feelings come from? Restorative accountability does not lead to self-rejection but to self-compassion and ultimately to self-acceptance. If anything, running away from harms committed—denying our relationship to harms done—constitutes self-rejection, because it rejects our reality and prevents us from confronting who we are, as if we could not handle facing ourselves and the reality of our lives.

Being held accountable also means finding out from those harmed what restitution they need and working to provide it. Offenders step up to the plate of doing whatever they can to put things right, no matter how long it takes. Making restitution affirms offenders' competence and establishes their dignity and self-respect. It feels good to own up to a harm and to work to make it right, just as it feels demeaning not to do so.

Another reason that holding perpetrators accountable transforms them is that, through the process, people who obviously felt isolated now learn how to build connections. The process forms relationships, and offenders experience something of what it means to be related. Even though the process is filled with pain and remorse, it is still transforming, suggesting that the slightest experience of being related can bring profound change.

Transformation is certainly what we colonizers need as a People, and we would be among the first to be blessed by the process of making things right. Holding ourselves accountable for the massive crimes embedded in our history and continuing—indeed, multiplying—in our present would help us become the kind of People we aspire to be but are not. By making ourselves come to terms with other Peoples' realities, we could discover coexistence—a way of being that depends not on conquest and oppression but on respect, honesty, integrity, and mutual good. Embracing our accountability could also effect a healing in our collective psyche of traumas going

back millennia—traumas that conditioned us to think in "me vs. not-me" terms. Instead of engaging in Darwinian, colonizer struggles for survival, we could learn how to "be a good relative," and we could discover that it is a better, happier, and more sustainable way to live.

⟨o⟩

Can restorative justice play a significant role in effecting this level of transformation? Yes, but only if we are serious about decolonizing. What does this mean? That is a huge question, and I can only begin to respond by trying to orient the restorative justice compass in a decolonizing direction. To start, restorative justice must set its sights on undoing colonization, since this is the core injustice, the root crime that must be addressed. To address the crime of colonization, decolonizing restorative justice means raising the questions that restorative justice typically poses but raising them on the level of Peoples—the level on which the crime of colonization has occurred:

- What happened in our history on this land?
- Who as a People was hurt and continues to be hurt?
- Who as a People caused the hurt and continues to benefit from it?
- What People-to-People amends could and should be made now?
- And what might it take for the Dakota People to be made whole?

Those of us who are the perpetrators and beneficiaries of colonization in Minnesota must be involved in addressing these questions, but we are not the ones to determine the answers. We must listen to what the Dakota have to say. In the process, we have to give up the power advantages as well as the presumptions of superiority that we have taken on as colonizers and instead humbly and sincerely work to make things right as equals with those of the Dakota Nation.

Certainly, decolonizing restorative justice means not using restorative justice to reinforce colonization. For example, using restorative justice as a better way to enforce obedience to colonizer institutions or to prop up the failing criminal justice system reinforces White supremacy and colonizer control. By contrast, a decolonizing premise is that the state of Minnesota is not the government of the Dakota People; it is their oppressor—the "might makes right" regime of the occupiers. On this premise, the restorative justice agenda is not to make Dakota people more comfortable in the White-dominated state of Minnesota or more willing to live under its rule; it is to establish a healthy nation-to-nation, People-to-People relationship that enables us to coexist respectfully as equals, as we do with Canada or France.

To get there, some serious amends must be made, and the process of making these amends is how respect is built on both sides. Indeed, everything we have learned about restorative justice says that we simply have to do the work that the healing process requires—and we discover what is required as we engage in it. If we commit to this process not as colonizers but as decolonizers, the restorative justice work is not something we do "to" Dakota people; it is something we do "with" the Dakota People.

◄o►

In 2004, I was invited to participate in the Dakota Commemorative March. Whether I will do so again in 2006, 2008, 2010, or 2012 will depend on the Dakota: What contribution, if any, can Whites, the colonizers, make by being present? In restorative justice, the victims of harm get to say what feels healing and what does not. Certainly the perpetrators and beneficiaries of harm are in no position to decide on these matters.

During the march, I saw the look on the faces of the Dakota, especially the elders, when they saw me—blond as can be, clearly White and not raised among them. I saw the effects of lifetimes of suffering at the hands of my fellow colonizers— nearly boiling water poured on children's hands in boarding schools as punishment for speaking their language, beatings and sexual abuse in schools, rapes and murders never even investigated much less brought to justice, children stolen from their parents, continually dehumanizing stereotypes and messages about them in colonizer society, exclusion from economic opportunities, yet complete denial that injustices had ever been done. Though not ungracious, the Dakota elders did not come up to me, shake my hand, and say how glad they were to see me there. How could they?

Restorative justice does involve bringing together victims and offenders, but only after considerable preparation has been done on both sides. Forcing those harmed to come together with those who have benefited from those harms prematurely could inflict greater damage, especially during times when the victims of harms want nothing more than to be left alone to grieve their loss. As for us colonizers, we are far from doing our preparation for such a meeting. Most of us have not seen the movie—we live oblivious to the immensity of harms done—so we are not even considering what preparation on our part would be necessary.

◄○►

Whatever my personal participation in future marches might be, I am profoundly grateful that I could be there in 2004. The experience is one I will never forget, and it has changed me far beyond what I could ever imagine that "sitting in a car" for seven days could do. Participating in the march has been a life-altering experience.

During the march, I felt that this was the most important place for me to be, and the rest of the world with all its busy-ness did not matter as much. The march seemed to occur outside of time. I suppose I felt this way because the march lifted me out of my everyday routine and gave me at week-long look at how we got to where we are. Holding a space for considering our course as Peoples is bound to be intense, and even when the conversations were light and joking, the deeper issues were always there.

My participation turned out to be a balance between being present and not being present, at least not in the sense of actually walking. I drove a support car and played Lakota music for the marchers through a speaker horn propped outside my car's sunroof. Marchers threw their coats and bottles of water in the car as the days warmed, and sometimes those whose feet hurt too much or who had developed an injury would ride a few miles. I was grateful that it worked out this way. I could bear witness to the history and support the marchers without intruding on their experience. It is ironic that, as much as I love to walk and walk an hour every day when I am at home, I went on a 150-mile march and ended up walking no more than two or three miles all week.

Though I live within driving distance of the march route, staying overnight in the church basements, gymnasiums, and community centers was a very important part of the experience. Sometimes the organizers arranged evening sessions when people were invited to share their thoughts and reflections about the day. Other times, we just had dinner and hung out. Different families and communities prepared feasts for us. The evenings gave us a chance to get to know each other and to reflect on the march. These times moved us to deeper places, so that by the next morning, something had shifted. The comments people made the night before stayed with me the next day, and I could tell from others' comments that they were experiencing the same.

Because I was driving behind the marchers and listening to Lakota/Dakota music (on top volume, so the marchers could hear it), I had plenty of time to think about the people in front of me—to wonder what they were feeling as we went along and what their ancestors felt 150 years earlier as they walked this route. I came to know everyone's walk, their hats and coats, and their back views very well. I could see relationships forming and friendships growing. I noticed which marchers enjoyed visiting with others and which preferred to walk in silence. Though I had to keep my concentration sharp because so many children were around, my experience was nonetheless very meditative. I was largely alone with my thoughts from sunup to sundown for the week.

I have so many memories. For example, I remember all of us waiting along the shoulder of a busy highway for the police to come and help us

cross the road. We were stopped a long time. The Lakota music was going, and traffic was speeding by on my left, so fast that my car shook. When I looked out into the trees in a marshy area to my right, though, it was as if I went back in time and could feel those who walked there before us—starving, sick, cold, wet, afraid, exhausted, grieving, yet persevering to save their children. I felt as if we were in two worlds at once, and somehow the world on our right seemed more real, more compelling. I didn't want to look to the left, and it felt jarring to do so.

I also remember a night in a parking lot. We were carrying our things into the basement of Turner Hall for the night. My friend, who is Sicangu Lakota, stopped and began singing "Kola Weksuye," "I remember my friend." It was a clear,

cold November night. He could not finish the song.

This parking lot was in New Ulm—perhaps the most terrible town for the original marchers to pass through. Settlers had been killed by Dakota warriors whose families were starving, and the surviving townspeople were full of revenge. It was here that White women poured boiling water on Dakota elders, children, and women, until their skin peeled off.

During our evening meeting, Dr. Chris Mato Nunpa, his daughter Dr. Waziyatawin Angela Wilson, her daughter, Autumn Wilson, Leo Omani, and Dr. Edward C. Valandra spoke about the history and what had happened in New Ulm. Some townspeople had been invited to this meeting. After the speakers, Dr. Mato Nunpa opened the microphone, and a White townswoman came forward. She invited the marchers to engage in reconciliation by agreeing to listen to some of the colonizers' stories and their accounts of settler losses during that time.

I did not sleep well that night. What the White woman said made me angry, and I was mad at myself as well for not speaking up. It sounded as if she said, "We suffered too, you know, so that makes it all equal." Yes, the loss of loved ones is always profound, but there is nothing remotely equal about what the Dakota experienced and what White settlers experienced, evidenced by the enormous differences in the lives of the two Peoples today. Whereas the settlers invaded someone else's territory and knew full well the risks of living here, the Dakota suffered invasion and occupation, theft of their homelands, fraud of every ilk, violations of treaties, betrayals, sadistic and murderous cruelty from soldiers and civilians alike, Governor Alexander Ramsey's statewide official policy of genocide and extermination, a harsh Minnesota winter in a concentration camp, forced removal from their ancestral homeland, and bounties on the head of any Dakota person who dared to stay. Yet this White-privileged colonizer had the gall to say what she did to the Dakota marchers in the basement.

I don't know the woman or her character, but her words provided a stark case of colonizer thinking, cloaked in the rhetoric of "reconciliation." Not once did she speak to the injustices that the Dakota speakers had raised. Not once did she acknowledge the crimes that enabled her to stand there on Dakota homeland. She came across to me—and, I later learned, to other marchers as well—as condescending, self-justifying, self-righteous,

self-servingly selective in the telling of history, unremorseful of the harms that her forebears had committed, and entirely unwilling to acknowledge the settlers' dishonest and downright inhuman conduct, which is what caused the 1862 war in the first place. If anyone, her own forebears are to blame for the settlers' deaths in New Ulm and Henderson, yet she failed to connect these dots. In her view, reconciliation evidently meant exchanging isolated stories of personal pain without regard to the actual context of historical events, not to mention their multigenerational consequences.

I felt ashamed, and as I said, ashamed of myself for not speaking up. Looking back, I now know I was so upset with her because I saw my own colonizer programming exposed, and it was ugly and shameful to behold. Yet it is also White shame—the racist, colonizer programming that has been instilled in me from the start—that prevented me from responding to this woman as I immediately wished I had done. African American minister and author Thandeka analyzes White shame and its twofold workings. First, we who are Euro-American are shamed into identifying ourselves as White early on, since that is how we gain our place of privilege in a power-over, colonizer hierarchy. Over half of her book, *Learning to Be White*, gives examples of White-on-White racist programming, in other words, examples of how Whites initiate each other into being racists and colonizers through emotional and sometimes physical violence against each other. This is how we "learn to be White." Second, once we internalize this shame—that is, once we internalize the White social "norm" that it is shameful *not* to act as racist colonizers—this shame controls our behavior, preventing us from taking action as antiracists and decolonizers, even when we consciously would hope that we would do so, as in my case here. Naturally, these dynamics of White-on-White shaming make it absolutely critical for us to develop White-on-White antiracist and decolonizing ways of interacting.[9]

As in this instance, being with the Dakota during the week inevitably made me see White colonizers differently, especially myself. I was aware of my legacy as a colonizer, and I could observe in myself how this has shaped me much more vividly than when I am among other Whites. Being in situations that make my programming more visible to me helps me, because I know that racist, colonizer programming is lethal stuff and that I have been conditioned by it since birth. Among other things, the march was a weeklong meditation on this programming: what it has done, what it continues to do, and how I personally figure in all of this.

Stopping every mile to put stakes in the ground to honor those who died during the 1862 Death March was inevitably powerful. When a marcher realized that a stake being put into the ground bore the name of an ancestor, history ceased to be abstract or remote. I will always remember the moment when Waziyatawin realized that her ancestor's name was written on a stake—her great-great-great-grandmother who had been killed by a soldier. She could not speak for her tears, so her father stepped in to continue telling their ancestor's story. I remember every detail of that stop—her face, her voice, her father's face and voice, her children coming to comfort her, the place where we were, the time of day, where people were standing, and the deep silence that followed her father's words, because so many people were weeping. I

also remember how hard it was to leave that place, how slowly we moved away.

Spending much of the week on dirt roads and along rivers gave me a different sense of the land as well. I gradually stopped seeing the land the way it is now with houses, telephone poles, roads, and SUVs scattered all over it, and I began to reflect on how it was before the White settlers came.

I also began to sense something about the relationship that the Dakota People have with their homeland and realized that their relationship is not diminished by White occupancy, which felt increasingly transient and ephemeral to me. The reason, as far as I could tell, is that the Dakota continue to have an intimate relationship with their homeland. In spite of dislocation and genocide, this has not changed.

Observing in some small way the depth and quality of this relationship, I also realized how profoundly we colonizers lack any comparable relationship with the land on which we live. Even the notion of having a two-way relationship with the land seems strange. Pondering this during the week, it seemed to me that, because we have not sought to "be good relatives" to either the Dakota People or the land, we continue here as intruders, false notes, no matter how long we have been here. It is not that we could not be here in a good way in principle. Rather, what makes our presence false is how we came here—that it was and remains so wrong. Those in restorative justice often repeat a saying that they have heard from Native Peoples: "You cannot get to a good place in a bad way." I imagined another movie:

A large and closely-knit family lives in a beautiful home that has been in the family

for generations, in fact, as long as anyone can remember. The home is well loved, tended, and cared for, and the people are happy. They also interact respectfully with the land around the home and have worked out respectful relations with plants and animals. Then one day, some gangsters arrive and gun everyone down. After the gangsters throw the dead bodies of the family members into a ditch, they move in, and they continue their violent way of life. They cut down all the trees around and kill the animals, and when they still need wood for fire, they pull off a piece of floor or the mantel. They don't honor the land or take care of the house; they just use things, consuming them as they go.

As colonizers, we would naturally say this movie image is overdrawn, since we do not see ourselves as rapacious gangsters, but I doubt the Dakota would agree. This land once had thick forests with trees fifteen feet in diameter, passenger pigeons so numerous that they blocked the sun, and buffalo whose herds covered the prairies. Aside from the questions of whose home it really is in this scenario or what has happened to this home since the invaders took over, who has a relationship to the place? Could the gangsters claim to have the same relationship to the place that the family had? If the gangsters wanted any kind of positive relationship with the place, what would they have to do to get it? What process would they have to go through in order to change their way of being there?

As I pondered such things on the march, I realized that being deeply connected to a place develops over generations. Moreover, it develops as people live in a place "in a good way," that is, with integrity and respect in every direction of their lives. "Being a good relative" to all beings is evidently essential to being in a place in a good way. If we fail to do this—if possessing is our only way of being in relation with a place—we will always be occupiers, because our very presence signifies disrespect, harmful intrusion, and violence.

Since our origin as White People is in Europe, we will never be Indigenous to North America, and so the land will never be "ours" or our homeland. But for those of us living here now as occupiers, we can address the realities of our occupation. We can learn the truth of how we came here, and we can challenge whether we want to continue being here in the worst of all possible ways. We can acknowledge that we live here as guests in another People's homeland, and we can inquire of our hosts whether we have behaved as guests well or badly. If badly, we cannot blame them if they fervently wish that we would leave. Until we confront how we are here, the authentic relationship that binds a People to the land in any legitimate way—a relationship based on mutual respect—will always be denied us. We will be here neither as Indigenous People nor as their guests but as offenders, violators—colonizers. I was reminded of what the great Dakota scholar, writer, and visionary, Vine Deloria Jr., wrote:

> Underneath all the conflicting images of the Indian one fundamental truth emerges—the white man knows that he is an alien and he knows that North America is Indian—and he will never let go of the Indian image because he thinks that by some clever manipulation he can achieve an authenticity that cannot ever be his.[10]

Behaving like gangsters and then trying "some clever manipulation" to cover our deeds will not make our presence here in any way legitimate.

By contrast, I glimpsed the Dakota People's authentic relatedness to the land not only in the marchers' words but also in their movements, gestures, tones of voice, and ways of interacting. Being respectful of place, land, and "all our relations" seemed simply the appropriate way to be. Indeed, the march itself is an example of this. The

« IF A PEOPLE AND THEIR HOMELAND SHARE A DEEP WOUND, IT IS RESPECTFUL TO ACKNOWLEDGE THAT WOUND AND WORK TO HEAL IT, JUST AS IT WOULD BE DISRESPECTFUL TO IGNORE THAT WOUND . . . »

march has to do with healing a terrible trauma that affected both the land and those who have lived there. Planning the event and taking the time to do it respect the land by maintaining a relationship of integrity. If a People and their homeland share a deep wound, it is respectful to acknowledge that wound and work to heal it, just as it would be disrespectful to ignore that wound, causing it to continue unhealed. Among the Indigenous Peoples of the world, the Dakota would not be alone in saying that the land remembers. My Celtic ancestors said the same.

For those of us who are occupiers and colonizers now, though, such values have not guided our relationship with the land. Because of our cultural paradigm and our history, we do not think in terms of having a relationship with the land that needs time and tending, neither would it occur to us to respect the land as we would our own mothers. We do not think that committing crimes on the land will damage our relationship to the place. According to our worldview, land is a commodity, an object of ownership, an inert "thing" that we possess, dominate, and exploit for profit. Indeed, our Bible tells us to "subdue" the earth and to "have dominion . . . over every living thing that moves upon the earth" (Genesis 1:28). Clearly, land falls into the "not me," "not us (not human)" category, so it would never occur to us to regard the land as our relative. To use theological terms, we would not consider having an "I–Thou" relationship with the land of Minnesota.[11]

The Dakota, by contrast, refer to their homeland as *Kunsi Maka*, Grandmother Earth, or *Ina Maka*, Mother Earth—one who has personality and who gives life. The desire to be in good relationship with her is as natural and important as being in a good way with our own mothers, and acting badly in her presence is like acting shamefully in front of our mothers. To be driven from their homeland is to be forcibly separated from family—from the original relative who gives the Dakota life as a People—and to return to walk in the footsteps of their ancestors on the body of their most shared relative is a profound experience. It is not about real estate. To begin to appreciate the power and depth of this relationship in even the smallest way and then to juxtapose this awareness with a knowledge of the history— that all the horrific things done to the Dakota were done precisely to separate them from their homeland—this is what I as a colonizer experienced on the march.

◄o►

Before closing my essay, I want to share something that occurred about a year after the 2004 March. I discovered that I am more personally related to this history and to the Dakota who suffered, as probably many other Whites are as well. During the march, it was clear that one of the most profound things that we can do as human beings is to acknowledge our relatives, and a crucial step in claiming our humanity is to recognize how related we are.

I was stunned, therefore, when at a conference in October 2005, I had the opportunity to hear Gabrielle Tateyuskanskan read her essay for this book. She described the inhumanity of Seth Eastman, a famous painter of Dakota people. Mr. Eastman had a daughter, Winona, with his wife Wakaninajinwin, a Dakota woman, but abandoned them both when Winona was born in 1832, declaring the marriage over. Thirty years later, Seth

Eastman, now remarried to a White woman, did not respond to a letter from his grandson and the son of Gabrielle's relative, Jacob Eastman, when he wrote to his grandfather telling him that he was imprisoned in Davenport, Iowa, and starving. Seth Eastman most certainly knew what was happening to his Dakota relatives during this terrible time of war, ethnic cleansing, executions, imprisonment, and extermination, and yet he did nothing to help or save them. Indeed, he had the position to do so, for he became the military governor of Cincinnati, Ohio, in 1863.

I am related to Seth Eastman through an ancestral cousin, Ebenezer Webster III, who married Seth Eastman's great aunt, Abigail Eastman. As I listened to Gaby read her article, I realized that I am related to a man who had a Dakota family and who made his fame and fortune painting images of Dakota people and Dakota life, yet when his own grandson needed him most for his survival, he turned his back on him and acted as if he did not exist. As Gaby asked in her essay, what kind of individual is this? What kind of society, culture, or People creates a person with such values?

If acknowledging relatives marks our humanity, his failure to respond to their life-or-death need marks a shocking inhumanity. His is a pattern I very much want to break, and the Dakota Commemorative March has given me one opportunity to do this. Whatever else I can do, I can at least bear personal and public witness to the terrible truth of what happened here to those to whom I am also related—something Seth Eastman chose not to do.

◄○►

Obviously, writing this article brings the march experience back to me, yet I have to say that not all of it is profound or wrenching. I also remember the foot rubs, the joking around, the morning meetings in the ladies room, the speculations about various sounds in the night, the eternal quest for coffee, the moments of rest before and after meals, the stories about blisters and aching feet and muscles, the evening rituals of setting up camp and the morning rituals of dismantling it—rituals such as hauling mattresses, sleeping bags, and luggage—and the feeling of being so tired at the end of the day in a way that felt so good.

I am grateful beyond words that the march is now a part of my life. Through this experience, I have become grateful to know who I am as a colonizer, because only then can I begin my life as a decolonizer. From a sense of despair, I once said to my Sicangu Lakota friend Edward Valandra, "This being White will be the death of me." Without missing a beat, he replied, "No, it will be your renewal."

Notes

1. About restorative justice, see Howard Zehr, *Changing Lenses: A New Focus for Crime and Justice* (Scottdale, PA: Herald Press, 1990); Howard Zehr, *The Little Book of Restorative Justice* (Intercourse, PA: Good Books, 2002); and Denise Breton and Stephen Lehman, *The Mystic Heart of Justice: Restoring Wholeness in a Broken World* (West Chester, PA: Chrysalis Books, 2001).

2. Listening to others' stories is central to any restorative justice process, because it generally has such transforming effects on everyone involved. Though all restorative justice practices provide spaces for listening, the process that teaches listening in the deepest and most transformative way is adapted from the Indigenous "talking circle" and is referred to among restorative justice practitioners as the "peacemaking circle process." See Kay Pranis, Barry Stuart, and Mark Wedge, *Peacemaking Circles: From Crime to Community* (St. Paul, MN: Living Justice Press, 2003).

3. Restorative justice draws directly in both philosophy and practices from Indigenous Peoples' traditional peacemaking ways worldwide. See *Justice As Healing: Indigenous Ways,* Wanda D. McCaslin, ed. (St. Paul, MN: Living Justice Press, 2005).

4. Michael Cousins, "Aboriginal Justice: A Haudenosaunee Approach," in *Justice As Healing: Indigenous Ways,* ed. Wanda D. McCaslin (St. Paul, MN: Living Justice Press, 2005), 141–59, especially 150–51.

5. Ella C. Deloria, "Some Notes on the Yankton," published in *Museum News* of the Dakota Museum, University of South Dakota (Vermillion, SD), March–April, 1967. The full text of her interview with Mr. Antelope is reproduced on the Web site of Living Justice Press: www.livingjusticepress.org under the listing "Indigenous Sources."

6. See Shari M. Huhndorf, *Going Native: Indians in the American Cultural Imagination* (Ithaca, NY: Cornell University Press, 2001).

7. See, for example, Donnarae MacCann, *White Supremacy in Children's Literature: Characterizations of African Americans, 1830–1900* (New York: Routledge, 1998).

8. A nonprofit organization devoted to helping Whites with the mechanisms and technicalities of returning land to Native Peoples—something like "Whites for Native Land Return"—could serve a valuable role and help build momentum for land return.

9. Thandeka, *Learning to Be White: Money, Race, and God in America* (New York: Continuum, 2000). On the subject of White racism in general, I have appreciated Paul Kivel's *Uprooting Racism: How White People Can Work for Racial Justice* (1996; revised, Gabriola Island, BC: New Society Publishers, 2002).

10. Vine Deloria Jr., "Foreword: American Fantasy," in *The Pretend Indians: Images of Native Americans in the Movies,* ed. Gretchen M. Bataille and Charles L.P. Silet (Ames: Iowa State University Press, 1980), xi–xiii.

11. I refer to the work of the Jewish theologian Martin Buber (1878–1965), who, viewing human life as being fundamentally about relationships, contrasted the "I–It" relationship with the "I–Thou" relationship. See Martin Buber, *I and Thou,* 2nd ed., tran. R. Gregory Smith (Edinburgh: T. & T. Clark, 1958).

2004 Dakota Commemorative March Photo Essay

DAVID MILLER

◄O►

List of photographs by David Miller in the order that they appear:

Bear Cronick, Neil McKay, Leo Omani, Alvin Kopas

Leo Omani

Autumn Wilson

Haza Win Prayer Stake

Alvin Kopas

Dakota Youth from the Lower Sioux Community

Mervel Jay La Rose Jr. and Talon Wilson

Transforming Lives by Reclaiming Memory
The Dakota Commemorative March of 2004

AMY LONETREE

◄○►

When people come back to their heritage, when they learn their language, when they march to reconcile a part of history that has never been acknowledged, then they are slowly putting together the pieces of their lives, like a puzzle.[1]

◄ Clifford Canku (Dakota) ►

As I sit down to write this essay the tears come, as they usually do, when I reflect on the Dakota Commemorative March. Where all this emotion comes from—grief, pain, anger, pride, joy, and love—will be what I hope to convey in this essay. I have given public presentations about my experiences on the march before, and I was overwhelmed by waves of emotion as I publicly shared my experiences. As a professional historian and college instructor, I am used to conveying to a wide range of audiences the painful and amazing stories that are the very core of the Native American experience in this continent. But why is it that when I speak about the Dakota March the emotions are so raw, so intense, that I find it impossible to speak on it without the tears?

Perhaps it is because the Commemorative March is all about the intersection of my personal and professional lives in ways that are so interwoven that I do not know where to begin

to separate the stories, nor would I even want to try. The march transformed my life in powerful and meaningful ways, and the words to express the depth of this transformation are at times elusive. But one of the most important sentiments to convey is my gratitude. I am grateful to all the generous and brave Dakota people who invited me to participate in their march and who made me feel so overwhelmingly proud to be part of this experience. And I feel gratitude for my ancestors, whose strength I drew upon every single step I took along the way.

I walked in November 2004 for reasons both professional and personal. As a Ho-Chunk woman, I walked in memory of my Ho-Chunk ancestors who, as a result of the ethnic cleansing policy of the time, were forced out of the state of Minnesota in 1863 along with the Dakota. I also walked to honor the stories shared by my father, Rawleigh Lonetree, who first told me about the painful history of the 1862 war and the mass hanging of the thirty-eight Dakota warriors in Mankato on the day after Christmas 1862. Perhaps most significantly, I wanted to be part of an event that acknowledged Indigenous women's history. The march gave me an important opportunity to honor my Ho-Chunk grandmother Ann Littlejohn Lonetree, who died in 2002, and her ancestral Dakota bloodline. As a historian who understands the importance of challenging the American master narrative and its silencing of Indigenous voices—especially the voices of women—in the telling of our history, I felt that this event gave me an opportunity to reclaim and honor the courage of Native women by walking in solidarity with the Dakota.

The Dakota Commemorative March is important on so many levels, and this essay will be a personal testament on the meaning of this histo-ric event in my life. What follows will be a series of reflections on the significance of this commemorative act and my critical engagements with its legacy. This essay also serves as the beginning of my contributions to the scholarship and reflective writing on the Dakota Commemorative March. These reflections underpin all of my scholarship on this inspiring event, which has forever influenced the way that I view the importance of making the Indigenous past present in our lives. The Dakota Commemorative March has given me tremendous gifts. It has helped me strengthen my voice as an Indigenous activist scholar, it has imbued my life with a greater appreciation of my family history, and it has strengthened my commitment to continuing the challenging task of reclaiming Indigenous history and memory and decolonizing the historical record.

THE FALLACY OF CLOSURE AND THE DANGERS OF "MEMORALIZED FORGETTING"

Before I began writing this essay, I watched a video on history and memory, *Public Memory: A Film about American Memorials,* which features some of the leading historians working in this area. Historian Kenneth Foote conveyed one of the most significant points for me as I consider the lasting legacy of the Commemorative March

My grandmother, Ann Littlejohn Lonetree, with her mother and sisters. Seated is my great-grandmother Rachel Whitedeer Littlejohn and behind her from left to right are her daughters Florence Littlejohn, Mary Littlejohn, and Ann Littlejohn (Lonetree), late 1920s/early 1930s. *(Photo courtesy of the Wisconsin Historical Society; Whi-35073.)*

when he stated, "Some . . . events do not have closure."[2] He and other scholars argued that some of the most painful and difficult events in American history will never be overcome even after being memorialized, nor should we delude ourselves into thinking that they ever could be. These tragic events are so painful and devastating and have had such a profound impact on who we are today, that it is futile to believe that we could ever achieve "closure" on them. Edward Linenthal, who recently completed a book on the memorializing of the Oklahoma City bombing, further articulates the futility of believing that closure is possible:

I don't want memorials to become part of the material expression of therapeutic culture. I think that one of the most obscene words in the English language is *closure*. And it's this pop psychology that evidenced the most profound moral disrespect for the searing events that people have gone through. How in hell do you go up, I don't care how many years after whether it's one or seventy-five, how do you go up to the mother of a murdered child in Oklahoma City and say: Well, have you reached closure? I mean that says so much about who we are and our desire to not deal profoundly with these indigestible events. Ok, so that's closed . . . we've learned the *lessons* . . . another really problematic word. The same with the term *healing process:* as if how people incorporate over time these violent events into what they consider and call the "new normal" which is a phrase I learned was not a glib phrase

but a really good phrase in Oklahoma City. That there's no old self to be put back together but a new self to be cobbled together out of searing experience. To think that this is some kind of regular process that you can look at in stages is just dopey.[3]

Linenthal's point that our society has a difficult time addressing, much less dealing with "the indigestible events" in our history certainly reflects how American society responds to the Native American past. The larger American society encourages us to seek closure; it tells us not to "live in the past" but rather to embrace a quick moment of reconciliation with the descendents of the perpetrators of the violence in our history, and then to move on, emphasizing to the world that we have survived. But how is this even possible? The devastation wrought in the name of Westward expansion and American Imperialism and the American Indian Holocaust of which the 1862 Dakota Death March is part have never been acknowledged. Why should we as Native people continually try to acquiesce to the all-consuming American desire for closure—that though our tribal nations have suffered in the past, we are all Americans now, and Indigenous people just like everyone else need to embrace the present.

It is futile for anyone to believe that these events could ever have "closure" and our commemorative events should never be framed as such. The Native American Holocaust encompasses many "searing events" in our history and no amount of time can ever diminish the pain we feel. That is not to say that we remain mired in the horror or that we think of ourselves only as victims. Through reclaiming memory of the tragic events of 1862, our communities are engaging in what Linenthal refers to as this *cobbling together of a new self out of "searing experience."* Through the Dakota March, the participants are demonstrating to the Dakota, as well as to other Indigenous people, the means to move forward. We are gaining strength born out of a new knowledge that emanates from our shared movement across the landscape. We learn to live in the present with an acknowledgement of the past, and we hope that we will have the strength to persevere just as our ancestors did.

Healing of Dakota communities is, therefore, an important overarching goal for the march, but it must also be made clear that this healing will never allow for a conscious forgetting of the searing events of 1862 in Minnesota history. It is futile and destructive to believe that this event will ever be forgotten, for as Edward Linenthal has stated, "memorialized forgetting is one of the most insidious processes that there is."[4] We must remain vigilant in our efforts never to forget and to continue our efforts toward decolonizing the historical record, now that the Dakota community has reminded everyone of the legacy of the 1862 war in our lives today.

WALKING TO EDUCATE: TELLING OUR STORIES OF THE 1862 DEATH MARCH

One of the purposes of the Dakota Commemorative March has been to educate the public about the continual legacy of the U.S.-Dakota War of 1862 and the forced removals that followed. This has included giving speeches and public testimonies to White people in the towns we stayed at in the evening after a long day of walking. March organizers and some participants also gave interviews to the local journalists of the towns we passed through.[5] These interviews, articles, and public presentations were designed to help raise the consciousness of people on the lasting legacy of the horrific events of 1862, and on the pain still felt by Native communities today. These moments of truth telling were difficult for some of the White people to face, and it was at these times that I experienced firsthand what Linenthal referred to, namely this all-consuming American desire for closure regarding horrific events.

A particular exchange that took place in the town of New Ulm, Minnesota, illustrates this point. We stayed in a community center in New Ulm following a particularly emotional day. We walked where Dakota oral historical accounts recall that White townspeople threw boiling water on the defenseless people back in 1862, burning many children, women, and old people. Upon our arrival, young children were attending dance classes on the upper levels of the community center, and later in the evening we ate dinner with local townspeople who came to hear us speak on the march.

During the speeches an important statement was made that I think represented the views of

« WE MUST REMAIN VIGILANT IN OUR EFFORTS NEVER TO FORGET AND TO CONTINUE OUR EFFORTS TOWARD DECOLONIZING THE HISTORICAL RECORD . . . »

many of the non-Native people we interacted with on the seven-day, 150-mile route. Though not usually stated so explicitly, we could still feel the undercurrents. On this evening in New Ulm, one of the White women in the audience took the microphone after listening to very powerful presentations by the marchers. The marchers had just been speaking on the significance of the original March: the hardships and atrocities that mostly Dakota women and children were forced to endure, what it feels like to walk in the path of the ancestors who suffered greatly on the original march, and how these stories needed to be told not only for the healing of our own communities, but for White people as well. In her remarks, the White woman expressed her wish that in the future the local White townspeople would be able to participate in the Commemorative March to tell their stories of their ancestors who had been killed in 1862. Though a good sentiment, I felt that she was suggesting that we stop emphasizing Dakota suffering, because, after all, White people suffered just as much, and that instead we should move toward a quick and speedy act of reconciliation.

I could not help feeling that my fellow marchers had similar reactions to what she said, for there was a noticeable silence in the room after she spoke. It is important to keep in mind that the marchers are a very articulate and vocal group comprised of community activists, scholars, artists, and tribal leaders. Silences usually do not last long in our midst. After this uncomfortable silence, one of the leaders of the march, Dr. Chris Mato Nunpa, found the words to speak. He said to her, with all due respect, that we have heard the White's stories. White stories about the loss of lives in their communities are the only stories

that have been remembered and honored on the landscape, and it is time for them to listen to us. Not much was said by the White people in attendance after Chris spoke, but his words served as an important reminder that we will not allow the impact of the Dakota ancestors' stories to be diminished.

To me this exchange speaks volumes and is representative of the reaction of many White people when the painful and horrific stories of the Indigenous experience in North America are discussed. In some cases they want us to be quiet—not to tell the stories again for fear that their deeply embedded understanding of who they are as Americans, and who their ancestors are, would be challenged. When we do tell these stories, they usually attempt to diminish our suffering by putting theirs on equal footing. It is difficult for Americans to accept that this nation was built on the pain and suffering of the Indigenous Peoples of this continent, and in this case that their privileged position and comfortable lives in New Ulm, Minnesota, had everything to do with the attempted destruction of the Dakota Nation in 1862.

DAKOTA 'COLLECTED MEMORY': HONORING AND REMEMBERING ALL OUR RELATIONS

One of the beautiful things for me about the Commemorative March is that it is not an effort toward a Dakota collective memory, but a bringing together of "*collected* memories" of the U.S.-Dakota War of 1862 and its significance for Dakota people. "Collected memories," a term advanced by historian James E. Young, are "the many discrete memories that are gathered into common memorial spaces and assigned common meaning."[6] Whereas collective memory suggests a fixed, monolithic view of memory that is imposed from the top down, "collected memory" embraces the diversity of memories that each individual brings. Collected memory allows for a bottom-up approach—a building of a community memory by a coming together of individual memories. Through the collecting of these individual memories, we build a "common understanding of widely disparate experiences and our very reasons for recalling them."[7]

In the case of the 1862 war, no singular narrative predominates in the Commemorative March participants' stories on the significance and meaning of this violent period in their history. Participants expressed a range of viewpoints and perspectives, and people came with a range of stories about the war, its aftermath, and how it has impacted their families. During the weeklong event and since, we have not emphasized only one particular story or response to the war to the exclusion of others. The war and everything that happened around it have been framed and understood as part of the colonization process, and this perspective has given us a deep understanding that the Dakota ancestors did the very best they could at a time of great hardship and suffering.[8]

After the devastation brought by invasion, diseases, forced assimilation, Christianity, the violence of the 1862 war, and the subsequent forced removals, we cannot say that there is only one response worth legitimating and acknowledging at times such as these. Perhaps in previous years, we as Native People have sought to emphasize only the stories of resistance to these devastating events and have ignored or relegated to the periphery stories of capitulation and assimilation. At the same time, Whites in Minnesota have always honored the stories of Dakota capitulation and assistance to their cause in their remembrances of the war. But when the 1862 war is framed as part of the colonization process, there is recognition that the difficult choices made by the Dakota ancestors reflected the horrific circumstances of the time.

The march organizers have allowed and advanced collected memory of this "searing event" by telling stories of their relatives who fought on both sides during the war. As Leo Omani, Dakota spiritual leader and Commemorative March organizer, stated, "We were torn apart. It was beyond our control. All of our People got torn by the Wasicu religion in our way. And it's hard to talk about those things. . . . It was tough. I know for all of us it was tough when we put those stakes in because we know our relatives, which side they were on, and we honored them. No matter which side they were on, it doesn't matter."[9]

I am reminded of a breakfast on the last day of the march that illustrates this point more fully. As we prepared for a final day of walking, the participants at my table reflected on the importance of creating a space where the range of Dakota responses to this devastating event could be discussed. A Dakota man who walked all seven days mentioned that within his own family, he had relatives who fought with Little Crow, and he also had members who had assisted the Whites. He mentioned how embarrassed he used to be about his relatives who he believed might have been part of the Hazelwood Republic, a group of Dakota who accepted Christianity in the nineteenth century and who called for assimilation.

Another person offered that she, too, had relatives who fought on both sides of the war and expressed the difficulties and challenges she faced in reconciling this aspect of her family history.

One of the most powerful and striking realizations that people came to is that this was a Dakota Civil War; it created deep divisions that are still very much a part of their contemporary lives. And, the great potential for these Commemorative Marches is to help heal the divisiveness that bitterly divided the Dakota as a People. In doing so, in embracing the multiple and difficult responses of the Dakota ancestors to this painful period in their history, they provide an inclusive space that promotes strength and healing to Dakota people today. By allowing for "collected memories" and their complexity, they are being generous with each other, their relatives, and their ancestors.

LEARNING COUNTER-NARRATIVES: MY FIRST INTRODUCTION TO THE HISTORY OF THE U.S.-DAKOTA WAR OF 1862

One of the most powerful points argued by Waziyatawin Angela Wilson in her work on the Commemorative March is that we as Native people, in this instance the Dakota people, live with assaults on our humanity when we are continually faced with monuments and memorials that honor the colonizers—the very leaders "responsible for the ethnic cleansing of our People."[10] We go through our daily lives with these assaults everywhere and Waziyatawin calls on us to "question those monuments and the ideologies they represent."[11] In questioning the "ideologies" embodied in these monuments, it is imperative that we teach our

children counter-narratives or counter-memories of these historical experiences. As Indigenous people, we need to continually remind people of our versions of the past as well as to continually name the violence that is part of America's deliberate forgetting of our accounts. Most of all, we have to tell our children these stories from the very beginning.

My desire to walk had everything to do with needing to remember and honor when it was that I learned this important lesson—namely, that the history of this country as told in school classrooms, in books, in the media, and in museums did not give voice to our stories and did not honor our memories. For me, that moment came when my father told me about the mass hanging of the thirty-eight Dakota warriors in 1862. When he told me what happened to the Dakota during the 1862 war, I felt most acutely the painful lesson that we had different truths from what I was being told in school.

It happened while I was in the third grade. I was excited to tell my father about the events of my day, which included a trip to the school library where I had checked out a biography of Abraham Lincoln. I proudly displayed the book and even offered to read a few pages for him before dinner. The book was a positive depiction of the "great emancipator of the slaves," the story of Lincoln that was confirmed in all of my history classes. At the time my father's response surprised me and it is one that I will never forget. Anger showed on his face as he told me, "Lincoln may have been a friend to Black people, but he was not a friend to the Indians. He was responsible for the killing of the thirty-eight Dakota warriors who were only fighting to save their homeland." He then went on to tell me about the U.S.-Dakota War, which at that time was referred to as the Great Sioux Uprising, and about my family connection to that story.

His counter-narrative to the one I had been taught and had read about in school was a lot for a third-grader to digest. As I stood holding the book about Lincoln and hearing for the first time about the mass hanging in Mankato, a story that I would not hear in history classes until my freshman year at the University of Minnesota, my desire to honor the different truths and memories of Native communities took hold. This desire would later define the direction of my life. In these moments of looking back, I realize that my interest in becoming a historian is firmly rooted in loyalty to family and community and in a desire for justice, rather than in an all-consuming desire to learn about the American past.[12]

Before he died in 1988, my father heard that they were building a memorial to the thirty-eight Dakota in Mankato and stated that he would like to see it. Sadly, we never had a chance to visit the memorial together, but my walking to remember the Dakota suffering during this period gave me an opportunity to honor not only one of the most painful and important lessons that I learned as a Native child, but also a story that has everything to do with the person I have become.[13]

The Commemorative March personifies the very essence of what a counter-narrative should be. By placing markers in the ground with the names of those on the original forced march, by educating non-Native people about the Dakota experience in the towns in which we stopped, and by producing scholarship and art that represents the reflections of the marchers on this transformative event, we are giving voice to the counter-memories that Native families hold. The American master narrative may have silenced and erased our versions of the past for many generations, but through this commemorative event we are reclaiming the past for current and future generations.

ANOTHER LAYER OF MEMORY TO A MULTI-LAYER MEMORY PROJECT: REMEMBERING HO-CHUNK REMOVAL IN 1863

I walked not only to honor the Dakota who were force marched in 1862, but also in memory of my Ho-Chunk ancestors, who were forced out of Minnesota at the same time, never again to have the same physical presence in the region that the Dakota call Minisota Makoce. The experience of the Ho-Chunk has been erased from the stories of the aftermath of the U.S.-Dakota War of 1862, and this erasure permeates every commemorative act and historical writing on the war to the present day. I wanted to participate in this march to finally assert a Ho-Chunk perspective on the story.

The history of the Ho-Chunk in Minnesota during the time of the U.S.-Dakota War of 1862—and our later forced removal from the state—is tragic. We were forced to relinquish our ancestral lands in Wisconsin and northern Illinois by 1837. We were then removed to reservations in Iowa (1840), northern Minnesota (1846), southern Minnesota (1855), and Crow Creek (1863). We fled the Crow Creek Reservation in South Dakota to Nebraska in 1864 where a reservation would later be established. Throughout these series of removals, many of my People stubbornly returned to their ancestral lands in Wisconsin and they eventually were able to attain homesteads in 1881. These removals, however, caused great divisions within our community, the legacy of which is still felt today.[14] At the time of the U.S.-Dakota War, my People lived on a reservation in Blue Earth County, near present-day Mankato, Minnesota. The story of our reservation experience echoes similarities to the Dakota People's experience: we, too, were subjected to corrupt government agents who withheld annuities from our people, leaving our leaders to beg for food to feed the children. Our experiences during the reservation era—as well as before—reflect the same injustices that other tribal nations endured: "invasion, oppression, conquest, and colonization."[15]

Almost as soon as we arrived on our reservation at Blue Earth, White citizenry began calling for our removal, eventually using the U.S.-Dakota War of 1862 as an excuse to force the Ho-Chunk from the state. A quote from a government agent at the time reflects the White's desire to rid the state of both tribal nations: "while it may be true that a few Winnebagos[16] were engaged in the atrocities of the Sioux . . . the exasperation of the people of Minnesota appears to be nearly as great toward the Winnebagos as toward the Sioux."[17] Although later official government reports confirmed that the Ho-Chunk remained on the reservation and did not participate in the war, Minnesota's ethnic-cleansing policy called for the removal of both tribes from the southern part of the state, and both

nations were sent to the Crow Creek Reservation in South Dakota in 1863.

As late as 2005, commemorative events and memorials addressing the significance of the 1862 war still exclude the shameful story of my ancestor's forced exile from the state of Minnesota. Why is this removal not remembered? Close to two thousand of my People were forced onto boats at Fort Snelling (the site of the Dakota concentration camp) in May 1863 and were sent to Crow Creek—a place so horrible that my ancestors immediately began digging out any trees they could find to make canoes so they could flee. Crow Creek was as a place of death far away from our ancestral lands. The removal of the Ho-Chunk, who even official government reports claim were not involved in the U.S.-Dakota War, speaks volumes about the deep-seated violent hatred of Indigenous People that is this nation's history. I am deeply committed, through future publications and my continual participation in the Dakota Commemorative March, to helping raise the consciousness of people, so that this deliberate forgetting of our removal, this violence, will cease.

> « IN OUR COLLECTED PHYSICAL MOVEMENT ACROSS THE MINNESOTA LANDSCAPE, WE WHO RECLAIMED MEMORY WILL BE FOREVER INSPIRED BY THIS EXPERIENCE. »

CONCLUSION: THE COURAGE TO SPEAK THE HARD TRUTHS

The experience of walking to honor the Dakota has given me a tremendous amount of strength that has infused all of my scholarship since. The events of the march and all the people whom I had the pleasure of walking with helped to strengthen my voice as an activist scholar. Upon my return to California, I spoke to everyone about this experience—how amazing, empowering, emotionally and spiritually enriching, and at times physically challenging the march had been for me. The Commemorative March gave me the strength to take important stands in my professional life and the courage to speak some of the hard truths even when it was difficult. I could not retrace with my own footsteps the horror endured by courageous women and children, and not be profoundly inspired to work to protect the way of life that these people heroically attempted to hold intact. In our collected physical movement across the Minnesota landscape, we who reclaimed memory will be forever inspired by this experience.

My participation in the Dakota Commemorative March has not only given me the courage to speak the hard truths, but it has also provided me an important opportunity to give voice to the stories of the women in my family. In my mind, the most significant legacy of this event is the honoring of Indigenous women in our past and present. Through the march we made Dakota women—their names, their stories, and their lives—visible and important. Though we live in a nation that has ignored the histories of Indigenous women—stereotyping or rendering us silent—by walking in the paths of the ancestors, we purposefully named those women and their suffering. Those markers stand on the Minnesota landscape to honor the Dakota grandmothers and relatives for their courage in the face of unspeakable hardships and cruelty. Scholar James Young states, "without having acted on memory we allow memory to be incomplete."[18] Through the act of walking, placing markers in the ground, and reading the names of the Dakota women, we are engaging in perhaps one of the most important acts of making Indigenous women present in the minds and hearts of contemporary communities. We are, as Young states, acting on memory, and by so doing, we are not allowing memory to remain incomplete.

—◦—

NOTES

1. As quoted in Diane Wilson, "Dakota Homecoming," *American Indian Quarterly* 28, nos. 1 and 2 (2004): 343.

2. As quoted in, *Public Memory: A Film about American Memorials*, prod. and dir. Amy Gerber, 68 min., FlatCoat Films, 2003, videocassette.

3. As quoted in, *Public Memory: A Film about American Memorials*.

4. As quoted in, *Public Memory: A Film about American Memorials*.

5. Several of the published articles (and after) were very good and reflected the importance of the Dakota Commemorative March of 2004. Nick Coleman's article published in the *Star Tribune* (the largest newspaper in the Minnesota), "To Remember Those Who Walked: Dakota Indians Retrace Minnesota's Trail of Tears" 12 November 2004, B1–2, was a particular standout. Coleman did an outstanding analysis of the significance of the Commemorative March that reflected his deep knowledge of Dakota history and the 1862 war.

6. James E. Young, *The Texture of Memory: Holocaust Memorials and Meaning* (New Haven and London: Yale University Press, 1993), xi.

7. James E. Young, "Memory and Monument after 9/11," lecture at Council for American Jewish Museum

Conference, January 2003. Available at http://www2.jewishculture.org/museums/cajm/cajm_young_lec_03.html (28 November 2005).

8. See Waziyatawin Angela Wilson, "Decolonizing the 1862 Death Marches," *American Indian Quarterly* 28, nos. 1 and 2, (2004): 185–215, and "Manipi Hena Owas'in Wicunkiksuyapi (We Remembered All Those Who Walked)" *American Indian Quarterly* 28, nos. 1 and 2 (2004): 151–169.

9. As quoted in, Waziyatawin Angela Wilson, "Voices of the Marchers" *American Indian Quarterly* 28, nos. 1 and 2 (2004): 325.

10. Waziyatawin Angela Wilson, "Decolonizing the 1862 Death Marches," 199.

11. Waziyatawin Angela Wilson, "Manipi Hena Owas'in Wicunkiksuyapi (We Remembered All Those Who Walked)," 157.

12. Waziyatawin Angela Wilson expressed a similar sentiment on her reasons for becoming a historian that reflects her commitment to community. See Angela Wilson, "Re: WHA and Indigenous History," 3 November 2003, <http://www.h-het.org/~west> (2 December 2005).

13. Diane Wilson writes beautifully on how many of the things that have happened in all of our lives, whether "acknowledged or not, has everything to do with the people we become." The counter-narrative

told to me by my father and that I have acknowledged above is an example of one of those experiences that profoundly influenced who I am today. See, Diane Wilson, "Dakota Homecoming," 348.

14. The Ho-Chunk today remain divided into two separate federally recognized communities. The Winnebago Tribe of Nebraska whose membership is estimated at 4,100 people, and the Ho-Chunk Nation of Wisconsin with 6,537 members. Though we are divided geographically, strong connections between the two communities are maintained.

15. Waziyatawin Angela Wilson "Manipi Hena Owas'in Wicunkiksuyapi (We Remembered All Those Who Walked)," 153.

16. Winnebago is the name given to us by outsiders, but in our language we are the Ho-Chunk (People of the Big Voice), the name that is now used officially by my tribal government—the Ho-Chunk Nation of Wisconsin. Winnebago is the name used by the United States government throughout our history.

17. As quoted in Mark Diedrich, compiler, *Winnebago Oratory: Great Moments in the Recorded Speech of the Ho-Chungra, 1742-1887* (Rochester, MN: Coyote Books, 1991), 89.

18. As quoted in, *Public Memory: A Film about American Memorials.*

Mending *Tiyospaye*

DIANE WILSON

◄o►

The first Dakota Commemorative March in 2002 shocked many of us with the realization of the depth of suffering and long-term consequences of colonization. When I look back on the second march in 2004, what comes first is the memory of tension, of grief confronted and challenged by a hostile world, and then offset, again and again, by the caring act of a single individual; a woman stood at the side of the road with a sign that apologized for the original march and gave us a bouquet of flowers.

Each day we were reminded of how White culture surrounds us like a circle of wagons. The march confronted these values by insisting that this history be remembered, our Dakota relatives honored, the circumstances that permitted it to happen be acknowledged, and the perpetrators and beneficiaries be held accountable. The march brought generations together whose lives have been shaped by the aftermath of the 1862 war: elders, parents, young adults, children. We have all been touched by these events, our lives molded by history and the invisible legacy we live with. The march gave our collective grief a place to be shared. Among us were many teachers who shared their knowledge, the side of the road sometimes acting like a makeshift classroom. And sometimes we learned simply by being present.

Around the fifth or sixth day, we suffered a terrible shock when one of the organizers, Mary Beth Faimon, was rear-ended in her car. We had been walking along Highway 169 all day. That part of the route provided endless worry about keeping the children safe and in line when their high energy sometimes made them forget about the traffic racing past. As we had done on the 2002 March, we placed a stake each mile that bore the name of two of the original marchers. Leo Omani sang as he pounded the stake with his Canadian hammer, and each of the marchers offered tobacco and prayers. By the end of the day, people were tired, cold, worried, and feeling the heavy weight of grief that accumulated as we moved closer to Fort Snelling. We had just finished walking late that afternoon when Mary Beth's car was hurled across two empty lanes by the truck that hit her from behind. She suffered whiplash and her car was totaled. That night we could hear her weeping as the trauma settled in her body.

The next day, a patrol car pulled over in front

of our caravan when we stopped to place a stake at the side of the road. Chris Mato Nunpa talked to the officer first through the open window of his police car. Finally, the patrolman got out and walked over to the group, his authority certain in each footstep, in the gun that rode on his hip. He came up to where we stood—silent, watchful, waiting to hear what he had to say. He told us that we could not put stakes in the public right-of-way, the strip of land that runs alongside each road and highway. Someone asked about the memorials that people leave for victims of car accidents. They're illegal, he said. Law enforcement turns a blind eye and allows families to leave these memorials for a year. But the stakes, our stakes, were illegal. He rattled off the numbers of a statute as if this settled the matter. He said that if we continued to pound stakes in the public right-of-way, we could be arrested. That next year we won't get a permit approved to do this march.

This is the moment I remember: Waziyatawin Angela Wilson said, in a voice made loud with anger, "We'll be placing a stake in another mile if you want to arrest us." He was young, this patrolman, and he could not stand up to her words. He could only nod his head and walk away, his message delivered, from whom we don't know, but the tone was clear: he shook a stick to intimidate, hoping that would be enough. For me, it might have been enough to change course, to rethink everything, to rationalize the safety of the children, elders, marchers. I had not yet fully understood

> « WE WERE MARCHING NOT ONLY TO GRIEVE FOR OUR ANCESTORS, I REALIZED, BUT ALSO TO CHALLENGE HISTORICAL INJUSTICE THAT HAS STOOD FOR MORE THAN 140 YEARS. »

the words spoken by Art Owen at the close of the first march when he told us, when you come to an obstacle it is better to go through it than around it; otherwise it might stop you the next time.

That night the women who organized this march gathered in the upper hall of the Shakopee community church where we were staying. Gabrielle Tateyuskanskan brought us together to discuss what should be done. I advocated not placing any more stakes, not risking the harm threatened by the patrolman. Let's use legal process, I said; let's establish a clear right to do this by battling it in the courts, by insisting on our permit. Angela sat on the floor next to Gabrielle, her tired feet stretched out in front of her. She said, No, this is Dakota land. We have every right to place stakes for our ancestors. There is no legal permit process to do this. We have the right because we are Dakota, this is our ancestral land, and we are honoring our ancestors.

Angela spoke the truth; this was originally Dakota land, most of it lost in duplicitous treaties, the rest seized after the 1862 war. We were marching not only to grieve for our ancestors, I realized, but also to challenge historical injustice that has stood for more than 140 years. And if moving through the patrolman's obstacle meant that we would be arrested, then that was exactly what we would do. Ultimately, as a group we decided to minimize the risk to the rest of the marchers by having only the women who were gathered upstairs place the stakes.

The next day passed without incident; we had

called the patrolman's bluff. No one appeared to harass the group for the duration of the march. The resistance and hostility from both the patrolman and some of the townspeople who came to dialogue was a test of our commitment—of the degree to which we would be willing to confront the forces that do not want these issues raised, who do not want to be reminded of the wrongs that have been done.

This is what I learned that day: that the internalized values of White culture are so pervasive that the most difficult first step is to see the effects of colonization. It is not enough to understand the trauma inflicted through policies like boarding schools and land allotment; they must be seen as part of a systemic process for dismantling a culture by force. When I spoke that night at the church, I used words I had learned growing up surrounded by White values. When I listened, I heard words that told me there was another way, one that had been trampled on, beat up, abused, but that still carried a strong message of hope and truth. It was like hearing a song I had almost forgotten, its melody familiar and strange all at once. It was also a hard lesson, the painful beginning of relearning Dakota ways.

My mother, who was with us in spirit, had tried all her life to forget the experience of boarding school and South Dakota's blatant racism, remaining silent in order to leave the past behind. Not until the first march did I begin to see how her silence—and that of many in her generation and mine—was a heartbreaking form of collusion, of allowing the legacy of colonization to continue unchallenged. Not until I became part of the march did I finally understand what it meant when I found my mother's photograph on a wall in a Rapid City museum as part of a display about boarding schools and the destruction of tiyospaye. The photograph was taken in 1940 at the Holy Rosary Mission School on the Pine Ridge Reservation.

The tiyospaye, which refers to the extended family, has been intrinsic to Dakota and Lakota culture long before contact with Euro-Americans. A good Dakota or Lakota must be a good relative, which means obeying a complex system of kinship rules that governs their relationships within their families and community and forms an essential part of the cultural values that contributes to a peaceful community. Understanding how people are related is an important aspect of the tiyospaye, and it is one of the reasons why Indian families are so aware of their ancestry. Among the government's efforts that contributed to the breakdown of the tiyospaye was the introduction of the boarding school system, which separated children from parents while reinforcing White cultural values. Land allotment policies in the late 1800s fragmented tribes even further by decimating the land base and introducing the concept of individual ownership, as opposed to the community.

To grow up without knowing my family's stories, or the Dakota culture, was to learn early on the lesson of shame about who I was and who our

---

« THIS IS WHAT I LEARNED THAT DAY: THAT THE INTERNALIZED VALUES OF WHITE CULTURE ARE SO PERVASIVE THAT THE MOST DIFFICULT FIRST STEP IS TO BEGIN TO SEE THE EFFECTS OF COLONIZATION. »

Holy Rosary Mission School on the Pine Ridge reservation, 1930s. Lucille Dion Wilson, third row up, third girl from left. *(Family photograph.)*

family had once been. Even that shame, however, is a tool of oppression, as it so easily prevents us from seeking the truth. It is far easier to hide behind denial, or addiction, or material comforts than to ask questions about a brutal history and to accept the full horror of what has been done to the Dakota People. It was an unwillingness to live this way that brought many of us to the march, to see and feel the limitations of old ways of thinking that have been determined by colonization and internalized racism, and to begin the healing process.

The marchers included many teachers who not only understood the meaning of this history but whose words and actions taught Dakota ways. Our spiritual leaders, Phyllis Redday and Gabrielle Tateyuskanskan, began each day with prayer, in itself an important lesson in the day's priorities. When Phyllis was called away to a funeral in Canada, Gabrielle helped keep the group's focus on the purpose of the march. The actions of many others—including Chris Mato Nunpa, Waziyatawin Angela Wilson, Leo Omani, Dottie Whipple—were a constant reminder of *community*, of the need to act on behalf of the people. Each person gave of themselves in whatever ways they could, as much as they could. As a need arose, an individual stepped forward to fill it. If a marcher was touched by grief, others came to offer prayers and comfort. Within this group, we were all responsible for each other, for the children who came with Tim Blue and Matt Pendleton, for the elders whose strength was limited, for the marchers who experienced pain or injuries from the long distance we walked each day.

We were also joined by two new marchers, Edward Valandra and Denise Breton, who are involved in writing and teaching about restorative justice, a process for healing that recognizes the effects of colonization. Learning about restorative justice offered hope that recovery was indeed possible, even from such great historical trauma as genocide. Within that context, the march offered healing on several levels: sharing our stories; an opportunity for grieving; the reeducation that was provided from the many teachers among us, both in academic understanding and spiritual lessons; and confronting the legacy of the march itself, beginning with its obscure, forgotten place in history. By participating, we were all given the chance to take responsibility—on an individual, family, and community level—for healing the harm that has been done to Dakota people. Those of us who came because of a break

with our Dakota culture learned to confront the consequences of colonization and assimilation, to insist on reclaiming this history, to experience the deep grief that is part of our loss, and to help others do the same.

Beneath the tension that lingered from the final days of the march, there is a sweet memory of the first, early days when we walked along the river on dirt roads nearly empty of traffic. As the sun melted the frost on the long grass and our breath rose like plumes on the cold morning air, we walked past deep woods with the river at our side. One morning we slowly approached a large, fenced field on our left, where four horses stood grazing. As we drew closer, their heads raised and they watched our slow-moving procession. They began to walk together at a measured pace, as if the rhythm of our steps inspired them to join us, in their own way. They trotted down the field, shoulder to shoulder, and then turned as a group, moving through a large loop, all the while remaining together, as if choreographed. They danced up and down the field, turning and wheeling, heads high, their bodies saying, We witness your grief, your long walk, your courage; we send you the strength of our own steps. We could all see that something miraculous was happening. These horses were dancing for us, and with us.

—◄◦►—

Voices of the Marchers from 2004

WAZIYATAWIN ANGELA WILSON

◄○►

THE PURPOSE OF THE MARCHES

What can we say about a forced removal? About the loss of a People's homeland, overtaken and overrun by a ruthless invading population? About the exile of a People denied their inheritance? And about the feeling that our people are now largely visitors to a land that still cries our names?

For many of us, the pain and sense of loss is so overwhelming that we seldom allow our conscious minds to dwell in that place of despair. But as soon as we do, the tears begin to flow. It has been four years since I have begun thinking and planning for our commemoration of the ethnic cleansing of our People, and still, the tears keep coming. At first, the tears came as I thought about the suffering and anguish endured by our grandmothers and grandfathers. Then the tears came for all that has been lost since. In my more foolish times, I think about when they might stop. Will it be after our fourth time walking in 2008? Or perhaps in 2012 when we commemorate the 150th year since the forced march? Or might it be when we can call our homeland ours again? Or is the landscape marked so deeply with

the memory of our genocide that all of our collective tears will never wash it away?

I tend to think the latter is true. I cannot imagine a time when we will not mourn what happened or even speak of our ancestors' suffering without solemnity and tears. Instead, like other sites of genocide, I think the horror of the event will never cease to affect and move all beings who allow themselves to feel empathy with our ancestors. What we feel, I believe, is inconsolable grief.

This has caused me also to ponder, then, what healing might mean in this context. If we are never "over" this event, what then is the purpose of the Commemorative March? We knew from the beginning that the spirits of our ancestors needed to be released through our memorial for them. As their descendants, we spoke their names and walked each mile for them, leaving our prayers and prayer flags along the way. We remembered their suffering, honored their strength, and cried for all they endured.

What we did not know when we took our first steps in 2002, however, was just how much we would be blessed in the process. I once believed that we could somehow be healed from our historical trauma. What I now feel is a slow, steady strengthening of our People, which may be a kind of healing after all, though different from the kind I initially envisioned. Our recognition of our ancestors' suffering is bringing a sense of unity to our People and reactivating a hunger for justice. Acknowledging the humanity of our ancestors awakens us to our own humanity—as well as to the realization that we, too, are worthy of justice and freedom from oppression.

of our humanity will survive; it must continue in our future generations if our nation is to survive.

THE SECOND MARCH BEGINS

This chapter creates a new story based on the perspectives of our relatives and allies who participated in the 2004 Dakota Commemorative March. This collective story is rooted in the present, in what is happening right now, but it is also

---

« WHAT I NOW FEEL IS A SLOW, STEADY STRENGTHENING OF OUR PEOPLE, WHICH MAY BE A KIND OF HEALING AFTER ALL, THOUGH DIFFERENT FROM THE KIND I INITIALLY ENVISIONED. »

In re-strengthening the connection to our ancestors and our homeland, we are re-strengthening our bonds as a nation. Our relatives are coming home, and we are embracing one another with joy and love. We have a long haul ahead of us, but we have begun a journey to reclaim all that was lost with integrity and righteousness—for ourselves, for our ancestors, and for our children yet unborn.

Since the first Commemorative March in 2002, our people have been coming home and wonderful things have been happening. We are creating new stories and a new chapter in our long history. As Gabrielle Tateyuskanskan reminded us in 2005 when we met at Lower Sioux for ceremony and feasting in honor of our ancestors, our stories are important and we need to pass them on, "so that our young people can know us as human beings and know Dakota people in their humanity and pass that on." Implicit in this sentiment is the notion that this sense

obviously deeply rooted in a past that defines our current context. As with the esssay "Voices of the Marchers from 2002," which relayed perspectives from the 2002 March, this essay highlights the insights and perspectives offered by the marchers in 2004.

One of the most positive aspects of these marches is the consistent sharing of our stories, reactions, and thoughts with one another (and occasionally with the Wasicu townspeople we met along the way). Many of the words expressed are never captured on tape; they happen as we are walking or as we gather at each mile marker to plant a stake in the ground, offer prayers, and comfort one another as we grieve. The words captured here are from the transcriptions of tape recordings made during our seven-day journey or shortly after the march when we gathered to talk about our experiences. Sometimes individuals expressed new thoughts, but more often individuals expressed thoughts that we all shared or feelings that we all felt and that continue to resonate with us. In gathering these testimonies, we are collecting a living history that will eventually become part of the collective Dakota memory regarding the Dakota Commemorative Marches of the twenty-first century.

The second Dakota Commemorative March held in 2004 was as amazing, inspiring, and uplifting as the first. When it was completed, participants felt the same sense of overwhelming emotion and positive feeling about the march. After the first march, a number of people commented that it was the best thing they had ever done. At the conclusion of the second march, Chris Mato Nunpa commented, ◀ *"Both were good, both were powerful, and both left me with the same feeling that I had the first time, that this was one of the best things I've ever done in my life. These two things together are the best thing I've ever done in my life."* ▶

In between the two marches, we became better prepared. If any of us had anticipated the magnitude of our undertaking back in 2001 when we began planning the first march, we probably would have been too intimidated to proceed. None of us realized what exactly we were getting ourselves into or how it would impact and define our lives. Even right after the first march, all we knew was that we needed to keep walking. We started to get an inkling about the doors we were opening, but we continue to be amazed at the seemingly endless journey upon which we have embarked. Once we invoked the spirits of our ancestors on the first march, it became apparent that, while they needed our help in being released through our honoring and remembering, we were the ones who really needed their help.

They have been obliging us ever since, telling us what we need to know when we need to know it, and though we don't yet understand much of what is being taught to us, we have faith that these understandings will come. It was clear that what began as a historical commemoration is in reality a spiritual journey for all of us. This essay, then, may be the last we write about this topic, as the path that we are being instructed to follow is only for Dakota eyes.

After the first walk, our women's march was gifted a pipe. When the pipestone carver and pipe-maker, Chuck Derby, began carving the bowl from the red pipestone for the pipe that he intended to give us, an image was revealed within the stone. The image is a woman's silhouette that looks startlingly like the photo of one of the Dakota women imprisoned at Fort Snelling during the winter of 1862–63, the photo we later chose for our 2004 Dakota Commemorative March T-shirts and which is included among the historical photographs in this book. While we appreciate how amazing such occurrences are, they do not surprise us, because we see them as signs that our ancestors are assisting us. When the pipe was gifted to us, our spiritual leader for the march, Phyllis Redday, became the pipe-carrier. So this sacred pipe in its beautiful Pendleton bundle led our march in 2004, and the walkers followed.

◀◦▶

We began this march with the prayers and good wishes of our brothers and sisters who are currently incarcerated. On the first day on the march, I shared with the group my recent conversation with George Blue Bird. He had called me the Friday before to tell me that they had everything set up and would be praying for us again. He told me that those supporting us included 270 people where he was in Sioux Falls, 190 people at Jameson prison, a couple other groups at other prisons he rattled off, including a women's prison, as well as some men at Stillwater prison (one of the Bellecourts had gotten word to them): all the Dakota/Lakota/Nakota people in these prisons would be praying for us. In George's facility, they received special permission to have ceremonies every day during the week of our walk. I told the group, ◄ *"So all of those men will be having pipe ceremonies, having inipi ceremonies, and they'll all be saying prayers for us. When he added up all of the men and women from these different prisons who he knew were having ceremonies for us or were praying on our behalf, there were nearly a thousand of them."* ►

I felt the same humility and overwhelming emotions when I heard this from George in 2004 as I did the first time he contacted me before the 2002 March to let me know they were praying for us. George has told me repeatedly that, as inmates, they identify with the people who were in the concentration camps, because they know what it is like to be imprisoned. This is one of the reasons why it is so important for them to be part of our walk. I told the group that day how much I appreciated their prayers and their generosity, ◄ *"Here are these men who are on the inside; they can't walk with us on the outside, they can't set foot on the grass, they can't be here with us, but they're giving so generously of themselves, giving so generously of their spirits. Again, I think that is a powerful testament to the way our People are, the best attributes of our People. And so I wanted to share all of that with all of you. All of those men*

and women who are incarcerated, they're praying for us and that gives me strength, and I'm sure all of you will feel the same." ►

Given our previous experience on the march and all the prayers that were said for us, the anxiety I felt before the first march was not there as we prepared to walk again in 2004. Instead I felt great anticipation. This time around, I knew who the core group of marchers would be, and I was looking forward to renewing the bond with the people I had come to love and admire on the last march. I was also looking forward to meeting the new people who would be walking with us, our Dakota relatives who were coming home and meeting other relatives. We gathered for inipi ceremonies at Dave Larson's house at Lower Sioux the night before the walk, and then my family and I went back to our hotel room at Jackpot Junction for the last night of sleeping in a bed for a while.

We awoke early the next morning to get our kids ready, quickly remembering the familiar morning routine of the last march. We had a hot breakfast brought in by the casino and began greeting one another, putting faces to the new people with whom we had communicated via telephone or e-mail in previous months, and introducing ourselves to those we didn't know. The planning committee had decided that with this march, we would limit the walking to about eighteen to twenty miles a day, and so we had to cut a few miles each day by caravanning to and from the starting and ending points.

November 7, we caravanned for the first time and gathered at the Lower Sioux Interpretive Center, a few miles from the community center where we had our breakfast. Dave Larson and Gabrielle Tateyuskanskan spoke a few words to

Our lunch stop on the first day, fire and food provided by the Anywaush family.

the marchers, and we were on our way, quickly stepping into the familiar pattern. We read the names on the first stake and planted them to mark our beginning. Then Deksi Leo's car took the lead to clear the way, followed by a Dakota woman carrying the bundle with the pipe. The usual caravan of cars fell in behind us, and Super Dave's On-Site Sanitation truck marked the tail end of our group.

That first morning we were greeted by horses along the way, and we were once again pleased with the sense of kinship we felt with the animals, as if they were welcoming us home and telling us that it is right that we are remembering and honoring our ancestors, that the land remembers who we are and what happened to her Indigenous children. We had a sack lunch provided by the Anywaush/Pigeon family from Upper Sioux, and Lorna Anywaush built a fire for us in one of the park-like areas along the side of the road. It was a cold and crisp November day, and we greeted with enthusiasm the smell of the campfire and the warmth it provided.

WHY WE CAME

That evening we caravanned back to Lower Sioux and slept on mattresses on the gymnasium floor in their community center. The end of the first day is always a bit of a shock, because people realize how sore their bodies already are and that they have to endure six more days of walking. But people already sensed the bond of kinship that was strengthening and the good feelings that were emerging. That first evening we gathered in the front room of the community center over coffee and shared our reasons for participating. Some of the stories were familiar. For example, Chris Mato Nunpa commented, ◀ *"I can say the main reason I'm here is very personal. I had a kunsi who was bayoneted in the stomach by a White soldier, and I had about four other relatives who were on the march as well, so I have a very personal interest in this march. So that's why I'm here and supporting our women leaders."* ▶

Leonard Wabasha said that he was participating because his ancestors were on this walk as well, but he also saw it as a way of uniting people, believing ◀ *"people can come together despite all the things that are happening in the world today."* ▶ Vanessa Rae Baker told us, ◀ *"I'm here to give thanks back to our ancestors, to feel what they went through and to give gratitude back to them, what they went through, what they suffered. When I was younger, I used to participate in the run from Fort Snelling to Mankato. I'm older now, I can't run, so I figured I'd try to walk and give thanks back to our ancestors."* ▶

Vanessa was there with her nephew Mervel, whom she either carried or pushed in a stroller the length of the walk. This image was one that each of us carried with us. Mato Nunpa commented, ◀ *"Today I saw a sight that I'll probably remember for a while. I saw a young Dakota woman pushing a child in a baby carriage, and I thought* *of this march of 1,700 people who were primarily women and children and elders, and I thought of all those mothers who were on that forced march who had little kids and how much more difficult that must have been back then."* ▶ Vanessa demonstrated her dedication to the march every day as she walked with her young nephew from beginning to end.

My husband, Scott Wilson, also spoke about his reasons for participating: ◀ *"I'm grateful for today and to be here again with all of you. It's so nice to see the familiar faces from two years ago and to meet the new faces today, all the new friends that we're all making. This community that meets every night and walks during the day gets really tight, and they become new members of your family. This is an ongoing process for me; that's why I'm here. About fifteen years ago now, I took Dakota history and culture at the University of Minnesota with Kunsi Carrie [Schommer]. And a couple of years later, I met this young lady, and we've been walking down this road ever since. It's an ongoing process as a Wasicu person coming to terms with the things that have gone on and that go on. It's a struggle, and it's not always about what's out there; sometimes it hits close to home, as it has for us in this last year [as we dealt with issues of colonialism in our extended family]. I'm here to support my wife and my family and to support my children, who have the great honor of being born Dakota in this world."* ▶

Lylis Wells came to participate in the march with her daughter, and it was beautiful to see a Dakota mother and daughter walking together. She discussed the importance of physically making this walk ourselves, drawing on the example of our elders, ◀ *"Now our days are filled up with this energy that we used to burn in gathering wood and having a healthy lifestyle; it was a lot of effort, just part of the deal. We have to make an effort to do that now, so some of us are kind of out of shape, and we have to kind of train to get in shape. But this is a good way of taking care of our bodies and taking care of our minds and spirits."* ❯

Dottie Whipple, who had been on the 2002 March and has served as a march organizer, told us at the end of that first day, ❮ *"This is my second year. The first year was just so powerful. I'm so glad this year that I get to be here the whole seven days. It's been wonderful this first day. . . . All the time when we're walking, I'm just giving thanks for those people who went before us and suffered, to hang in there, with what they did, so that we're still here. And we're able to do this. I've found through my life that these things that we do are always so healing with the people who are there, the people who are with us. . . . It's just a win-win the whole time . . . except my foot aches."* ❯

Debbie Robertson, who walked with Dottie that first day, relayed a conversation they had: ❮ *"Dottie and I were walking today, and she said, 'I hope our parents are up there looking down on us, proud of us.' And I said, 'Yes, I'm sure they are, and I'm sure the ones who walked are also happy that we are remembering them.' It was very powerful. For a while there, I thought, what am I doing here? I could have been home, my leg hurt so bad. But it was really nice, and I wouldn't change it for the world."* ❯

She and Dottie expressed what we all felt. Most of us were drawn to the march out of love for our ancestors. We wanted them to know they were remembered and that we had not forgotten their sacrifice and suffering. As a consequence, we all

experienced a sense of fulfillment that made all our aches and pains worth every step.

SUPPORT FROM OTHER INDIGENOUS PEOPLE

Other Indigenous people came to support the event and to walk with us for a variety of reasons. Myla Vicenti Carpio (Jicarilla Apache, Laguna, Isleta) arrived from the Southwest to participate. She later articulated her reasons for participating: ❮ *"My connections to the marchers and their ancestors were deeply rooted in our shared historical and contemporary relationships and experiences. Like the Dakotas and many other Indigenous Nations, the federal government force marched the Jicarillas to southern New Mexico onto Mescalero Apache lands in 1883. Therefore, my participation in the march not only strengthened my connection to my ancestors' histories and experiences but also empowered me to march in solidarity, in healing, and with compassion."* ❯ Indeed, the ethnic cleansing of Indigenous Peoples was a common occurrence in nineteenth-century America, and hundreds of thousands of Indigenous people were affected by it.

Amy Lonetree traveled from northern California to participate, and she did so in part because she, like Myla, is a dear friend to my family and me. However, she had her own reasons for participating as well. Amy is Ho-Chunk, but she also has some Dakota ancestry, and the march offered a way for her to pay homage to that bloodline. But her connection as a Ho-Chunk woman to the Dakota of 1862 is strong for other reasons as well. As she explained to us that first evening, ❮ *"When I did research on Ho-Chunk history in*

Minnesota, I learned as a student and as a historian that after the U.S.-Dakota War of 1862, my People, who were on a reservation in Mankato, were rounded up and sent to Crow Creek as well. We lost our lands in Minnesota; we were happy in those lands. We had given up a reservation at Long Prairie . . . and we were given a reservation in Southern Minnesota. . . . But we lost those lands after the war. The U.S. government sent us out of Minnesota as well." ▶

By participating in the march, Amy was re-establishing a historical connection that we, as Dakota People, have with the Ho-Chunk Nation. Not only were they our neighbors for centuries—people with whom we frequently traded and intermarried—but they were also the people who faced removal and exile with us.

HONORING INDIGENOUS WOMEN'S HISTORY AND EXPERIENCE

Yet these were not the only reasons for Amy's participation. She continued, ◀ *"And finally, I am here because, as an Indigenous woman and as a historian, I know that so much about American Indian women—our history, our experience—is not in the historical record. And I think what's so beautiful here is that you put those markers in the earth to honor these women."* ▶

In the field of Indigenous history, Amy and I both know too well that ordinary Indigenous women are almost entirely absent from the written historical record. Writers of Indigenous history, who themselves are still marginalized among American historians, have most often illuminated the lives of Indigenous male, military, and spiritual leaders. Their attention to Indigenous women

has been minimal at best. Amy elaborated on this idea a few days later saying, ◀ *"As an Indigenous woman, I know how our stories have been silenced and erased. As Indigenous people, we talk about how our stories have been marginalized, but that's even more true about the stories of Indigenous women and their courage. I wanted to honor the courage and the bravery of those Dakota women who were on this march in 1862. And I have to say that as I participate—and this is my first year—as we walk and we stop every mile, and we take out a marker with the name of a person who was the head of the household, and typically it's a woman, and we put those in the earth, and they have red ties on them, it is such a beautiful experience. And as I watched my Dakota friends and colleagues and relatives say their prayers and put their tobacco down, I am just so proud to be an Indigenous woman, because I see how much we care about our relatives. And that is a really beautiful thing."* ▶

My daughter Autumn Wilson was fourteen years old on the 2004 March, and she also saw the need to enter this information into the written historical record. Building on the comments Amy had expressed earlier, Autumn stated through tears her concerns about the lack of knowledge about events like this within the dominant society, ◀ *"Like Amy was saying, it's not documented, nobody knows. I mean, I go to school, in the history books, it's not there. Nobody knows. And so many people, when I try to tell them, they won't listen. Their ears are deaf to that, because they have this image implanted in their heads that the United States can do no wrong. I feel bad, because I know different. And for the majority of those people, they never will. They can't know what's been done here, because they won't open their eyes,* and that hurts." ▶ The emotion conveyed in Autumn's voice made it clear that the portrayal of our history matters, and it affects the lives of our young people every day.

WASICUS' REASONS FOR PARTICIPATING

One of the issues that has become increasingly clear since we first walked in 2002 is that our greatest Wasicu allies are those people who are capable of critical self-reflection. Many liberal-minded Wasicus would be happy to support the march if it in no way jeopardized their power base, their status, or their ideologies, but if they were to begin to feel threatened by what we were doing, their support would fade away amidst rationalizing excuses. While those folks might eventually become allies, as long as they remain in denial, they cannot support our cause, nor can we feel good about their superficial participation in our march.

We suspect such people are drawn to participating to ease their guilty consciences rather than to support the liberation of our People. While they are a long way from the colonizers who revel in their privilege and power and feel no regret or responsibility for the suffering of the oppressed, their inability to take responsibility for their role in the oppression of others means the outcome is the same for the oppressed.

At the other end of the spectrum are those people who believe in their complicity in our oppression and who want to help us challenge the institutions and forces that maintain our subjugation. They understand our interconnectedness and they support our struggle for liberation, because they recognize it as their struggle too.

In 2004, we had such Wasicu allies present, and two of them gave eloquent explanations of the reality of colonization, of White participation in our oppression, and of the possibilities for future justice. For example, because she works in the area of restorative justice, Denise Breton told us that first evening, ◀ *"I'm very much committed to Whites righting historical harms and going on the healing path that involves healing for us, because it takes really, really sick people to do such things. So I'm very grateful to be here and to be part of this."* ▶ In making her agenda explicit by acknowledging the wrongs that were perpetrated in 1862 and realizing her role in helping to right those wrongs, she could be immediately embraced by us as a supportive ally.

Similarly, Mary Beth Faimon relayed her own ancestry, understanding fully that she comes from a family of Wasicu settlers who were in southern Minnesota in 1862 when the war broke out: ◀ *"My great-grandmother was born in 1861. Though it may go deeper than that, I don't know. But there reaches a point where I think we all have to connect with our roots, and when we go deep down, we start intertwining and mingling with other groups with our roots too, which leads to the shared history of it. I want the truth to be known."* ▶ This honesty, coupled with the recognition of the need for justice, allows us to contemplate the dream of a mass movement of Wasicus in Minnesota who would assist us in reclaiming our homeland.

DEALING WITH THE PAIN OF THE STORIES

As we shared our reasons for participating in the march, I discussed the importance of my grand-

Lunch by the side of the road.

mother's story to my life. It was her story about the original 1862 march that in many ways prepared me for the possibility of participating in this Commemorative March—or even realizing the need for it. I told our relatives gathered at Lower Sioux about some of my realizations about my grandmother's stories: ◀ *"I grew up spending a lot of time around a grandmother who took the time to share a lot of stories with me. She died over a decade ago now, and as I get older, I realize more and more the impact of her stories on me. I'm thinking more and more about this now, because I am working with her stories again that I recorded back in 1990 when my daughter was just a newborn. One of the things I've realized is that when I go back over her stories and when I think about the impact of her stories, so many of them are stories of suffering. They're stories filled with pain, with anger, with hurt, in some cases a sense of betrayal, and at the same time they are also stories of incredible hope, because they're stories of survival. . . .*

"She would tell these stories over and over again, and they were hard stories to listen to, because there was so much pain there, but it was important to her that we remember those stories, that we pass them on to our children, and I think it was so important because it was about survival, it was about how we continue living as a People." ▶

Lylis Wells spoke clearly about the need for us to address our own grief and release ourselves from a state of victimage. In reference to the pain we encounter, she said, ◀ *"Sometimes in our ceremonies we let that go. . . . We have strong grandmas and grandpas, and that's because they let it go."* ▶ Indeed, our elders did not let their grief overwhelm them on a daily basis, because they also had to engage life. So she encouraged us, ◀ *"Look over your grief; deal with your grief. Our grandmas and grandpas could be laying down crying and stuff, but they're not; they're strong. They're walking around; they're saying they're proud; they're laughing; they're healing. So this is . . . a really good process; it makes us stronger, we're not* victims, we're empowering ourselves, we're empowering the next generation." ▶

Lydia "Toyo" Conito was also there with us that evening. She had participated in our ceremonies the night before, and now she was with us to share her own family stories. She told us, ◀ *"I have a story that you should hear, because when you are walking, my kunsi and unkan, their spirits are going to be alive and well. I can't be there with you, but I want you to put your tobacco out when you get that feeling in your heart for them."* ▶

Then she explained to us that her mother said that her ◀ *"kunsi's mother, the mother and the father, they met at Fort Snelling when they were taken to Fort Snelling. That's where they met, and they also fell in love; I say they fell in love; I like romance. But they met there."* ▶ This was such an important story for us to hear. So often we get mired in the heaviness of our grief, and we can forget that as human beings, we also experience joy.

During both of our marches, one of the consistent characteristics was that we experienced great pain as we delved into the difficult stories about this painful episode in our history, but we also experienced great joy as we found relatives, teased one another, and felt the strength and love of our relatives. When we know the nature of our people today, we must also recognize the nature of our ancestors in 1862.

When I spoke a little while later, I discussed how during the previous week I had talked to my students about the Diné People who were force marched on their Long Walk to a concentration camp at Bosque Redondo, a place they called *Hweeldii*, "The Place of Despair." I told them, ◀ *"There must have been happy stories, there must have been marriages, children must have been born,*

people must have shown their love for one another, they must have laughed at times, they must have still sung their songs, they must have still said their prayers, and you know all of these things because that's what human beings do." ▶

The same is true about our people both along the walk and at Fort Snelling. Even in times of suffering, we need to remember that people were also falling in love. After Lydia's comments, I continued, ◀ *"I hope the Anywaush family comes later, because they have a grandmother who was carried on her grandmother's back for 150 miles when she was three years old. If you think about the love that that grandmother would have had for her grandchild in order to carry her on her back for 150 miles, that's true love. That is the best that human beings can offer this world. That's how our People were, and that's how our People are today."* ▶

These are the stories that teach us about our humanity. Frequently when I think about the horrible conditions that our ancestors faced in 1862, I realize that many of them must have simply wanted to end their own suffering and die. But on this forced march, these women, many of them elderly, kept walking footstep after footstep. They wanted our People to survive, so they kept walking. They did so out of love for the children and grandchildren who were by their sides, but they also did so out of love for our nation more broadly. They wanted our People to live. That, too, is true love.

CONFRONTING THE CONSEQUENCES OF COLONIZATION

Lydia went on to tell us more about her family's experiences as a consequence of 1862 and the subsequent colonization of our People. ◄ *"I was always asking her, 'Kunsi, how come you could put that pipe away and be a Christian? How could you do that? How could you give up all your medicine and your stuff that you know? How could you do that?' I could never understand it. But she said that when they were at Fort Snelling, they agreed to be baptized so that they couldn't be killed. They were baptized so that they wouldn't be killed. That still didn't make sense to me. I still don't understand it. One of these days, that kunsi is going to be answering all my questions. But my relatives, my unkanna [grandfather], my grandma, my mom and dad, they're all very, very devout Christians, and I said, well how can that be? I just can't understand how that could be. But anyway, my mom said that kunsi said that in the religion they talked about, this man called Jesus was so close to our beliefs as Dakota People, and she said that's why it was so easy for them to say they'd be baptized. Number one, they would have been killed. Number two, this man that they heard them preach about was a very powerful man."* ► Then she told us that when her mom died, she picked up the pipe. Her stories demonstrate both the good and bad experiences of 1862.

The consequences of colonialism can be seen in a variety of ways. While the influence of Christianity is one way, the disconnection of our people from our traditions is another. Alvin Kopas drove from Sisseton, South Dakota, to participate in the march, and as he revealed his reasons for participating, it was clear that he, like many of us, was coming home. ◄ *"I just recently got in touch with my heritage. . . . In rediscovering my heritage, I found out that my relatives were on this [original Death March], and I felt compelled to come. It's*

such an honor to take part in this. In some respects as a Dakota, I feel lost today as to know what to do; that's also why I'm here. I'm looking for answers. I'm trying to find the right way." ►

Along the march, he realized he was related to Dave and Diane Wilson. As Mato Nunpa said at one of the mile markers, ◄ *"They found out they were relatives, because they were all related to the person whose name was on the stake."* ► Al walked the whole way with us, and we all inherited a relative when he came back to our homeland to participate in the march.

REUNITING DESCENDANTS, RELATIVES

Indeed, the importance of finding relatives was a major theme throughout the first Commemorative March, and it will remain a central theme as long as we continue to walk. We know that the colonization process has been largely about the disconnection of ourselves from our lands, traditions, and each other, so the antidote to that is reconnecting with our lands, traditions, and relatives.

On the very first day, Deksi Leo Omani described one way that our being forced to leave our homeland has made our reconnection to one another more difficult. He stated, ◄ *"From oral history back home, we were doing our genealogy years ago in Canada in northern Saskatchewan. What we found was that a lot of our older relatives, our parents and grandparents, have a lot of names, a number of Dakota names and a number of English names, and we're trying to figure out exactly what it meant, because we wanted to find out our roots. . . . Well why is that? Through oral history, that's what they told us. It was because the Wasicus down here, they put a bounty on our people's heads, and the U.S. Army was looking for us all over. It didn't matter where, whether it be here or Canada."* ▶

Because of the threat of being caught and killed, Dakota people in Canada developed a variety of strategies to protect themselves, including using multiple names. As a consequence, finding our relatives can be challenging. Yet the desire and need for that reunification are compelling. Deksi Leo relayed his thoughts about this in New Ulm, ◀ *"A number of years ago, my tahansi Chris had come up to Canada to look for their relatives. To me, that's where the healing journey began, the connectedness, because of the incident that we're talking about tonight happened, all of our People were scattered all over."* ▶

During the march, we had the opportunity to hear many family stories about the women and children who were on the original march and their family networks. The descendants of Mazaadidi, for example, participated in force in this march, and they came from all over the country to do so. Reuben Kitto arrived from Florida to participate, and others came from the Twin Cities area, like Ramona Stately. One of my students, Randilynn Boucher, came up from Arizona, and she is a part of the Mazaadidi family as well. They supported the march in numerous ways, including walking with us, feeding us, and erecting their tipis at the concentration camp site to meet us when we arrived at Fort Snelling. My father, Chris Mato Nunpa, later commented on their participation, ◀ *"I also learn stories, more and more stories, as people come forth and say, 'My relatives were on that march.' For example, the Mazaadidi family came because they had relatives who were on that march. That was really good,*

and this is going to be happening more as the word gets out. People are going to be saying, 'Hey, I had relatives. I think I want to participate as well.' So that's going to happen more. We'll learn the names of more and more people, and we'll learn about the descendents of those 1,700 who were on that march." ▶

REUNITING THE OCETI SAKOWIN OYATE

The need for reunification reaches beyond the eastern Dakota and stretches to our other relatives to the west. Fundamentally, we are all part of the Oceti Sakowin, or the Seven Council Fires, which includes the Bdewakantunwan, Wahpekute, Sisitunwan, Wahpetunwan, Ihanktunwan, Ihanktunwanna, and the Titunwan. Yet during this violent history of genocide and colonization, everything possible has been done to divide us and to destroy our cultural cohesion as a People. Bringing the Oceti Sakowin back together will strengthen and heal us collectively, and we are slowly working to make these connections. Edward Valandra, Sicangu Lakota from Rosebud, reminded us of this connection early in the march. When discussing his reasons for participating, he said, ◀ *"I also believe that as we support each other, the entire Nation will be strengthened. Malakota, Madakota, Manakota [among the eastern groups, we would say Damakota, meaning "I am Dakota"], it's all one to me. So it's good to be here with my relatives."* ▶

Deksi Leo Omani conveyed similar thoughts, ◀ *"We were always one, and that word* Oceti Sakowin *is strong. It gives us that identity that was our governing system, our checks and balances that upheld our moral values. I say 'pidamayaye do' to our relatives from Yankton and Rosebud who are here to be with us, for we are one."* ▶

While Deski Leo and many of our Canadian relatives realize that our traditional territory extended well into what is now called Canada, we know that the flight from Minnesota occurred as a consequence of the war. Whereas previously our people would have traveled back to our homeland at will, after 1862 that was no longer a possibility. So meeting in our homeland is a means of reconnecting that was lost to us post-1862. Beth Brown, a Dakota language student at the University of Minnesota, relayed similar thoughts, ◀ *"I feel like 1862 was a year of the Dakota People being scattered all over the map. With the march, it was like people from all over the map came back together and were together again. I think the march serves as a symbol to remind people that this is Dakota makoce, Dakota land,*

and I feel like it's a symbol of return that kind of helps heal the exile." ▶

She is highlighting an important connection between the return of the People to the land and the healing that ensues. I also commented on this, ◀ *"When we come together like this, what we're doing is we're getting to know one another again, and we're finding out how we're connected to one another. That, in itself, is really healing. It's really important."* ▶

CHILDREN AND YOUNG PEOPLE ON THE MARCH

Fundamental to our future as a People are our young people, and on this 2004 March, we had a whole group of students from the Lower Sioux Community who walked with us as well as many of the children of the adult marchers. Many of us were thrilled that they wanted to participate, and

Anthony Rangel carrying one of the staffs.

we were happy to know they were learning about our history in a very personal way. I hope that we will also be able to hear their reflections on the march. They brought an energy to the walk and also reminded us of all the young people who would have been on the original march in 1862. Ron "Bear" Cronick commented later, ◀ *"It was good to see all the youth from Lower Sioux walking with us those days. They came here, and they also carried the eagle staffs; they really enjoyed carrying the staffs in the front."* ▶

Phyllis Redday also appreciated their participation, stating after the first day, ◀ *"I was real pleased with the walk, and I say thank you to the little* takozas, *all the little children, who gave me strength. I said, 'Well, I'm just going to walk a mile or two,' but I ended up doing four, which is real well for me."* ▶

The walk also gave the young people an opportunity to learn about our culture and about how we can show respect to the spirits of our ancestors. Deski Leo remarked, ◀ *"We are going through this healing process, and it is really important to reconnect with our relatives and for our younger ones to learn too. Today I really enjoyed the walk, seeing all these young ones out there. But it's also a learning process for us and our younger ones, too. . . . I mentioned that the younger ones should be aware, that they should not get past [in front of] the* canunpa, *the sacred pipe; until then, things didn't really settle down. I noticed, thinking back, that's what was happening: some of those younger ones were passing the* canunpa *later on during the day. It was causing a lot of chaos, and emotions were really running high. So that's what I'm learning. That's also a learning for us, too, and for our younger ones—to let them know about those things."* ▶

DEALING WITH WHITE RACISM

While on the march, instances of racism always arise, and they can affect the marchers' morale if they are not addressed in some way. Many of them are quite minor. That first day, for example, Deksi Leo told us, ◀ *"There was that car at the end that tried to impress us by that last stake we put up; it came flying by and raised a lot of dust there to get onto Highway 10. Then fifteen minutes later it came flying by again and parked at the end of the road there. He wasn't helping. But just let it pass, because we are not here for them. We're here for us and for our healing, and that's what we need to think about."* ▶

These kinds of reminders helped us maintain our focus and not deviate from our mission on the walk. As we prepared for the resistance we might face each day, it helped to understand what we might come up against or what kind of reactions we might get from Wasicus along the way. The night before we walked into New Ulm, Mary Beth discussed a portion of our upcoming route, ◀ *"We're going to be walking a part of 29, and we're going to be walking down into Milford Township. I have a current Milford directory platt map over here that you can look at it. But what I want to note particularly is the Anson Henley farm that is on here. We're going to be walking right past it. . . . The Henley farm family lost twenty-one members on that August day. . . . So we're walking through that township, just to alert you that we're opening their wounds. . . . There are going to be old sentiments in that soil, and maybe in the people too, because some of the descendants still live there. . . . Because there is so much animosity, maybe we have to reopen the wounds and let them bleed out, maybe."* ▶

Similarly, my father expressed a need for us to prepare ourselves for what was to come, ◀ *"The other thing that I was thinking about, too, is that tomorrow night, we're going to be dealing with Wasicus. It was good to hear these stories, and it strengthens us and encourages us. Tomorrow when we deal with people at New Ulm—for example, when my daughter talks about her grandmother and tells the stories of hot, scalding water being poured upon our people—we need to be strong, and we need to encourage each other."* ▶

SEEKING JUSTICE, NOT "RECONCILIATION"

In some ways, dealing with whatever animosity is present in White townspeople is getting more difficult to endure. Though we understand that we need to build Wasicu allies if justice in Minnesota will ever be realized, reconciliation between the Dakota Oyate and the White Minnesotans is not a possibility. My father, Chris Mato Nunpa, publicly acknowledged this in New Ulm, using his own experience and observations to illustrate this point: ◀ *"I got crucified by many Dakotas, by many Indigenous people, back in 1987 when we used the term 'reconciliation'. . . . I suggested that term because that was the 125th anniversary of what happened in 1862 and because I knew Wasicus really like that term. It sounds good—'reconciliation.' I also knew what it meant, but I was just doing it for the political purpose. Governor Perpich, at the suggestion of the Minnesota Historical Society (which they got from the Dakota Studies Committee), called it the 'Year of Reconciliation' from December 26, 1986, to December 26, 1987. Lots of fellow Dakotas, they didn't like that term at all.*

You see, 'reconciliation' means that people were together once, and then somehow they got estranged, and then they came back together. As far as our people can tell, there was never that unity with Wasicus. Strangers came to this land and they took it. I don't know of any point when there was a oneness." ▶

Nonetheless, 'reconciliation' remains a term that Wasicus find comfortable and reassuring. When we use the term amongst ourselves, we are referring to the reconciliation that has to occur among our Peoples within the Oceti Sakowin, as we heal from the factionalism we have endured as a consequence of colonialism. With the door closed to reconciliation with White townspeople, though, tensions may mount. In this context, having Wasicu allies to vocalize and model rhetoric and action supportive of our cause becomes increasingly important, especially as Dakota people begin telling some of our stories and expressing our views.

During the evening meeting with the townspeople in New Ulm, my father began once again by sharing some of his personal reasons for participating, which meant describing the death of his grandmother who was stabbed by a White soldier. For him, the suffering did not end with her death but has continued forward since that day in 1862: ◀ *"That night, the relatives went back to where the killing took place and couldn't find the body. The body had been thrown in the creek after what had happened, but they didn't find the body in the creek. So we don't know where the body is and so, the general society, they like to talk about 'closure.' When other people are missing and they find them, then they feel like they have closure. But a lot of the Dakota people never had closure, and we didn't get to go through the traditional prayers, the songs, the rituals, and the* wokiksuya wotapi, *what we call over here 'the remembrance feast,' that's held one year after a loved one dies. We didn't get to do any of that. And so we still don't know where those people who were killed on the march are, and those hundreds of people who were killed at the concentration camp at Fort Snelling, we don't know where they are either."* ▶

Mato Nunpa then went on to discuss how perspectives on these events differ according to who is observing them, who is involved. For example, the perspectives of those who break the treaties will differ from those who have their treaties broken, those who steal the land from those who have their land stolen, and those who were perpetrators of genocide from those who were victims of genocide. He said he did not know whether the two sides could ever agree, but he asked the group, ◀ *"Can the stealers of the land agree with the people who feel their lands were stolen? I don't know, you have to answer that question."* ▶

As Dakota people committed to seeking justice, we know that we will never subscribe to the colonizers' perspective regarding the broken treaties, land theft, and genocide, and we are training the next generation to continue the struggles in which we are currently engaged. Will the colonizers ever begin to see things from our perspective? I think they will eventually, if only to ease their own sickness and suffering, but that is years down the road. My father closed his initial comments by stating, ◀ *"We're dealing with tough stuff, but in the process of healing for both sides, one thing that has to be put on the table is the truth, the truth. Especially with land, with land*

theft, it has to be put on the table, and we have to talk about it." ▶

RECLAIMING OUR HISTORY THROUGH OUR STORIES AND TRUTH-TELLING

When I spoke next, I continued his discussion about the importance of remembering and telling the truth: ◀ *"When September 11 happened in this country, one of the phrases you saw all over the place after 9-11 was, 'We will never forget, we will never forget.' And I think that is a really significant idea, it's a significant concept, and it's one that we, as Dakota People, share or believe in when we think about our own history, especially with everything that happened here in Minnesota in 1862. For us, the stories that have been carried on are stories of resistance; they're stories of survival; they're stories that indicate a conception of the world that is different from that of the dominant society. It is a conception that celebrates Dakota defense of homeland; it celebrates Dakota violence against invaders; it celebrates the martyrs who gave their lives defending our land, our way of life, our women and children, and that's what we have been taught to believe.*

"When I started doing research for the Commemorative March by researching the historical march that occurred in 1862, one of the things that became apparent to me was that the story that I grew up with, that my grandmother shared, is the most detailed account yet documented. It was a story conveyed in the oral tradition, a story that I heard many, many times throughout my lifetime, until I began saying the same kinds of phrases that my grandmother would say. And I'd like to share with you that account. . . .

"I've asked my daughter to read it in part be-

cause I think the wind affected my eyes today and everything seems a bit blurry, but I also wanted my daughter to read this because she is someone who is a carrier of this story now. One of the last memories that I have of my grandmother before she passed away is of her holding my daughter, who was just a baby still, on her lap and telling her the stories. And when I saw that, I knew my grandmother must have done that with me when I was a baby. Of course, I don't remember it much, but I know I heard the stories all through my childhood and into adulthood. When I saw her beginning this training process with my own daughter, it really hit me that this is very important. These stories are very important. And it's very important for our People's survival that they get passed on." ▶

My daughter, Autumn, then stood up and shared Maza Okiye Win's account of the 1862 Death March as told in her great-grandmother's voice, that of Elsie Two Bear Cavender (see "Decolonizing the 1862 Death Marches" in this volume for the written version of this story).

While some of our families have specific stories about these horrific events in our past, many others do not. In the midst of warfare, removal, diaspora, and colonization, the carriers of the stories sometimes died before they could pass them on; in other cases, they remained too fearful to tell the stories. For us, we cannot go to textbooks to find our perspectives represented, so we work on recovering these stories. Deksi Leo reminded us about this need to reclaim history: ◀ "Our history has been stolen from so many of our Peoples who we know are Indigenous to this land. Now we are so scattered all over the country, over Turtle Island, and we need to go back and reclaim our history. . . . Because of disease and warfare, and because of people renaming us and renaming our bloodlines, we've lost so much of our history that we need to claim back, and we're in this process of doing that. And we need to do it the hard way through this healing process that we're going through, through these memorial walks. I thank our women, pidamayaye do, to all our winyans (women) for picking up from the first march and carrying on this process of healing." ▶

While Americans may not find the link between history and healing readily apparent, for a People whose history has been denied, the link is direct and powerful: reclaiming our history has everything to do with our healing. He continued with his discussion of healing, saying, ◀ "You need to cry in order to begin that healing process. And each time we've come the last two years, the last march, and today and yesterday, tears happened in our hearts and in our minds with both men and women, and that's something that needs to happen. The way we talk needs to happen also. And the solutions that we suggest and offer need to be acknowledged, so our voices will begin to be heard by those elected to various positions of power. Because I know—and no doubt they also know—that we need to come to terms with the past." ▶

AFFIRMING OUR BASIC HUMANITY

Edward Valandra then picked up on these themes. After a few laughs and teasing, he moved into a more serious discussion of how the recent presidential elections had involved a major debate over values—family values in particular—yet Wasicus seem unable to understand why we might be upset about crimes perpetrated against our ancestors and family members, or why we might be concerned when we cannot find their bodies. To attempt to place our love of family within contexts that the dominant society might be able to understand, he used more familiar examples: ◀ *"What was one of the first things that happened after the Civil War when the slaves were so-called freed? The first thing they did was to begin to look for their relatives. They traveled all over the South to find their relatives. And that's in their oral history. They searched high, they searched low, they traveled hundreds and hundreds of miles to locate a father, a mother, a grandfather, a grandmother, an uncle, an auntie, a son, a daughter; it is not a unique experience to our People. So you have to understand that it's not just an Indian thing. . . . Missing in Action, MIAs in Vietnam, their families are still searching for them, still searching. Vietnam has ended, but families are still searching for their lost loved ones. And what happens when they find one? It's flashed across the headlines. . . . Even 9-11, think about that: those people are still looking for relatives. So when we talk about this, we're talking about reconnecting, finding our people who have disappeared."* ▶

It saddens me that in the twenty-first century, we still have to put forward such arguments, because they seem so basic to all human beings. Yet because society has denied us our humanity, we must continue to defend our positions relentlessly and to point out that we are not different in this respect from other humans.

WHITE ON WHITE: DEMANDING ACCOUNTABILITY FOR GENOCIDE AND ITS COVER-UP

In New Ulm, as we were meeting with White townspeople and after a number of Dakota people had spoken, both Mary Beth and Denise stepped forward to eloquently engage a critical and essential discourse. Many of these comments were presented so well that they have been included at length here. Mary Beth began by describing again her own family history: ◀ *"My heritage is German and Moravian, and my great-great-grandmother was born in Minnesota in 1861. So I don't know how long my ancestors were here prior to that, but my roots go to at least 1861. And my roots have reached the ground underneath and have entangled with the roots of Dakota People. So this march for me has been very emotional, leaving me with mixed emotions in the sense that, mixed in with German ancestry, I feel a great deal of sadness about what happened to the German people, the settlers, but I feel a greater sense of sorrow for what has happened to the Dakota People.*

"I want to come from a perspective of looking at perpetrators and bystanders. In our generation, we are bystanders in looking at what happened, and we have an obligation as bystanders to speak the truth. There may have been bystanders, and there certainly were in 1862, people who had no voice or a limited voice, or who were silent and never expressed what they believed or thought to be true and right, but it is our obligation now, for those who are the descendants of those settlers, to listen, to read, to research, and to look at what is going on today and to not be bystanders to what is happening to the Oyate and to all Indigenous Peoples in the United States and elsewhere as well.

"In my looking at historical grief and in looking at trauma and violence, there is a theme that has been expressed by a psychiatrist, a woman psychiatrist, who has studied and written about working with violence and the perpetrator. I'd like

you to think about this, because the perpetrator of these crimes was our very own U.S. government, and Governor Alexander Ramsey, General Sibley, and Colonel William Rainey Marshall. Unfortunately, I'm living in a town named after Marshall. He was one of the architects and engineers of this removal—the man who deliberately brought the Dakota through New Ulm and Henderson. So let me tell you this, and I want you to think about it. What does the perpetrator do?

"This is from Judith Herman: 'In order to escape accountability for his crimes, the perpetrator does everything in his power to promote forgetting. Secrecy and silence are the perpetrator's first line of defense. If secrecy fails, the perpetrator attacks the credibility of the victim. If he can't silence him or her absolutely, he tries to make sure that no one listens. To this end, he marshals an impressive array of arguments, from the most blatant denial to the most sophisticated and elegant rationalization. After every atrocity, one can expect to hear the same predictable mythologies: it never happened; the victim lies; the victim exaggerates; the victim brought it upon himself or herself; and in any case, it is time to forget the past and move on. The more powerful the perpetrator, the greater is his prerogative to name and define reality, and the more completely his arguments prevail.'

"So what did we learn about Minnesota history in sixth grade? What did we learn in high school? And for those of us who went on to higher education, what did we learn there? It was silenced. It was not spoken. And if it was, and if stories were told by Native people, it was said that they exaggerated, they lied, or it didn't happen. And so we continue this genocide of people with our denials. What is it that is our responsibility? What is that

responsibility to search out truth and to search out what happened? And where do we find it?

"Although I have not done extensive digging—more casual inquiries at the Minnesota Historical Society—I find it interesting that there are no daily journals of William Rainey Marshall. Where are the daily logs, the morning reports—all that is part of military protocol? It doesn't exist—not that we can find. Every now and then, one might stumble across a journal. And we happened to stumble across a journal entry by a young soldier at Fort Ridgely. As their Web site says, they have a research library, which is a book shelf behind the counter. He happened to have one that was only discovered in 1984. So where are these journals? What has happened to them? Were the atrocities so great that they were destroyed? And if you have nothing written in the White world, the history didn't exist, and any oral stories are exaggerations. They aren't reliable, they are lies, and anyway, it's time to forget the past and move on. So what is our accountability as bystanders? What is our responsibility? That is the question that we have to answer for ourselves, because we clearly have those responsibilities. . . .

"We need to name what happened here as state-sponsored genocide. And what could be clearer than placing bounties on any man, woman, or child? Ramsey's policies were clearly genocidal. The first time I visited Alexander Ramsey's house in St. Paul, I went into the garage—this was twenty years ago—and there was a video on Ramsey and a quote that was very clear and direct stating that his position was for the extinction and removal of the Dakota People from Minnesota, extermination. It's pretty clear what the intentions were.

"And we need as Minnesotans—as White Minnesotans who have roots here in that period of time and later—to declare that anything with Ramsey's name on it be extinguished. There is nothing in Germany named 'Hitler Avenue,' or 'Hitler Township,' or 'Hitler County.' Germans would be outraged, but we aren't. We celebrate Ramsey as a hero. I learned just recently, which probably everyone in Mankato knows, that Sibley Park—which is located next to the Land of Memories of Park where the Dakota have the Makato Wacipi every year—was the site of the Mankato concentration camp for the men. So perhaps we should rename Auschwitz 'Hitler Camp.' 'Hitler Park,' let's call it. Let's acknowledge, then—we need to acknowledge what happened in these places.

"We do not have Minnesota history in this state. I learned about the lakes and the trees, who the first [White] settler was, and that they made treaties, but they never told me what a treaty was, or that that's how we got all this land—nothing about what happened on this land. We all, as White people, need to read the treaties. There are Web sites that give the text of the treaties in full with notations. These sites show where the treaties were signed by the Dakota in good faith, by all Peoples in good faith, and how, when they got to Congress, articles were removed, particularly those that defined territory and defined payment. That's fraud, don't you think? That's a contract. Those issues need to be addressed as well. We have, as White Minnesotans, a lot of work to do. And some of us are at that certain age where we have time on our hands and that is what we can do. Pidamayeye." ▶

WHITE ALLIES: WHY THEY'RE NEEDED, AND WHY THEY'RE SCARCE

After Mary Beth spoke these powerful words calling for accountability and action by White Minnesotans, my father articulated why it was important to have non-Indigenous allies address these issues as well. He said, ◀ "One of my White colleagues at Southwest Minnesota State University is a retired historian, and he says to me, 'You know Chris, I can say the same things that you say,' but he says, 'I can get away with it.' But if I say it, you know I'm going to really get crucified; I'm going to get reported to the dean or to the provost when I say those things. And there's a lot of truth to that. That's why it's really good to have a Wasicu woman up here to say that." ▶

Interestingly, when my father made very similar comments in 2002, Frederick Wulff, a retired professor from a local Bible college, wrote several letters to the editor of the local newspaper complaining about the outrageous arguments made by Mato Nunpa (see Mato Nunpa's chapter for a further discussion of what was said). Because of the racism and colonialism that is still part of everyday reality for Indigenous people, Wasicu people are less likely to challenge, discredit, or disbelieve comments made by other Wasicus.

Yet Wasicu fear and cowardice tends to prevent many non-Indigenous people from taking a stand on these issues, even if they share some of the same thoughts, because many are afraid of what they might lose in the process. Mato Nunpa went on to explain that, after his series of written exchanges with Wulff in the local newspaper, some Wasicus contacted him privately to express their support: ◀ "So then I wrote back to them, and I said, 'Hey, why don't you think about writing a letter to the editor?' One of them was very honest and said, 'I admit it, I'm a coward.' She didn't want to write what she thought because she was afraid that she would get her fellow Euro-Americans angry at her here in New Ulm. Another said, 'My husband owns a business, and I'm afraid he'll face reprisals.' So she didn't want to write a letter to the editor either. A third one said, 'I work for a state-funded institution, so I can't, I'm not free.' So I was just thinking, that seems to be the way it is—not just in New Ulm but in any small town. There's no freedom of opinion. You have to agree with what the majority says." ▶

Furthermore, what typically happens when allies take up the cause of the oppressed is that they begin to be treated like the oppressed, and most Wasicus do not want to receive that kind of treatment.

It was important that these Wasicu allies voice their critical perspectives, not only because all the marchers were exhausted, but also because we knew those comments would be accepted more easily by White audiences if they came from White speakers.

DOING JUSTICE BETWEEN PEOPLES: WHAT DOES IT TAKE TO MAKE THINGS RIGHT?

Denise then picked up where Mary Beth and my father left off by discussing Dakota-Wasicu relations from a restorative justice perspective: ◀ "As I was driving through here behind the marchers, I looked at the big houses, horses, barns, and very wealthy areas where we walked by playgrounds and houses with huge playground equipment just for their own children, and there's a lot of beauty, but I thought, we committed genocide for this? This is what we committed genocide for? It was just a very powerful day.

"I believe Chris wanted me to talk about my background in restorative justice. . . . I run a small nonprofit publishing company devoted to restorative justice. Restorative justice is the idea of doing justice as healing rather than doing justice as punishment; it looks for alternative ways of resolving hurts, harms, conflicts, and crimes. It started with victim-offender mediation among the Whites. Its roots, of course, are Indigenous.

"To give you a sense of how it's approached, one of the things that we've learned—or that the restorative justice movement has learned in the thirty years that it's been practiced among Whites in the criminal justice system—is accountability. That means holding the perpetrators or the offenders accountable for what they've done. And this is done as part of the offender's transformation and for the dignity of the offender.

"One of the things that has brought me to participate in this march is the need to take what we've learned in restorative justice and apply it to healing historical harms—addressing harms between Peoples. That's not something that the movement is doing right now, but it seems like a very logical and necessary next step. Otherwise, what sense does restorative justice make? It doesn't mean much if you don't take it to these deeper levels. So naturally those of us who are in restorative justice say, okay, if we need to hold the offender accountable, then we need to hold ourselves accountable for what was done and for the crimes our ancestors did, crimes against humanity, from which we benefit. I live on land that could have been bought by killing a Dakota man or many men, I don't know, or women and children for the bounty. So we need to hold ourselves accountable and that's for my dignity and my healing.

"Another fundamental principle of restorative

justice is hearing the stories. We need to hear the stories. We need to know what happened. That's a very fundamental piece. The first book we published is Peacemaking Circles, *because the talking circle process is being used for creating alternatives to incarceration. One of the most important things is to go around the circle, a talking circle, and to hear the stories of everyone who has been involved. We know in South Africa that the Truth and Reconciliation Commission was very important in their national healing, even though there are many criticisms of that—still it was an important step. I understand from Edward and Angela that you are working on this as well—talking about a truth and reconciliation commission for dealing with the history in this country of genocide.*

"A third thing that is very important in restorative justice that we've learned is the importance of apology—a heartfelt, genuine, and authentic apology, a sense of real deep remorse for what has happened, for what has been done, and for how it continues to have profound effects on generations now. It's not something that's just in the past; it's very much lived now (as in, who's living in the big houses and who's living in the prisons). It's very much an issue now. We've learned that, so we need to be doing that.

"And then the last thing we have learned in restorative justice is that all the people who are connected to the harm should come together and ask: What can we do to make things right? An apology most certainly is not enough. It has to be followed by action and there are so many dimensions to this, but land return and reparations—these are two of many, many actions that we need to take. That's the core issue: What needs to be done to make things right?

"I also want to underscore that when I hear about what has happened, I think, my gosh, how sick, how traumatized, how screwed up the White people were who did these things—and how screwed up we remain as long as we don't deal with them. We know from the study of multigenerational trauma, we know from European history, and, for those of you who've read Alice Miller's book* For Your Own Good, *we know how really deeply traumatized were the people who were doing this stuff.*

"So it's clear that we need our healing too. I think we see that now with recovery issues, we have a population where addiction rates are off the charts among White people—both process addictions and substance addictions. Addictions don't come from healthy people. The greed that goes on in the world, well, we could really talk a long time about that; suffice it to say, there's a need for healing. I think addressing historical harms can be the most profound place to start in our healing work and the foundation for a kind of healing that will bless us White people and will help make us whole. It wouldn't kill us to do justice, I'm thinking. Thank you very much, my Oceti Sakowin Oyate friends, for allowing me to be a part of this healing journey." ▶

After Denise's comments, at least one Wasicu came forward to attempt to address the message that both she and Mary Beth were trying to convey. Hank Campbell, the pastor at the United Church of Christ in New Ulm, discussed the importance of confession in the faith community, and he agreed, ◀ *"I think we need to listen and acknowledge."* ▶ He discussed the role of White people and churches coming into the land, bringing in ◀ *"boarding schools, bringing in culture, overlaying culture along with religion, which was not respectful of the people."* ▶ He went on to say, ◀ *"Justice and peace are certainly a part of the Christian faith community message and probably most religions as well. We need to be striving for that, for hope. I have hope that there can be healing, that there can be coming together, that there can be reconciliation. I think that there has been some of that along the way, but we have a past that we need to continually confess, that's part of the universal human brokenness, really. I mean, all of our cultures and all of our traditions do have a brokenness that is part of the human condition, the way that I see it. Certainly the history around the 1860s was a real picture of brokenness in the European, White community."* ▶

His comments offer hope that, as we continue to pursue our quest for accountability and justice, we may at least have some common ground from which to begin.

WHY THE MARCH IS NOT A GOOD FORUM FOR EDUCATING WHITES

While there was some basis for hopeful partnering in the future concerning issues of justice for the Dakota People, there were also causes for concern. For example, one of the townspeople who has been quite supportive of the Commemorative Marches demonstrated an inability to distinguish between Dakota acts of violence in defense of a homeland and Wasicu acts of violence perpetrated against a People for the purpose of eliminating them from their homeland and taking over their lands and resources. Despite my father's earlier comments about the inevitable difference in perspective between the Dakotas and Wasicus, this townsperson proceeded to explain that she hoped to work toward reconciliation. She

suggested that perhaps some day we could all walk together, and at each site the Wasicus could watch and listen to our stories of what happened there, and then we could listen to their stories about what happened. She believed that if both sides could do that, then we could move just a little bit closer together.

Most of us from the march were deeply disturbed by her comments, but we were also too exhausted to think about challenging her comments at that moment. Unfortunately, she was not the only White townsperson who felt that way. Later that evening, another Wasicu woman approached Dave and Diane Wilson privately and said, "Well, you killed us too!"

In future marches, we will have to consider whether we want to engage Wasicu townspeople in this way. We conceived of the march as including an educational project—as an opportunity to educate White Minnesotans about the shameful history of Dakota annihilation and White settlement of the state. We viewed it as our opportunity to tell the truth. However, we weren't banking on the fact that we would be spiritually and physically exhausted as we attempted to do this educating. This became apparent the first day of the walk in 2002 when we arrived in Sleepy Eye and felt the awkward attempt at reconciliation by those townspeople. After walking approximately twenty-five miles, most of us could barely move, and we were simply not prepared to challenge the ideas that we opposed. All we wanted was to rest with the support and comfort of other marchers, but we had to rally for the ensuing discussion. I remember feeling not just incredibly emotional but also incredibly uncomfortable.

Many of us spend the seven days of the march

emotionally raw. As we walk, mile by mile the defenses that we have built over the years peel away layer by layer, until we are emotionally laid bare. Emotions emerge that we didn't even know were there, and the tears and laughter flow in abundance. Our senses are so heightened that we find ourselves acutely aware not only of our own feelings but of what others are feeling too. We know immediately when someone in our midst is hurting, and we reach out to comfort and support that person, knowing that others will later be supporting us. And because we feel our physical pain so deeply, we empathize with others and take on their pain. We share our humanity with one another at the deepest levels.

It is in this context that White townspeople met with us and engaged in this dialogue, but what followed seemed to be dialogue that both sides were unprepared to have with each other. The marchers were emotionally and spiritually prepared to engage with each other about the meaning of the Commemorative March, because we had been contemplating the experience every single mile and had spent many hours engaging one another in such discussions. We were not, however, prepared to effectively engage a more hostile Wasicu audience—or even one in denial about the ongoing colonization and their participation in it.

Recently, my friend Jason Weber pointed out to me that the White townspeople were indeed not at all prepared to address these issues in any meaningful way. They essentially came to our gathering as a respite from their daily lives, and they simply were not prepared to engage with us on the same level. They had not been stripped of the defenses, and they were not in the vulnerable

places we were, nor were they emotionally and spiritually prepared to address the profound pain that is present whenever genocide of a People is discussed.

Fortunately, we have always had a few among us who are less physically drained and who are prepared to address issues for us when we are too weak to do so. My father is usually one of those people. In New Ulm, after hearing the comments from that Wasicu townsperson, he was able to politely state to the group, ◀ *"That's a good idea, but it's just that we know plenty about what happened to the White people in this country. We don't know too much about the Dakota, because that's been suppressed. The perpetrators do not want that to be known."* ▶

Although we did not discuss it at the time, we all recognize that both Wasicu and Dakota people committed acts of violence, but we do not view the violence in the same way. The two acts are not morally equivalent: invading the land is not morally equivalent to defending the land. It may be that our efforts to educate the public about our event and the history behind it will have to occur outside of those seven days; those seven days must be reserved for discussions among ourselves and our closest allies.

COLONIAL POWER: POLICE HARASSMENT AND THREATS

Perhaps the most poignant reminder of our differing perspectives and agendas came on the sixth day of the march when a state trooper stopped our procession. As my father later recounted, ◀ *"The highway patrolman came with his lights flashing, pulled in front of us, stopped in front of us, and held up our procession. Leo and I went over to talk to him, and he quoted some Minnesota statute, threatened us, and said we were violating the law and that he could arrest us and take us to jail. Then he said that not only to me and Leo, but he said that to the whole group of marchers as well. That's when Angela just said, 'A mile down the road, we're going to pound in another stake.' But, fortunately, there was no confrontation."* ▶

We had not expected police harassment this far into our journey, but a couple of events the previous day had apparently precipitated this police intervention. First, when we were walking along Highway 169 (a divided highway), a vehicle in the oncoming lanes of traffic across the divider must have braked to look at our marchers and caused an accident. While no one was physically injured, the accident drew increased attention to our march. Second, later that same day, Mary Beth Faimon's car was hit from behind, and the impact sent her careening into the ditch. Her car was totaled, but her life was saved only because her car landed perfectly between a telephone pole and a road sign. She suffered leg injuries, however, from which she is still recovering. After these events, the state apparently received a flurry of complaints regarding the distraction we were creating by pounding prayer stakes into the ground. We were told that we had no permit to engage in such acts and that the state was unaware that we had been doing that without permission.

When the police officer stopped us, he told the group of marchers, "The stakes are not to be placed in the right-of-way of the roadways. . . . You can be cited and taken to jail for a misdemeanor offense." My father spoke up at that point: "I told him that I can't tell the marchers not to do that, that we're honoring our ancestors and relatives. So there is a conflict between state law and honoring our ancestors." The officer replied, "I'm telling you that if we see you doing that, we are supposed to cite you." It did not matter that we had encountered numerous roadside memorials erected by family members of car accident victims for their lost loved ones; somehow our memorials were illegal and worthy of citation and arrest, while theirs were not. As my father later reported to the *Dakota Journal*, ◀ *"When he asked if we were going to deliberately disobey the law, I told him, 'No, we are going to deliberately honor our ancestors.'"* ▶ Fortunately, at that point in the day, we were close to our destination, and we were turning onto reservation land at Prior Lake. But we knew this was an issue we would need to quickly address, since our status as colonized people was made instantly clear in that brief engagement.

When *News from Indian Country* solicited comments about the 2004 Commemorative March a few weeks later, I wrote about this incident: ◀ *"The attempt of state authorities to dictate the parameters of our actions was reminiscent of the same kind of colonial power seen in 1862. We were extremely disheartened by the fact that, as Dakota people walking in 2004, we were not free to walk in prayer to honor our ancestors without colonial interference. We had a decision to make about what to do as we faced the prospect that some of us might be arrested for honoring our ancestors in this way. As a group, the Dakota women who were the primary organizers for the march agreed that we would be the ones to place the stakes in the ground on the last day, so that if arrests were made, we would bear the brunt of that burden. As it turned out, on the last day, state officials left us alone as we placed the remaining stakes in the ground, and no arrests were made.*

"However, this warning raised important issues regarding our relationship to the colonial government and the extent to which we should seek state 'permission' to honor our ancestors in future marches. It also reminded us that, in spite of whatever perceived strides have been made in recent decades, we are still denied the most basic access to and freedoms in our ancestral homeland." ▶

This particular event was an extraordinary learning experience for all of us. While some of us were adamant about continuing unabated, even if it meant citation and arrest, others were interested in exploring possible ways to reach a compromise with law enforcement. For example, we knew that, since we had marchers from Canada, including Deksi Leo, we had to be conscious of the fact that if they were arrested, they might be prevented from crossing the border in the future, and as a group, we had an obligation to protect them as much as possible. We also had many children with us for whom we needed to be responsible.

Because the contentious issue seemed to stem from us placing "structures" in the ground in the area reserved for approved road signs, some people questioned the state trooper about the possibility of placing the stakes further inland from the road. We were told that was not an option because we would then be infringing on private property. Others suggested that perhaps we could lay the prayer stakes on the ground rather than stake them upright in the ground, but we felt that would be too disrespectful.

In the end, it was the small group of women

from the planning committee who made the decision on this matter. We decided we would risk arrest, but we didn't want anyone else to suffer the consequences of our decision. This experience demonstrated, however, the varying responses to colonialism. While our situation was not the life-or-death struggle that our ancestors experienced in 1862, the flight, fight, or capitulate responses were still very much present. It was important for us to make our decisions consciously, fully aware that this is precisely how factionalism takes root in a community.

We are currently in the process of getting together a legal team that could assist us if arrests are made during the next march. Some people believe that resistance will only increase in the coming years. In the follow-up meeting held one month after the 2004 March, Mary Beth Faimon stated, ◀ *"I think the resistance is going to become stronger, and there is going to be a real effort to stop us from going on 169, and we have to do it because that is the fort road that goes to Fort Snelling. That is where people died, and some do not want that history to be heard. . . . The roles of men and women, the White people from 1862, are going to be replayed on these other walks in modern times. No one is going to bayonet anyone in the stomach, but they're going to arrest them. But if we know something is going to happen and if we are just prepared mentally, we will do what needs to be done when that happens."* ▶

On the other hand, it is entirely possible that, if arrests are made in the future, more people will rally to support our efforts. The image of Dakota women of all ages being arrested for placing prayer stakes in the ground in our ancestral homeland would not cast law enforcement in a positive light. It would likely outrage Indigenous people and morally minded Wasicus, especially the faith-based communities, who might rally to defend our right to religious freedom.

HEALING AS A PEOPLE: OUR RECONCILIATION

In spite of the intrusion by law enforcement, the last day of the march proceeded without mishap. We again rose early, had a hot breakfast, said our prayers, and made our way to the first mile marker of the day. The sun was shining, and it was a beautiful day. As we headed toward the Mendota Bridge just a few miles from the fort, the same quiet we experienced in 2002 came over the marchers. The tears flowed for many in heavy sobs, as the realization of concentration camp imprisonment settled into the consciousness of the marchers. We were almost there. The last stretch was heavy with the weight of grief.

For that last segment of the journey, Leonard Wabasha handed my father the shackles his ancestor, Chief Wabasha III, had been forced to wear in 1862 and asked that I carry them into Fort Snelling. I was deeply honored and humbled by that request, and when that cold iron was placed in my hands, I wept. As I carried those shackles across the Mendota Bridge and into the lands where our ancestors were imprisoned, something profound happened. Compassion filled my heart, and I understood at my core that all of our People suffered deeply during the war and as a consequence of colonialism, no matter which side we were on. While I had understood this intellectually for years, it took the experience of me carrying those symbols of oppression—the shackles

of someone who had sided with General Sibley at the end of the war—to teach me that important lesson. I think I did more growing, maturing, and healing during those last two miles than I had in all the miles past.

This event had a similar effect on my father, Chris Mato Nunpa. At the follow-up meeting about the march in December 2005, he commented, ◄ *"It took Lenny, a young man, to bring about healing for me. . . . I guess it just reminds me again about the effects of colonialism. Because of the colonizers' way of doing things, their behavior and their values that were forced upon our People, our people had to make horrible, horrible choices, and everyone who made those choices did so not just for himself or herself, but thinking about the safety and security of his or her family."* ►

He went on to describe a similar reaction to people like John Other Day, who led sixty-two Wasicu refugees to safety at the beginning of the war and then served as a scout and ally to them against other Dakota people. Mato Nunpa then stated, ◄ *"When I thought about it, I was able to see John Other Day in a different light as well. I guess the point I'm making is that all of us who are descendants of people living back then, we've got our own issues to deal with in terms of historical grief and trauma and real anger, real resentment . . . As Dakota People, we need to do a lot of healing."* ►

I had similar thoughts and questions at the end of our first day of walking: ◄ *"I think much of this walk is about this reunification of our nation, and it's not easy, because the United States government worked very hard to divide our People. And they succeeded in many ways. Because we've had family on all sides, one of the issues that I've had to reconcile is, how do you make amends*

Edward Valandra with his T-shirt
signed by march participants.

*with this past when our People were so
divided?"* ►

The march allows us to address these
issues and to develop a sense of compassion for all of our People, regardless of
their ancestors' actions. That conscious
recognition of the colonizers' divisive
strategies and the various responses to
colonialism that we employ allow us to
make good choices for the future in a
more unified way—a way that will help
us all resist colonial institutions and reclaim what we have lost.

RECONNECTING WITH OUR ANCESTRAL HOMELAND

Part of this reclamation is about finding our relatives, as so many marchers have experienced, but it is also about reconnecting with the land. After the march, Dottie Whipple remembered those first days of walking with special fondness. She said, ◄ *"I think the best part for me was being able to walk through the valley for quite a ways. Those first couple days, that was so beautiful. It was nice and quieter and safer. Because it was through the valley, it seemed more like what it would have been like for the original marchers. That's the part that I enjoyed."* ►

Scott Wilson made similar comments about

the first day's journey, ◄ *"We didn't take it for granted when we lived here; we knew it was a beautiful and powerful place, but after you're gone and the longer you're gone, when you come back, it just pounds you in your heart and in your spirit. It's so beautiful here, and it's so wonderful to be back. And today, walking in the Minnesota River valley again, it's such a powerful place and so good for our souls to be back here."* ►

Everyone felt this connection to land in different ways. Since human beings in the twenty-first century rarely take the time to walk 150 miles in any landscape, this daily experience of touch-

Phyllis Redday and Randilynn Boucher.

ing the earth through mindful walking proved healing and moving. Mary Beth Faimon reflected on this as well: ◀ *"The other real point that has happened for me is a deeper understanding of this land, and it makes me feel very sad. I feel very sad inside about being here, because the land is not mine and is not the land of the United States of America. It's the land of the Dakota People. I think that is something that I am becoming more in touch with, and it's hard to acknowledge. I've listened to Chris for almost eight years now, and I hear what he says, but to really feel what he says really hurts inside. And I think the walk is bringing me more in touch with that."* ▶

The reconnection to land is made more poignant because of the sense of loss. My father frequently articulated this in different ways along the march. He addressed everyone gathered in New Ulm saying, ◀ *"This land, it was given to us by the Creator, Wakantanka, the Great Mystery, and the Bdewakantunwan origin story places our Dakota Garden of Eden where the Minnesota River joins the Mississippi. That's* Maka Cokaya Kin, *the center of the earth. And it wasn't a Jew who was born there, and it wasn't a Norwegian who was born there, it wasn't Germans who came out of there; it was Dakotas who came out of there."* ▶

The loss of ancestral homeland, the site of a People's creation, is a loss of profound proportions. Deksi Leo Omani described the connection between land recovery and healing in his discussion of events in Canada: ◀ *"The federal government in Canada has come to the table and has agreed with the provincial government, what you'd call the state government, to look at claims of losses, and they're beginning to settle them now. The state took almost 150 years to do it, but they're doing it. I think in the United States, that's what needs to happen to begin this healing process from land loss. Until that happens, we will all need to struggle to come to terms with the past that has happened both in Canada and the United States."* ▶

Implicit in his statement is a recognition that justice will eventually be a part of the healing process and that this justice must in some way include land recovery.

"IT WASN'T MEANT TO BE AN EASY WALK"

Clearly, our thoughts on how the march may be a healing event are transforming as we continue to walk. While we can feel that some healing is tak-ing place, maybe in the form of strengthening, we also do not cease to feel the pain. Rather than initiating a grieving process that would bring an end to the grief and leave us healed from these wounds, walking in remembrance of our ancestors seems to raise more questions about what happened and increases our desire for more answers. These are the more difficult aspects of the walk, but as Ron "Bear" Cronick stated later, ◀ *"It wasn't meant to be an easy walk. I was telling Anthony [Rangel], that young one from Lower Sioux, and I told Autumn [Wilson] that same thing, 'This isn't meant to be easy, because a lot of the women and a lot of our elders walked in the winter with the snow and everything, and if they couldn't make it, the soldiers either killed them or tortured them.' So even though a lot of us had blisters on our feet and our legs were really sore, I still wanted to walk, because I knew our elders, our grandmas, did the walk. . . . We need to think about our people who suffered worse than us."* ▶

One of the most difficult aspects of this experience is the void we face when we try to find out what happened to our relatives who disappeared. My father raised interesting points concerning the walk and the desire to know what happened to the bodies of our loved ones. As he reflected on the march, he shared these thoughts with the marchers, ◀ *"Each time I do this, it gets me a little closer to my thoughts, my real feelings about all the historical trauma, historical grief that I am still carrying with me. I think about the fact that we don't even know where exactly the death of my kunsi occurred. We know it happened near a creek or a river and that her body was thrown in the creek or river. So this time, for me personally, when we were in Henderson and we crossed that*

At another mile marker stop.

Rush River (it's a little creek, I don't know why they call it a river), I wondered, is this the place? And then when we left Henderson and we crossed the bridge over the Minnesota River, then I thought to myself again, I wonder if that's the place. . . . A whole lot of Dakotas living today, they experienced the same thing my family experienced—that is, the deaths, the killings, the murders of their loved ones—and they don't know where those bodies are, and we face the realization that we will probably never know where those bodies are, except probably through ceremonies." ▶

For many of us, the sense of grief we feel takes a heavy toll. Dottie later recounted that just after we left Henderson, the name on a stake belonged to her husband Harlan's relative, a great-great-grandfather. She said she was glad to be there when we put that stake into the ground. She then described the difficult section of the journey that followed as we went up to where we put my family's Haza Win marker into the ground, and many of us were extremely emotional, ◀ *"All the way starting from Henderson when we were going up that hill, it just seemed so powerful. For me, it was a time to be more quiet. I was just trying to be introspective and look around us to see what I could see. Then when she [Angela] broke down, I stopped to take a rest, and I rode with Mary Beth. I think I was telling her what was going on then. There are different times when I think of the People, then I feel like I need to break down or something, but I didn't because I just had to keep on going. I didn't really have that opportunity. But then it just came. And it just came in big sobs, and I just cried and cried and sobbed. It's been three years since we've been doing this. I've been doing a lot of healing my whole life, well not my whole life. I didn't really start until I was about forty-three, and then I started dancing and learning more about traditional things. So I tell people now that every step I take in my moccasins is healing, for dancing and all that. And I've been able to take part in healing conferences. I've needed all of that, and this is part of that too. For me, this is a real opportunity to heal and to understand and to get more into what really went on, because we read it over and we don't understand. So this has been so powerful for me."* ▶

THE POWER OF COMING TOGETHER TO MAKE THE MARCH HAPPEN

The march could not have been completed without the help of many people, but the second march seemed much easier to organize, because there was an increased division and assignment of tasks. This allowed all of us to participate more fully. Dottie, who was one of the core organiz-ers, commented, ◀ *"I think probably the most important thing was all the people—the people who supported us, the marchers—and how everyone got along. Also, all the work that went into it beforehand was good, organizing the people who volunteered to provide us lunch. It was wonderful to have lunch, to sit and rest a while, and to have enough to eat. That was great, and those people are certainly to be thanked. . . . I know it takes a lot of work for people on the outside, so I appreciate the work that people did behind the scenes, because it was wonderful to be able to just walk."* ▶

Similarly, when my father compared the first and second marches, he observed a big change in the planning aspect, ◀ *"Something that was really different from my point of view was the fact that we had so many people helping. . . . So for me, I could just go on the walk and feel it and enjoy the company of the marchers. As usual, it was good to experience it together. It was good to eat together, talk together, cry together, laugh together, and feel pain together—feel the blisters and aching legs. I still remember Ed Valandra and John [Provost] toward the end. Their feet were really full of blisters and sore. And I remember John—I think you guys heard me kidding him on Saturday—John showed me how to put on shoes. He put on his socks first, and then he'd sit there, then he'd put on his shoes, and he'd sit there, and then finally he'd lace them. It was a three-step process to put on his shoes. But they kept walking every day."* ▶

Because Mato Nunpa did not spend so much of his time running from place to place—being a "gofer," as he put it—he was able to appreciate the little things that united all of us. Amy Lonetree commented one time when she stood up to speak, ◀ *"I don't know if you saw me get up, but*

Picking up our sack lunches from the Fuller family.

it takes me a while. I was saying to a few people, 'Geez, I thought I was in better shape than this, and I can barely walk.' I know for me, it's not easy to walk, and I know that other people here are struggling too, but it's really beautiful to see how they keep going." ▶

Mary Beth commented about the communal eating and sleeping together, ◀ *"It was important for me to sleep with the people, not to sleep someplace else. There was a calmness, there was a reverie, and there was a community again that was formed with everyone who was there."* ▶

We could all laugh about cold showers—or no showers—tease about who got to the shower first and had the hot water, who was snoring, who was the last to wake up: all the very human things that people living in a community share.

After arriving at Fort Snelling, we planted the remaining stakes in a circle at the concentration camp site, and we said our last prayers to Wakantanka and the spirits of our ancestors. We enjoyed sandwiches and fruit there. It was bright and sunny, and we all felt tremendous joy from finishing what we had set out to do. On the other hand, we all felt the pangs of hurt that come from saying good-bye to loved ones. After visiting a while and taking a few hours to rest, those who were able to do so met up again at the American Indian Center in Minneapolis for our final dinner together, a few honor and round dance songs, and more discussion about the march. Then we said our good-byes, knowing we might not see one another again until our 2006 Commemorative March.

In the meantime, we hope that other Dakota people will step forward to tell their family stories about the forced removal of our People from our homeland, and we hope they will walk with us in

Irene Howell, Sharon Odegard, Dottie Whipple, and Alvin Howell in Henderson.

2006, 2008, 2010, and 2012. To all of you reading this, I want to tell you that it is safe to tell your stories, because the people of the Oceti Sakowin will stand by your side and share your pain. We will honor your ancestors and the many sacrifices they made. Until then, we will continue our daily lives and daily struggles, and we will continue to educate people about what happened in Minnesota in 1862. When our historical representation of our past is contested, we will be there to stand up and tell our stories about what has happened to our People. The experience of the march has given us the courage to continue to speak the truth in our everyday lives, and it has rekindled a desire for justice. As Gabrielle Tateyuskanskan has written, ◀ *"My historical grief will not find peace until the crimes against the 1,700 vulnerable prisoners find justice. Until this happens, I will continue to walk in the beauty of the Minnesota River valley, acknowledge my spiritual tie to the earth of Dakota origin, work for social change by seeking recognition of Dakota historical trauma, and bear witness to the disappeared."* ▶

Many of us who walked in 2002 and 2004 feel exactly the same way. We'll see you in 2006. *Han mitakuyapi owas'in.*

Wounded Hearts

GABRIELLE WYNDE TATEYUSKANSKAN

◄o►

In 1862 the promise of life's suffering was delivered by a brutal mob.
Shouting, "Exile, Deportation & Capital Punishment."
The whisper of the mind's moral conscience,
Too faint to be heard.

Dakota ancestors journeyed through their despair,
Toward wisdom's understanding.
Passing fires fueled by medicine bundles and visible prayers.
Hope and fragile happiness were on the journey
Carried by the unborn.

Walking with the ancestors in 2002,
Precious gift my inheritance.
Wise teachers to guide the walk in my mortal skin.
A brief journey in comparison,
Marked with honorable names and visible prayers.
A legacy for the unborn,
A road of moral courage.

Humanity, Justice & Peace speak to the living,
Giving strength to wounded hearts.

Afterword

◄◦►

The Dakota Commemorative Marches have breathed life into our struggle to reclaim our homeland and our dignity in the dawn of the twenty-first century. As we begin to prepare to walk again in 2006, we face a host of old and new issues. The usual activities busy our schedules. We are fundraising, preparing publicity materials, making logistical decisions, and preparing our bodies for the arduous event. Yet we are also making preparations for the possibility of police arrest and harassment along the length of the march and have solicited the help of attorneys and other allies who will come to our aid.

In addition, we are contemplating more deeply the role of Wasicu participants and supporters. While we want to make sure that this event remains an Oceti Sakowin event, we also believe there are key ways our Wasicu allies can offer their assistance and support. One form of assistance might come through our Wasicu allies advancing the political issues surrounding the forced march. Some of these allies have suggested lining the streets as our caravan comes through and supporting the marchers by carrying such signs as "We Will Never Forget Minnesota's Genocide," "We Support Justice for Dakota People," "We Need Accountability for Genocide," and "Land Acquisition Is Not Worth Genocide." Others have suggested that Wasicu participants could assist us by helping to serve as a buffer by walking between the Dakota marchers and traffic. As the time draws nearer, we will post our collective thoughts on these topics to our Dakota Commemorative March Web site.

We learned this year that Molly Schoenhoff's vision for a red planting project along the length of the march just might be realized earlier than we anticipated. The Center for Changing Landscapes at the University of Minnesota is currently engaged in developing such a plan along one portion of the march route, using indigenous plants and rocks to mark the trail. They should complete their plans by Summer, 2007, and we hope various community groups will help implement them.

Since we marched in 2004, new concerns have emerged regarding the Fort Snelling site. The Minnesota Historical Society (MHS) has jurisdiction over the historic fort that sits on top of the bluff overlooking Bdote. It was from this fort that cannons were aimed at the tipis in the concentration camp on the flats below during the winter of 1862–63. The MHS is requesting an appropriation of $22.6 million from the Minnesota state legislature to preserve and revitalize Fort Snelling. In essence, the MHS wants to re-fortify the fort, further entrenching this icon of American imperialism in the Minnesota landscape. At the urging of Brenda Child and without input from the Dakota community, the University of Minnesota created a plan for an Ojibwe and Dakota language institute that would be housed in

Fort Snelling

the existing Fort Snelling buildings as part of the renovation.

While the Dakota community is nearly unanimous in its desire to save our language, most of us feel that Fort Snelling, a site of genocide, is not the appropriate place for such an institute. At a February 9, 2006, meeting that the University of Minnesota belatedly sponsored to discuss this project with the Dakota community, the 140 people in attendance—most of whom were Dakota—soundly rejected the proposal. Many of us present found it appalling that Anishinabe people would ignore our deep history at this particular site and would support further Ojibwe encroachment on Dakota lands.

As Dakota People, we lay claim to this area not only as a site of genocide but also as a site of genesis. The Bdewakantunwan Dakota creation story places Dakota origin at this Bdote, and thus this land is considered to be wakan by our People. No other population in the world has such a claim to this specific site. Our task, then, has been to determine how we can honor the site as our place of genesis and genocide, and this is a task that can be determined only by Dakota people.

After the recent community discussion, a group of us (Dakota people and our Wasicu allies) have launched a campaign to *Take Down the Fort*. While this is meant in a literal way—we want the fort demolished—it is also meant to symbolize something much greater. Precisely because the fort stands as a symbol of American imperialism, the eradication of the fort symbolizes a resurgence of Dakota resistance to colonialism and a new era in the reclamation of Dakota homeland. If Wasicu Minnesotans are looking for a concrete way to support Dakota efforts, they can assist us by helping us to eradicate the most prominent symbol of White hegemony on the Minnesota landscape—to take down Fort Snelling. For further information about this campaign, see: http://www.takedown-thefort.com.

This is not the only way in which the Dakota People are reclaiming this area. My father, Chris Mato Nunpa, and Jim Anderson from the Mendota community are being hauled into court because of a citation they received from Homeland Security for collecting water from the sacred Cold Water Spring in the Bdote area. Their experience is a testament to the absurd extent of colonial imposition in the Dakota homeland. It is extremely ironic that Homeland Security, a U.S. government agency, is citing Dakota people for committing the outrageous act of collecting water

in *our* homeland. The U.S. has appropriated the term *homeland* to suit colonial purposes. It is an ingenious and effective way to maintain colonial authority over Indigenous lands and resources, while denying the only people actually entitled to use the term *homeland* even basic access to their ancestral lands and resources. My father and Jim expect a lengthy legal battle as a result of their exertion of Dakota Aboriginal rights, and they will be using the rights guaranteed in the Treaty of 1805 to justify their actions in court.

Our struggles do not end there. As a direct consequence of the Dakota Commemorative Marches, we are also contemplating pursuing a truth commission process in the state of Minnesota with the help of our allies in the restorative justice movement. We learned from our spiritual walks that telling the truth about the injustices perpetrated against us is both healing and empowering. As we speak the truths that have been silenced and suppressed, we allow ourselves to exert a humanity that the dominant society has denied. While we may never stop grieving the human injustices from the past and present, we can use the truth-telling process to strengthen ourselves and to engage in a powerful struggle for liberation and justice in our homeland. Wasicu Minnesotans have yet to acknowledge the shameful past of how they came to dominate our lands; they have yet to hold themselves accountable to the truth; and they have yet to initiate a system of reparative justice. A truth commission would compel action in all of these areas.

One thing is certain. There is an incredible amount of work that needs to be done to address the legacy of 1862 and its aftermath between and

Bdote, the site of origin of the Dakota People

among both the Dakota Oyate and the Wasicu people who invaded and colonized our homelands. In taking no action, both populations become complicit in the ongoing colonization and suppression of the inherent rights of the original People of the land we call Minisota Makoce. How will the future generations characterize your role in the Dakota struggles for justice in the twenty-first century?

Waziyatawin
Gold Canyon, Arizona
April 12, 2006

Glossary of Dakota Terms

◄○►

ate, father

Ate Wakan Tanka, Father, Great Mystery

Bdote, now called Mendota, which literally means the joining or juncture of two bodies of water

candi, tobacco

canku, road

canpahmihma kawitkotkoka, crazy cart

canunpa, the pipe

cinye, older brother to a man

Dakota, M'dewakantonwan (Dwellers by Mystic Lake), Wahpekute (Shooters of the Leaves), Wahpetonwan (Dwellers in the Leaves), and Sissitunwan (Dwellers by the Fish Campground). These are historical spellings from documents; today, many Dakota write Bdewakantunwan, Wahpekute, Wahpetunwan, and Sisitunwan.

Damakota, "I am Dakota" (Dakota speakers)

deksi, uncle

Eci Nompa Woonspe, The Second Chance Learning Center

Eya, also Iya, a character from stories who was a voracious, human-eating giant

Han mitakuyapi owas'in, Hello all my relatives (female speech)

Hecetu welo, "That is right," used to end an oratory

"Heun oyate nipi kte!" "Therefore the People will live," or "That the People may live."

hocokata, center of the circle

ic'esi, male cousin for a woman

ina, mother

Ina Maka, Mother Earth

inipi, purification or sweat ceremonies

koda, friend

kunsi, grandmother

Kunsi Maka, Grandmother Earth

Kuwa wo, sunka! Come here, dog, and help out!

Lakota, Titunwan (Dwellers on the Plains)

Mahkato, Blue Earth, now referred to as Mankato, Minnesota

maka cokaya kin, the center of the earth

makoce, Dakota land

Malakota, Madakota, Manakota, "I am Lakota, I am Dakota, I am Nakota" (Lakota speakers)

Manipi Hena Owas'in Wicunkiksuyapi, "We Remember All Those Who Walked," the Dakota Commemorative March

Mini Sose Wakpala, The River That Runs Fast or the Missouri River

Mini Sota, generally translated by the Eastern Dakota as slightly cloudy (almost clear) water that reflects the skies, though some people suggest that it comes from sota (pronounced sho-ta) which could be translated as "Smokey Water"

Minisota Makoce, Land Where the Waters Reflect the Skies (Mato Nunpa's translation)

Mitakuye, my relative

Mitakuye Owasin, mitakuye owas'in, Mitakuye Oyasin, all our relations, we are all related

Nakota, Ihanktunwan (Dwellers at the End) and Ihanktunwanna (Little Dwellers at the End)

Oceti Sakowin, Seven Council Fires

okiya, to help or assist someone, also to talk with

oyate, nation

Oyate Ceyapi Wopakinte, Wiping of the Tears

Paha Sapa, Black Hills

pidamayaye do, thank you in male speech

pidamayeye ye, thank you in female speech

Si Tanka Oyate Wokiksuye, Remembering Big Foot's People

sunka, dog

tahansi, cousin, male to male

takoza, grandchild

takozas, grandchildren

tiospaye, also spelled tiyospaye, extended family, part of a complex system of kinship

toska, nephew

tunkasida, grandfather

Unci Maka, earth

unkan, unkanna, both mean grandfather in Dakota. The "na" at the end is a diminutive expressing affection and is usually used when a grandfather is very old

unsika, pitiful

wacekiye, to acknowledge to relatives

Wacewakiye (Revering Relatives)

wacipi, dance or powwow

Wakantanka, The Great Mystery; also Wakan Tanka, Creator

Wasicu, White

Wasicu caze, English name

winyan, woman

wopida k'a woyuonihan wotapi, a thanksgiving and honoring feast

wopila, giving thanks

wokiksuya wotapi, the remembrance feast

wokiksuye k'a woyuonihan, remembering and honoring

wozapi, fruit pudding, usually refers to blueberry pudding among the Minisota Dakota

Author Biographies

◄○►

George Blue Bird is a Lakota language speaker, writer, and artist from the Pine Ridge Reservation in South Dakota and part of the Native American Council of Tribes at the State Penitentiary in Sioux Falls, South Dakota.

Denise Breton, Celtic in ancestry, White American in upbringing, taught at the University of Delaware's philosophy department for nearly twenty years. She coauthored four books, including *The Paradigm Conspiracy: Why Our Social Systems Violate Human Potential and How We Can Change Them* and *The Mystic Heart of Justice*. In 2002, she cofounded Living Justice Press (LJP), a nonprofit publisher in restorative justice. She currently serves as LJP's executive director.

Myla Vicenti Carpio is Jicarilla Apache, Laguna, and Isleta. She is currently an assistant professor in American Indian Studies at Arizona State University.

Lisa Elbert received her Masters of Arts in U.S. History (2005) and in Teaching English as a Second Language (2006) from the University Minnesota and she hopes to continue working in education and research pertaining to Dakota language, history, and instructional technology. She is author of *Wicoie Yutokcapi Wowapi: Verb Companion to Dakota Iapi*.

Mary Beth Faimon, MSW, LCSW, is an Assistant Professor in Social Work and Director of Social Work Field Education at Southwest Minnesota State University in Marshall, Minnesota.

Amy Lonetree (Ho-Chunk) received her Ph.D. in Ethnic Studies from the University of California, Berkeley, where she specialized in Native American History and Public History. She is an Assistant Professor of Native American Studies at Portland State University and a recent recipient of a UC Berkeley Chancellor's Postdoctoral Fellowship for the 2004–2006 academic years. With Amanda J. Cobb, she is currently working on an edited volume on the Smithsonian's National Museum of the American Indian.

Craig Marsden was born and raised in Minnesota. He received an MFA from NYU Film School and is based in New York City. He is currently completing a documentary on the legacy of Euro-American settlement in southwestern Minnesota.

Chris Mato Nunpa is Wahpetunwan Dakota and is an associate professor of Indigenous Nations and Dakota Studies (INDS) at Southwest Minnesota State University in Marshall, Minnesota. His current book project is entitled *A Sweet Smelling Sacrifice: The Bible, Genocide, and the Indigenous Peoples of the United States*.

David Miller is a photographer who was transplanted from Omaha, Nebraska, to Phoenix, Arizona, in 2002. He graduated from Arizona State University in 2006 with a BFA in Photography and a Minor in American Indian Studies.

Leo Omani is a former chief of the Wahpeton Dakota Nation near Prince Albert, Saskatchewan. He received his Masters of Education degree in 1992 and is currently enrolled in an interdisciplinary Ph.D. program at the University of Saskatchewan.

Molly Schoenhoff teaches and practices graphic design as a means of drawing attention to contemporary social issues. She is an Assistant Professor of Graphic Design at Arizona State University.

Ramona Kitto Stately is an enrolled member of the Santee Dakota Nation. Both of her Dakota great-great-grandparents were exiled from the state of Minnesota in 1863. She works in Indian Education in Minnesota and is dedicated to keeping the history of the Dakota Nation alive. "As we journey through this life, we must look back and know where we came from and tell our ancestors stories in order to walk in balance and in peace into the future."

Gabrielle Tateyuskanskan is a jingle dress dancer, visual artist, poet, speaker, and educator who lives with her family in the community of Enemy Swim on the Sisseton-Wahpeton Reservation in South Dakota.

Edward Valandra is Sicangu Lakota and was born and raised on the Rosebud Reservation. He received his B.A. from Minnesota State University at Mankato, Minnesota, his M.A. from the University of Colorado, Boulder, and his Ph.D. from SUNY Buffalo. He is an assistant professor at the University of California at Davis and is the author of *Not Without Our Consent: The Lakota Resistence to Termination, 1950–59* (University of Illinois Press, 2006). His research focus is the revitalization of the Oceti Sakowin Oyate (People of the Seven Council Fires).

Diane Wilson is a creative nonfiction writer whose essays and memoir use personal experience to illustrate broader social and historical context. Her first book, *Spirit Car: Journey to a Dakota Past*, is a historical memoir about cultural identity and heritage (Minnesota Historical Society Press, 2006). She currently works as a freelance writer and editor from her home in Shafer, Minnesota.

Waziyatawin Angela Wilson is Wahpetunwan Dakota and is from the Pezihutazizi Otunwe in southwestern Minnesota. She is the author of *Remember This! Dakota Decolonization and the Eli Taylor Narratives* (Nebraska, 2005) and is the co-editor of *For Indigenous Eyes Only: A Decolonization Handbook* (School of American Research, 2005) and *Indigenizing the Academy: Transforming Scholarship and Empowering Communities* (Nebraska, 2004). Waziyatawin is currently working to create Oyate Nipi Kte, an organization dedicated to the decolonization of Indigenous Peoples in the United States.

Index

agenda of, 46; brutality of, 20;
and celebrations of, 53–54; as
defining "truth" and history,
85, 174; habits of, 222–23; and
holding accountable, 16–17;
institutions of, 225; and law
enforcement system, 18, 185–87,
190, 286–89; mentality of, 144;
programming of, 223–24, 226,
231–32; relationship to colonized, 187; and Whites as, 134,
181–83, 185, 270; work of, 175,
290. *See also* Wasicu

Columbus, Christopher, 183

Commemorative March; evolution
of, 93, 262–63, 292; goals of,
1–2, 7, 10–11, 13, 15, 17–18, 20,
92, 104, 130–31, 136, 195, 257–58,
262; as historical commemoration, 264; of Jicarilla People,
173; role of men in, 177–78, 187,
189–90; as spiritual journey,
264; walks in support of,
125–26; as war crime scene, 171

community organizing: as social
work action principle, 90

concentration camps: 67–70, 85,
96, 117–19, 152, 202, 265, 289; at
Bdote, 114, 167; at Davenport,
Iowa, 170, 193; of Diné, 69, 272;
and forced march to, 43, 50,
166; at Fort Snelling, 9, 278; and
Hitler, 74, 78, 130, 142; list of
Dakota families imprisoned at,
22–24; at Mankato, 9, 47, 139;
photo of, 31; photos from, 32–35,
37–38; and Ramsey, 76, 231

condemned Dakota men, 2–3, 7,
108, 189, 193, 196–97; attacks
on, 57–59, 203, 205, 207–209;
forced removal of, 47, 50,
56–59, 139, 202–203; names of,
25–30

Conito, Lydia "Toyo," 272–73

conquest, 1, 3, 48, 57, 61, 77, 130,
136, 171, 227, 254

contributors; to March, 18–19, 81,
100

Cook-Lynn, Elizabeth, 131

counter-narratives, 252–53

Cousins, Michael, 214

creation story, 114, 167, 300–301.
See also genesis

crimes against humanity, 70,
73–74, 77, 171, 217, 225, 283

critical consciousness, 20, 63, 92

Cronick, Ron "Bear," 276, 292;
pictured on 177, 238

Crooks, George, 58–59

Crow Creek, 47, 50, 55, 129, 180,
193, 253–54, 269

culpability, 44, 62

Dakota First Nations of Canada,
117

Dakota Meadows School, 19, 107,
109, 139, 144

Dakota Studies Committee, 130,
277

Davenport (Iowa), 47, 50, 137, 170,
193, 236

Death March, 11, 50, 96, 180, 185,
192, 279

Debo, Angie, 69

decolonization, 148, 223, 232;
agenda of, 12, 14; of history, 9,
247, 249; meaning of, 178; and
naming colonialism as root
harm, 17, 224, 227–28; role
of colonizers in, 20, 236; as
violent, 62–63

Deloria, Ella, 187–89, 214

Deloria, Vine, Jr., 234

Derby, Chuck, 264

diaspora, 3, 12, 47, 125, 152, 279

Diné, 272

disappeared people, 168, 169, 171,
296

divide and conquer, 45–46

Dowans'a, 141

Dowlin, Bruce, 144

Duta Win, 79

Eagle Head's Band, 23

Eastman, Abigail, 236

Eastman, Charles, 170. *See also*
Ohiyesa

Eastman, Emmett, 184

Eastman, Jacob, 169–70, 236; photo
of, 170. *See also* Tawakanhdiota

Eastman, Seth, 170, 235–36

Eastman, Winona, 235

Eci Nompa Woonspe, 100, 106, 147

Eitinger, Leo, 85

Elbert, Lisa, 15–16, 134; biography
of, 305

empowerment, 6, 39, 116, 178, 268,
271–72

Erlich, John, 91

ethnic cleansing, 9, 14, 68–70, 123,
180, 186, 262, 268; beneficiaries
of, 131; citizen involvement in,
62; as crime against humanity, 77–78; and Hitler, 73–74,
78; of Ho-Chunk People, 246,
253–54, 269; Minnesota's state
policy of, 2, 5, 67, 170; phases
of, 3, 8; and Ramsey, 53, 76, 78;
totality of, 4; White celebrations of, 53–54, 252

ethnocide, 61, 128

exile: of Dakota people from our
homeland, 47, 125, 145, 262, 275;
of Ho-Chunk people, 254, 269

expulsion, 2, 6, 49

extermination, 6, 63, 217, 220, 222,
236; and beneficiaries of, 72,
131; and Bible, 75; and Hitler,
71, 74; and imperial expansion,

46, 49, 53, 84–85; Minnesota's policy of, 85; Ramsey's policy of, 76, 78, 166, 183, 231, 281; settler demand for, 105; U.S. policy of, 69, 95; White culpability for, 62. *See also* genocide

Faimon, Mary Beth, 10, 142, 151, 192, 257, 270, 276, 280–82, 287–88, 291, 295; biography of, 305; and work on march, 107, 132–34

factionalism, 127, 277, 288; healing from, 289–90; honoring all factions, 147

Fanon, Frantz, 62

"farmers," 46

flight, 85, 96, 180, 275

Foote, Kenneth, 247

forced dependency, 4

forced march, 74, 77–79, 85, 96, 117–19, 130, 181; and attacks on Dakota prisoners, 56; and children on, 149, 267, 272; and decolonizing commemoration of, 88, 92; as first phase of ethnic cleansing, 2–4, 7–9, 50; of Jicarilla Apache People, 173–74, 268; and Nazi Germany, 142; personal connections to, 51–53, 79–80, 125, 192–94; and Trail of Tears, 68–69; and trauma and violence of, 166, 187, 189. *See also* ethnic cleansing

forced removal, 121–22, 217, 221, 231, 251, 295; and bounties, 85; and confiscation of treaty lands, 85; and confronting injustice of, 172, 262; devastating consequences of, 63–64, 90; as ethnic cleansing, 53; of Ho-Chunk People, 253–54, 269; of Jicarilla Apache People,

173; successive waves of, 49–50. *See also* ethnic cleansing

Fort Ridgely, 5, 155, 197–200, 203, 281

Fort Snelling, 98, 128–29, 173, 209; arrival of 2002 and 2004 marchers at, 82, 89, 113–15, 125, 147, 149–51, 155–56, 177, 289, 295; as concentration camp, 6–9, 11, 43, 56, 67, 74, 78–79, 96; Dakota removal from, 50; and deaths on the way to, 100, 119; as destination of 1862 march, 15, 47, 50–51, 54, 101, 117, 119, 196; and events of commemorative march, 11, 13, 151, 183; and forced conversions at, 273; Ho-Chunk removal from, 254; photo of, 300; and relatives imprisoned at, 140; and role in ethnic cleansing, 85; route to, 197–98; as site of genocide, 299–301; spiritual run from, to Mankato, 15, 92, 184, 267; as strategic to colonial expansion, 3, 121–22. *See also* concentration camps; ethnic cleansing

Fort Sumner, 69

fractionation, 46, 147

Freire, Paulo, 43, 63

Frenier, Louise, 156

Frenier, Narcisse, 156

Frenier, Rosalie, 156

"friendlies," 46, 50

friendship between Dakota and Wasicu, 61

Fuller, Audrey, 19, 103; in photo, 295

Gebhard, Darla, 135, 141

genesis: site of, 300–301. *See also* creation story

genocidal policies, 10, 62, 74, 84, 87, 145

genocide, 95, 128, 172, 174, 179, 182–83, 217–20, 222–25, 231–32, 261, 278, 283; and *Bible*, 75; as celebrated by colonizers, 53–54, 131; and citizen complicity in, 62; dealing with pain of, 18, 93, 286; and Fort Snelling as site of, 300–301; and impact on land, 123, 262; Minnesota's policy of, 49, 73, 78, 142, 145; naming U.S. history of, 11, 15, 43, 87, 281, 284; ongoing damage of, 9, 274; and scholarship on, 78; and UN Genocide Convention on, 9, 71, 87; and U.S. compared with Nazi Germany, 71, 73–74; and White denials of, 281; and White women's participation in, 58. *See also* ethnic cleansing; extermination

Glanville, Amos, 203, 205, 207

Good Road's Band, 23

Good Voice, Ernest, 118

Good Voice, Robert, 118

Great Commission, 71

grieving, 189, 261, 271–72, 301; as process, 136, 292

Gustavus Adolphus College, 18, 81, 109–10, 128, 143

Haza Win, 79, 103, 105, 294; photo of planting stake with her name, 103

healing, 39, 294; from colonization, 18; and Commemorative March as, 119, 147, 152, 160, 175, 177, 195, 260, 268, 276, 279; as distinct from reconciliation with Whites, 129–33; and grieving, 136, 279; and land, 235, 275, 278, 292; meaning of, 262–63; need community for, 61; between Peoples, 215, 224–26;

The Dakota Commemorative Marches

Contact Information

Web site: www.dakota-march.50megs.com/

◄○►

If you would like to send letters of support, donations, and ideas, if you are offering to help, or if you would like further information about the marches, you may contact any of the following members of the Dakota Commemorative March Committee:

Gabrielle Tateyuskanskan
PO Box 183
Waubay, SD 57273
Tel. (605) 947-3419

Waziyatawin Angela Wilson
11046 E. Walking Stick Way
Gold Canyon, AZ 85218
Tel. (480) 813-1387
waziyatawin@gmail.com

Dottie Whipple
109 Driftwood Drive
Redwood Falls, MN 56283
Tel. (507) 627-1091
hdwhipp@newulmtel.net

Mary Beth Faimon
802 Lawrence Court
Marshall, MN 56258
Tel. (507) 537-4080
faimon@iw.net

Diane Wilson
26366 Red Wing Avenue
Shafer, MN 55074-9614
Tel. (651) 257-7105
dianewilson@frontiernet.net

Chris Mato Nunpa
5690 250th Ave.
Granite Falls, MN 56241-3655
Tel. (320) 564-4348 (h); (507) 537-6118 (o)
matonunpa@earthlink.net or
matonunpa@SouthwestMSU.edu

About Living Justice Press

A nonprofit, tax-exempt publisher on restorative justice

Founded in 2002, Living Justice Press (LJP) is a 501(c)(3) nonprofit organization whose purpose is to publish and promote alternative works about social justice and community healing. Our specific focus is on restorative justice and peacemaking. Within this field, our concentration is two-fold: first, to promote the understanding and use of peacemaking circles as a means to deal with conflict in many different settings as well as to promote justice as a way of life; and second, to publish the voices of those "in struggle" for justice. Our books seek to apply what we have learned about healing harms between people to the larger challenge of healing harms between Peoples.

Our first two books, *Peacemaking Circles: From Crime to Community* by Kay Pranis, Barry Stuart, and Mark Wedge, and *Justice As Healing: Indigenous Ways* edited by Wanda D. McCaslin are being used extensively by tribal courts and First Nations communities, law schools, colleges (for courses ranging from Native studies to philosophies of life to dispute resolution to criminal justice), churches, law enforcement and probation departments, schools, youth centers, families, and, of course, community justice programs across the country and around the world.

Thank you for the time and thought you have given to our publications. We are also deeply grateful to those who have chosen to support us financially. Because publishing is so expensive, and because we try to keep the price of books as low as we can, we could not make them available without such support. Above all, we appreciate your telling your family, friends, colleagues, and communities about our books, because that is how books get into the hands of those who need them. Thank you.

In this spirit, Living Justice Press makes books available to groups and communities (10 books or more) at a discount when you order directly from us.

We invite you to add your name to our mailing list, so we can inform you of future books, and we look forward to hearing from you.

◄o►

2093 Juliet Avenue, St. Paul, MN 55105
Tel. (651) 695-1008 • Fax. (651) 695-8564
E-mail: info@livingjusticepress.org
Web site: www.livingjusticepress.org

Closing Reflections

—◄○►—

In our ancestral homeland

Lights flashing
The highway patrolman
quoted some
Minnesota statute
"You can be cited
and taken to jail"
a misdemeanor offense

We are not free
to walk in prayer
to honor our ancestors
without colonial interference

In our ancestral homeland

Our people
    scattered
        all
            over
The Wasicus
    put a bounty
        on our heads
The U.S. Army
    looking for us
        here
            Canada
It
    didn't
        matter
            where

With the march people came back together

We didn't
      go through
    the traditional prayers
      the songs
        the rituals
          the wokiksuye wotapi
They couldn't
    find the body

They met
  at Fort Snelling
    They also fell in love
      Even in times of suffering
        that's what human beings do

The truth
has to be put
on the table
Especially
land theft
We have to
talk
about it

Wasicu allies
　committed
　　to righting
　　　historical harms

In our generation
we are
　　bystanders
We have
an obligation
　　to speak the truth
We continue
this genocide
　　of people
　　with our denials
We need
to hold
　　ourselves
　　accountable
We need
to hear
　　the stories
We need
to know
　　what happened
I want
　　the truth
　　　to be known
　　　　For my healing

Every mile
we stop
say prayers
put tobacco down
to honor
the courage and bravery
of those Dakota women
A beautiful experience
I am proud
to be
an Indigenous
woman

We're empowering ourselves
We're empowering the next generation